THE POLITICAL ECONOMY OF JAPANESE SOCIETY
VOLUME 2

The Political Economy of Japanese Society

Volume 2

Internationalization and Domestic Issues

Edited by

BANNO JUNJI

OXFORD UNIVERSITY PRESS

1998

Oxford University Press, Great Clarendon Street, Oxford OX2 6DP

Oxford New York

Athens Auckland Bangkok Bogota Bombay
Buenos Aires Calcutta Cape Town Dar es Salaam
Delhi Florence Hong Kong Istanbul Karachi
Kuala Lumpur Madras Madrid Melbourne
Mexico City Nairobi Paris Singapore
Taipei Tokyo Toronto Warsaw

and associated companies in
Berlin Ibadan

Oxford is a trade mark of Oxford University Press

Published in the United States by
Oxford University Press Inc., New York

British Library Cataloguing in Publication Data
Data available

Library of Congress Cataloging in Publication Data
The political economy of Japanese society / edited by Junji Banno.
A revision and translation of the 7 vol. ed. published 1990–1992
by the University of Tokyo Press.
Includes bibliographical references and index.
Contents: v. 2. Internationalization and Domestic Issues
1. Japan—Economic conditions—1945– 2. Japan—Politics and
government—1945 I. Banno, Junji, 1937– .
HC462.9.P5719 1997 330.952'04—dc21 97–23116

ISBN 0–19–828034–3

1 3 5 7 9 10 8 6 4 2

Typeset by Graphicraft Typesetters Ltd., Hong Kong
Printed in Great Britain by
Bookcraft (Bath) Ltd
Midsomer Norton, Somerset

Contents

List of Figures

List of Tables

List of Contributors

BANNO JUNJI Professor of Japanese Political History, Institute of Social Science, University of Tokyo

HARADA SUMITAKA Professor of Civil Law and Sociology of Law, Institute of Social Science, University of Tokyo

HIROWATARI SEIGO Professor of German Law and Sociology of Law, Institute of Social Science, University of Tokyo

HIWATARI NOBUHIRO Associate Professor of Contemporary Japanese Politics, Institute of Social Science, University of Tokyo

INAMOTO YONOSUKE Professor of French Law and Land Law, Faculty of Real Estate Sciences, Meikai University

KAWAI MASAHIRO Professor of Economics, Institute of Social Science, University of Tokyo

KOIKE KAZUO Professor of Human Resource Management, Faculty of Business, Hosei University

NITTA MICHIO Professor of Industrial Relations, Institute of Social Science, University of Tokyo

OSAWA MARI Associate Professor of Social Policy and Gender Studies, Institute of Social Science, University of Tokyo

WADA HARUKI Professor of Russian History and Korean Studies, Institute of Social Science, University of Tokyo

Introduction

BANNO JUNJI

It is a historical fact that by the 1980s, Japan had become an economic giant second only to the United States. Many people predicted that this economic strength would continue in the 1990s, and that, as a result, Japan would surpass the USA in economic terms. We now know that this prediction was not to be fulfilled. The main purpose of this book and its companion volume, published earlier this year, is to re-examine Japan's economic strength of the 1980s in the light of the changed trends of the 1990s.

The first of these two volumes analysed the structures of the Japanese political economy which encouraged continuous economic growth from 1955 to 1990, focusing on such phenomena as 'Japanese management', 'the Japanese employment system', and 'one-party dominance' in politics, and analysing their historical origins. In this second volume, we analyse the 'problems' that were caused by rapid and continuous economic growth before the 1990s.

During the 1980s, Japan was faced with critical problems in her relations with foreign countries and their peoples. The most conspicuous was the US–Japanese 'economic war', but the frictions created by overseas Japanese firms' relations with their local employees also raised important issues. While Japanese finance and Japanese firms were 'exported' overseas, foreign workers were 'imported' into Japan. Since Japan had long been a 'closed nation' in terms of immigration, this sudden inflow of foreign workers created legal and cultural problems. Japan's rapid economic growth in the 1980s also caused increasing dissatisfaction among the peoples of other Asian countries. The self-satisfaction of many Japanese in the 1980s contrasted sharply not only with Japan's pre-war and wartime crimes against Asian people but also with her post-war attitude to those crimes. Within Japan, rapid economic growth in the 1980s also produced various domestic problems, such as rapid increases in land prices, the increasing disadvantage experienced by women both in the workplace and in the home, and the growing number of aged people who were not well cared for either by their children or by central or local governments.

By the late 1990s, some of these international and domestic problems had changed in nature or become less urgent than in the 1980s, while others had become much more urgent than before. This volume demonstrates, however, that the problems themselves are far from solved.

In Chapter 1, Kawai examines the causes of the rise and decline of Japan as a creditor nation. As he shows, Japan's status as a world creditor nation is declining in spite of the continuous increase in her net external assets. In addition to his detailed macroeconomic analysis, which explains the changing nature of Japan's net external asset position in the 1980s and 1990s, his prediction that the rapid ageing of the population will produce future economic difficulties is closely related to the arguments in Chapters 5 and 6, which deal with women and old people respectively.

In Chapter 2, Koike criticizes facile arguments for or against introducing 'Japanese management' to Asian countries. Without research based on proper analysis of conditions for blue-collar workers in Japan and other Asian countries, he argues, we will reach no correct conclusion as to whether 'Japanese management' is suitable as a model for other countries. In this chapter, Koike presents some results of his research on Asian blue-collar workers' conditions, including the term of employment, the range and frequency of change in the nature of work practices, and the promotion system in terms of both wages and status. In the early 1990s, when the first draft of this chapter was written, however, Japanese and other Asian firms could not wait until proper research had been completed. Now that so-called Japanese management is losing popularity, on the other hand, Koike's call for empirical comparative research on Japanese, American, European, and Asian blue-collar workers seems even more persuasive.

Hirowatari's analysis of and conclusions concerning foreign workers' 'problems' (Chapter 3) also seem more relevant today than in the 1980s. From 1989 to 1991, the number of legal foreign workers increased continuously, but after the collapse of the 'bubble economy' the number began to decrease and in 1995 it fell to about 72 per cent of the peak year (1991). We are now in a good position to reconsider not only Japan's attitude to short-term foreign workers but also the legal and social systems relating to long-term immigration in general.

Wada's essay (Chapter 4) is particularly important because it analyses postwar attitudes to Japan's war crimes and colonial crimes of the pre-war period. It is evident that the simple description of crimes against Asian people is not sufficient if Japanese attitudes to the past are to change. In the negotiations leading up to the Sino-Japanese Peace Treaty of 1952, the Japan–Republic of Korea Treaty of 1965, and the Japan–China Treaty of Peace and Friendship of 1978, Wada argues, the Japanese government did its best not to recognize its responsibilities to China and Korea for wartime and colonial crimes. Japanese attitudes to other Asian countries in this context were quite different from attitudes to the USA and to European nations, and in this regard Japan has been consistent since 1895 when she colonized Taiwan. At the time of Japan's annexation of Korea in 1910, the Twenty-One Demands to China of 1915, the Manchurian Incident of 1931, and the outbreak of the Sino-Japanese War in 1937, not only the government, but also many opinion-leaders outside the government, paid great attention to Western reactions but little attention to those of Asian nations. As Wada's essay suggests, Japan's neglect of Asian responses to her actions in both the pre-war and post-war periods has exacerbated the difficulties in Japanese relations with the rest of Asia.

The three chapters in Part II (Chapters 5–7) analyse domestic problems created by the process of Japan's economic growth in the 1980s. While the land problems analysed by Inamoto changed in nature in the 1990s, domestic problems relating to women and old people have become more serious in the post-bubble period.

In Chapter 5, Osawa emphasizes the increase in the gap in wages between male and female workers at the very moment when Japan's economic growth was reaching its peak. This implies the decrease of that gap in the recession period of the 1990s, but that does not mean that female workers' wages increased. In the post-bubble period, while the unemployment of female workers increased, their wages did not increase. Thus conditions for female workers became much worse than in the bubble period. More striking is the fact that the basic gap in wages (excluding overtime) between male and female workers was almost the same over the twenty-five years between 1970 and 1995. Overall, women workers' wages have been about 60 per cent of male workers' wages during the last twenty-five years.

Osawa's main argument is that the disadvantageous conditions experienced by women at work encourage discrimination against them at home. It is difficult to say definitively which is the main cause, but Osawa's essay clearly shows that home and workplace are inter-related.

In addition, Osawa's chapter leads us to reconsider Kawai's earlier essay and Harada's later chapter on the ageing society. As has already been mentioned, Kawai warned of both the decrease in quantity and quality of labour and the decrease in savings likely to be caused by rapid population ageing. If both trends do in fact occur, they could conceivably be compensated for by the mobilization of women's labour. If women become more liberated both in their workplaces and in their homes, the losses in manpower and savings caused by population ageing will easily be made good.

This point is closely related to an understanding of the problems of the ageing society. Despite the commonly held image, the increase in numbers of aged people is not greatly affecting women's situation in the workplace or at home. If we look at the composition of Japanese families in 1990, about 60 per cent were nuclear families and more than 13 per cent were composed of aged people alone. The proportion of three-generation families was only 13 per cent. Moreover, some of those three-generation families encourage the wives to work outside the home. In short, the ageing society itself does not discourage women from working outside the home. As Osawa emphasizes in her chapter, either management at the workplace or husbands in the home are responsible for the low number of women workers.

The same figures, however, have a different significance for old people themselves. The decrease in three-generation families and the increase in nuclear families consisting solely of old people mean that old people are no longer able to rely on the Japanese family system. In 1975, when the proportion of the population aged 65 or over was about 8 per cent, the proportion of three-generation families was still more than 17 per cent. In contrast, in 1995, when the proportion of the population aged 65 or more increased to 14.5 per cent, that of three-generation families declined to 13 per cent. While the aged population increased, the proportion of three-generation families decreased. It is obvious that the role of central and local governments in the welfare of aged people must be increasing. Harada's essay in Chapter 6 provides a detailed analysis of this issue.

Land problems in Japan changed markedly between the bubble and the post-bubble period. The Japanese attitude to land ownership, however, has not changed greatly over the two periods. The criticism by Inamoto in Chapter 7 of this attitude should be borne in mind by those who might wish for a recovery in the land price. Land should exist first for public and private use, only secondly as a commodity in itself, and not at all for speculation.

In addition to the chapters which deal with international and domestic problems, this volume includes two chapters (Part III) that analyse the structures of the Japanese political economy. The reason for this is very simple. With the rapid increase of unemployment and the collapse of the political dominance of the Liberal Democratic party, many arguments appeared predicting the end of the 'Japanese employment system' and the '1955 political system'. Thus, the chapters by Nitta and Hiwatari were added to update the analyses presented in the previous volume.

PART I

Internationalization

1

Japan as a Creditor Nation: What is Happening to its Net External Assets?*

KAWAI MASAHIRO

I. Introduction

Japan experienced large and persistent current account surpluses throughout the 1980s and the first half of the 1990s while accumulating considerable amounts of net external assets. Based on the external asset-liability data, it became the world's largest *net* creditor nation in 1986 and the world's second largest *gross* creditor nation in 1988, surpassing the United States in the first category and the United Kingdom in the second. Japan's ascendance to the status of a leading creditor nation was accompanied by a rapidly deteriorating net external asset position in the United States. According to the stock data based on market value, the United States became a net debtor nation in the late 1980s for the first time since the end of the First World War and is now the world's largest net debtor. Figure 1.1 demonstrates not only the dramatic changes in the two countries' net external asset positions but also their contrasting movements in the 1980s and 1990s. (Net investment income also exhibits similar movements.) Japan's creditor status once posed the pressing question worldwide of what Japan might do with its powerful financial resources. Japanese investors and institutions were considered capable of exerting a large influence on the rest of the world. In the post-bubble period of the 1990s, however, Japan's net external position, though still on a continuous growth path, no longer appears to be a big issue, and is less threatening to other parts of the world.

This chapter clarifies distinct characteristics of Japan's expanding net external assets, examines the causes of its rapid accumulation of net external assets, and explains why Japan's net creditor status attracts less attention in the 1990s than it did in the 1980s. Section II overviews recent developments in Japan's net external asset position by studying two data sets of external assets and liabilities (stock data) and net investment income in the balance of payments (flow data). The compositional patterns and distinct characteristics of Japan's net external asset position are explained and compared with those

* The author is thankful to David Leheny and Andrew Robertson for their editorial assistance.

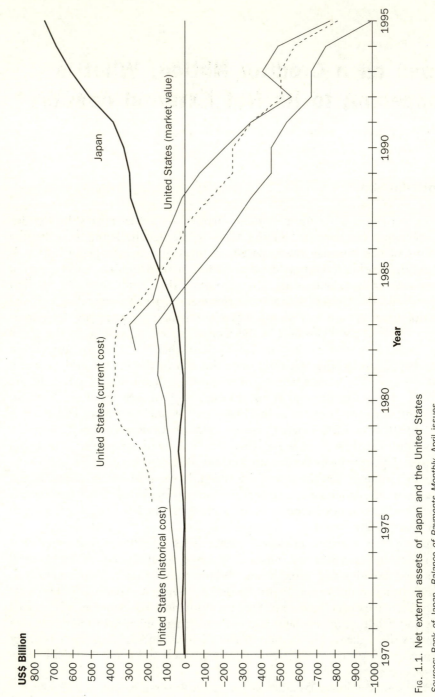

Fig. 1.1. Net external assets of Japan and the United States

Sources: Bank of Japan, *Balance of Payments Monthly*, April issues.
US Department of Commerce, Survey of Current Business, June 1986, June 1988, June 1991, June 1992, July 1996.

of other major industrial countries. Section III analyses the causes of the rapid accumulation of Japan's net external assets by focusing on current account and capital account transactions, and the underlying savings-investment balances. This section will argue that several factors contributed to the expansion of Japan's net external assets in the 1980s and 1990s:

(a) strong international competitiveness in high value-added, highly income-elastic manufacturing products;
(b) high household savings relative to corporate investment in equipment and structure;
(c) liberalization of capital controls in the first half of the 1980s;
(d) divergent macroeconomic conditions in the United States and Japan; and
(e) fluctuations in asset prices, including those of foreign exchange, stocks and shares, and land.

Section IV specifically considers the consequences of the burst of the recent 'bubbles' and the post-bubble recession, which exhibits the weakness and fragility of Japan despite its status as largest net creditor nation. This section explains what is different in the 1990s in comparison to the 1980s. Section V summarizes the chapter and presents future prospects for Japan's net external asset position.

II. Japan's Net External Asset Position (NEAP)

1. Stock data and flow data

There are at least two statistical measures that express a country's net external asset position (NEAP). A direct measure is the difference between a country's gross external assets and liabilities while an indirect measure is the difference between a country's receipts and payments of income due to cross-border investment. The stock balance between gross external assets and liabilities is readily available in official publications; Japan's Ministry of Finance has been publishing external asset and liability data (and their composition) annually since 1971 (see Appendix Table A1 for a complete set of statistics) and the Economic Planning Agency has been publishing the summary statistics as part of national income and wealth data. Net investment income is reported as part of the current account of Japan's balance of payments (see Appendix Table A2). Since net investment income is the fruit of past investments abroad, it can be postulated that a capitalized value of net investment income presents another measure of the NEAP.

Figure 1.2 plots these two measures of Japan's NEAP as a ratio of Gross Domestic Product (GDP). The direct measure of NEAP (i.e., the stock data), depicted by the solid curve, is constructed as the difference between gross

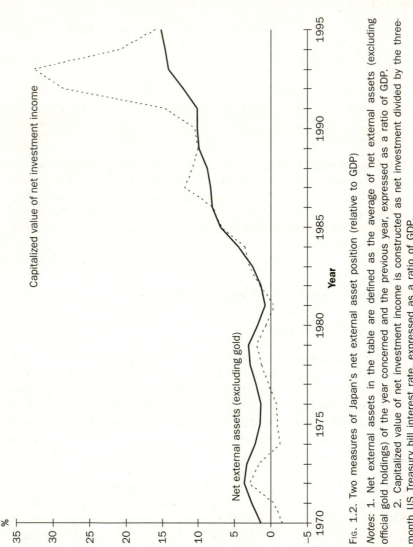

FIG. 1.2. Two measures of Japan's net external asset position (relative to GDP)

Notes: 1. Net external assets in the table are defined as the average of net external assets (excluding official gold holdings) of the year concerned and the previous year, expressed as a ratio of GDP.

2. Capitalized value of net investment income is constructed as net investment divided by the three-month US Treasury bill interest rate, expressed as a ratio of GDP.

Sources: Ministry of Finance, *Monthly Statistics on Government Finance and Banking*, No. 255 (June 1973), No. 374 (June 1983).

Bank of Japan, *Balance of Payments Monthly*, various issues.

International Monetary Fund, *International Financial Statistics*, various issues.

external assets, excluding official gold holdings, and gross external liabilities, expressed as a ratio of GDP. The indirect measure (i.e., the flow data), depicted by the dotted curve, is constructed by capitalizing net investment income using the annual average of three-month US Treasury bill interest rates as a discount factor and expressing the capitalized value as a ratio of GDP. Official gold holdings are excluded from the stock data due to the fact that gold does not bear interest and the stock and flow data must be comparable with each other. In any case, gold holdings, valued at the official price, relative to GDP, are small. Not surprisingly, the two data series move together in a parallel fashion with a correlation coefficient of 0.91 for the 1970–95 period. Both data sets show that Japan's NEAP remained stable as a trend throughout the 1970s when oil-price increases plagued the economy twice, and started to rise sharply in the mid-1980s. Though the pace of NEAP growth slowed down a little towards the end of the 1980s and early 1990s, it continued to rise until 1995.

While moving closely with each other, the two data series exhibit some discrepancies. First, the stock data show that Japan has been a net creditor nation since the start of the 1970s,[1] while the flow data indicate that Japan was never a persistent net creditor country until 1982. According to the flow data, Japan's NEAP fluctuated between negative and positive numbers throughout the 1970s and early 1980s, and it was only in the first half of the 1980s that net investment income started to register a persistent surplus. Second, the flow data exhibited a smaller NEAP than did the stock data until the beginning of the 1980s, while this trend has been reversed in the 1990s.[2]

There are several reasons for a discrepancy between the stock data and flow data. One obvious reason is that neither data set is completely accurate. It is known that the data for external assets and liabilities do not reflect true economic values because most of them are evaluated at historical costs. The Ministry of Finance makes valuation adjustments every year when it publishes the annual data, but the adjustment procedure is not clearly stated and the adjustments appear to be far from complete.[3] The data for investment income, which are considered more accurate because of the reporting requirements imposed on commercial banks (authorized foreign exchange banks) by the Foreign Exchange and Foreign Trade Control Law, have not captured all the investment income flows. For example, reinvestment by Japanese firms' affiliates abroad has not been treated as part of investment income so that reported investment income tends to underestimate true values.

Another possible reason for a discrepancy between the stock and flow data is that the rates of return on external assets and liabilities are different. The ex-post rates of return, reported in Table 1.1, reveal that external assets earned less than did external liabilities until 1981, but that this trend was completely reversed in 1982 and remained so through 1993. In essence, although Japan has always been a net creditor nation on a stock basis since the late 1960s, it never registered a persistent surplus on net investment income until the

TABLE 1.1. Ex-post rates of return on external assets and liabilities

(%)

Year	Direct Investment		Indirect Investment		Total	
	Assets	Liabilities	Assets	Liabilities	Assets	Liabilities
1972	7.6	11.5	4.0	4.4	4.2	4.8
1973	6.3	18.2	5.8	6.1	5.8	6.7
1974	6.3	16.7	7.0	9.5	6.9	9.8
1975	6.8	15.1	6.3	7.6	6.3	7.9
1976	6.8	15.1	5.3	6.3	5.5	6.7
1977	7.6	17.0	4.6	5.8	5.0	6.2
1978	5.9	16.0	5.2	5.9	5.3	6.2
1979	5.9	18.7	7.2	7.0	7.1	7.4
1980	7.3	15.9	7.6	7.8	7.5	8.1
1981	6.5	17.4	8.8	9.4	8.5	9.5
1982	5.9	15.1	8.7	8.1	8.4	8.3
1983	6.7	16.4	6.2	5.5	6.2	5.7
1984	6.3	17.5	6.1	5.6	6.1	5.8
1985	6.2	18.0	5.6	5.1	5.7	5.3
1986	5.2	22.4	5.0	4.4	5.0	4.6
1987	5.3	19.9	5.5	4.6	5.5	4.7
1988	4.0	20.6	6.0	5.2	5.9	5.4
1989	3.5	23.3	6.5	5.8	6.3	5.9
1990	2.7	23.7	7.2	6.5	6.7	6.6
1991	2.9	18.7	7.8	7.1	7.3	7.2
1992	3.3	13.6	7.5	6.7	7.0	6.7
1993	3.3	11.5	7.5	6.8	7.0	6.9
1994	3.7	10.8	7.1	6.8	6.7	6.9
1995	3.2	13.0	8.0	7.8	7.4	7.9

Note: The ex-post rate of return is calculated as investment income received (or paid) divided by the average asset (liability) stock, where average asset (or liability) stock is the average of the end-of-the-year stocks of the year concerned and the previous year.

Source: Bank of Japan, Balance of Payments Monthly, various issues.

beginning of the 1980s due to the low rate of return on external assets relative to external liabilities. Only in the first half of the 1980s did a persistent and rising surplus on net investment income start to emerge and did Japan truly become a net creditor nation on the basis of both stock and flow data.

2. The composition of Japan's net external assets

To analyse the causes of the rise in the NEAP, one must understand what types of net external assets the Japanese investors accumulated. Let us examine changes in the pattern and composition of Japan's NEAP over time.

Table 1.2 summarizes the composition of Japan's NEAP based on the stock data. Net external assets are broken down into those of the private sector and the government sector, and each sector's net external assets are further broken down into long-term and short-term net external assets. Private long-term net external assets include direct investments and securities investments among others.

The table demonstrates that the government sector has always been a net creditor since at latest the beginning of the 1970s, while the private sector had almost always been a net debtor until 1981. This means that Japan's net creditor position until 1981 was made possible by the official holdings of net external assets that exceeded private net external liabilities.[4] In 1982, however, the private sector became a net creditor and has since increased its net external assets substantially, contributing to the rapid expansion of Japan's total NEAP. Out of the rise in total NEAP between 1980 and 1995 (US$ 737 billion), the private sector accounted for 71 per cent and the government sector accounted for 29 per cent.

Among the private NEAP, long-term net external assets, such as direct investments and securities investments, rose substantially while short-term net external assets underwent a big swing. An important compositional shift can be observed in long-term net external assets in the 1980s and 1990s. The net position of direct investments saw the most persistent and highest growth between 1980 and 1995 (US$ 260 billion). The net position of securities investments also rose between 1980 and 1995 (US$ 229 billion) but with substantially greater fluctuations than direct investments. Several explanations for such a compositional shift will be offered in Section III.

It must be pointed out that, as private long-term net external assets grew, private short-term net external assets exhibited a pronounced swing, declining by US$ 298 billion between 1980 and 1990 and rising by US$ 261 billion between 1990 and 1995. This big swing was due to private monetary movements, which represent short-term capital transactions by authorized foreign exchange banks (including all city banks, many large regional banks, Shinkin Banks, some credit cooperatives, semi-government banks, and postal savings). These commercial banks had large net external debts in the 1970s and 1980s due to the fact that their non-banking customers needed to finance export, import, and other business activities; the commercial banks borrowed short-term funds abroad and lent them to domestic non-banking customers. Due to the increased demand for such external short-term funds in the non-banking sector as well as in the commercial banks themselves,[5] their short-term net external debts rose substantially in the 1980s. Since the rise in short-term net external liabilities was accompanied by a rise in long-term net external assets, Japan was effectively engaged in large-scale international financial intermediation by borrowing short and lending long. This was also a time when Japanese commercial banks, securities firms, and insurance companies expanded their

TABLE 1.2. Composition of Japan's net external assets

(US$ million)

	1971	1975	1980	1985	1986	1987	1988	1989	1990	1991	1992	1993	1994	1995
Private sector	-7,088	-10,302	-16,659	104,450	138,541	146,494	147,571	158,839	218,835	285,545	393,056	448,837	489,938	505,053
Long-term	-495	12,931	31,760	172,682	272,512	386,290	459,737	496,238	565,542	524,810	553,367	572,087	571,283	590,652
Direct investments	514	6,238	16,342	39,231	51,557	68,004	100,364	145,207	191,591	219,494	232,547	242,911	256,363	276,144
Securities investments	-3,490	-3,591	-8,305	60,901	114,322	173,471	172,332	159,791	229,292	188,308	224,069	239,262	221,313	220,678
Loans	-1,620	3,282	13,216	45,659	68,012	96,368	122,602	118,189	72,059	41,542	23,732	16,370	18,941	17,103
Trade credits	4,853	6,734	9,752	23,472	31,959	37,154	48,768	52,850	47,134	47,290	44,546	42,066	42,095	41,619
Other	-752	268	755	3,419	6,662	11,293	15,671	20,201	25,466	28,176	28,473	31,478	32,571	35,109
Short-term	-6,593	-23,233	-48,419	-68,232	-133,971	-239,796	-312,166	-337,399	-346,707	-239,265	-160,311	-123,250	-81,345	-85,599
Monetary movements	-1,471	-13,471	-32,816	-61,265	-127,450	-209,901	-262,909	-266,833	-254,367	-162,693	-84,789	-51,852	-8,453	72,530
Other	-5,122	-9,762	-15,603	-6,967	-6,521	-29,895	-49,257	-70,566	-92,340	-76,572	-75,522	-71,398	-72,892	-158,128
Government sector	16,861	17,320	28,193	25,371	41,810	94,250	144,175	134,376	109,224	97,527	120,563	161,980	199,036	243,095
Long-term	2,211	5,823	8,832	6,287	11,288	23,710	61,307	75,508	66,521	75,635	103,715	129,038	173,084	183,412
Loans	1,809	5,083	15,282	23,209	33,492	43,098	55,544	60,464	60,927	77,285	88,261	103,608	121,073	134,622
Other	402	740	-6,450	-16,922	-22,204	-19,388	5,763	15,044	5,594	-1,650	15,454	25,430	52,011	48,790
Short-term	14,650	11,497	19,361	19,084	30,522	70,540	82,868	58,868	42,703	21,892	16,848	32,942	25,952	59,683
Monetary movements	14,877	12,103	21,790	23,093	36,191	78,253	92,725	68,115	50,894	30,408	26,141	43,764	38,068	73,268
Other	-227	-606	-2,429	-4,009	-5,669	-7,713	-9,857	-9,247	-8,191	-8,516	-9,293	-10,822	-12,116	-13,594
Total net external assets	9,773	7,018	11,534	129,821	180,351	240,744	291,746	293,215	328,059	383,072	513,619	610,817	688,974	748,140
Long-term	1,716	18,754	40,592	178,969	283,800	410,000	521,044	571,746	632,063	600,445	657,082	701,125	744,367	774,065
Short-term	8,057	-11,736	-29,058	-49,148	-103,449	-169,256	-229,298	-278,531	-304,004	-217,373	-143,463	-90,308	-55,393	-25,926

Note: The Japanese-yen data for 1995 are converted into US dollars by using the end-of-the-year exchange rate of 102.91 yen per US dollar.

Source: Bank of Japan, *Balance of Payments Monthly*, April issues.

international operations with the surging wealth from the asset market boom. They emerged as some of the most powerful financial institutions in the world.

International financial intermediation suddenly collapsed, however, in the 1990s when the growth of private long-term net external *assets* slowed and the growth of private short-term net external *liabilities* stopped and began to reverse its previous trend. In essence, Japanese commercial banks simply stopped borrowing short-term funds abroad and started to make repayments of past debts, thus decumulating short-term net external liabilities. This was the period when the asset market boom collapsed and the financial position of almost all Japanese financial institutions was greatly damaged.

The government sector also played a role in accumulating net external assets. Its role was conspicuous at the times of rapid yen rate appreciation and the consequent intervention in the foreign exchange market. For example, in 1987, due to persistent current account deficits in the United States and the lack of autonomous private capital inflows (see Marris (1987) and Krugman (1988)), serious fears of free fall in the external value of the US dollar mounted in the world currency markets, thereby putting precipitous downward pressure on the US dollar. The Bank of Japan (together with the central banks of other major industrialized countries) stepped in to support the dollar and accumulated foreign exchange reserves. When another round of rapid yen appreciation occurred in 1995, the Bank of Japan engaged once again in large-scale interventions to prevent further yen appreciation and added to its foreign exchange reserves. Though there were times when downward pressure on the Japanese yen forced the Bank of Japan to sell US dollars from 1989 through 1991, and more recently in late 1996 and early 1997, the overall position of the Bank of Japan's foreign exchange reserves rose on average, thus contributing to an expansion in Japan's NEAP.

To summarize, the rapid expansion of Japan's NEAP in the 1980s and 1990s was essentially private-sector driven, though it was supplemented by occasional official intervention in the foreign exchange market when private capital outflows were drying up. The private sector accumulated net external assets mainly in the form of direct investments and securities investments, though securities investments were much more volatile than direct investments. Improvement in the private short-term net external asset position was also an important factor behind the continuous expansion in the NEAP in the 1990s when the growth of long-term net external assets reached a plateau.

3. International comparisons

It is useful to compare Japan's NEAP data with those of other major industrial countries. Tables 1.3 and 1.4 summarize stock and flow data of external assets and liabilities for four major industrial countries.

TABLE 1.3. Gross external assets and liabilities and net external assets of Japan, the USA, the UK, and Germany

(US$ billion)

Year	Japan			United States			United Kingdom			Germany		
	Assets	Liabilities	Net Assets	Assets	Liabilities	Net Assets	Assets	Liabilities	Net Assets	Assets	Liabilities	Net Assets
1970	–	–	4.7	165.4	106.9	58.5	49.0	40.4	8.6	51.0	34.8	16.3
1971	32.8	23.0	9.8	179.0	133.5	45.5	61.4	51.3	10.1	61.6	44.3	17.4
1972	43.6	29.7	13.9	198.7	161.7	37.0	66.3	52.1	14.2	69.5	51.4	18.1
1973	47.6	34.5	13.0	222.4	174.5	47.9	71.5	58.9	12.6	91.2	67.7	23.5
1974	55.9	47.0	8.9	255.7	197.0	58.7	180.4	175.0	5.4	114.7	81.1	33.5
1975	58.3	51.3	7.0	295.1	220.9	74.2	199.5	194.0	5.5	122.9	85.9	37.0
1976	68.0	58.4	9.6	457.6	281.7	175.9	222.4	214.2	8.2	152.3	108.5	43.8
1977	80.1	58.1	22.0	519.0	328.5	190.5	273.6	261.4	12.2	181.4	130.2	51.2
1978	118.7	82.5	36.2	627.3	398.8	228.4	340.2	312.9	27.3	232.9	173.2	59.7
1979	135.4	106.6	28.8	792.9	450.0	342.9	443.3	415.7	27.6	258.7	207.6	51.1
1980	159.6	148.0	11.5	936.3	543.7	392.5	550.8	507.7	43.2	249.1	216.0	33.1
1981	209.3	198.3	10.9	1,004.2	629.9	374.3	630.3	568.0	62.3	241.3	215.1	26.3
1982	227.7	203.0	24.7	958.8	693.8	265.0	671.8	601.5	70.2	251.0	218.0	32.9
1983	272.0	234.7	37.3	1,127.6	835.5	292.1	705.7	625.1	80.6	234.3	201.9	32.4
1984	341.2	266.9	74.3	1,125.2	952.2	172.9	721.0	629.2	91.8	231.5	193.1	38.5
1985	437.7	307.9	129.8	1,295.6	1,159.8	135.8	857.8	751.1	106.7	339.5	288.5	51.0
1986	727.3	547.0	180.4	1,577.7	1,441.3	136.4	1,062.5	916.0	146.5	501.7	404.8	96.9
1987	1,071.6	830.9	240.7	1,722.3	1,650.9	71.3	1,301.6	1,180.2	121.4	665.7	496.5	169.2
1988	1,469.3	1,177.6	291.7	1,949.7	1,935.0	14.8	1,403.1	1,287.8	115.3	689.5	479.8	209.7
1989	1,771.0	1,477.8	293.2	2,251.4	2,328.6	-77.2	1,536.5	1,450.3	86.2	863.6	595.0	268.6
1990	1,857.9	1,529.8	328.1	2,178.1	2,389.8	-211.7	1,757.0	1,743.6	13.3	1,100.0	751.1	348.9
1991	2,006.5	1,623.4	383.1	2,315.0	2,664.0	-349.0	1,775.8	1,755.4	20.4	1,145.8	817.6	328.2
1992	2,035.2	1,521.6	513.6	2,285.6	2,854.0	-568.4	1,779.3	1,745.7	33.7	1,174.7	881.0	293.7
1993	2,180.9	1,570.1	610.8	2,750.3	3,162.9	-412.5	2,055.9	2,000.7	55.2	1,276.0	1,033.2	242.8
1994	2,424.2	1,735.3	689.0	2,825.8	3,318.3	-492.5	2,170.2	2,117.3	52.9	1,449.2	1,233.1	216.1
1995	2,722.5	1,974.4	748.1	3,352.9	4,126.6	-773.7	2,489.8	2,431.7	58.1	1,671.9	1,484.5	187.4

Notes: 1. The US data are based on historical costs for 1970–5, current replacement cost for 1976–81, and market values for 1982–present.
2. The exchange rates used to convert the UK and German data are their respective rates at the end of the year, obtained from IMF, *International Financial Statistics*. The Japanese data are expressed in US dollars.

Sources: Bank of Japan, *Balance of Payments Monthly*, April issues; Department of Commerce, US Government, *Survey of Current Business*, June issues; Central Statistical Office, UK Government, *United Kingdom Balance of Payments* (Pink Book), various issues; Deutsche Bundesbank, *Monthly Report*, May 1981, August 1983, October 1984, October 1986, October 1989; International Monetary Fund, *International Financial Statistics*, CD-ROM.

TABLE 1.4. Investment income of Japan, the USA, the UK, and Germany

(US$ billion)

Year	Japan			United States			United Kingdom			Germany		
	Received	Paid	Net Received	Received	Paid	Net Received	Received	Paid	Net Received	Received	Paid	Net Received
1970	0.71	0.92	-0.21	11.75	5.52	6.23	3.59	2.16	1.43	1.97	2.02	-0.05
1971	0.98	1.03	-0.05	12.69	5.44	7.25	3.74	2.40	1.34	2.49	2.27	0.22
1972	1.62	1.26	0.36	14.69	6.54	8.15	8.51	7.02	1.50	2.91	2.56	0.35
1973	2.65	2.16	0.49	21.67	9.64	12.03	12.07	8.81	3.25	4.06	3.44	0.62
1974	3.56	4.00	-0.44	27.64	12.11	15.53	14.52	10.99	3.53	4.97	4.61	0.36
1975	3.61	3.89	-0.28	25.42	12.58	12.84	14.56	12.60	1.96	5.04	4.10	0.94
1976	3.46	3.66	-0.20	29.29	13.32	15.97	15.09	12.29	2.79	5.56	4.26	1.30
1977	3.72	3.61	0.11	32.19	14.21	17.98	15.40	14.94	0.46	5.88	5.70	0.18
1978	5.26	4.38	0.88	42.13	21.61	20.52	21.47	19.93	1.54	8.70	6.17	2.53
1979	8.97	6.95	2.02	64.10	32.91	31.19	37.25	34.69	2.56	11.06	9.32	1.74
1980	11.12	10.26	0.86	72.52	42.13	30.39	55.07	55.48	-0.42	13.18	11.26	1.92
1981	15.82	16.59	-0.77	86.52	52.39	34.13	74.88	72.34	2.54	12.96	12.44	0.52
1982	18.32	16.60	1.72	85.35	57.10	28.25	77.59	75.06	2.53	13.32	14.51	-1.19
1983	15.60	12.52	3.08	81.97	54.56	27.41	64.36	60.07	4.29	13.56	11.95	1.61
1984	18.77	14.54	4.23	92.95	69.57	23.38	68.52	62.79	5.73	14.61	11.03	3.58
1985	22.11	15.27	6.84	72.27	66.14	6.13	66.81	63.93	2.88	15.04	11.77	3.27
1986	29.09	19.61	9.48	80.97	70.00	10.97	69.40	62.59	6.81	21.49	17.26	4.23
1987	49.25	32.58	16.67	100.78	91.30	9.48	78.62	72.27	6.35	28.33	24.24	4.09
1988	74.82	53.81	21.01	129.07	115.73	13.34	100.59	92.48	8.11	32.18	27.63	4.55
1989	101.82	78.39	23.43	152.53	138.65	13.88	121.00	115.19	5.81	41.67	29.84	11.83
1990	122.18	98.97	23.21	160.30	139.41	20.89	141.44	139.02	2.42	60.74	42.61	18.13
1991	140.38	113.68	26.70	137.01	121.17	15.84	136.07	135.93	0.14	69.34	49.67	19.67
1992	142.11	105.89	36.22	119.05	107.86	11.19	120.51	114.98	5.53	75.53	58.70	16.83
1993	147.45	106.05	41.40	119.90	110.16	9.74	111.19	107.89	3.30	73.66	59.60	14.06
1994	154.50	113.48	41.02	141.71	145.84	-4.13	119.43	106.07	13.36	73.97	66.17	7.80
1995	191.45	146.37	45.08	182.69	190.66	-7.97	146.94	131.87	15.07	92.81	90.89	1.92

Notes: 1. The data are expressed in the SDR until 1981 for Japan, the United States, and Germany and they are converted into US dollars using the annual average SDR exchange rates.
2. The original data for the United Kingdom are expressed in US dollars.

Sources: IMF, Balance of Payments Statistics, Yearbook 1977, 1982, 1984, 1989, 1990, 1995, and 1996. IMF, International Financial Statistics, Yearbook 1996.

Table 1.3 compares Japan, the United States, the United Kingdom, and Germany regarding their stock measures of gross external assets and liabilities and net external assets. The data are taken from national and IMF statistics and expressed in US$ million.[6] The stock data in the table indicate that Japan had the smallest net external assets of the four countries until 1982 but that, as a result of rapid accumulation in the 1980s, it surpassed Germany in 1983, the United Kingdom in 1985, and the United States in 1986.[7] In terms of the size of gross external assets and liabilities, Japan had the smallest of the four countries until 1982, but it exceeded Germany in 1983 and the United Kingdom in 1988, excepting UK gross external liabilities, which almost always exceed those of Japan. The gross external assets and liabilities of the United States are still the largest of all in size. In essence, Japan became the world's largest net creditor nation while accumulating gross external assets more rapidly than gross external liabilities.

Table 1.4 compares the same four countries concerning their investment income received from and paid to the rest of the world, which represent flow measures of external assets and liabilities. The data are taken from the IMF's balance of payments statistics for international comparison. On the basis of net investment income received, Japan became a larger net creditor nation than Germany in 1984, the United Kingdom in 1985, and the United States in 1987. The investment income data show, however, that the United States was a net creditor country until 1993 even though it had turned a net debtor country four years earlier on the basis of stock data. A similar divergence between the stock and flow data is also observed for other countries.

To summarize this section, while it is not possible to obtain accurate statistics of Japan's NEAP because of the lack of truly reliable data, we can safely conclude that Japan accumulated huge amounts of net external assets and established itself among the world's leading net creditor nations in the latter half of the 1980s. This was made possible by a rapid expansion of private long-term net external assets in the 1980s that exceeded the growth of short-term net external liabilities, and by a substantial improvement in private short-term net external asset positions in the 1990s when the growth of long-term net external assets slowed down.

III. The Current and Capital Accounts and the Savings–Investment Balance

Japan's accumulation of considerable amounts of net external assets and its becoming the world's largest creditor nation in the 1980s, followed by its maintenance of that status in the 1990s, suggests that the causes of this shift can be found specifically in the 1980s and 1990s. This does not mean, however, that the underlying conditions behind the remarkable expansion of Japan's NEAP emerged suddenly in the 1980s. It is argued that long-term, structural factors and factors specific to the 1980s and 1990s both played important roles in the growth of Japan's NEAP. Long-term, structural factors include (a) the dynamically changing comparative advantage of the Japanese manufacturing industry, such as a shift to high value-added, highly income-elastic manufacturing products, and (b) high rates of savings by the Japanese household sector relative to the rates of investment by the corporate sector. Factors specific to the 1980s and 1990s include (c) Japan's liberalization of exchange and capital transactions during the first half of the 1980s, (d) divergent macroeconomic developments in the United States and Japan, and (e) fluctuations in Japanese asset prices, particularly the yen/dollar exchange rate, stock and share prices, and land prices.

As is well known, a change in a country's NEAP is identical to the current account or the negative of the capital account, which in turn is the same as the savings–investment balance:

$$\text{NEAP} - \text{NEAP}(-1) = \text{Current Account}$$

$$= - \text{ Capital Account}$$

$$= \text{Savings} - \text{Investment}.$$

A rapid and continuous expansion of Japan's NEAP, therefore, means that Japan has been running current account surpluses and that Japanese investors and firms have been investing abroad, thereby accumulating net claims against the rest of the world. This process has been supported by the excess of Japanese savings over investment. Since certain autonomous elements existed in the current account, the capital account, and the savings-investment balance, let us examine factors affecting each one by one.

1. The current account

Japan has been running persistent current account surpluses since 1981 when the economy recovered from the second oil-price shock. Accumulation of persistent current account surpluses led to a massive build-up of net external assets.

Current account surpluses in the 1980s were caused principally by merchandise trade surpluses (Appendix Table A2). The merchandise trade account has been in surplus since the mid-1960s, even at times of oil-price shocks in the 1970s. Trade surpluses widened considerably in the 1980s until 1987 and, after the brief period of decline in 1988–90, rose again in the first half of the 1990s. The services and transfers accounts were stable and in deficit throughout the period, so that they cannot be judged as an element contributing to persistent current account surpluses.

TABLE 1.5. Trade balance of selected commodity categories

(US$ million)

Exports	1960	1965	1970	1975	1980	1985	1986	1987	1988	1989	1990	1991	1992	1993	1994	1995
Foodstuff	256	344	648	760	1,588	1,316	1,476	1,546	1,695	1,687	1,646	1,822	1,929	2,007	2,038	2,124
Crude materials and fuels	112	156	215	629	1,271	1,256	1,398	1,649	1,718	2,115	2,379	2,400	2,883	3,278	3,797	4,255
Textile products	1,223	1,582	2,408	3,719	6,296	6,263	6,874	6,917	6,908	6,862	7,195	7,943	8,590	8,239	8,385	8,943
Chemical products	181	547	1,234	3,889	6,767	7,698	9,484	11,662	13,964	14,776	15,872	17,475	19,118	20,199	23,669	30,213
Iron and steel products	388	1,290	2,844	10,176	15,454	13,566	12,706	12,610	15,321	14,789	12,509	13,612	13,331	14,524	14,842	17,488
Machinery and equipment	1,035	2,975	8,941	30,004	81,481	126,179	155,027	171,077	196,965	205,471	215,097	236,641	256,828	274,388	300,837	330,903
Others	860	1,558	3,028	6,576	16,950	19,360	22,186	23,760	28,346	29,475	32,250	34,632	36,971	38,276	42,032	49,011
Total exports	4,055	8,452	19,318	55,753	129,807	175,638	209,151	229,221	264,917	275,175	286,948	314,525	339,650	360,911	395,600	442,937
Imports																
Foodstuff	548	1,470	2,574	8,815	14,666	15,547	19,186	22,395	29,120	31,012	31,572	34,473	37,289	39,413	46,652	51,120
Crude materials and fuels	2,951	4,846	10,528	37,301	93,752	73,834	54,423	61,122	66,330	73,649	85,199	81,923	78,734	75,693	76,354	86,165
Textile products	19	57	314	1,310	3,180	3,886	5,027	7,624	10,631	13,283	12,805	13,660	15,328	16,569	20,390	24,540
Chemical products	265	408	1,000	2,057	6,202	8,073	9,733	11,845	14,830	15,948	16,045	17,412	17,355	17,964	20,216	24,817
Iron and steel products	88	141	276	189	894	1,479	1,762	2,484	4,625	5,068	4,584	5,503	3,787	4,067	4,065	5,896
Machinery and equipment	435	760	2,298	4,286	9,843	12,372	14,699	19,123	26,661	32,376	40,863	42,851	42,853	46,634	59,591	85,068
Others	185	487	1,891	3,905	11,991	14,348	21,578	24,922	35,157	39,511	43,731	40,915	37,675	40,330	47,473	58,488
Total imports	4,491	8,169	18,881	57,863	140,528	129,539	126,408	149,515	187,354	210,847	234,799	236,737	233,021	240,670	274,742	336,094
Net exports																
Foodstuff	-292	-1,126	-1,926	-8,055	-13,078	-14,231	-17,710	-20,849	-27,425	-29,325	-29,926	-32,651	-35,360	-37,406	-44,614	-48,996
Crude materials and fuels	-2,839	-4,690	-10,313	-36,672	-92,481	-72,578	-53,025	-59,473	-64,612	-71,534	-82,820	-79,523	-75,850	-72,415	-72,558	-81,910
Textile products	1,204	1,525	2,094	2,409	3,116	2,377	1,847	-707	-3,723	-6,421	-5,610	-5,717	-6,738	-8,330	-12,005	-15,597
Chemical products	-84	139	234	1,832	565	-375	-249	-183	-866	-1,172	-173	63	1,763	2,235	3,453	5,396
Iron and steel products	300	1,149	2,568	9,987	14,560	12,087	10,944	10,126	10,696	9,721	7,925	8,109	9,544	10,457	10,777	11,591
Machinery and equipment	600	2,215	6,643	25,718	71,638	113,807	140,328	151,954	170,304	173,095	174,234	193,790	213,975	227,754	241,246	245,836
Others	675	1,071	1,137	2,671	4,959	5,012	608	-1,162	-6,811	-10,036	-11,481	-6,283	-704	-2,054	-5,441	-9,477
Total net exports	-436	283	437	-2,110	-10,721	46,099	82,743	79,706	77,563	64,328	52,149	77,788	106,629	120,241	120,858	106,843

Sources: Bank of Japan, Economic Statistics Annual, various issues; Balance of Payments Monthly, various issues.

Table 1.5 summarizes the net exports of major commodity categories. It is observed that Japan's large merchandise trade surpluses in the 1980s were brought about primarily by increases in the net export of machinery and equipment and by decreases in the net import of crude materials and mineral fuels. Japan has long maintained a trade pattern of importing raw materials and mineral fuels while exporting manufactured products. In the 1980s and 1990s import values of foreign raw materials and mineral fuels declined while imports of manufactured products, including both intermediate and finished products, rose. At the same time, exports of manufactured products, particularly machinery and equipment, exploded. Dependence on foreign raw materials and mineral fuels was reduced partly due to declines in their international prices and partly due to the increased efficiency in their use and the development of energy-saving technologies.

Over the years, Japan has been shifting the weight of manufacturing exports from low value-added, labour-intensive products to high value-added, technology- and human-capital-intensive products. Starting with light-industry products such as textiles, the weight of exports shifted over time to heavy-industry products such as iron and steel, and to machinery products such as colour television sets, motor vehicles, machine tools, and semi-conductors. This shift reflected dynamic changes in Japan's comparative advantage. Keen competition among firms in the domestic market and scale economies due to growing domestic demand made the Japanese manufacturing industry one of the most efficient producers of high value-added and highly income-elastic manufactured products. Although the dynamically changing comparative advantage of the manufacturing industry was not the direct cause of large merchandise trade surpluses in the 1980s, it was definitely a fundamental, underlying factor. Without it, Japan would not have experienced such explosive net export behaviour in the key manufactured products.

Following Ueda (1988) and Kawai (1994), let us investigate the major determinants of Japan's net exports by running a simple OLS regression. The estimated regression equation reveals that Japanese net exports relative to GDP for the period 1975.I to 1996.IV is explained primarily by the real effective exchange rate of the yen, relative levels of real domestic demand in Japan and six other major industrialized countries, and the real oil price.[8] Specifically, relative real domestic demand is identified as quantitatively the most important variable affecting Japan's net export, while the effects of the real effective exchange rate and the real oil price, though significant, are smaller. The quantitative impact of US macroeconomic fluctuations on Japanese net exports turns out to be large because fluctuations in the US economy strongly affect Japan's external demand. In the 1990s, the relatively low domestic demand in Japan in the face of the post-bubble recession has contributed to its continuing surplus in net exports. This may well have been aided by the real depreciation of the yen during the 1989–91 period.

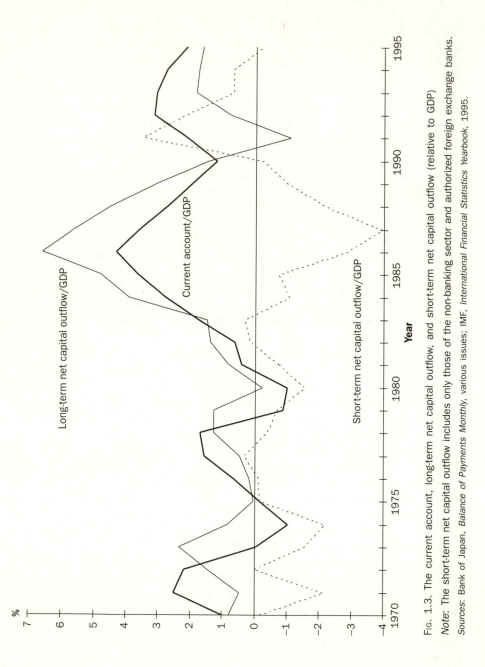

Fig. 1.3. The current account, long-term net capital outflow, and short-term net capital outflow (relative to GDP)

Note: The short-term net capital outflow includes only those of the non-banking sector and authorized foreign exchange banks.

Sources: Bank of Japan, *Balance of Payments Monthly,* various issues; IMF, *International Financial Statistics Yearbook,* 1995.

2. The capital account

Overall trends

Japan's capital account recorded large deficits (net outflows) throughout the 1980s and 1990s (see Appendix Table A2). This led to the accumulation of net claims against the rest of the world.

The long-term net capital outflow moved in a parallel fashion with the current account.[9] This is demonstrated clearly in Figure 1.3, which depicts the movements of the current account and long-term and short-term (private) net capital outflows, expressed as percentages of GDP, for the period 1970 through 1995.[10] The rise and fall in the current account was accompanied by a rise and fall in the long-term net capital outflow throughout the period under consideration. The magnitude by which the long-term net capital outflow exceeded the current account in the mid- to late 1980s is striking. The current account movement had also been accompanied by a rise and fall in the short-term net capital outflow until the early 1980s, but these two started to exhibit divergent movements from the historical pattern thereafter. The short-term net capital outflow has also exhibited negative correlation with the long-term net capital outflow since 1984.

The fluctuation in the long-term net capital outflow was associated with a remarkable expansion and contraction in the net outflow of securities investment (Appendix Table A2). The share of net securities investment outflows in total long-term net capital outflows rose rapidly in the mid-1980s, reaching a peak of 77 per cent in 1986. Then it started to decline. The share continued to decline and registered net inflows in 1991, but started to recover strongly afterwards. The net outflow of direct investment grew steadily in the latter half of the 1980s. Despite a surplus (net inflow) in the long-term net capital account in 1991, the net outflow of direct investment remained steady and persistent.[11] Other components of long-term capital flows, such as loans and trade credits, were less important in magnitude than securities and direct investment. Securities investment was clearly the principal vehicle through which Japan accumulated long-term net external assets in the mid- to latter part of the 1980s, while direct investment persistently contributed to net capital outflows.[12]

Private short-term net capital outflows started to move in the opposite direction from long-term net capital outflows in 1984. When Japan's long-term net capital outflows expanded rapidly in the mid-1980s, private short-term net capital *inflows* also grew quickly. As long-term net capital outflows declined quickly in 1987 and after, short-term net capital *inflows* also started to shrink. Essentially, Japan was engaged in large-scale international financial intermediation by borrowing short and lending long in the mid- to latter part of the 1980s. During this period Japan's long-term net capital outflows were financed by the current account surplus (domestic excess savings over investment) as well as by short-term net capital inflows. However, such international financial intermediation disappeared suddenly in the 1990s due to the fact that net outflows of long-term capital slowed down and net outflows of short-term capital expanded.

Securities investment

It is generally pointed out (see Ueda (1990) and Kawai (1991, 1994)) that three factors contributed to the surge of securities investments in the 1980s and the mid-1990s: (a) Japan's liberalization of capital controls in the first half of the 1980s; (b) the high real interest rate abroad, particularly in the United States, relative to Japan; and (c) Japan's rising stock and share prices in the second half of the 1980s.

First, there is no doubt that the rapid rise of securities investment abroad was made possible by a series of measures to liberalize government regulations on international capital transactions. The first major deregulation occurred in December 1980 when the Ministry of Finance drastically revised the Foreign Exchange and Foreign Trade Control Law to liberalize, in principle, all foreign exchange and capital transactions. This revision was designed to ensure freer mobility of capital into and out of Japan. None the less, an elaborate system for checking and monitoring capital transactions was retained, and regulatory restrictions on foreign securities investment were still in place, thereby hindering complete integration of the Japanese financial and capital markets with the rest of the world. The second impetus for capital flow liberalization was given by the Yen/Dollar Agreement of May 1984 reached by the Japanese Ministry of Finance and the US Treasury Department, which forced the Ministry of Finance to implement additional measures to liberalize cross-border capital transactions and internationalize the Japanese financial system (see Frankel (1984) and Fukao (1990) for details). The third measures came out when existing restrictions on foreign securities holdings, such as ceiling limits on the amount of foreign securities held by life and non-life insurance companies, pension trusts of trust banks, etc., were relaxed incrementally.

As a result of these liberalization measures, the Japanese financial and capital markets became virtually integrated into world markets by the mid-1980s and the Japanese investors could start accumulating foreign securities at a rapid pace to achieve a desired portfolio mix. This autonomous stock adjustment appears to have taken place over several years, perhaps in the mid- to latter part of the 1980s, which led to a massive build-up of foreign securities.

The second factor that has contributed to large net outflows of securities investment is the high long-term real interest rate abroad relative to Japan. It is well documented that the expansionary fiscal policy and the consequent rise in real domestic demand in the United States under the first Reagan administration led to a high US real interest rate. It attracted capital from all over the world just as Japanese investors were beginning aggressively to acquire large quantities of foreign securities in a more liberalized institutional framework. Over and above the autonomous rise in the demand for foreign securities, which was prompted by the liberalization measures, the higher real interest rate in the United States was an added inducement for foreign securities investments.

The third factor leading to the rapid rise of securities investment abroad is the effect of Japanese asset prices, particularly those of stocks and shares and of land. In the 1980s, the Japanese stock market witnessed one of the biggest booms in its history with an impressive 25 per cent increase (per annum) in the Nikkei Stock Average between 1983 and 1989. Figure 1.4 plots the rate of change in the Japanese stock and share prices and land prices as well as the rate of growth of nominal GDP. It indicates that the stock and share prices rose substantially in the mid- to latter part of the 1980s and that the prices collapsed in the 1990s. A rise in Japanese stock and share prices stimulated securities investment abroad for two reasons. The first was the wealth effect. A rise in stock and share prices raised the value of Japanese investors' over-all financial wealth, thereby stimulating demand for various types of financial assets, one of which was foreign securities. The second reason concerned the regulations imposed on the distribution of capital gains. With a continuous rise in stock and share prices, Japanese investors accumulated large capital gains, realized or unrealized, in their portfolios. Several important institutional investors, however, were not allowed to distribute current and past capital gains to their clients. For example, Article 86 of the Insurance Law prohibited life insurance companies from distributing capital gains to policy holders for prudential reasons; only income gains could be distributed. In the face of increased competition among financial institutions due to liberalization in the domestic financial system, life insurance companies tried to convert capital gains into income gains in order to offer attractive rates of return to their policy holders. The income gains obtained from foreign securities yielding high nominal interest rates, such as those denominated in US, Canadian, and Australian dollars, could be distributed to the policy holders, while possible capital losses due to foreign currency depreciation could be offset by capital gains in the stock market. As long as stock and share prices rose and were expected to rise, securities investment abroad was justified.[13] This, in turn, meant that if the stock market were to collapse, securities investment abroad would no longer be justified.

Indeed, the net outflow of securities investment declined sharply in the first part of the 1990s when the Japanese stock and share prices declined sharply as a result of the Bank of Japan's tight monetary policy. The Nikkei Stock Average declined 38 per cent from ¥ 38,130.0 at the end of 1989 to ¥ 23,740.5

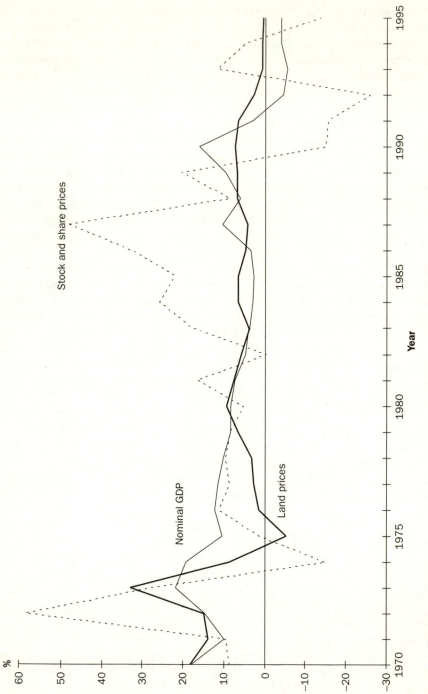

Stock and share prices

Nominal GDP

Land prices

Year

FIG. 1.4. The rates of change in stock and share prices, land prices, and nominal GDP

a year later, and the market remained stagnant in 1991 and 1992. In the face of large capital losses in the stock market, the financial institutions and institutional investors no longer had an incentive to purchase foreign securities because of the risk of potential exchange losses that could no longer be offset by capital gains elsewhere.

The recovery of net outflows of securities investment since 1993 may be explained by the low interest rate due to the Bank of Japan's shift to a lax monetary policy to cope with the collapsing stock market and ailing commercial banks with bad loans. Low interest policy and a rebound of the stock and share prices contributed to the expansion of securities investment abroad.

Direct investment

Japan's direct investment abroad was not large in magnitude until the mid-1980s but the rise has since been remarkable. The recent globalization of business activities has been a natural underlying factor behind the rise in Japanese direct investment, and the most important macroeconomic factor since 1985 has been an appreciation of the yen exchange rate against the major international currencies. As Figure 1.5 demonstrates, the real effective exchange rate of the yen, measured as the IMF's relative normalized unit labour costs, appreciated abruptly and drastically between 1985 and 1988 and between 1990 and 1995. The sharp yen rate appreciation stimulated direct investment abroad from two channels.

First, steep yen rate appreciation meant a dramatic shift in Japan's international price competitiveness. The real effective value of the yen, based on relative normalized unit labour costs, appreciated by 39 per cent between 1985 and 1988 and by 55 per cent between 1990 and 1995. To cope with the new international relative prices, many firms in the manufacturing sector producing with high labour contents and low value-added were forced to move part or all of their production base from the home market to foreign countries where production costs were lower. They invested particularly in the growing East Asian economies.[14]

The second channel through which the yen rate had a positive impact on Japan's direct investment abroad was the 'liquidity' or 'wealth' effect. Insofar as yen appreciation made Japanese firms relatively more 'wealthy' in the sense of the increased collateral and liquidity, it enabled them to finance direct investment relatively cheaply compared to their foreign competitors. The Bank of Japan also injected abundant liquidity into the economy in the latter half of the 1980s to cope with the high yen rate, and toward the mid-1990s to cope with the stock market collapse. This rise in liquidity partly explains the growth of Japan's direct investment abroad.

Econometric evidence reported by Kawai (1994) is clearly consistent with the view that real appreciation of the yen induced net outflows of direct

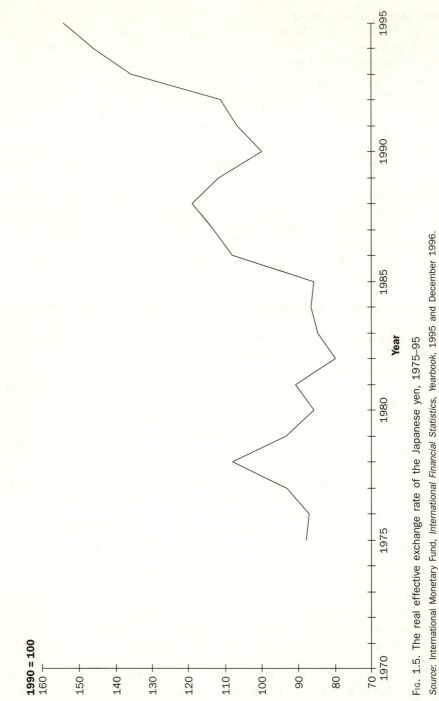

FIG. 1.5. The real effective exchange rate of the Japanese yen, 1975–95

Source: International Monetary Fund, *International Financial Statistics, Yearbook,* 1995 and December 1996.

investment. The positive impact of the real exchange rate, though small in magnitude, is extremely robust regarding specification changes.

3. The savings and investment balance

That Japan experienced persistent current account surpluses and accumulated considerable amounts of net external assets in the 1980s and 1990s reflects the fact that its residents spent less than they produced, or saved more than they invested. The excess of savings over investment was transferred abroad in the form of claims against the rest of the world. To fully understand the underlying causes of the rapid expansion of Japan's NEAP, therefore, its savings and investment behaviour must be examined.

Figure 1.6 depicts Japan's net savings and net investment as percentages of GDP. The figure shows that both the savings rate (net savings relative to GDP) and the investment rate (net investment relative to GDP) declined over time as a trend, while maintaining a fairly close relationship with each other. The two rates averaged about 22.5 per cent in the first half of the 1970s and declined to 17 per cent (for the investment rate) and 18 per cent (for the savings rate) afterwards. They moved very closely with each other until the beginning of the 1980s when the relation became loose. For example, the correlation coefficient between the two rates was 0.90 in the 1970–80 period and declined to 0.70 in the 1980–95 period. The correlation between savings and investment has loosened since the beginning of the 1980s because of the increased liberalization of international capital transactions and integration of the Japanese and world financial markets. Liberalization of capital movements and financial market integration have made domestic investment less constrained by domestic savings.[15] When the savings rate declined in the beginning of the 1980s, the investment rate declined faster. When the savings rate rose in the mid- to late 1980s, the investment rate also rose and narrowed the gap with the savings rate, but investment never caught up to savings. When the savings rate declined again in the 1990s the investment rate also declined. The excess savings, which have been in place since the beginning of the 1980s, have been transferred abroad mainly in the form of securities and direct investment.

Figure 1.7 breaks down Japan's savings–investment balance by economic sectors as a percentage of GDP. The economic sectors considered here are the household sector (including unincorporated enterprises), the business corporate sector, and the government sector (including the central and local governments as well as the social security account). The negative of the foreign sector corresponds to Japan's current account. It is observed that the household sector maintains a consistently high savings–investment balance without large fluctuations and that the corporate sector maintains a negative balance

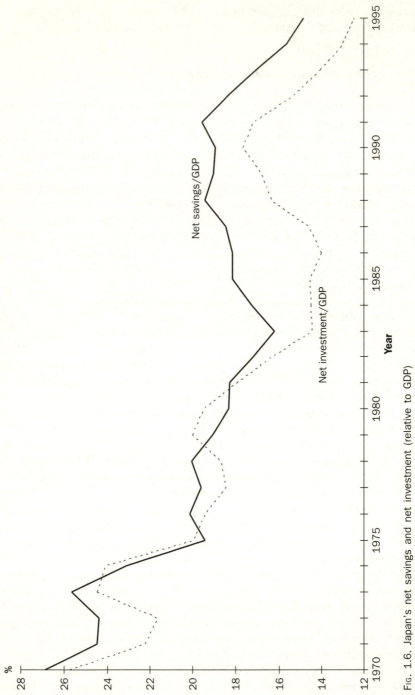

FIG. 1.6. Japan's net savings and net investment (relative to GDP)

Sources: Economic Planning Agency, Government of Japan, *Annual Report of National Income*, various issues.

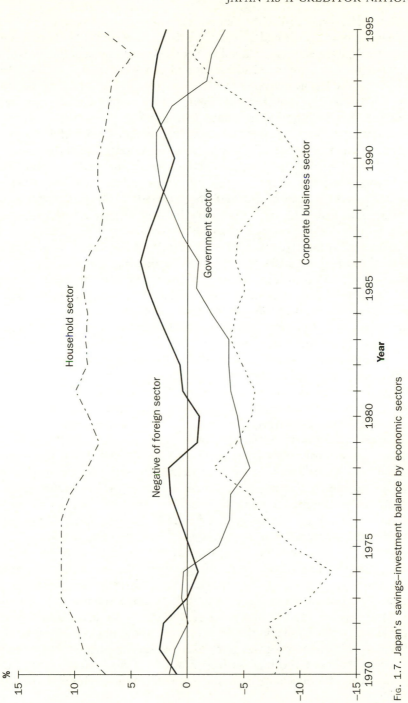

Household sector

Negative of foreign sector

Government sector

Corporate business sector

Year

% 15 10 5 0 -5 -10 -15

1970 1975 1980 1985 1990 1995

FIG. 1.7. Japan's savings–investment balance by economic sectors

Sources: Economic Planning Agency, Government of Japan, *Annual Report of National Income,* various issues.

which fluctuates cyclically with general economic activities over time. The government sector, which had a negative balance in the mid-1970s as a result of mounting budget deficits, changed its fiscal stance to reconsolidation in the late 1970s, gradually improved its savings–investment balance in the 1980s, and finally succeeded in reversing the balance from red to black in the latter half of the 1980s. The government savings–investment balance once again deteriorated in the 1990s due to a deep recession.

The current account used to be strongly correlated with the corporate savings–investment balance until the late 1970s. In contrast, the current account moved in parallel with the government balance in the early to mid-1980s; Japan's rising current account surplus in this period was clearly associated with a sharp reduction in budget deficits (see Ueda (1988)). Changes in the current account since the late 1980s have been accompanied by changes in the corporate savings–investment balance, despite the opposite changes in the fiscal balance. In other words, in the latter half of the 1980s, active private investment more than offset the cyclically improving government balance and led to a reduction in the current account surplus. In the 1990s stagnant private investment more than offset the cyclically deteriorating budget deficits and led to an expansion in the current account surplus.

It must be pointed out that, in the United States, the government savings–investment balance worsened rapidly in the 1980s, particularly during the Reagan administration. Even though the US economy enjoyed its longest peacetime expansion in history, and consumers and firms increased their spending, the budget deficit did not decline. This was a departure from historical patterns. Essentially, the United States and Japan adopted fiscal policies that were radically divergent from each other in the 1980s; the United States ran an expansionary fiscal policy by increasing budget deficits and Japan a contractionary fiscal policy by reducing budget deficits. From the view of savings–investment balances, part of Japan's large current account surplus was attributable to the contrasting fiscal policies between the two countries. The reduction in the current account surplus in the late 1980s and its rise in the 1990s, however, should be explained respectively by active and stagnant corporate investment, rather than by changes in fiscal policies.

While the persistently large savings–investment balance of the household sector was not the direct cause of the rise in Japan's current account surpluses in the 1980s and 1990s, it was one of the long-term, structural factors behind it. The household balance, though it declined slightly from an average of 10 per cent in the 1970s to 8 per cent in the 1980s and 1990s, was high and stable over time. Unlike in the United States, it did not decline even when the economy continued to grow, nor did it rise in the post-bubble recession in the 1990s. Without the high savings rate of the household sector, Japan would not have experienced persistent current account surpluses in the 1980s and 1990s.

A large number of factors have been suggested as possible explanations for Japan's sustained high savings rate for the household sector.[16] Horioka (1992) finds that among them the demographic structure of the Japanese population is a major (if not the dominant) determinant of not only the high level of Japan's savings rate but also of trends over time in Japan. That is, he argues that the low ratio of the aged population to the working-age population in Japan is the major cause of the high level of Japan's savings rate relative to the US level, and that the age structure of the population is one of the few factors that can, by itself, explain the observed pattern in Japan's savings rate.

IV. Japan as a Fragile Creditor Nation?

Japan's current account continues to be in surplus and its net external assets continue to expand even in the 1990s as the economy is damaged by a long, deep recession in the aftermath of the burst of the 'speculative bubbles'. The rising NEAP in the 1990s, however, does not seem to be taken as something threatening to the rest of the world, which is a big change from the experience of the 1980s. In the 1980s, it was feared by many observers in the United States, Europe, and elsewhere that the Japanese, with awesome financial resources, were buying up their countries. Not only have such sentiments faded away in the 1990s, but also Japan is now considered as a fragile creditor nation. Why?

1. The post-bubble recession and overhang of non-performing loans

What is clearly different in the 1990s is the fact that the economy has entered a long period of deep recession, following the burst of the bubbles in the stock and land markets in the 1980s. The burst of the bubbles led all types of financial institutions to difficulties due to mounting non-performing assets. Many commercial banks had extended loans to firms and speculators with land as collateral. A decline in land prices to levels below the loan value meant that borrowers could no longer make repayment even when they sold their land. A decline in stock and share prices reduced values of assets held by many finanical institutions.

Commercial banks felt the pinch, and there is some evidence that they limited loans even to prudent firms due to the overhang of non-performing loans. They viewed foreign loans and investment as equally risky and reduced the scale of international operations. In addition to reducing the asset portfolio, they chose to make repayments on their past short-term borrowings from abroad and reduced activities on the liability side. This led to large net outflows of short-term capital, improving the short-term net external asset position for the economy as a whole. Institutional investors, such as life insurance companies and trust banks, were also weakened by non-performing loans and became extremely sensitive to taking exchange risks through foreign securities investment. They virtually stopped acquiring foreign securities until 1993 when they resumed foreign securities investment.

The net result is that the current account surplus was financed largely by short-term capital outflows rather than long-term capital outflows in the first few years of the 1990s. The absence of long-term net capital outflows was the major event that took place in the face of the burst of asset price bubbles.

2. Exchange rate fluctuations

The yen/dollar exchange rate has exhibited wild fluctuations as ever since the end of the 1980s. First, a substantial yen rate depreciation occurred in 1989–91, followed by a gradual and persistent yen rate appreciation culminating at a level just around 80 yen to the US dollar in the spring of 1995. The yen rate then started to reverse the trend in the summer and continued to depreciate, reaching about 120 yen per dollar early in 1997. Yen rate appreciation in the 1992–5 period created another round of foreign direct investment by Japanese firms, which were forced to move part of their home production base abroad. The subsequent yen rate depreciation, however, has been causing some problems for those firms that invested abroad, as it can have a negative impact on firms that rely on procurement of foreign parts and components and imported intermediate products.

Exchange rate fluctuations also increase exchange risks for investors engaged in foreign securities investment because most of the debt instruments are denominated in foreign currencies. Japan is distinct in comparison to earlier creditor nations, such as the United Kingdom before the First World War and the United Sates in the post-Second World War period, in that Japan holds most of its net external assets in the form of foreign-currency denominated instruments, while the United Kingdom and the United States held their net external assets mainly in the form of the pound sterling and the US dollar, respectively. Despite its large net debtor status, the United States can continue to borrow from abroad in US-dollar denominated instruments. The inability of Japanese investors to lend in the Japanese yen poses the serious question of how to protect the real purchasing power of their wealth invested abroad. This is an important source of fragility of Japan as a creditor nation.

It must be pointed out, however, that yen appreciation raises the real purchasing power of yen denominated financial instruments held by the Japanese, while reducing the real purchasing power of foreign-currency denominated financial assets. Since the Japanese investors tend to accumulate foreign-currency denominated external assets, it is imperative that they diversify their portfolios to maximize real purchasing power of wealth at a minimum risk. This requires them to be competent and prudent global fund managers.

3. An ageing society

The proportion of the aged in the composition of the Japanese population has been rising more rapidly than in most other industrialized countries. This single fact overshadows the future course of the Japanese economy. Rapid population ageing, in the sense of the rising number of the elderly and the declining number of young in the total population in Japan, is a product of a large decline in the fertility rate and a marked lengthening of the average life-expectancy. This has several important macroeconomic implications (see Yashiro and Oishi (1993)). First, there is a negative impact on the labour market through a declining labour force and an increasing share of older workers in the total labour force. Second, there is a negative impact on the capital market due to falling savings rates as a result of the rising proportion of the elderly to the working-age population. Third, there is a negative fiscal impact with an increasing share of the elderly causing substantial transfers of income from the working generation to the retired generation through tax and social security systems. Essentially, an ageing society means that the proportion of the elderly to working-age people rises and greater burdens are borne by a smaller number of young people to support the society.

All these factors tend to indicate that Japan's savings rate will decline drastically, leaving less financial resources directed to capital investment, and that Japan will eventually experience current account deficits in the early part of the twenty-first century. Japan's creditor nation status, therefore, may be quite short-lived. As the current account turns into a deficit, there may be downward pressure on the value of the Japanese yen, reducing the real purchasing power of yen denominated assets. This would mean a grim future for Japan.

The declining savings rate, however, does not have to lead to current account deficits if investment also falls together with savings. Noguchi (1994) basically makes such a point. He argues that as national savings decline gradually, business investment will also decline. The reason is that the real return on capital falls with a declining labour force, unchanged labour-augmenting technical progress, and an inelastic labour supply response to population ageing, which in turn reduces the rate of investment. He obtained through simulation the result that Japan will continue to experience current account surpluses in the 1990s, even rising surpluses in the 2000–10 period, but will eventually face a deteriorating current account by the year 2015 and afterwards. Yashiro and Oishi (1993) argue that the negative impact of the rapidly ageing population on savings and investment can be mitigated by stimulating labour-augmenting technical progress and by extending the working life of older workers. They maintain that, with appropriate policies, reasonably high savings and investment can be sustained.

V. Conclusion

This chapter has presented data on Japan's NEAP, explained the recent patterns and compositions of NEAP accumulation, and examined the causes of the rapid rise in net external assets in the 1980s and 1990s.

Japan's NEAP started to expand rapidly in the 1980s due to the aggressive accumulation of long-term net external assets by private agents. This trend continued into the 1990s when decumulation of short-term external liabilities played a more important role. Factors that led to the expansion of Japan's NEAP include:

(a) Japan's dynamically changing comparative advantage and the consequent strengthening of its international competitiveness in high value-added, highly income-elastic manufacturing products;
(b) high and stable household savings reflecting the underlying demographic structure in Japan;
(c) Japan's liberalization of exchange and capital controls in the early 1980s;
(d) macroeconomic conditions in the United States and Japan and the induced changes in their real domestic demand; and
(e) changes in asset prices, such as the real interest rate, the real exchange rate, stock and share prices, and land prices.

To summarize this analysis, when the US economy entered a long expansion in 1983, government fiscal deficits emerged and persisted. The growth of real domestic demand alongside structural budget deficits raised the US long-term real interest rate. This attracted capital from all over the world, including Japan. Japanese investors who had just been freed from exchange and capital controls found it profitable to purchase dollar denominated securities for their global portfolio diversification. Long-term capital outflows in the form of foreign securities sky-rocketed, leading to an appreciation of the dollar and depreciation of the yen. Rising real domestic demand in the United States twinned with yen depreciation stimulated Japanese net exports, particularly those of machinery and equipment. Japan had established its competitive industrial base to provide those manufactured products highly demanded in the United States and other industrial countries. The Plaza G5 Agreement in September 1985 attempted to correct the strong dollar and to force dollar depreciation, but the pace of dollar depreciation accelerated too rapidly and the yen appreciated too steeply. This led to the Louvre Accord of February 1987, where the G7 countries decided to prevent further depreciation of the dollar and Japan agreed to adopt an expansionary monetary policy. The low interest rate policy continued well into 1989, keeping the official discount rate at the historically low 2.5 per cent level between February 1987 and May 1989. The great inflation of asset prices ensued, generating bubbles in the stock and land markets, which had to be dealt with later by an extremely tight monetary policy. The low interest rate and the subsequent boom in the stock market kept Japanese investment in foreign securities at high levels in the latter half of the 1980s. As the Bank of Japan shifted its monetary policy to squeeze liquidity out of the economy, the Japanese interest rate started to rise and the stock and share prices started to fall. The monetary tightening was so severe that the stock and share prices virtually collapsed by the end of 1990, which eventually ended one of the longest expansions of the Japanese economy. The collapse of the stock market damaged the financial positions of commercial banks and institutional investors who were no longer willing to take additional exchange risks and reduced the net outflow of securities investment to a significant degree. The year 1991 witnessed net inflows of securities, loans, and trade credits and a surplus in the overall long-term capital account. The short-term net capital outflow became dominant together with direct investment that had been persistently rising as a result of the steep yen appreciation since 1985. It was only toward the mid-1990s that foreign securities investment started to be active once again, as the Bank of Japan took a lax monetary policy to revive the stock market and rescue those ailing financial institutions with bad loans.

Thus the macroeconomic developments in the United States and Japan and the consequent changes in real domestic demand and real asset prices, together with Japan's relaxation of exchange and capital controls, were directly responsible for the expansion of Japan's NEAP in the 1980s. Japan's NEAP continued to expand in the 1990s. At the same time it is important to reiterate that high household savings in excess of corporate investment sustained the current account surplus.

Even when the Japanese economy recovers from the post-bubble recession, it is overshadowed by the rapid ageing of the population. It is likely that both savings and investment will decline in a rapidly ageing society and the future prospects of Japan's current account remain uncertain. If Japan can take appropriate policy actions to enhance labour-augmenting technical progress and to encourage older workers to continue to supply labour and to save, one need not be pessimistic about the future course of Japan as a creditor nation.

References

Eichengreen, Barry. 'The Responsibilities of a Creditor Nation', *Annals of the Institute of Social Science*, Special Issue, *The Advanced Industrial Societies in Disarray: What are the Available Choices?*. (March 1989), Institute of Social Science, University of Tokyo, 77–107.

Feldstein, Martin and Horioka, Charles. 'Domestic Saving and International Capital Flows'. *Economic Journal*, 90 (June 1980), 314–29.

Frankel, Jeffrey A. 'The Yen–Dollar Agreement: Liberalizing Japanese Capital Markets'. *Policy Analyses in International Economics*, No. 9 (December 1984), Institute for International Economics (Washington, DC).

Fukao, Mitsuhiro. 'Liberalization of Japan's Foreign Exchange Controls and Structural Changes in the Balance of Payments'. *Bank of Japan Monetary and Economic Studies*, 8 (September 1990), 101–65.

Horioka, Charles Yuji. 'Future Trends in Japan's Saving Rate and the Implications thereof for Japan's External Imbalance'. *Japan and the World Economy*, 3 (April 1992), 307–30.

Kawai, Masahiro. 'Japan's Demand for Long-term External Financial Assets in the 1980's'. *Asian Economic Journal*, 3 (September 1989), 65–115.

—— 'Japanese Investment in Foreign Securities in the 1980's'. *Pacific Economic Papers*, 201 (November 1991), Australian National University.

—— 'Accumulation of Net External Assets in Japan'. in Ryuzo Sato, Richard M. Levich, and Rama V. Ramachandran (eds.), *Japan, Europe and International Financial Markets: Analytical and Empirical Perspectives*. (Cambridge: Cambridge University Press, 1994), 73–123.

—— 'The Japanese Yen as an International Currency: Performance and Prospects'. in Ryuzo Sato, Rama Ramachandran, and Hajime Hori (eds.), *Organization, Performance and Equity: Perspectives on the Japanese Economy* (Boston, London, and Dordrecht: Kluwer Academic Publishers, 1996), 305–55.

—— 'Japan's Trade and Investment in East Asia'. in David Robertson (ed.), *East Asian Trade after the Uruguay Round* (tentative) (Cambridge: Cambridge University Press, 1997), 209–26.

—— and Urata, Shujiro. 'Are Trade and Investment Substitutes or Complements?: An Empirical Analysis of Japanese Manufacturing Industries'. in Hiro Lee and David W. Roland–Holst (eds.), *Economic Development and Cooperation in the Pacific Basin: Trade, Investment, and Environmental Issues* (Cambridge University Press, *forthcoming* 1997).

Krugman, Paul. 'Sustainability and the Decline of the Dollar'. in Ralph C. Bryant, Gerald Holtham, and Peter Hooper (eds.), *External Deficits and the Dollar: The Pit and the Pendulum* (Washington, DC: Brookings Institution, 1988), 82–99.

Marris, Stephen. 'Deficits and the Dollar: The World Economy at Risk'. *Policy Analyses in International Economics*, No. 14, Updated edition (August 1987), Institute for International Economics (Washington, DC).

Noguchi, Yukio. 'Japan's Fiscal Policy, Population Aging, and External Balance'. In Hans-Eckart Scharrer (ed.), *Economic and Monetary Policy Cooperation: The EC and Japan* (Baden Baden: Nomos Verlagsgesellschaft, 1994), 125–42.

Sinn, Stefan. *Net External Asset Positions of 145 Countries: Estimation and Interpretation*, Kieler Studien 234, Institut für Weltwirtschaft an der Universität Kiel (J. C. B. Mohr (Paul Siebeck): Tubingen, 1990).

Ueda, Kazuo. 'Perspectives on the Japanese Current Account Surplus'. *NBER Macroeconomics Annual*, 3 (Cambridge, Mass.: MIT Press, 1988), 217–56.

—— 'The Japanese Capital Outflows'. *Journal of Banking and Finance*, 14 (December 1990).

Yashiro, Naohiro and Oishi, Akiko. 'Population Aging and the Saving–Investment Balance in Japan'. A paper presented to the NBER–JCER Joint Conference 'The Economics of Aging' (December 1993).

APPENDIX TABLE A1. Japan's external assets and liabilities, 1971–95

	1971	1972	1973	1974	1975	1976	1977	1978	1979	1980	1981	1982
Total assets	32,753	43,595	47,551	55,942	58,334	67,990	80,060	118,725	135,365	159,580	209,257	227,688
Long-term assets	11,270	16,185	24,733	28,984	32,357	36,899	42,085	63,299	83,663	87,881	117,090	139,451
Private sector	7,626	11,404	18,806	22,242	24,522	27,786	31,177	46,467	62,141	66,504	89,269	110,025
Direct investments	1,851	2,574	4,546	6,559	8,322	10,313	11,958	14,329	17,227	19,612	24,506	28,969
Trade credits on exports	4,950	5,228	6,191	6,805	6,832	7,403	8,791	10,753	10,468	9,773	13,225	15,905
Loans extended	330	1,472	3,969	4,641	4,984	5,384	4,322	8,785	14,938	14,839	18,944	23,228
Securities investments	348	1,950	3,898	4,083	4,104	4,158	5,595	12,204	19,003	21,439	31,538	40,070
Other	147	180	202	154	280	528	511	396	505	841	1,056	1,853
Government sector	3,644	4,781	5,927	6,742	7,835	9,113	10,908	16,832	21,522	21,377	27,821	29,426
Trade credits on exports	175	184	270	328	330	330	330	429	575	689	1,148	1,124
Loans extended	2,476	3,074	3,874	4,558	5,497	6,568	8,022	12,894	16,574	15,507	19,936	20,436
Other	993	1,523	1,783	1,856	2,008	2,215	2,556	3,509	4,373	5,181	6,737	7,866
Short-term assets	21,483	27,410	22,818	26,958	25,977	31,091	37,975	55,426	51,702	71,699	92,167	88,237
Private sector	6,241	9,040	10,567	13,439	13,162	14,486	14,764	21,964	31,087	46,047	62,912	63,927
Monetary movements	6,020	8,864	10,003	13,085	12,947	14,295	14,457	21,364	29,946	45,158	61,074	61,117
Other	221	176	564	354	215	191	307	600	1,141	889	1,838	2,810
Government sector	15,242	18,370	12,251	13,519	12,815	16,605	23,211	33,462	20,615	25,652	29,255	24,310
Monetary movements	15,235	18,365	12,246	13,518	12,815	16,604	23,212	33,463	20,614	25,648	29,252	24,308
Other	7	5	5	1	0	1	-1	-1	1	4	3	2
Total liabilities	22,980	29,728	34,535	46,999	51,316	58,416	58,080	82,511	106,588	148,046	198,339	203,006
Long-term liabilities	9,554	13,147	10,061	9,843	13,603	18,402	19,575	29,276	35,958	47,289	70,335	77,645
Private sector	8,121	11,683	9,025	7,991	11,591	15,586	16,048	22,892	27,573	34,744	49,738	53.097
Direct investments	1,337	1,645	1,602	1,867	2,084	2,208	2,229	2,841	3,422	3,270	3,915	3,998
Trade credits on imports	97	141	130	124	98	93	80	66	38	21	5	0
Loans received	1,950	1,764	1,694	1,504	1,702	2,075	1,758	1,921	1,815	1,623	1,478	1,325
Securities investments	3,838	7,351	4,940	3,722	7,695	11,161	11,908	17,976	22,209	29,744	43,982	47,076
Other	899	782	659	774	12	49	73	88	89	86	358	698
Government sector	1,433	1,464	1,036	1,852	2,012	2,816	3,527	6,384	8,385	12,545	20,597	24,548
Loans received	667	624	493	452	414	379	341	306	268	225	178	149
Securities investments	235	217	204	183	509	1,434	2,186	5,078	8,117	12,320	20,419	24,399
Other	531	623	339	1,217	1,089	1,003	1,000	1,000	0	0	0	0
Short-term liabilities	13,426	16,581	24,474	37,156	37,713	40,014	38,505	53,235	70,630	100,757	128,004	125,361
Private sector	12,834	15,581	23,369	36,008	36,395	38,339	36,075	48,089	64,805	94,466	120,980	118,809
Monetary movements	7,491	8,356	13,468	24,676	26,418	28,387	26,865	36,735	50,208	77,974	100,619	100,103
Other	5,343	7,225	9,901	11,332	9,977	9,952	9,210	11,354	14,597	16,492	20,361	18,706
Government sector	592	1,000	1,105	1,148	1,318	1,675	2,430	5,146	5,825	6,291	7,024	6,552
Monetary movements	358	726	708	619	712	955	1,505	3,733	3,852	3,858	3,922	3,864
Other	234	274	397	529	606	720	925	1,413	1,973	2,433	3,102	2,688
Total net assets	9,773	13,867	13,016	8,943	7,018	9,574	21,980	36,214	28,777	11,534	10,918	24,682
Long-term net assets	1,716	3,038	14,672	19,141	18,754	18,497	22,510	34,023	47,705	40,592	46,755	61,806
Private sector	-495	-279	9,781	14,251	12,931	12,200	15,129	23,575	34,568	31,760	39,531	56,928
Direct investments	514	929	2,944	4,692	6,238	8,105	9,729	11,488	13,805	16,342	20,591	24,971
Trade credits	4,853	5,087	6,061	6,681	6,734	7,310	8,711	10,687	10,430	9,752	13,220	15,905
Loans	-1,620	-292	2,275	3,137	3,282	3,309	2,564	6,864	13,123	13,216	17,466	21,903
Securities investments	-3,490	-5,401	-1,042	361	-3,591	-7,003	-6,313	-5,772	-3,206	-8,305	-12,444	-7,006
Other	-752	-602	-457	-620	268	479	438	308	416	755	698	1,155
Government sector	2,211	3,317	4,891	4,890	5,823	6,297	7,381	10,448	13,137	8,832	7,224	4,878
Trade credits	-492	-440	-223	-124	-84	-49	-11	123	307	464	970	975
Loans	2,241	2,857	3,670	4,375	4,988	5,134	5,836	7,816	8,457	3,187	-483	-3,963
Other	462	900	1,444	639	919	1,212	1,556	2,509	4,373	5,181	6,737	7,866
Short-term net assets	8,057	10,829	-1,656	-10,198	-11,736	-8,923	-530	2,191	-18,928	-29,058	-35,837	-37,124
Private sector	-6,593	-6,541	-12,802	-22,569	-23,233	-23,853	-21,311	-26,125	-33,718	-48,419	-58,068	-54,882
Monetary movements	-1,471	508	-3,465	-11,591	-13,471	-14,092	-12,408	-15,371	-20,262	-32,816	-39,545	-38,986
Other	-5,122	-7,049	-9,337	-10,978	-9,762	-9,761	-8,903	-10,754	-13,456	-15,603	-18,523	-15,896
Government sector	14,650	17,370	11,146	12,371	11,497	14,930	20,781	28,316	14,790	19,361	22,231	17,758
Monetary movements	14,877	17,639	11,538	12,899	12,103	15,649	21,707	29,730	16,762	21,790	25,330	20,444
Other	-227	-269	-392	-528	-606	-719	-926	-1,414	-1,972	-2,429	-3,099	-2,686

Notes: 1. The Ministry of Finance reports that the net external asset positions for the years 1967, 1968, 1969, and 1970 are respectively: -916, 270, 1,714, 4,674 (all in US$ Million). See *Monthly Statistics on Government Finance and Banking*, No. 255 (June 1973).

2. The Ministry of Finance reports the statistics for the year 1971 in its *Monthly Statistics on Government Finance and Banking*, No. 374 (June 1983).

3. The Japanese-yen data for 1995 are converted into US dollars at the end-of-the-year exchange rate of 102.91 yen per US dollar.

Sources: Ministry of Finance, *Monthly Statistics on Government Finance and Banking*, No. 255 (June 1973), No. 374 (June 1983), other issues. Bank of Japan, *Balance of Payments Monthly*, April issues.

(US$ million)

1983	1984	1985	1986	1987	1988	1989	1990	1991	1992	1993	1994	1995
271,956	341,208	437,701	727,306	1,071,631	1,469,347	1,771,003	1,857,862	2,006,521	2,036,238	2,180,880	2,424,231	2,722,525
170,905	229,184	301,297	476,136	646,181	832,669	1,019,218	1,096,085	1,247,847	1,315,551	1,412,928	1,548,571	1,676,786
138,051	191,946	264,458	424,704	565,100	728,168	901,736	973,626	1,090,059	1,132,193	1,195,622	1,278,501	1,386,590
32,178	37,921	43,974	58,071	77,022	110,780	154,367	201,441	231,791	248,058	259,795	275,574	295,977
18,110	22,824	23,603	31,992	37,189	48,791	52,866	47,138	47,300	44,569	42,077	42,100	41,619
29,266	40,601	46,870	69,211	97,469	123,663	137,084	130,074	141,239	143,411	152,123	158,287	159,703
56,115	87,578	145,748	257,933	339,677	427,218	533,781	563,815	632,129	655,491	696,016	753,618	835,128
2,382	3,022	4,263	7,497	13,743	17,716	23,638	31,158	37,600	40,664	45,611	48,922	54,174
32,854	37,238	36,839	51,432	81,081	104,501	117,482	122,459	157,788	183,358	217,306	270,070	290,195
1,165	1,189	1,062	1,423	1,664	1,885	1,750	1,425,000	1,468,000	1,404,000	1,417,000	1,423,000	1,322,000
22,473	24,491	23,293	33,558	43,145	55,570	60,471	60,927	77,285	88,261	103,608	121,073	134,622
9,216	11,558	12,484	16,451	36,272	47,046	55,261	60,107	79,035	93,693	112,281	147,574	154,251
101,051	112,024	136,404	251,170	425,450	636,678	751,785	761,777	758,674	719,687	767,952	875,660	1,045,739
75,492	84,761	108,753	207,876	343,261	538,802	666,712	682,068	685,401	646,897	668,261	748,553	861,384
72,087	77,562	99,719	194,713	320,171	502,256	627,846	644,519	640,828	599,888	607,796	670,505	781,557
3,405	7,199	9,034	13,163	23,090	36,546	38,866	37,549	44,573	47,009	60,465	78,048	79,827
25,559	27,263	27,651	43,294	82,189	97,876	85,073	79,709	73,273	72,790	99,691	127,107	184,355
25,556	27,261	27,650	43,294	82,175	97,869	85,072	79,708	73,272	72,789	99,690	127,099	184,346
3	2	1	0	14	7	1	1	1	1	1	8	10
234,697	266,862	307,880	546,955	830,887	1,177,601	1,477,788	1,529,803	1,623,449	1,521,619	1,570,063	1,735,257	1,974,385
102,794	113,222	122,328	192,336	236,181	311,625	447,472	464,022	647,402	658,469	711,803	804,204	902,721
76,551	83,738	91,776	152,192	178,810	268,431	405,498	408,084	565,249	578,826	623,535	707,218	795,938
4,364	4,458	4,743	6,514	9,018	10,416	9,160	9,850	12,297	15,511	16,884	19,211	19,833
16	24	131	33	35	23	16	4	10	23	11	5	0
1,320	1,266	1,211	1,199	1,101	1,061	18,895	58,015	99,697	119,679	135,753	139,346	142,600
69,948	77,081	84,847	143,611	166,206	254,886	373,990	334,523	443,821	431,422	456,754	532,305	614,450
903	909	844	835	2,450	2,045	3,437	5,692	9,424	12,191	14,133	16,351	19,065
26,243	29,484	30,552	40,144	57,371	43,194	41,974	55,938	82,153	79,643	88,268	96,986	106,783
124	103	84	66	47	26	7	0	0	0	0	0	0
26,119	29,381	30,468	40,078	57,324	43,168	41,967	55,938	82,153	79,643	88,268	96,986	106,783
0	0	0	0	0	0	0	0	0	0	0	0	0
131,903	153,640	185,552	354,619	594,706	865,976	1,030,316	1,065,781	976,047	863,150	858,260	931,053	1,071,665
125,064	145,900	176,985	341,847	583,057	850,968	1,004,111	1,028,775	924,666	807,208	791,511	829,898	946,983
107,308	130,098	160,984	322,163	530,072	765,165	894,679	898,886	803,521	684,677	659,648	678,958	709,027
17,756	15,802	16,001	19,684	52,985	85,803	109,432	129,889	121,145	122,531	131,863	150,940	237,955
6,839	7,740	8,567	12,772	11,649	15,008	26,205	37,006	51,381	55,942	66,749	101,155	124,672
3,765	3,590	4,557	7,103	3,922	5,144	16,957	28,814	42,864	46,648	55,926	89,031	111,078
3,074	4,150	4,010	5,669	7,727	9,864	9,248	8,192	8,517	9,294	10,823	12,124	13,604
37,259	74,346	129,821	180,351	240,744	291,746	293,215	328,059	383,072	513,619	610,817	688,974	748,140
68,111	115,962	178,969	283,800	410,000	521,044	571,746	632,063	600,445	657,082	701,125	744,367	774,065
61,500	108,208	172,682	272,512	386,290	459,737	496,238	565,542	524,810	553,367	572,087	571,283	590,652
27,814	33,463	39,231	51,557	68,004	100,364	145,207	191,591	219,494	232,547	242,911	256,363	276,144
18,094	22,800	23,472	31,959	37,154	48,768	52,850	47,134	47,290	44,546	42,066	42,095	41,619
27,946	39,335	45,659	68,012	96,368	122,602	118,189	72,059	41,542	23,732	16,370	18,941	17,103
–13,833	10,497	60,901	114,322	173,471	172,332	159,791	229,292	188,308	224,069	239,262	221,313	220,678
1,479	2,113	3,419	6,662	11,293	15,671	20,201	25,466	28,176	28,473	31,478	32,571	35,109
6,611	7,754	6,287	11,288	23,710	61,307	75,508	66,521	75,635	103,715	129,038	173,084	183,412
1,041	1,086	978	1,357	1,617	1,859	1,743	1,425	1,468	1,404	1,417	1,423	1,322
–3,646	–4,890	–7,175	–6,520	–14,179	12,402	18,504	4,989	–4,868	8,618	15,340	24,087	27,839
9,216	11,558	12,484	16,451	36,272	47,046	55,261	60,107	79,035	93,693	112,281	147,574	154,251
–30,852	–41,616	–49,148	–103,449	–169,256	–229,298	–278,531	–304,004	–217,373	–143,463	–90,308	–55,393	–25,926
–49,572	–61,139	–68,232	–133,971	–239,796	–312,166	–337,399	–346,707	–239,265	–160,311	–123,250	–81,345	–85,599
–35,221	–52,536	–61,265	–127,450	–209,901	–262,909	–266,833	–254,367	–162,693	–84,789	–51,852	–8,453	72,530
–14,351	–8,603	–6,967	–6,521	–29,895	–49,257	–70,566	–92,340	–76,572	–75,522	–71,398	–72,892	–158,128
18,720	19,523	19,084	30,522	70,540	82,868	58,868	42,703	21,892	16,848	32,942	25,952	59,683
21,791	23,671	23,093	36,191	78,253	92,725	68,115	50,894	30,408	26,141	43,764	38,068	73,268
–3,071	–4,148	–4,009	–5,669	–7,713	–9,857	–9,247	–8,191	–8,516	–9,293	–10,822	–12,116	–13,594

APPENDIX TABLE A2. Japan's balance of payments, 1970–95

	1970	1971	1972	1973	1974	1975	1976	1977	1978	1979	1980	1981
Current account	1,970	5,797	6,624	-136	-4,693	-682	3,680	10,918	16,534	-8,754	-10,746	4,770
Merchandise trade	3,963	7,787	8,971	3,688	1,436	5,028	9,887	17,311	24,596	1,845	2,125	19,967
Services	-1,785	-1,738	-1,883	-3,510	-5,842	-5,354	-5,867	-6,004	-7,387	-9,472	-11,343	-13,573
Net investment income	-209	-47	367	490	-451	-273	-204	115	900	2,011	854	-763
Other	-1,576	-1,691	-2,250	-4,000	-5,391	-5,081	-5,663	-6,119	-8,287	-11,483	-12,197	-12,810
Unrequited transfers	-208	-252	-464	-314	-287	-356	-340	-389	-675	-1,127	-1,528	-1,624
Capital account (a)	-2,241	-6,324	-7,262	2,731	4,736	1,266	-3,797	-11,575	-16,801	6,421	13,861	-5,263
Long-term capital account	-1,591	-1,082	-4,487	-9,750	-3,881	-272	-984	-3,184	-12,389	-12,976	2,324	-9,672
Direct investments	-261	-150	-554	-1,946	-1,810	-1,537	-1,878	-1,624	-2,363	-2,659	-2,107	-4,705
Securities investments (b)	234	753	-597	-2,576	-926	2,729	2,958	637	-2,813	-1,583	9,360	4,443
Loans	-548	-574	-1,881	-3,351	-1,368	-1,129	-1,191	-796	-6,306	-8,271	-2,784	-5,269
Trade credits	-780	-855	-313	-1,060	-678	-55	-576	-1,401	-164	1,255	-733	-2,746
Other	-236	-256	-1,142	-817	901	-280	-289	0	-743	-1,717	-1,412	-1,395
Short-term capital account, private	358	4,966	-13	6,380	9,978	742	732	-2,332	3,781	6,755	16,285	8,651
Private nonbanking	724	2,435	1,966	2,407	1,778	-1,138	111	-648	1,538	2,735	3,141	2,265
Authorized foreign exchange banks	-366	2,531	-1,979	3,973	8,200	1,880	621	-1,684	2,243	4,020	13,144	6,386
Short-term capital account, official (c)	-1,008	-10,208	-2,762	6,101	-1,361	796	-3,545	-6,059	-8,193	12,642	-4,748	-4,242
Changes in foreign exchange reserves	-903	-10,836	-3,130	6,119	-1,272	703	-3,789	-6,244	-10,171	12,692	-4,905	-3,171
Errors and omissions	271	527	638	-2,595	-43	-584	117	657	267	2,333	-3,115	493

Note: (a) Minus sign indicates deficits or net capital outflows.

(b) Gensaki transactions are entered as short-term capital.

(c) Constructed as—(current account + long-term capital account + private short-term capital account + errors and omissions).

(d) The Japanese-yen data for 1995 are converted into US dollars by using the period average exchange rate of 94.06 yen per US dollar.

(e) The data for private short-term capital account with single asterisks (*) for 1995 are obtained by calculating the annual increase in the stock of private short-term assets.

Sources: Bank of Japan, Balance of Payments Monthly, various issues.

APPENDIX TABLE A3. Japan's long-term capital transactions, 1970–95

	1970	1971	1972	1973	1974	1975	1976	1977	1978	1979	1980	1981
Japanese capital	-2,031	-2,231	-5,020	-8,468	-4,063	-3,392	-4,559	-5,247	-14,872	-16,294	-10,817	-22,809
Direct investment	-355	-360	-723	-1,904	-2,012	-1,763	-1,991	-1,645	-2,371	-2,898	-2,385	-4,894
Securities investment	-62	-195	-1,188	-1,787	-141	-24	-146	-1,718	-5,300	-5,865	-3,753	-8,777
Stocks and shares	n.a.	n.a.	n.a.	n.a.	-37	7	0	-7	-124	-575	213	-240
Bonds	n.a.	n.a.	n.a.	n.a.	-90	41	64	-735	-1,897	-3,385	-2,996	-5,810
Yen-denominated external bonds	n.a.	n.a.	n.a.	n.a.	-14	-72	-210	-976	-3,279	-1,905	-970	-2,727
Export credits	-787	-863	-324	-1,048	-672	-29	-571	-1,388	-142	1,288	-717	-2,731
Loans extended	-628	-594	-1,684	-3,038	-1,136	-1,295	-1,525	-472	-6,299	-8,102	-2,553	-5,083
Others	-199	-219	-1,101	-691	-102	-281	-326	-24	-760	-717	-1,409	-1,324
Foreign capital	396	1,149	533	-1,282	182	3,120	3,575	2,063	2,483	3,318	13,141	13,137
Direct investment	94	210	169	-42	202	226	113	21	8	239	278	189
Securities investment	252	940	696	-591	-785	2,753	3,104	2,355	2,487	4,282	13,113	13,220
Stocks and shares	n.a.	n.a.	n.a.	n.a.	-1,102	596	-112	-778	-807	329	6,546	5,916
Bonds	n.a.	n.a.	n.a.	n.a.	237	922	1,707	2,034	2,461	1,743	5,331	5,936
External bonds	n.a.	n.a.	n.a.	n.a.	80	1,235	1,509	1,099	833	2,210	1,236	1,368
Import credits	7	8	11	-12	-6	-26	-5	-13	-22	-33	-16	-15
Loans received	80	20	-197	-313	-232	166	326	-324	-7	-169	-231	-186
Others	-37	-37	-37	-126	1,003	1	37	24	17	-1,001	-3	-71
Long-term capital account	-1,635	-1,082	-4,487	-9,750	-3,881	-272	-984	-3,184	-12,389	-12,976	2,324	-9,672
Direct investment, net	-261	-150	-554	-1,946	-1,810	-1,537	-1,878	-1,624	-2,363	-2,659	-2,107	-4,705
Securities investment, net	190	745	-492	-2,378	-926	2,729	2,958	637	-2,813	-1,583	9,360	4,443
Stocks and shares, net	n.a.	n.a.	n.a.	n.a.	-1,139	603	-112	-785	-931	-246	6,759	5,676
Bonds, net	n.a.	n.a.	n.a.	n.a.	147	963	1,771	1,299	564	-1,642	2,335	126
External bonds, net	n.a.	n.a.	n.a.	n.a.	66	1,163	1,299	123	-2,446	305	266	-1,359
Trade credits, net	-780	-855	-313	-1,060	-678	-55	-576	-1,401	-164	1,255	-733	-2,746
Loans, net	-548	-574	-1,881	-3,351	-1,368	-1,129	-1,199	-796	-6,306	-8,271	-2,784	-5,269
Others, net	-236	-256	-1,138	-817	901	-280	-289	0	-743	-1,718	-1,412	-1,395
Reference: Current account	1,970	5,797	6,624	-136	-4,693	-682	3,680	10,918	16,534	-8,754	-10,746	4,770

Note: 1. The Japanese-yen data for 1995 are converted into US dollars by using the period average exchange rate of 93.97 yen per US dollar.

2. The data with double asterisks (**) for 1995 are based on new balance of payments statistics and, therefore, not comparable to the previous years' data.

Source: Bank of Japan, Balance of Payments Monthly, Various issues.

(US$ million)

1982	1983	1984	1985	1986	1987	1988	1989	1990	1991	1992	1993	1994	1995
6,850	20,799	35,003	49,169	85,845	87,015	79,631	57,157	35,761	72,901	117,551	131,448	129,140	109,550
18,079	31,454	44,257	55,986	92,827	96,386	95,012	76,917	63,528	103,044	132,348	141,514	145,944	133,935
-9,848	-9,106	-7,747	-5,165	-4,932	-5,702	-11,263	-15,526	-22,292	-17,660	-10,112	-3,949	-9,296	-14,982
1,718	3,082	4,231	6,840	9,473	16,670	21,032	23,442	23,204	26,724	36,218	41,409	41,000	44,867
-11,566	-12,188	-11,978	-12,005	-14,405	-22,372	-32,295	-38,968	-45,496	-44,384	-46,330	-45,358	-50,296	-59,849
-1,381	-1,549	-1,507	-1,652	-2,050	-3,669	-4,118	-4,234	-5,475	-12,483	-4,685	-6,117	-7,508	-9,403
-11,577	-22,854	-38,746	-53,160	-88,303	-83,122	-82,427	-35,149	-14,884	-65,070	-107,100	-131,188	-111,362	-123,506
-14,969	-17,700	-49,651	-64,542	-131,461	-136,532	-130,930	-89,246	-43,586	37,057	-28,459	-78,336	-82,037	-82,358
-4,101	-3,196	-5,975	-5,810	-14,254	-18,354	-34,695	-45,144	-46,271	-29,358	-14,494	-13,628	-17,050	-22,287
2,117	-1,876	-23,601	-43,032	-101,432	-93,838	-66,651	-28,034	-5,028	40,978	-26,191	-62,748	-48,944	-52,267
-8,083	-8,462	-11,999	-10,502	-9,315	-16,309	-15,293	-4,682	16,930	25,027	8,276	-3,831	-17,368	-12,377
-3,245	-2,581	-4,934	-2,788	-1,876	-536	-6,957	-4,011	671	3,926	5,288	5,396	3,753	4,986
-1,657	-1,585	-3,142	-2,410	-4,584	-7,495	-7,334	-7,335	-9,888	-3,516	-1,338	-3,525	-2,428	-3,013
-1,544	-3,547	13,265	9,912	56,897	95,666	63,981	29,403	7,835	-119,212	-80,037	-29,400	-31,594	13,455*
-1,579	23	-4,295	-936	-1,609	23,865	19,521	20,811	21,468	-25,758	-7,039	-14,426	-8,897	85,913*
35	-3,570	17,560	10,848	58,506	71,801	44,460	8,592	-13,633	-93,454	-72,998	-14,974	-22,697	-72,458*
4,936	-1,607	-2,360	1,470	-13,739	-42,256	-15,478	24,694	20,867	17,085	1,396	-23,452	2,269	-54,603
5,141	-1,234	-1,817	-197	-15,729	-39,240	-16,183	12,767	7,842	8,073	295	-26,904	-27,256	-57,660
4,727	2,055	3,743	3,991	2,458	-3,893	2,796	-22,008	-20,877	-7,831	-10,451	-260	-17,778	13,956

(US$ million)

1982	1983	1984	1985	1986	1987	1988	1989	1990	1991	1992	1993	1994	1995
-27,418	-32,459	-56,775	-81,815	-132,095	-132,830	-149,883	-192,118	-120,766	-121,446	-57,962	-73,608	-110,232	-124,332
-4,540	-3,612	-5,965	-6,452	-14,480	-19,519	-34,210	-44,130	-48,024	-30,726	-17,222	-13,714	-17,938	-22,305
-9,743	-16,024	-30,795	-59,773	-101,977	-87,757	-86,949	-113,178	-39,681	-74,306	-34,362	-51,670	-83,607	-92,866
-151	-661	-51	-995	-7,048	-16,874	-2,993	-17,887	-6,256	-3,630	3,012	-15,329	-14,057	72**
-6,076	-12,505	-26,773	-53,479	-93,024	-72,885	-85,812	-94,083	-28,961	-68,202	-35,634	-29,913	-64,101	-90,235**
-3,516	-2,858	-3,971	-5,299	-1,905	2,002	1,856	-1,208	-4,464	-2,474	-1,740	-6,428	-5,449	-11,945**
-3,239	-2,589	-4,937	-2,817	-1,836	-535	-6,939	-4,002	681	3,928	5,293	5,407	3,758	5,001
-7,902	-8,425	-11,922	-10,427	-9,281	-16,190	-15,211	-22,495	-22,182	-13,097	-7,623	-8,169	-7,744	-10,268
-1,994	-1,809	-3,156	-2,346	-4,521	-8,829	-6,574	-8,313	-11,560	-7,245	-4,048	-5,462	-4,701	-6,649
12,449	14,759	7,124	17,273	634	-3,702	18,953	102,872	77,180	158,503	29,503	-4,728	28,195	41,893
439	416	-10	642	226	1,165	-485	-1,054	1,753	1,368	2,728	86	888	-3
11,860	14,148	7,194	16,741	545	-6,081	20,298	85,144	34,653	115,284	8,171	-11,078	34,663	40,549
2,549	6,126	-3,610	-673	-15,758	-42,835	6,810	6,998	-13,276	46,779	8,731	19,992	48,995	51,134**
5,030	2,359	3,454	4,524	-2,109	6,675	-21,628	2,400	16,991	21,241	-8,194	-221	521	-9,787**
4,281	5,663	7,350	12,890	18,412	30,079	35,116	75,746	30,938	47,264	7,634	-30,849	-14,853	-17,874**
-6	8	3	29	-40	-1	-18	-9	-10	-2	-5	-11	-5	-10
-181	-37	-77	-75	-34	-119	-82	17,813	39,112	38,124	15,899	4,338	-9,624	-2,121
337	224	14	-64	-63	1,334	-760	978	1,672	3,729	2,710	1,937	2,273	3,633
-14,969	-17,700	-49,651	-64,542	-131,461	-136,532	-130,930	-89,246	-43,586	37,057	-28,459	-78,336	-82,037	-82,439
-4,101	-3,196	-5,975	-5,810	-14,254	-18,354	-34,695	-45,184	-46,271	-29,358	-14,494	-13,628	-17,050	-22,308
2,117	-1,876	-23,601	-43,032	-101,432	-93,838	-66,651	-28,034	-5,028	40,978	-26,191	-62,748	-48,944	-52,317
2,398	5,465	-3,661	-1,668	-22,806	-59,709	3,817	-10,889	-19,532	43,149	11,743	4,663	34,938	51,207**
-1,046	-10,146	-23,319	-48,955	-95,133	-66,210	-107,440	-91,683	-11,970	-46,961	-43,828	-30,134	-63,580	-100,022**
765	2,805	3,379	7,591	16,507	32,081	36,972	74,538	26,474	44,790	5,894	-37,277	-20,302	-29,819**
-3,245	-2,581	-4,934	-2,788	-1,876	-536	-6,957	-4,011	671	3,926	5,288	5,396	3,753	4,991
-8,083	-8,462	-11,999	-10,502	-9,315	-16,309	-15,293	-4,682	16,930	25,027	8,276	-3,831	-17,368	-12,389
-1,657	-1,585	-3,142	-2,410	-4,584	-7,495	-7,334	-7,335	-9,888	-3,516	-1,338	-3,525	-2,428	-3,016
6,850	20,799	35,003	49,169	85,845	87,015	79,631	57,157	35,761	72,901	117,551	131,448	129,140	109,655

2

The Internationalization of the Japanese Firm: Japanese Working Practices and Indigenous Asian Workplaces*

KOIKE KAZUO

I. The Issues

1. Initial premisses

The theme of this chapter is the internationalization of the Japanese firm. The particular issue of inquiry here is the extent to which the working practices of Japanese firms are transferable to workplaces in other Asian countries, or whether a basic modification of practices is essential. There are two significant reasons why this issue, which may at first appear to be mundane, can be viewed as the main qualitative appearance of internationalization.

First, transferability is important for a firm's internationalization or, more generally, multinationalization. According to applied research on multinational companies,[1] the basic requirement for direct investment in another country is advanced management resources, but this tends to change over certain stages. The initial investment period requires the management of manufacturing technology—namely making new goods—but when the goods have become standardized and are distant from the platform of advanced management resources, processing technology comes to the forefront. Processing technology consists of two stages, and the central condition for competitiveness shifts over time from the hard technology of machinery to soft technology. The core of this soft technology is actually nothing other than workplace practices. Whether such practices are applicable or whether instead they cause a problem in the host country is a crucial question.

Second, much of the existing research is seriously deficient in that a conclusion is reached without the essential points being investigated. In order to pursue the above issue, the first task before anything else must be an inquiry into the nature of Japanese working practices and working practices in other Asian countries in order to find out their differences and similarities. There have been a number of papers that have failed, however, to investigate these

* Translated by Mary Saso.

aspects directly and have simply made assumptions about working practices. The reason for this failure is that, with just a few exceptions, previous research has often been limited to superficial questionnaire surveys mainly among Japanese joint ventures.[2] If Japanese joint ventures are the only ones observed, assumptions will be made inevitably without investigating either indigenous companies' working methods or those of Japanese companies within Japan, and, as a result, a completely realistic picture will not be provided.

2. Job rotation

Many texts offer so-called job rotation as a universal Japanese working practice, but what is meant by job rotation in this case? If a Japanese workplace were to be observed attentively for assessment, even for a short while, one should first consider dividing the workforce into blue-collar and white-collar workers. Then, in the case of blue-collar workers, the following questions should be asked:

1. Even over a medium-term period of three to five years, can it be said that each worker sticks with one job assignment and does not move to other jobs within the workshop?

2. Taking the long term of ten years or more, does each worker move between three to five job assignments in one workshop?

3. Is there job rotation between assignments under the jurisdiction of a group leader in one workshop? (Between five to ten workers there is usually one group leader, who may spend the whole day in productive activities. This kind of definition is essential for international comparisons.)

4. Is there job rotation between almost all of the assignments in one workshop? (A workshop is defined as the area of activity under one foreman. Depending on the occupation, there are usually between fifteen and forty workers under the jurisdiction of a foreman, who in a maximum supervisory role generally spends the whole day supervising workers.)

5. Is there job rotation between clusters of technically-related workshops?

6. Is there transfer between workshops that are scarcely related technologically?

The meaning of job rotation differs greatly between each of the above categories. Often it seems to be tacitly assumed, without actually being specified, that (6) is applicable to Japan and (1) to Asia. Under that assumption, without following the results of careful research concerning production workers, there could be a double mistake. First, there is no rotation in the workplaces of large Japanese companies in the sense of (6), as it occurs only as an emergency response at times of employment adjustment. Instead, at the most, job rotation takes the form of either (4) or (5). Second, although workplaces should be actively observed to find out whether Asian countries practice (1) or not, this has not actually been done.

The character of each of the above categories, especially (6), is discrete, and the kinds of costs and benefits associated with job rotation must be considered accordingly. In the case of (6) there is only a tenuous technical relationship, and the costs would be very high since any job rotation would require the worker to learn new skills from scratch, and he would not be using his earlier skills. About the only time when benefits would be greater than costs here would be in the case of avoiding redundancies, and on that account (6) is only adopted as an emergency refuge at times of employment adjustments. On the other hand, for categories (2) to (5), where job rotation takes place within the same workshop or between neighbouring workshops, there is a technical relationship. Any costs are few, since previously acquired skills are transferred, and workers can even improve their skills through wider experience.

Trouble could be expected in any workplace in any country if there were no workers with experience of more than one job assignment. Let us consider, for example, the case of absentee workers. Regardless of the country, it is impossible never to experience absences from work. Workers also take leave. At such times, if no substitute can be found to perform the assignment of the absentee, nothing can be done. This is why there are relief men in US auto assembly plants. These men practise job rotation in the form of (3) or (4), and naturally their wages are rather high.[3]

A real difficulty—when circumstances do not fall under either (1) or something similar—lies in grasping the comparative differences between (2), (3), (4), and (5) in order to make the right categorization. Since the area of job rotation is wider among these categories, the skill levels are higher. The workers' ability to respond to absenteeism has already been mentioned, but know-how in dealing with non-routine tasks or problems is also important.

Problems can appear in any workplace, and defective products are an example of this. The ability to diagnose the cause of defects in products is crucial in avoiding their reappearance. If a diagnostic ability is lacking, machines will continue to produce defective items. If workers can detect the cause of a problem, a recurrence can be effectively prevented, which will greatly improve efficiency. The real source of efficiency on modern Japanese shop floors lies in the fact that many production workers have this kind of deductive power. Their knowledge of the production process and the machines' structures provides them with the ability to detect the cause of defects. After all, defective items result from a machine operating oddly. To acquire this kind of knowledge, as wide an experience as possible of the production path is necessary. On that account, the kind of job rotation in category (5) would probably be most beneficial, while (2) would be least helpful.[4]

In general, just asking in a questionnaire whether job rotation is utilized without touching on the above sorts of issues would be meaningless. To a surprising extent, an underlying theory is required for an investigation to be effective. If there is resistance to the word 'theory' (though I consider just this kind of discussion to be theoretical), then one may say that a theory is simply a precise building up of concepts. For that purpose a really close observation of Japanese shop floors is essential. Indeed the key to a successful international comparison lies with practices in one's own country being thoroughly examined and investigated.

3. Seniority wages

Quite similar comments are pertinent to the concepts of so-called lifetime employment, seniority wages, and enterprise-based unions. These concepts are often adopted as a test of the transferability of Japanese methods. I have discussed this issue elsewhere, but here I would like to write a few words about seniority wages in particular.

Economic theory suggests that, essentially, wages are determined according to the job, and are not expected to rise in line with age and length of service. In contrast, according to the conventional view, seniority wages depend not on each job, but on length of service and age. However, if one actually looks at seniority-wage systems in large Japanese companies, regardless of whether the systems are for production workers or white-collar workers, they include the three features of pay according to the job grade, yearly incremental pay rises, and pay by merit assessments.

Wages are not decided by each individual's job, but, through the job grade element, wages do reflect skill improvements in the medium term. Naturally, if the job grade and degree of skill differ between two workers, there is a wage differential, even though their lengths of service and educational backgrounds may be similar. Moreover, even for workers with the same job grade, there can be wage differences depending on their performance or on the degree of improvement of their skills in the short term, or, in other words, on their merit assessments. In order to encourage skill formation over the long term, there is the system of incremental rises in wages, which is advantageous for those who are in long-term employment.

It should be remarked that these three kinds of elements of pay are actually normal features of white-collar salaries in large western European companies. Unfortunately, the presence of these features cannot be adequately confirmed, as good data are lacking, but any differences with Japan seem to be at most in the length of the period for incremental rises for those with the same job grade, or in other words in the number of years employed before hitting the ceiling. It appears that in large western European companies this ceiling occurs after five to ten years on the same job grade, but the ceiling is higher in Japan.

If these kinds of features are excluded from an investigation and just a simple questionnaire is used to ask about whether or not there are seniority wages, the survey will probably be far removed from reality.

4. The issues to be investigated

The above discussion does not mean of course that there has been no case-study research in ASEAN (Association of South-East Asian Nations) work-places. One example is the work of the ASEAN Kenkyu-kai (ASEAN Study Team) led by Imano Koichiro,[5] where issues that could not be revealed in a questionnaire-type survey were studied through the direct observation of workplaces. However, since only Japanese subsidiaries or joint ventures were included in the study, the above problems could still not be avoided.

Yahata and Mizuno surveyed fifteen companies operating in Thailand.[6] These companies were parts makers supplying Japanese automobile producers, and employing an average of 200 employees each. Yahata and Mizuno's valuable investigation of job rotation showed clearly that, whereas there was fairly active rotation within the workshop, there was hardly any job rotation between workshops. This distinction may be clearer than others, but the division of job rotation into the two simple categories—within the workshop and between workshops—does not serve to distinguish between the above-mentioned (2), (3), and (4) categories, nor between categories (5) and (6). Thus, making a comparison with, in particular, Japanese small and medium-sized companies would be difficult. In any case, the main object of this survey was not job rotation but rather the division of labour between firms. Another survey of plants in several Asian countries was carried out by Odaka and others, but without an adequate investigation into job rotation.[7]

Probably the best research study is Shiba Shoji's survey of thermal power stations.[8] His investigation went as deeply as possible into the two issues raised above. He made a direct comparison of workplaces of exactly the same type, namely thermal power stations in eight countries, comprising Canada, America, Japan, and five other Asian countries. The investigation was excellent as he spent over a month in each enterprise and he even collected individual personnel records. It was masterly research work, and has not been matched elsewhere. This research was, however, limited to thermal power stations, which are, whether private or public, a non-competitive industry in every country. Moreover, it is likely that in this industry the influence of the country installing the equipment and teaching the know-how is easily absorbed. In the case of a competitive industry, which has to compete to be successful, it would probably be necessary to modify working practices to make them more appropriate for the host country's conditions. Thus there is even more reason to investigate competitive industries.

Looking back on such research projects demonstrates the necessity of incorporating the above two issues, namely both to clarify Japanese work practices and to analyse work methods in indigenous firms. Yet the first issue was not explored, as I have already shown. On the other hand, there have until now been only a few research projects on the second issue, apparently confined to the previously discussed Shiba survey, the Yawata–Mizuno survey, and the Odaka survey, in addition to a survey by Koike and Inoki in Thailand and Malaysia.[9] Although there are some excellent surveys on agricultural areas, they become suddenly silent when it is a question of the economy. Fortunately there are surveys on indigenous firms in Singapore, Indonesia, Thailand, and India. The observations are not deep, but I wish to record them here, because there is really not enough basic material available concerning the internationalization of Japanese firms.

With reference to these surveys, I would like to comment on the prospects for the internationalization of Japanese firms in ASEAN and to make a comparison with western European and American firms. If an observation of all so-called Japanese working practices were to be attempted, the investigation would become too wide. The focus here, therefore, will be on the most basic factors that prescribe working practices, namely skill formation and measures taken to foster skills. The initial methods for skill formation are either off-the-job training: (OffJT) or OJT. In the case of the latter, both spans—the horizontal and the vertical—of the actual content of experience over the long term should be investigated, because the training depends on accumulated experience. The horizontal span is measured by the extent of work experience, the meaning of which can be found in the scale of job rotation mentioned earlier. The vertical span or depth of experience is said to be what production workers can do in coping with the previously mentioned problems. Concerning the promotion of skill formation, we will first examine whether remuneration is made according to the job or whether payment is made in line with a long-term improvement of skills. In addition, apart from wages, we will observe whether advancement to higher positions takes place through the promotion of foremen from below in the ranks, or through appointments based on having a higher level of qualifications or educational background than the production workers. This issue in the case of highly industrialized countries could appear to be an indicator that would be better left alone, but in developing countries it is truly an important first index.[10]

The second section observes three case studies of indigenous firms in Singapore and in the third section a look, though somewhat superficial, will be taken at workplaces in Indonesia, Thailand, and India. In the fourth section, with reference to those examples and previous research, the prospects for the internationalization of Japanese firms' working practices will be considered and the issues will be grasped.

II. Indigenous Firms in Singapore

The significance of examining Singaporean companies lies in their being among the most advanced in South-East Asia. Thus Singapore provides a reference point when considering what kind of work practices will be adopted in the future when incomes in South-East Asia rise. Also, even now, South-East Asian countries are already said to be looking to Singapore as a model.

Research in the workplaces of indigenous firms is, as far as I know, confined to the Shiba survey introduced earlier. But there are labour surveys in the case of Japanese joint ventures, including surveys carried out by Koshiro,[11] by Harada,[12] and by Imano and Yahata.[13] Though these surveys did not extend to covering Singaporean local firms at all, there are some references to indigenous firms. In addition, there have been JETRO (Japan External Trade Organization) surveys of Singapore.[14] In general, the following assertions about the workplace customs of non-Japanese firms in Singapore tend to prevail:

1. The scope of duties required is made precisely and individual responsibilities are clear.[15]

2. The methods for skill formation being western in style and systematically organized differ from Japanese on-the-job training (OJT) methods.[16]

3. As a result, the wage system, which is based on pay according to each job, differs from the so-called seniority wage system in Japan.[17]

4. On the basis of the above trends, an external labour market has become dominant and labour mobility is high. Internal labour markets with internal promotion have not become established.[18]

Such trends have been strongly highlighted by the Koshiro and Harada surveys. However, the Imano–Yahata survey is more cautious in saying that, without there yet having been a survey of indigenous firms, judgement should be reserved. None the less, the above assertions are consistent with the impressions of personnel managers in Japanese companies seen in various texts. But does that necessarily mean that their impressions are accurate? To reiterate, these surveys have not looked at Singaporean local firms. Fortunately I was able to visit some Singaporean firms, albeit just three, in 1986. I conducted interviews on two occasions for two case studies, but in the third case study I was only able to visit once. The interviews were rather unstructured, but I dare to report the results here because information in this area is so very scarce.

1. A mass-production workplace

Rotation every two hours

I will first look at an atomizer factory with 200 employees. It takes time to establish a horizontal span of experience in the form of job rotation within the workshop taking place as a usual workplace custom. Yet a clear trend

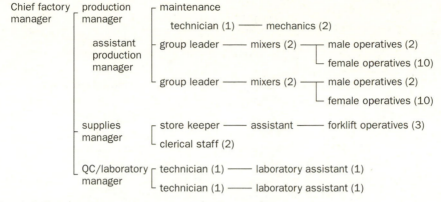

FIG. 2.1. Factory organization: a mass-production workplace

could be recognized here, even though this plant had only been established for five years at the time of the case study.

To consider the width of experience one must first look at the organization of the workplace. Figure 2.1 shows the manufacturing relationships in the plant. In manufacturing are engaged two groups, each of which has a total of fifteen workers comprising two mixers, two male operatives and ten female operatives. The quality control department, which becomes relevant when considering the depth of experience, has five staff. One issue concerns how these staff and the manufacturing line workers assign non-routine tasks and quality checks.

The impression conveyed from Figure 2.1 is probably that the conditions are such that the two groups are assigned to sections of the line and divide the work systematically. However, in reality the situation is completely different. There are five manufacturing lines in this plant requiring different numbers of workers with the total reaching forty workers, which greatly surpasses the thirty described above. The fact is that all five lines may not be operating depending on demand conditions and, since the required number of workers is only nominal, changes are made to correspond with the quantity of output. Thus the two groups do not systematically assign jobs, but instead often take on a tangle of assignments. The prevailing belief is that the assignment of duties is distinct, suggesting an inflexible and fixed arrangement under which job assignments could not easily be changed. The facts deviate greatly from this.

Let us observe the degree of flexibility by entering an atomizer line with many workers. The meaning of job rotation cannot be understood unless the job content is at least roughly described. This line is making sprayers for household insecticides. The compressed insecticide is packed in metal cans with a height of 20 cm and a diameter of about 8 cm. After being sealed with

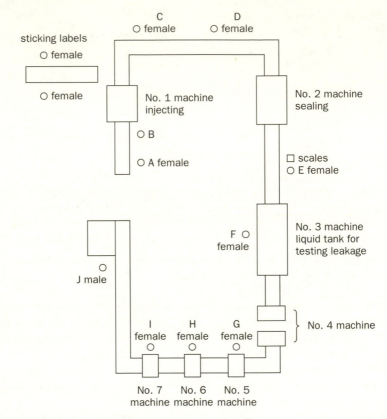

Fɪɢ. 2.2. Layout of mass-production workplace: atomizer line

a lid at the top, these cans are packed into boxes. As shown in Figure 2.2, woman A stands at one end of the line as she lines up the metal cans on top of the belt; B watches the injection machine; while C and D attach the inner cap and position the nozzle at the head. The sealing is carried out by machine. Subsequently E weighs the cans, though in fact the weight is automatically measured and those cans whose weight is excessive or insufficient are automatically expelled from the line. E places the expelled cans on hand-operated scales. If the weight problem continues, E informs the group leader, who takes measures to find out the cause of the problem and to deal with it. If any problem remains, a mechanic from the maintenance department is called. Meanwhile, F carries out a leakage test in a liquid tank. Any leakage of air is also checked at that point and a report is made to the group leader. G is in charge of watching the machine for fixing the caps, while H checks the way of fixing the cap and I watches the machine for packing the cans in boxes. J piles up the output packed in boxes on a side platform. As this is a job requiring a good deal of physical strength, it is assigned to a man.

In practice, job rotation takes place systematically every two hours. The pattern of job changes works out in this manner: after two hours the women at positions A and B go to the posts at C and D, while the incumbents there go to E and G. The two workers who attach labels also participate in the job rotation. The above rotation takes place among all the female operatives, while in the case of the men, those at F and J change their positions every two hours. Still, on this day, one male operative was absent and so a woman had taken over. In other words, job rotation between men and women also sometimes takes place.

The same kind of job rotation can be seen on the other lines as well. On the first day I visited the insecticide line, one male and three female operatives were in position and, in fact, exchanged places every two hours. This rotation had first been effected because of the ideas of the assistant production manager, who wished to equalize burdens. The assistant manager had experienced being employed by a Japanese subsidiary, so on that account it might be risky to see this as originally a Singaporean practice. None the less, job rotation could be seen in other case studies, and even if this were due to experience in Japanese companies, it should be remarked that the practice has been preserved. If Singaporean and Japanese practices were like oil and water, how could the Japanese way be maintained? Also, the flexibility of the arrangements can be judged from the number of people on the insecticide line on that day. The required number for this line is originally one male and four female operatives making a total of five, but the work is being done by fewer on that day. When there are insufficient operatives, a mixer or even a mechanic from the maintenance section joins the line.

Unusual operations

At this point the doubt may arise that perhaps experiencing many jobs would not be really significant for skill formation because the work is simple. This is a reasonable doubt in respect of what has been so far described, but in fact no reference has yet been made to an important part of the work, which is the response to changes and to unexpected problems.

The most easily seen change is that of product variations on one line. The presence of an ability to handle the setting-up efficiently through changing the jigs and tools to meet the product changes is necessary. About four or five kinds of product are produced on each of the five lines; and the jigs and tools must be adjusted at least once a day. More importantly, there are unexpected problems that require attention in dealing with continued product defects or malfunctioning machinery. Let us observe this kind of work on the atomizer line seen earlier.

There are both machines that are relatively easy to operate and those that are somewhat difficult to operate, on which tools are changed. In the case of the more simple machines, a male operative and a mixer do the work. With the difficult machines, such as the machinery for injection and sealing or cap fixing, a mechanical engineer and the group leader take charge, while at the same time teaching their know-how to the mixer. In the case of problems, the operative merely reports the trouble to the group leader and does not deal with it by himself or herself. For inspecting airtight leakages, the male operative goes no further than confirming the location of the leak. Seeking the cause and handling it are mainly the responsibility of the group leader or, at times, the mixer. When they cannot handle the problem, a mechanical engineer is summoned. Generally speaking, small problems mostly end up being dealt with by the group leader. This observation was not only made by the assistant production manager of the line, but was also asserted by the engineering chief.

The group leader was internally promoted. If the group leader had a com-pletely different career path from the operatives, the skill formation of the male operatives would be confined to a shallow depth. However, both the group leader and the mixers were internally promoted from below. The former prac-tice of recruiting the mixers externally has been changed, so that now, out of four mixers, all but one—who was left over from a prior scheme—were previously operatives. As is shown on Table 2.1, one of the group leaders had also been promoted from operative through mixer to group leader, while the other entered the company as a mechanic in the maintenance section and later became a group leader. Under such conditions, it must be agreed that the skills making up a male worker's career do not simply stop at operating the line, but also include responding to variations and troubles. This kind of internal promotion is not incompatible with a high degree of labour mobility. Even if a worker is mobile, only one or two years after entering the com-pany, he settles down and starts on the internal promotion system.

However, the career stops at this point and does not extend any higher. If one could say that the assistant production manager had come from below, then the situation would resemble a Japanese workplace where the super-visors or *kakarichō* have been promoted from below, but in this case he had graduated from a technical college and so his career had no connection with that of a production worker. The career dividing lines are more distinct in the quality-control section, since the bosses had graduated from technical colleges and the assistants from high schools,[19] and assistants cannot appar-ently be promoted to superior positions. This factor would be a deterrent to a desire for improving one's skills.

Another measure for promoting skill formation does, however, exist, which is a wage system that encourages employment over the long term. Although there is no wage table on account of this being a small firm and interviews are inadequate for collecting such data, one can at least understand that the starting wage is determined by educational level and that pay is differentiated by job-grade rises in yearly increments. Since a male operative earns around

TABLE 2.1. Workers' careers: mass-production workplace, Singapore

	Age (yrs)	Length of service	Education	Career
Manufacturing department				
Group leader		5 yrs		Operative → mixer → group leader
Group leader				After similar experience elsewhere recruited as a mechanic → group leader
Male operative J		6 mths		Unrelated experience elsewhere
Maintenance chief	45	4 yrs	Primary school	Group-leader experience in many companies, always in maintenance
Maintenance mechanic		3 yrs		Mechanic elsewhere; recruited through newspaper advert
Maintenance mechanic		3 yrs		NIC 3rd Class, mixer for 2 years, then mechanic for 1 year
Quality control department				
Officer		1 yr	Technical high school	Female; experience elsewhere
Officer		2.5 yrs	Technical high school	Female; experience elsewhere
Assistant		10 mths	O levels[a]	Female; promoted from operative
Assistant		2 yrs	O levels[a]	Relevant experience elsewhere

[a] National examinations taken at the age of 16.

S$400 (Singaporean dollars), a mixer around S$500, and a group leader about S$650, one could speculate that the wage gain is roughly 50 per cent under internal promotion. However, it would be better to study wage systems by turning to other detailed case studies of wage structures.

2. A ship repair yard

The nature of the work

Let us look at a ship repair yard where a fairly high level of skills is required. There are just 110 blue-collar workers, but when including 30 staff and 100 to 150 contract workers the total number of employees becomes roughly 300. As the parent company is a new large shipbuilder, this shipyard cannot be said to be merely small or medium sized. The yard had been in business for ten years at the time of the interviews and so workplace practices had become fairly well established.

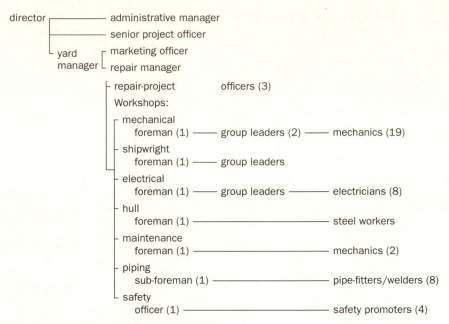

Fig. 2.3. Organizational chart: ship-repair yard

The organizational chart in Figure 2.3 shows that the repair section, which is the main part of the shipyard, is composed of seven workshops. In the machining workshop, which has the largest number of workers, nineteen mechanics are working in small groups of three to four under one foreman and two group leaders. Another small group made up of just contract workers may be brought in depending on the volume of work. I was told that contract workers and regular employees do not work in the same group. Contract workers are divided into skilled and unskilled workers, with the former earning rather higher wages than the regular workers. Although regular employees are sometimes transferred into contract-worker positions, they apparently prefer to seek employment stability by becoming regular employees.

According to the foreman of the mechanical section, the workers there are divided into three groups: the A group, the B group, and those in the machining workshop. The A group and B group each take eight mechanics, who make up a total of four small groups, each made up of four people. They are responsible for repairing the engine and other mechanical equipment of a ship requiring maintenance. There is no difference between the work of each of the four groups, since any group works on any part of any piece of ship equipment. They simply respond to requirements according to whether work is rushed or slack. Since they are responsible for a variety of ships and parts, they are all-rounders in handling mechanical equipment.

The remaining machining workshop is responsible for the parts required for repairing machinery and equipment. The four mechanics are stationed in a small hut, where each kind of multi-use machine tool—such as lathes, milling machines, shapers, and drilling machines—is lined up. These men have been recruited on account of their being experienced in mechanical work. The leader is responsible for the difficult jobs and he assigns the work to the other three workers. The leader as well as two of the mechanics have been employed in this machining workshop for ten consecutive years. The fourth mechanic, whose experience has been confined to a short period in another company and who has only been employed here for two years, is at present learning machining work from the leader.

The actual arrangements are not fixed in the way usually supposed. There are deliberate exchanges of workers between the machining workshop and the A and B repair unit groups. The leader and the two experienced mechanics from the machining workshop go to the repair units when required, thereby acquiring extra knowledge about ships' engines and mechanical equipment. The youngest mechanic in the workshop is still inexperienced, but I was told that the plan was that in the future he would also rotate. On the other hand, the two workers in the repair units who are able mechanics sometimes go to assist in the machining workshop when the work load is heavy there. The other workers in the repair units go to assist also in the hull and electrical workshops. At 10:00 a.m. every Monday, Wednesday, Friday, and Saturday, the foremen hold a meeting to discuss assistance between workshops in response to differing workloads. Thus actual conditions are very different to the common belief that a worker only does work falling under his own occupation.

Pay according to job grade

One question that arises is how a worker can form such wide-ranging skills. In this case study, skill formation starts from having had experience in other companies, as can be seen from Table 2.2, which shows the careers of individual workers. Skills are not dependent on training and qualifications from outside the company. Until a few years ago, the plan had been that workers who had completed their apprenticeships in the parent company should make up the core workforce, but after successive quittings, the plan had been changed to recruiting fully skilled workers from other companies. In fact, in the sample of workers whose careers I surveyed, only the foremen and some of the supervisors had completed their apprenticeships in the parent company, while all the others had become experienced in other similar companies.

Even so, one should not jump quickly to the conclusion that experience within the company is treated lightly. The remuneration system shows realistically that the converse is true. Even when the job title is the same, wages rise yearly so that there is a large gain depending on years of service. Union members, who are made up of group leaders and those below, as shown on Table 2.3, are divided into six occupational grades. Wages are not only paid to everyone in each grade according to a range-rate system; for those with

TABLE 2.2. Workers' careers: ship-repair yard, Singapore

	Age (yrs)	Length of service (yrs)	Education	Job grade	Career
Mechanical workshop					
Foreman	28	7	O levels[a]		Trained in parent company → mechanic → group leader → came to this yard as foreman
Sub-foreman A			O levels[a]		Worked as a mechanic in parent company
Sub-foreman B			O levels[a]		Worked as a mechanic in parent company
Machining shop					
Group leader		10			Experience elsewhere as a mechanic; machining shop group leader since entering company
Mechanic 1 (substitute leader)		10		4	Always been in machine shop
Mechanic 2		6		3	Experience elsewhere as a mechanic
Mechanic 3		2			Before employment was semi-skilled mechanic
Shipwright workshop					
Foreman		7			Parent company trainee → group leader → appointed as foreman in this yard
Sub-foreman				5	Promoted from steel worker
Sub-foreman				6	Promoted from steel worker

[a] National examinations taken at the age of 16.

the same occupational title, wages rise to the levels given in upper grades as well. Taking the case of mechanics, for example, workers holding the third class of the National Training Certificate, which they attained by completing a daily year-long training course in a vocational training school after leaving junior-high school, have been ranked in the occupational second grade. In that grade not only are there incremental wage rises, but also the workers' ranking will eventually rise to the occupational third grade. Those who have had experience in another company are considered to be skilled and can start at the occupational third grade. Wages rise yearly within the wide boundaries of the third grade from S$450 to S$800. The extent of yearly wage increments displayed in the table are the lowest guaranteed amounts and are boosted through merit payments. Moreover, many workers, such as the first mechanic in the machining workshop observed earlier, advance to the fourth grade. The upper limit has become $875, which is 90 per cent greater than the starting

TABLE 2.3. Wage table: ship-repair yard, Singapore

Job title	Job grade	Minimum wage ($)	Maximum wage ($)	Annual increment
Unskilled worker }	1	350	450	20
Tea lady }	2	400	550	25
Steel worker				
Mechanic				
Machinist				
Pipe welder/fitter	2	400	550	25
Electrician	3	450	800	30
Crane driver	4	550	875	35
Safety promoter				
Trainee technician				
Draughtsman				
Clerical assistant				
Typist				
Store assistant				
Purchasing assistant				
Group leader }	5	650	975	40
Technician }	6	750	1,100	45
Clerk, typist }				

point in the third grade. This must be said to be quite a considerable gain. If a worker becomes a group leader, the wage gain is even greater. As a rule, earlier experience elsewhere has an impact on the initial wage, but later on it is experience within the company that appears to have the greater impact. Under such an arrangement, a considerable development in skills could be expected as long as assessments and upgrading proceed efficiently.

However, there are conditions that severely limit skill formation, namely the shallowness of the career. Shop-floor workers can only go as high as some of the group leaders. Many of the group leaders and all of the foremen have had different careers from those of the shop-floor workers. They completed their apprenticeships in the parent company, worked there, and transferred to this company later. That fact must strongly limit the shop-floor workers' desire for raising their skills.

3. A plant for maintaining aircraft engines

Handling every part

The remaining case study is of a maintenance plant that requires an extremely high level of skills involving the disassembling, repair, and reassembling of air-craft engines. As is well known, aircraft engines must be regularly taken apart, checked and maintained after a certain number of flying hours. This is not a mass-production workplace, since many kinds of aircraft engines are handled. The disassembling and reassembling of one engine takes two weeks, and, in particular, a high level of skills is required. The workplace had been set up twelve years before the time of the interviews, which is probably a sufficient period for workplace customs to have become established. The building is new and well arranged with about 350 employees. The work first involves the assembly section, which takes apart the engine that has been carried in. The quality management section inspection staff then check the disassembled parts and divide them into those that need repairing and those that do not. After the former have been routed to the repair section and returned, both sets of parts are collected by the assembly section for reassembling and adjustment.

Table 2.4 displays the structure of the assembly section in which the work both begins and finishes. The section is divided into three large assembling

TABLE 2.4. Organization of assembly section: engine-maintenance plant, Singapore

	Personnel numbers					
	Engineers of foremen	Assistant engineers	Group leaders	Mechanics 1st class	Mechanics 2nd class	Apprentice mechanics
Assembly section chief						
1st division chief						
J1 engine assembly line	1	1	1	4	3	2
J2 engine assembly line	1	1	1	4		
Electrical parts	1			2	1	2
Gear box etc.	1			3		
Fuel accelerator assembly line	1		1	5	6	
2nd division chief						
J1/JT1 engine assembly line	1		1	5	2	
J3/H2 engine assembly line	1	1	1	6	1	3
Engine adjustments				7		
3rd division chief						
T3 engine assembly line	1			3	2	1
V/A engine assembly line		1	1	5		
Inspection area		1	1	6	5	2

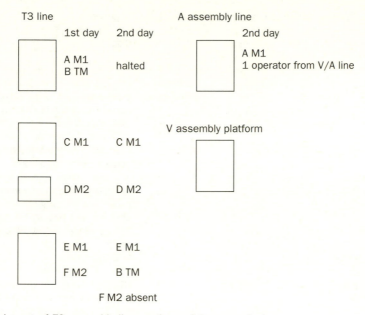

T3 line

1st day   2nd day

A M1
B TM   halted

C M1   C M1

D M2   D M2

E M1   E M1

F M2   B TM

F M2 absent

A assembly line

2nd day

A M1
1 operator from V/A line

V assembly platform

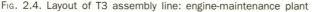

FIG. 2.4. Layout of T3 assembly line: engine-maintenance plant

divisions, each of which is made up of two assembling lines and two or three attached work groups. Since I interviewed the foreman of the T3 assembly line twice, I will use this line as an example. As is shown in Figure 2.4, rather than thinking of a conventional assembly line, one should picture the area as containing work platforms several metres apart on which the seated workers are engaged in careful reassembling. There are three small groups made up of pairs ranging from first- and second-class mechanics to apprentices. On the first day that I visited the line, a first-class mechanic A and an apprentice B were assembling large parts on one of the work platforms. The second small group was made up of a first-class mechanic C, who was installing the engine blades; on a rather small platform next to him was a second-class mechanic D, who was assembling small parts. The third group was made up of mechanics E and F.

The responsibilities of these three small groups are not necessarily fixed. Instead, there is a variety of responses to changing conditions in the work. One engine can be separated into nine large parts. The three groups are either made responsible for these parts, or else they each set about working with different engines. The engineer does assign the work, but apparently in the case of a first-class mechanic, he has to do any part of the work. In fact, as is clear from the assignments on the second day shown on Figure 2.4, the small groups are not fixed and often change. On the second day, the work of the first small group was halted and mechanic A moved to the neighbouring

TABLE 2.5. Workers' careers: engine-maintenance plant, Singapore

T3 assembly line	Age (yrs)	Length of service	Education	Career
Foreman		8 yrs	Technical high school	Entered after 1 year's experience in a shipbuilding yard; apprentice technician for 3 years, then experienced 3 lines in this assembly section as a sub-foreman before moving to present position; offJT overseas
A.M1 mechanic 1st class	late 20s	6 yrs		NTC 3rd Class; entered as apprentice mechanic without experience elsewhere; worked on next line but has always been on T3 line since its setting up in 1982
B.TM. apprentice mechanic		1 yr 3 mths		NTC 3rd Class
C.M1 mechanic 1st class		10 yrs		NTC 3rd Class; no experience elsewhere; first 6 months on V/A line but has always been on T3 line since its setting up in 1982; 6 months' offJT in Canada
D.M2 mechanic 2nd class		2 yrs		NTC 3rd Class; experience as a mechanic elsewhere; just become M2
E.M1 mechanic 1st class		12 yrs		NTC 3rd Class; entered as apprentice mechanic; 7 years' experience on V/A line before T3 line; offJT overseas
F.M2 mechanic 2nd class				NTC 3rd Class; no experience elsewhere; just become M2 after being apprentice mechanic
3rd assembly chief	34	13 yrs	Technical high school	Aircraft maker maintenance engineer: this plant's inspection engineer and chief; 3 years in present position; offJT overseas
Maintenance section chief	38	8 yrs	Technical high school	Experience in 5 other companies; as laboratory assistant, technician, electrical division chief; 3 years in present position after being maintenance engineer
Quality control section chief	34	5 yrs	O-levels[a]	Completed 2 years VITB machine assembly course; experience in 3 other companies starting as a shipbuilding company's apprentice, then experienced areas including

Table 2.5. (cont'd)

T3 assembly line	Age (yrs)	Length of service	Education	Career
				QC technical work and tool-work shop chief; has always been in QC section in this plant and in present position for 3 years
Responsible for QC in 3rd assembly division		7 yrs		Apprentice mechanic → mechanic 1st and 2nd Class → mechanic 1st Class; first did assembly work on V line and T3 line before becoming line inspector in March 1986

[a] National examinations taken at the age of 16.

line, while apprentice B entered the third small group as F was absent. Mechanics C and D did not rotate during these two days, but of course they do change positions on other days. In sum, there is frequent rotation within the line. Even between lines, as long as they are in the same division, as in the example of A above, job rotation does occasionally appear to take place. However, rotation which goes beyond the division is rare, because, as I was told, it would not be possible to let go of the talents of a first-class mechanic. In practice, staying on the line where one first arrived appears to be the norm from the individual careers shown on Table 2.5. At first glance it may be thought that the range of job rotations is narrow, but within that range a worker is handling various parts of an engine. The content of the work has a wide scope, because this is non-mass-production work with only six engines being maintained in one month.

Quality inspection

The actual work content deals much more with inspections and unusual operations, rather than simple assembly work. For example, first-class mechanic C is installing the engine blades, but the job entails measuring each blade, examining each closely, and making sure that their direction is uniform after being installed. The inspection categories and standards are based on those in the manual from the engine-production company and are set by the quality-control section. None the less, the work done by C is complex and he first corrects any defects or unexpected problems by himself. If malfunctions continue in any case, they are dealt with by the line technician or the maintenance staff. A first-class mechanic is expected to handle any problems. Even a second-class mechanic will grapple with some problems and the technician will later inspect his work.

One technician said that the leading part in quality inspections is taken by the assembly-line workers. In general, however, it is thought that when the onset of industrialization is recent, the 'separate system' is dominant. Under this system, difficult operations such as quality inspections and dealing with the unexpected are not expected of assembly-line workers, but of more highly qualified technicians and others instead.[20] Even in this plant, at first glance, it seems that the separate system is being followed. Somebody has been assigned to be in charge of quality control in the workplace. In the quality-control division, there are sections for parts control and for manufacturing-process control; the former judges the necessity of repairing the parts that have been disassembled while the latter's responsibility is to check the quality of the work on the shop floor. However, only one inspector is assigned to each assembly division and the core of the inspection work is taken by the line workers. Moreover, the process-inspection chief has had previous experience of the T3 line and the V/A assembly line in the role of third assembly chief. His career path is clearly connected up. For that reason, it would probably be better to view the structure of responsibilities as following the 'integrated system'.

Under the integrated system, the line workers are not only doing assembly work, but are also responsible for dealing with problems. This process can often be seen on contemporary Japanese shop floors.

But what of shallow measures taken toward fostering skills for shallow internal promotion? How do line workers acquire the know-how for quality inspections and the handling of problems? The study of individual careers shown on Table 2.5 reveals four special features. First of all, attention should be drawn to the third-class mechanics. Apparently, at this plant the recruitment level encompassed not just the six shown on the table, as fourteen were recruited in total in that year. Secondly, there are evidently some workers without experience in other companies. Of the four whom I interviewed, three were without outside experience. This point cannot be generalized as it must be noted that this is a rather unusual and particularly excellent company in Singapore. In any case, the recruits work as apprentice mechanics for eighteen months, during which time they receive an OffJT course within the company for four days. Subsequently, they are promoted to become second-class mechanics. Then, after passing the internal-company test for each kind of job category, they become first-class mechanics. Those who do not pass the test apparently move to another company. Thirdly, when someone is to be promoted to first-class mechanic, he sometimes receives OffJT overseas where he participates in a course that lasts several weeks and is run by an overseas engine manufacturer. Not everyone has this opportunity, but on this assembly line, there were four who had participated in an overseas course; namely, the foreman, C, E, and the section chief. Fourthly, though this kind of written work and OffJT seem to be held in high esteem, the core is OJT in the workplace; and when a worker reaches a line, rarely does he change to another line; rather, he is promoted to first-class mechanic on that line. Thus, the first-class mechanic progressively learns through experience how to deal with problems as well.

Workers are remunerated in a way that fosters skill formation over the long term. The initial pay for an apprentice mechanic was S$420 (at the time of the interviews). This rose to S$470 after the trial period. The minimum starting pay rate for those second-class mechanics with experience in other companies was S$550; and though annual merit assessments widened differentials, the wages for most second-class mechanics were around S$600. A newly qualified first-class mechanic would earn between S$680 and S$690, but the upper limit of S$1,400 was high. Thus, over fifteen to twenty years the rate of pay rose to be three times greater than that of a worker beginning as an apprentice mechanic. Even compared to a second-class mechanic, it was 2.5 times greater. Wage rates do not hit a ceiling after a worker becomes a first-class mechanic; instead rates should be said to resemble somewhat the Japanese system of job-grade-based payments. For those who are promoted to group-leader positions, the upper limit to wages is that much higher.

The other measure to foster skills through vertical career development or, in other words, through promotion to leading positions is, however, shallow, since production workers do not reach the level of foreman. All of the foremen had graduated from a higher level of school and held formal qualifications. Shop-floor workers could reach no higher than group leader or, in some cases, they could transfer to become process chiefs for quality control. It cannot be said, therefore, that the measures for fostering skills were wholly satisfactory.

4. Conclusion

Because actual observation of workplaces was scarce in other studies, very different conclusions from prevailing beliefs have been reached, despite the limitations of being based on only three case studies. First, it is quite customary for workers in indigenous Singapore companies to engage in several different jobs within the workshop in response to demand conditions. Where the required level of skills is not high, such as in a mass-production workshop, job rotation takes place every two hours, but even in non-mass-production workshops with high skill requirements, it is usual for a worker to take on several assignments. The reality of this differs from the kind of conditions where a worker would only take on fixed duties.

Secondly, the shop-floor workers also carry out rather unusual operations; namely, dealing with product variations and problems. On a mass-production shop floor, male workers deal with product changes in the first half of their careers, while in the second half they handle unexpected problems.

Thirdly, workers acquire the skills to handle changes and unusual operations mainly through experience in the workplace. The prevailing view is
that external labour markets, in which workers attain higher positions by
acquiring higher qualifications in external courses, are the dominant system.
However, job rotation is practised right from the first stage of a worker's
career and, subsequently, there is internal promotion within the company.
This is not just the tale in large companies, but can be seen as well in medium-
sized companies with between 100 and 300 employees.

Fourthly, the wage system also encourages long-term service and brings
about skill improvements through experience within the company. It is commonly thought that wages in Singapore cannot be expected to rise when a
worker stays in the same duties under an external labour market system.
However, in these three case studies, wages do rise by up to two or three
times in quantity, even where the workers' duties do not change. During that
interval the job grade would also rise. There are payments for merit assessments as well. In fact, this system is close to the Japanese practice of wages
by job grade. If a worker can get that practical benefit of higher pay, he has
an incentive over the long term to raise his skill level.

Fifthly, there is the proviso that measures to foster higher skill levels are
partly lacking in some essential respects in Singapore. Vertical promotion as
part of a career path is shallow. The career path does not extend as far as
becoming a foreman and stops at the group-leader level. If workers cannot
hope to attain higher-status positions, their will to improve skills will be
obstructed. The reason for a shallow career path is certainly not that the
application of Singapore workers is low. As has already been seen, production workers are handling product variations and problems. They seem to
display a rather higher aptitude than production workers in Indonesia, as
will be discussed later, or workers in Thailand as reported elsewhere.[21] One
causative factor for the shallow career path is probably the excessive weight
placed on educational results in Singapore society.

III. Indigenous Companies in Indonesia and Thailand

As a part of a survey being carried out by the UN Regional Development
Centre, in the summer of 1981, I visited the three cities of Lucknow in India,
Ubon Ratchathani in Thailand, and Yogyakarta in Indonesia, where I could
carry out interviews in indigenous companies and observe shop-floor activities.[22] Since I visited each place only once, the case studies were rather
limited and based on short interviews. At most, I could gauge only the scope
of a worker's experience, in terms of both the horizontal span—measured by
the extent to which different jobs were experienced—and the vertical span—
seen in whether group leaders and foremen are promoted from below. I did

not investigate how workers responded to product variations or to problems, since at the time I had not yet developed the appropriate analytical framework. Nor did I inquire into the remuneration system. Since other studies of indigenous shop floors are scarce, I shall have to display the case-study results here as an important resource, although the research was carried out more than ten years ago. These results could also be valuable in that they come from a study of small and medium-sized companies in regional cities.

1. Processing-industry shop floors in Indonesia

In Yogyakarta, I visited the nine plants shown in Table 2.6, but here I shall take up the case study of the powdered milk manufacturing plant, where I conducted relatively detailed interviews. The plant had been established in 1954, but during the 1970s it was completely renovated with modern equipment and expanded from 250 employees in 1972 to 420 in 1981. It is a plant that can appropriately be called part of a processing industry.

The plant is divided into eight divisions: manufacturing, finishing, packing, machinery, electricity, store, management, and research and development. The manufacturing division is the largest, accounting for 120 workers. As is shown in Figure 2.5, there are two lines in the manufacturing division. Each line is made up of four sections: an infusion section; a mixing section; a drying section and a hygiene section. These sections operate under a single foreman and each utilizes about fifteen or sixteen workers divided into four units. There are four gangs for three shifts in three of the four sections. Only in the hygiene section, which is responsible for arranging things and cleaning, are there two shifts. If the mixing section is taken as an example, one unit is made up of four workers—group leader, first operator, second operator, and assistant.

A worker's career begins with the assistant's position in each section and progresses through first and second operator to group leader. A worker who starts in the hygiene section will sometimes rotate to other sections. At present, graduation from a senior-high school is a condition for recruitment, and if one looks at the diffusion rate of senior-high schools at this time, it must be said to be quite a high qualification. The majority of the present employees are only primary-school graduates and it is they who have become group leaders. Nevertheless, I was told that there is also the possibility from now on of not being promoted unless one is a high-school graduate. The reason is that, in this workplace, excessive weight seems to be given to qualifications, while shop-floor experience tends to be underestimated. Promotion to group leader depends not only on length of service, of course, but also on assessments and tests; not every worker can be promoted. Still, all the group leaders so far have been promoted from below.

There is also rotation between sections. For example, the first operator in the infusion section sometimes rotates with the first operators in the drying

TABLE 2.6. Workers' careers: plants in Yogyakarta, 1981

Plant	No. of employees	Horizontal career span		Vertical career span: up to			State or private	Year founded	Rate of growth
		Group-leader unit	Foreman unit	Group leader	Foreman	Section chief			
powdered-milk	420	**	**	*	*	*	semi-state	1953	fair
agricultural machinery I	850 assembly * machinists –		–	*	*	–	private	1953	rapid
agricultural machinery II	300	*	–	*	*	–	state	1918	slow
Auto-repairs	100	*	*	*	*	*	private	1974	rapid
Leather	300	–	–	*	–	–	private	1968	rapid
Sugar-cane	1,500	*	–	*	–	–	state	1955	slow
Water-glass	90	*	–	**	–	–	private	1975	rapid
Tiles	100	*	–	*	–	–	private	1976	rapid
Batik	110	–	–	*	–	–	private	years ago	fair

** indicates 'highly prevalent'.
* indicates 'exists'.
– indicates 'rather rare'.

```
Department——assistant ┌ line no. 1
     head                   foreman      1 per shift

                              ┌ infusion section    4 per shift
                              │   chief (1), operators (2), assistant (1)
                              │ mixing section     4 per shift
                              │ drying section     4 per shift
                              └ hygiene section     2 per shift

                    └ line no. 2
                      rather similar to line no. 1
```

FIG. 2.5. Organization of powdered-milk plant: Yogyakarta

section and in the mixing section. Though this is not a regular rotation, it is a directive clearly given by the manufacturing-division manager, who said during the interview that he wanted workers who have had experience of the main jobs in the division. This is not, however, a requirement for all the workers, being confined to those with good results, while the rotation is at most limited to within the division. The vertical span of the workers' careers is remarkable. All of the foremen have been promoted from below as is the case with even some of the assistant managers. As only the division manager had definitely graduated from university, this was the cut-off point for the production workers' careers. Still, their careers were quite broad with both good horizontal and vertical spans.

2. An Indonesian auto-repair shop

Such broad careers are not only found on the shop floors of processing industries, but can also be recognized in an auto-repair shop. At the time, as far as I knew, the main machine plants in a developing country were auto-repair shops, so I made sure to visit this type of industry. However, rather than simply an auto-repair shop, the object of this case study should be called the equipment-maintenance division of a large auto-sales company. There were only ten employees when the company started up in 1974, but by 1981 there were around 100 employees, so the company's growth has been remarkable.

There are also sales and management divisions, but the structure of the maintenance division alone is as shown in Figure 2.6. There are four workshops, namely engine maintenance, body maintenance, servicing, and tool-keeping. The engine maintenance workshop is divided into two groups—electrical repairs and general repairs—with about five workers in each group.

The company likes to recruit young graduates of technical high schools. In fact, in that year all of the six recruits had graduated from technical high schools and had completed twelve years of education. Despite having been to a technical high school, the worker actually masters the job after entering

Fɪɢ. 2.6. Organization of auto-repair shop: Yogyakarta, 1981

the workplace in this auto industry. In the case of the engine workshop, the entrant is first in the general-repair group and is responsible for easy jobs such as checking the radiator. He then gradually takes on more difficult tasks. After mastering the jobs in the general-repair group, he moves to the electrical group, where all the workers have already experienced the general-group work. In other words, the span of experience spreads over the whole workshop.

The vertical span is also remarkable, since this division's group leaders, three foremen, and even its division manager were all promoted from below. However, a career here is not finished at the point of becoming a foreman or section chief. Some of the employees move to the office area to do sales work or management. Thus white-collar and blue-collar careers are not rigidly separated.

Skill formation is not only determined by OJT. There is also OffJT. In the initial stages of the workers' careers, the foreman assembles the young workers after working hours to give classes on auto mechanics. Workers who have achieved good results in the classes and in their daily work can participate in a course on auto mechanics run by Indonesia-Toyota and thereby obtain the 'Toyota Dealer' qualifying licence which is issued there. In this company, eight people hold the third-class licence, three people the second-class, and just one person, the repair manager, the first-class licence.

A worker's career need not be confined to this company. More than a few former employees have become independent by setting up their own companies for auto repairs. The diffusion rate of cars in Indonesia has increased very rapidly, so there is a large demand for auto-repair shops. Since there is a possible future of becoming independent, workers have a will to study over a broad range of topics. If they think that with diligence they can work for themselves, they will not dislike having a wide range of experience. Even though this is a natural phenomenon, it is often overlooked and needs to be mentioned.

Let us return again to Table 2.6, which shows the nine places I visited. It should be clear that the above two cases are certainly not exceptional, since in seven out of the nine case studies, jobs were being rotated within the group-leader unit. Rotation beyond the group-leader unit was only found in these two cases. Also, in all nine cases the vertical career permitted promotion as far as group-leader positions, and in four of the cases up to the foreman level. Certainly, in the two cases discussed in detail, careers are broad. However, in the other cases there is rotation within the group-leader unit as well.

3. A Thai auto-repair shop

Our survey results for indigenous Thai workplaces have already been published.[23] In addition, however, I separately visited the five small and medium-sized companies shown in Table 2.7 in a regional city called Ubon Ratchathani near the Cambodian border. Let us examine the auto-repair shop here, for such a plant is the classic machine shop for a country at this early stage of industrial development. Briefly, there were about fifty employees apparently working hard. In fact, it would be more appropriate to call the plant a machine works rather than an auto-repair shop. About forty machines, such as lathes and drilling machines, and mostly made in Taiwan, are installed there and the workers take apart the engines of old cars for grinding and repairing before reassembling. Thus, the work somewhat resembles that of making new engines.

The workplace is divided into the lathe-operating group and the welding group. The youths who enter the jobs have had no previous experience in this kind of work and have had around six years of formal education at the elementary-school level. For about the first three years they are employed as

TABLE 2.7. Workers' careers: plants in Ubon Ratchathani, 1981

Plant	No. of employees		Horizontal career span: within		Vertical career span: up to		
			Group-leader unit	Foreman unit	Group leader	Foreman	Owner of small company
Auto repairs	50		**	*	*	–	**
Machinery	20	welders	*	*	*	–	*
		turners	*	–	*	–	**
Liquor	230		*	*	*	*	–
Rice mill	15		*	–	*	–	*
Tapioca	20		–	–	*	–	–

** indicates 'highly prevalent'.
* indicates 'exists'.
– indicates 'rather rare'.

assistants, carrying parts, and learning how to do simple welding or lathe operations, while gradually taking on more difficult tasks. Even when they have become lathe operators or welders after three years, they still go on to do more difficult jobs and their wages continue to rise.

The workers rotate to do other jobs beyond the group. A welder will go to assist the lathe-operating group and become responsible for simple lathe operations, and vice versa. Not all the workers rotate, however; only those who are enthusiastic. For example, a keen lathe operative will learn welding tasks when a welding machine is vacant, not simply because of management objectives but also for his own motives.

In the same way as the workers in the Indonesian auto-repair shop, some of the workers are hoping that in the future they will be able to be independent and have their own auto-repair shops. They wish, therefore, to learn not only how to do lathe operations but welding tasks as well. In general, if workers know of advantages for themselves, they will work hard. However, the vertical span of a career here only reaches as far as group leader and does not encompass the foreman level.

These kinds of trends were also more or less common to the other four places I visited. As is shown in Table 2.7, there is job rotation within the group-leader unit in four out of the five case studies, while in three cases rotation extends more widely to the foreman's unit. In all cases the vertical career span includes group leaders, but in only one exceptional case does it extend to the foreman's position. On the other hand, the road to owning a small business is open in four of the cases. In general, these case studies can be said to resemble somewhat general workplace trends in Indonesia.

4. The Indian case

In Lucknow, which is a central city in the Punjab region with a population of more than 1 million, I observed five small companies and a scooter-assembly plant employing 1,500 workers. Each of the small companies, located on an industrial estate set up by the regional government, is of a compact scale with about twenty workers. I shall take up the example of a plant where the couplings for plastic pipes are moulded. There are two plastic exuding machines in the centre of the workshop, being operated by twelve workers. In the tool shop, in addition, three workers are making metal dies with lathes and drilling machines, while another three are employed as packers. The plastic exuding-machine workshop is divided into three units, each made up of two operatives and two assistants. One exuding machine is operated by one operative and one assistant in a shift.

With actual observation of the work, I realized that the operative and the assistant, either regularly or irregularly, exchanged their duties. An assistant is usually promoted to operative. Out of the present six operatives, two are

TABLE 2.8. Workers' careers: plants in Lucknow, 1981

Plant	No. of employees	Horizontal career span:	Vertical career span: up to		Independent or sub-contractor
		Group-leader unit	Group leader	Foreman	
Pump production	11	*	*	–	independent
Plastic extrusion	20	*	*	*	independent
Ignition switches	20	*	*	*	sub-contractor
Speedometers	23	*	*	–	sub-contractor
Die casting	20	*	*	*	sub-contractor

* indicates 'exists'.
– indicates 'rather rare'.

from another company, but that is because a second machine has recently been brought in. Indian workers are said to be mobile, but out of the six operatives, four have been employed there for five or six years. When one considers that this company had been established for no more than nine years, one should rather say that the workforce is stable. The tool shop is different in that workers with experience in other companies have been engaged there.

None the less, workers in the tool shop and the exuding-machine shop do assist each other. When the delivery date is close, the members of the tool shop go to help in the exuding-machine shop. Apparently, the reverse also happens, though with less frequency. This kind of rotation between groups is clearly a management policy, being, it was suggested to me, a natural way of dealing with orders in a small organization. Often said to be a special Japanese work practice, this type of rotation can even be recognized in India, where work practice in this respect is thought to run directly counter to the Japanese system. I was told that, in order to encourage job rotation, those practising it receive, of course, a good merit assessment; they also have no risk of being laid off in a recession and, moreover, there is a greater possibility of their being promoted to the foreman level. The span of promotion is not too short as well, since the single foreman in this plant has been promoted from below. The reality of this situation is very different from the image of India as a 'qualifications society'.

It can be seen from Table 2.8 that the above trends are fairly common in the other case studies. In all five cases there is job rotation within the group-leader unit, and in three out of the five cases, the foreman has been promoted from below. The large scooter plant is no exception in terms of the breadth of workers' careers, either. One of the foremen on the final assembly line with seventy-eight workers told me that he rotated the workers in order that one worker should experience seven or eight different assignments as a necessary measure to be able to cope with unexpected situations such as needing substitutes for absentees. When a worker has experienced more assignments, his merit assessment improves and there is a greater possibility of his moving to the inspection division, which is everyone's hope. The vertical career span does not, however, reach as far as a foreman's position. The foreman has a higher level of educational qualifications than the production workers. The plant manager emphasized that there was no notion at all that a foreman could emerge from among the workers on the shop floor in the future. I was told that the educational level of the production workers could in no way equal that of the foreman.

IV. The Feasibility of Japanese Working Practices

The topic of this chapter has been whether Japanese work practices could be transferable to ASEAN workplaces. In the light of the case studies discussed above, and with reference to the results of the detailed research of six indigenous Thai companies and five indigenous Malaysian companies, which have been recorded elsewhere, are Japanese work practices indeed transferable as set above?[24]

To answer this question, the Japanese approach must first be clarified. I believe that the nucleus of Japanese practices is made up of the two following aspects. First, there is the know-how to deal with changes and problems, which can be called workplace software techniques or, more simply, skills. As has been mentioned repeatedly, the foundation of such skills is wide-ranging experience. In other words, we need to find out both the horizontal span of experience and also the depth of experience by paying attention to workers' responses to changes and problems. Second, incentives for fostering this kind of skill formation must be established. To know whether such incentives exist, attention should be paid both to whether remuneration will rise in line with the formation of higher level skills, and also, since remuneration is not just a function of salary, to whether the way is open for production workers to be promoted to higher positions, in particular to becoming foremen.

1. Breadth of experience

Asian workplaces outside Japan are said to have usually adopted western working practices with fixed duties and specialization and with little rotation between jobs. For that reason, attempts to estimate the degree of transferability of Japanese practices have been made using ambiguous indices such as whether or not there is job rotation. At the very least, however, the span of experience must be considered through the following questions, outlined at the begining of this chapter:

1. Do production workers stay in just one job?

2. Do production workers experience between three to five positions?

3. Do production workers experience all the main positions within a group leader's unit?

4. Do production workers experience all the main positions within a foreman's unit?

5. Do production workers experience positions in a cluster of technically related workshops?

Sometimes a comparison is made between the case of (1) where the job is never changed, and that of job rotation (6), as mentioned earlier, between unrelated positions. However, this comparison is confusing the definition of the issue by taking cases that are too far apart. In practice, job rotation case (6) would obstruct skill formation in its capacity as an emergency refuge, as it were, and it is qualitatively completely different from the cases up to and including job rotation (5), as mentioned earlier.

In contemporary Japanese workplaces, speaking very roughly, it appears that there is job rotation in large companies, where its nature is either like (4), within the workshop, or (5), between technically related workshops. In small and medium-sized companies there seems to be a mixture within the same company of production workers rotating between three to five positions as in (2), while others are changing jobs within (3), the group leader's unit, or (4), the foreman's unit. Sometimes there may be a small fraction of the workforce who move also between the technically related workshops in (5). On average, therefore, the scope of job rotation in smaller companies is narrower, but at the same time there is variety in the scale of rotation.[25]

In respect of the above classification, I could naturally not find any case at all of there being (1), no job rotation in Asian workplaces. Even in small workplaces, production workers experienced between three to five job assignments as in (2), and in many places the scope of job experience widened to within the group leader's unit. Furthermore, the span was sometimes as wide as that of (4) the foreman's unit in Singapore, Thailand, and Indonesia. I did not ever recognize, however, the (5) kind of job rotation between technically related workshops. In general, the scale of job rotation is narrower than in large Japanese companies, but it can be said to be only marginally narrower than in small and medium-sized Japanese companies.

These trends are consistent with our survey results for six case studies of indigenous Thai companies and five of indigenous Malaysian companies. Of course, our studies are a long way from being proved to be statistically significant in terms of numbers, but since we are not blest with other dependable surveys, we can probably adequately estimate the feasibility of transferring Japanese practices in terms of widening the breadth of experience from this point. It seems that, until now, the view that production workers outside Japan retain specialists and fix assignments, and the judgements reached as a result of this view, have all been based on preconceived ideas without even visiting indigenous workplaces.

2. Know-how for problem solving

Asian production workers outside Japan have been said to do only what they are told to do. However, the Singapore case study has suggested that production workers who handle problem-solving are certainly not an exception. If attention is paid also to the latter half of a career, problem-solving is clearly not just the job of technicians with high qualifications, but also the job of shop-floor production workers. Unfortunately I was not able to enquire into this point in either the Indonesian company or the small and medium-sized Indian companies, but on another occasion I recognized that, among the production workers, there were those engaged in problem-solving when I was carrying out interviews in indigenous Thai and Malaysian company workplaces. Compared to Japanese workplaces, however, the number is much smaller. Whereas in the Japanese case about nine out of ten will be engaged in problem-solving, in the Thai case studies only one or two out of ten could be counted.[26] Nevertheless, in the Singapore case studies, where a high degree of skills is required, many were doing so. Therefore, if policies are adopted to promote problem-solving, this kind of know-how will probably become fairly well diffused. Of course, when the onset of industrialization is relatively recent, the level of that kind of problem-solving would be lower. Thus, there are surely sufficient prospects for applying Japanese methods, which stress problem-solving.

3. Incentive measures

These kinds of high-level skills are not something which can be formed without any effort. It is often suggested that, in Japan, skills can be formed simply out of a spirit of loyalty to the company, but if an appropriate remuneration system is lacking, there will ultimately not be any real formation of skills. A company cannot achieve an appropriate system by paying wages according to each job. Even if assignments are the same, when the workers have previously had differing degrees of experience, their spans of experience differ and the degree to which they can contribute through being able to substitute for absent workers is different. Also, even if the assignments are the same, the workers' contribution can differ greatly depending on their skill in problem-solving. Appropriate compensation cannot be achieved by giving a wage according to the job.

First of all, since experience is accumulated over the long term, it is necessary for the pay system to be advantageous for those giving longer service by providing them with regular increments. In addition, wages should reflect improvements in skill levels. Payments based on the job grade, which reflect jobs and skill improvements over the medium term, can compensate for a rise in skills regardless of individuals' jobs. Merit assessments would probably also be required to express the difference in skill improvements for those in the same job grades.

In practice, pay systems for both production workers and white-collar workers in large Japanese companies are based on the three pillars of job-grade-based pay, regular increments, and merit payments. However, in Asian workplaces outside Japan pay systems are said to be absolutely unlike the above, since wages are paid according to each job, following western European practice. Nevertheless, if one actually observes indigenous companies, the above three pillars can in fact be seen in most countries and in most cases. I use the word 'most' not because there were cases where the converse was true, but only because there were some cases where I did not carry out inquiries into the pay system. Even in the case of Singapore, which is thought to have had the strongest influence from western Europe, in occupations with the same name, job grades do rise. Even within the same job grade, there are regular pay increments and merit payments, as has been seen earlier. Also, In these cases there is no lack of incentive measures to promote the formation of higher skill levels. The next stage will be arrived at when the degree of skill improvements is clearly written down according to standards for assessment and raising job grades. In the case of Japanese companies, it is written down in the workplace in the form of the work chart.[27]

4. Promotion to foreman

Remuneration does not only consist of cash wages. Compensation is augmented through promotion to higher positions and also through the chance for the worker to go even further. Attention has been paid, in particular, to the possibilities of being promoted to the foreman level. In all industrialized countries, most foremen have been promoted from among the production workers. This is not necessarily always the case in developing countries, and so it is necessary to investigate this issue.

In fact once this point is reached in our analysis, differences do appear among ASEAN countries. In all the Thai case studies during the 1987 survey, the foreman had been promoted from below.[28] In the smaller-scale Thai survey (1981), promotion stopped at the group-leader level in four out of the five cases and in only one case had the foreman been promoted from below. In roughly half of the cases observed in the Indonesian survey (1981) and the Malaysian survey (1987), the foreman had been promoted from below. In Singapore, in contrast, the foreman had not been promoted from below in every case study. Instead, foremen with a higher level of qualifications than production workers had been appointed. The same was true of the case study of a large company in India. However, in all the countries and case studies, the group leaders had been promoted from below.

Foremen in both large and small Japanese companies have been promoted from below, which in this respect is a practice similar to policies in western European and North American companies. But Japanese companies' policies go further in that many sub-section chiefs in higher positions are also promoted from below. The vertical span of the production worker's career in Thailand, Malaysia, and Indonesia is one step shorter than in industrialized countries such as Japan. Even so, group leaders as well as half the foremen in the case studies above have been promoted from below. Under such circumstances, if standard operating practices were formed to enable promotion to the foreman level, quite a high degree of skill formation could be fostered.

Such practices, however, do not occur in large companies in Singapore and India. However much effort is expended by production workers, they cannot rise to the level of foreman. This being the case, why should anyone make an effort and set about acquiring difficult skills? This point suggests that measures to foster skill formation are not sufficient.

The justification given by these companies' managers is that, since the technical level of production workers is still low, they cannot be entrusted with that level of responsibility. This statement may be appropriate in India, but Singapore, where production workers on the shop floor achieve high skill levels, is different. The proportion of Singapore production workers who handle unusual operations and deal with problems is not low, and is higher than in Thailand and Malaysia. This observation is supported by a variety of indicators such as the diffusion rate of education. Why then should promotion from below to the level of foreman not be apparent? My hypothesis is that the reason lies in Singaporean society's excessive bias towards educational performance. Overwhelming stress is given to the school people graduated from and the marks they received. This approach to choosing Singapore's élite vividly shows the extreme emphasis given to these kinds of educational results.

5. Conclusion

When the kind of perspective adopted above has been used, it becomes evident that most Japanese working practices are transferable to ASEAN workplaces. Promotion to the foreman level could be a problem, but as a lengthening of the vertical career would be welcomed by production workers, any resistance to this practice would be limited. In practice, Japanese joint ventures in ASEAN do promote all their foremen from below. This is also true in Singapore. With this kind of groundwork, business results of Japanese joint ventures in South-East Asia should compare favourably with those of

Japanese joint ventures in the USA. Indeed, looking at both company profitability and growth of employment, the performance of Japanese joint ventures in Thailand is good, greatly surpassing performance levels in the USA.[29] This evidence suggests a problem in the transferability of Japanese work practices to Europe and the USA. This is not the place to go into the details, but I would like to make a few comments.

Transferability to Europe and the USA

Without displaying the evidence here, if a hypothesis were made out of the two essential parts of Japanese work practices, the formation of high-level skills would appear to a certain extent to be transferable. However, effecting the measures needed to foster skill formation at a higher stage would surely take more time.

Adopting a somewhat general way of speaking, it may be said that, because skill formation is the software of technology, as long as there are the conditions and the will to use that software, implementation will not necessarily be difficult. To put the point concretely, widening the scope of workers' experience is possible. As has already been pointed out, there are relief workers in US auto-assembly plants. If there were no relief workers, it would not be possible to substitute for workers who are absent or on leave. The necessity of widening the span of their experience to that extent is already sufficiently acknowledged and has been partially put into effect. Also, in the case of problem-solving, surveys of Japanese joint ventures have reported that it takes place on the shop floors of Japanese subsidiaries and has been generally welcomed by the production workers.[30]

The remaining issue rests with the incentive measures apparent in the pay system. This is not an aspect of technology, but is, rather, a part of a social system. In Europe and the USA, where a long tradition in labour-management relations has already been established, measures that are not in line with that tradition would have difficulty in being accepted. Thus, particularly in unionized large companies' workplaces, the pay for each job is determined and the three pillars of payment for job grade, regular increments, and merit payments are not found. It would not be correct to say that production workers never receive regular increments, but the examples are extremely few and the period during which increments are received is short. When the job assignment and the workplace are the same, increments are confined to just the trainee period of, at most, about two years and do not reflect a rise in status. In particular, merit payments are strongly opposed by labour unions, due to a fear of favouritism leading to injustice. Opposition arises when there is a worry that the foremen and supervisors would assess workers' loyalty to them rather than assess their skills and work. Certainly, merit assessments are not free from a fear that, however they are devised, they must still be subjective. As a result, for example, I do not know of any case studies that observed full assessments on the shop floors of Japanese joint ventures in the USA.

Does this mean that there is little prospect in the West for transferring the Japanese working practices seen earlier? In my opinion it would be going too far to say that there was no prospect at all.

First, the opposition to merit assessments is not culturally part of the western tradition. Whether in the USA, Britain, Germany, or Sweden, merit assessments of white-collar workers are made. Also, payment reflects the job grade, and there are regular increments. White-collar workers now account for the majority of workers. Their numbers have increased more rapidly than those of blue-collar workers due to the growing services economy. As this is the case, why do production workers refuse to adopt what is already accepted practice in their own country in the more numerous higher salary group? If one looks at the history of working hours, leave, and the welfare system in these countries, it is apparent that production workers' practices have come closer to the white-collar system. Why this is not the case with their pay systems is difficult to assert.

Second, a trend towards white-collar pay systems for production workers can already be recognized. If inadequate material may be acceptable as a basis for this assertion, it appears that merit assessments are gradually becoming more widespread for production workers in large companies and, subsequently, in unionized companies. The proportion rose from as few as 2 per cent of companies engaging in merit assessments for their production workers in 1977, to 24 per cent in 1986.[31] Also, though there are not any relevant data, when I visited three large unionized companies in Sweden, one of the companies had introduced assessments for production workers as well. Another symptom of this trend is evident in the appearance of skill-based payments for US production workers.[32]

A much broader time scale would be required for their implementation in the West than for the ASEAN countries, but Japanese work practices could be universally transferable as long as the appropriate measures were adopted.

3

Foreign Workers and Immigration Policy*

HIROWATARI SEIGO

I. Identifying the Problem

1. In the beginning there was 'illegal work'

A chronological glance at *Homu nenkan* (Justice Annual), the Japanese Ministry of Justice's annual report of its activities, reveals that during the period of high economic growth from the 1950s, the main thrust of the Immigration Bureau's operations was directed at illegal entry from the Korean Peninsula. From 1951 to 1969 the total number of illegal entrants prosecuted was 31,562, or an annual average of 1,661, of whom North and South Koreans accounted for 29,740, or 94.2 per cent. This was at a time when 300,000 foreigners were entering Japan annually (1965 figure).[1]

Now, it is known that on three occasions—in 1967, 1973, and 1976—cabinet approval was given to the idea that so-called unskilled foreign workers would not be introduced into Japan, but the fact that particular trends in the entry of foreigners—what we might call 'push factors'—formed the backdrop in each instance is not particularly evident from the Immigration Bureau's reports of its activities.[2]

The 1980s saw a change in the situation. The reports began to point out the large increase in the number of people illegally remaining in Japan, while in 1985, for the first time, the category of 'illegal work' was used and the number of illegal workers prosecuted began to be reported. The number, which had been 5,269 in 1985, climbed to 14,314 in 1988, and for the first time since it began to rise in 1979, the gender balance was reversed. In 1989, the number increased further to 16,608, a 'trend toward multinationalism' was identified, and it was reckoned that the total number of illegal workers would surpass 100,000. In that year more than three million foreigners entered Japan.

One of the main aims of the December 1989 revision of the Immigration Law (revision of the Immigration Control and Refugee Recognition Act) was

* Translated by Colin Noble.

the rectification of the illegal work situation. It established provisions for punishment of employers who allowed 'illegal work activity' and brokers who acted as intermediaries; and enforcement was strengthened. At this point a legal definition was given to 'illegal work' activity, which had hitherto been no more than a statistical term. It was prescribed as 'any activity engaged in by persons outside their residence status, persons who have entered Japan illegally, or persons who have remained in Japan illegally, and for which remuneration or other income is received' (clause 73, paragraph 4).

Thus, in the late 1980s, 'illegal work' became one of the most important categories in terms of the Immigration Law.[3] The number of illegal workers has continued to increase in the 1990s—from 29,884 in 1990 to 32,908 in 1991; 62,161 in 1992; and 64,341 in 1993.[4]

2. The so-called '1991 issue'

As is well known, the agreement on legal status, which was based on the 1965 normalization treaty between Japan and Korea, stipulated that in order to secure the legal status of Korean residents of Japan, they would be granted permanent residence permits on application. Under the terms of the agreement, permanent residence permits based on the agreement would be granted on application to:

1. persons who had resided in Japan since before 15 August 1945 and their children who were born on or after that same date and who had resided in Japan continuously up to 17 January 1971, the final date of the application period; and

2. persons born on or after 17 January 1971 to persons granted permanent residence permits pursuant to 1 above.

Under these terms, the children of persons of category 2 above—those referred to as third generation residents of Japan—are excluded from permanent residence permits based on the agreement. It is probable that, at the time of the agreement, the issue of third generation residents was considered to be an uncertain one for which it was thought that review at a later date would be appropriate. It was stipulated that, in the event of a request from the Korean government, the Japanese government would enter into discussions on this matter before 16 January 1991. Contact between Japanese and Korean authorities on the issue was initiated at the end of 1985.

The 1991 issue is therefore at the moment 'the issue of the legal treatment of descendants of those with permanent resident permits based on the agreement'.[5] However, North and South Korean residents of Japan, and lobbyists for the preservation and expansion of their rights, as well as the Korean government, suggested that the 1991 issue should be one that addresses a comprehensive resolution to the issue of Korean residents in Japan (i.e., overall improvement of their legal treatment), rather than the tidying up of the loose ends of the 1965 normalization treaty (i.e., the issue of the third generation).[6]

Progress on the '1991 issue' has been evident since Japan and South Korea exchanged a memorandum signed by the foreign ministers of both nations on 10 January 1991.[7] On 26 April 1991, the Special Law for the Handling of Immigration Affairs of Persons who have Divested Themselves of Japanese Nationality on the Basis of Peace Treaties with Japan (Special Immigration Law) was passed. This law provided for a single permanent residence status (referred to in the law as 'special permanent residents') covering 'persons divested of citizenship on the basis of peace treaties and the descendants of persons divested of citizenship by peace treaties'. By this means, the issue of the legal status of 'third generation descendants of the agreement' was resolved.[8]

As at 1994, the number of Koreans resident in Japan was about 600,000, while the number of registered foreigners including temporary visitors was 682,276. A look at the historical record shows that the number of Korean residents in Japan in 1911, the year following the annexation of Korea, was 2,527, while in 1920 it was no more than 40,755. The number rose after the start of the Showa period (to 419,009 in 1930) and increased sharply during the war (to 1,241,315 in 1940, and about 1,940,000 in 1944).[9]

After the war, by March 1946, approximately 1.3 million people had returned to Korea, but those who remained for various reasons were stripped of their voting rights (which they had exercised before the war as subjects of the empire) without the issue of citizenship being resolved (i.e., they still held Japanese citizenship).[10] With the promulgation of the Alien Registration Order (Imperial Decree No. 207) on 22 May 1947, they became 'deemed aliens', having to register, and, based on the 19 April 1952 directive of the Director of the Ministry of Justice Civil Affairs Bureau concerning resolution of citizenship, they ultimately lost their Japanese citizenship and became 'aliens' at the time the peace treaty came into effect on 28 April 1952, regardless of their own volition.[11]

Despite the fact that efforts have been made to give stability to the legal status of Korean residents of Japan, there are still various problems with their situation. One document that suggests directions toward solution of the problems is the 'Zainichi Kankoku/Chosenjin no Shogu Kaizen ni Kansuru Teigen —Hirakareta Nihon Shakai to Higashi Ajia no Akarui Shorai o Motomete' (Proposals for Improvement in the Treatment of Korean Residents of Japan —Seeking an Open Japanese Society and a Bright Future for East Asia) put forward by ninety people, led by Onuma Yasuaki in Tokyo on 23 April 1990.

According to this document, the principle that is fundamental to the solution of this issue is 'the creation of an environment in which [they] live in Japanese society in an equivalent capacity to a Japanese, while retaining their ethnic dignity'. The foundation of such a policy would be the achievement of permanent resident status as foreign long-term residents, involving 'the guarantee in principle of rights that are the equivalent of those of Japanese nationals, with the exception of a few areas such as suffrage at the level of national politics and qualifying to take up duties in the civil service that relate directly to the principle of the nation state'. In concrete terms this means taking positive steps to abolish discrimination in employment, particularly increasing the number of foreigners employed as civil servants and teachers; assurances of ethnic education; the establishment of a cultural foundation and guaranteed access to it; effectively no deportation; making the system of their re-entry into Japan work on the same basis as passports for Japanese nationals (the issuing of five-year multiple re-entry permits with permits denied for the same reasons as those under passport legislation); and exemption from the obligation under the alien registration law to be fingerprinted and to carry one's alien registration certificate at all times. In broad terms, the demand is for establishment of a policy committee on foreign long-term residents.[12]

3. The relationship between the old and the new 'foreign problem'

The problem of illegal workers has arisen because of the existence of a bottleneck, in the form of a legal system that does not accept 'unskilled workers' at a time when the increase in the number of foreigners seeking work opportunities in Japan and the shortage of labour in certain areas of the domestic labour market have led to a matching of supply and demand. If one were to argue that the problem of illegal work were a matter of economic factors rupturing the legislative framework, analysis of the various structural factors, which induce international labour movements, and of the domestic market, which seeks foreign workers, would become important, but since such analyses are beyond the scope of this non-specialist writer, they will not be dealt with directly here.[13]

The issue of how to interpret the flow of workers and immigration from the developing countries to the developed countries in the 1980s and 1990s is not particularly one faced uniquely by Japan. France and Germany, which actively introduced foreign workers in the high-growth period of the 1960s, suspended recruitment of foreign workers and shifted to a policy of restricting new entries after the first oil shock (i.e., after 1973), while in the 1980s they made their restrictive policies even clearer. As pointed out by the Ministry of Labour's 'Gaikokujin Rodosha Mondai Kenkyukai' (Working Group on the Foreign Worker Problem), chaired by Koike Kazuo, Japan's present policy of not admitting unskilled foreign workers is comparable to the western European tendency to restrict new access, and, viewed comparatively, it is not particularly 'closed' per se.[14] However, in light of the fact that France and Germany already have more than four million foreign workers and their families, and, moreover, have responded positively in terms of accepting refugees from areas such as Indo-China, it is not necessarily fair in international terms for Japan to rationalize its own policy by referring to the western European trend toward restricting new access.

The issue of Korean and Taiwanese residents of Japan is unique to Japan as it originates in the history of imperial Japan. However, if one were to see these people and their families as settled foreign workers who work, have families, and have their home base in a foreign country, then one could find similarities with the problems faced by 'foreign workers and their families who have become immigrants' in France and Germany.

The 'Proposals for Improvement in the Treatment of Korean Residents of Japan' mentioned above was extremely significant in that it dealt with 'residents of Japan' prescriptively at two levels—first, they were at one time under Japanese colonial rule and held Japanese citizenship; and secondly, they are foreign long-term residents who have completely settled into Japanese society. The significance arises from the fact that the first point enables the foundation to be laid for the necessity of special consideration by the Japanese state, while the second provides a start for enabling issues common to other foreign long-term residents of Japan to be sorted out, in addition to making comparisons with the treatment of foreign long-term residents of France and Germany possible.

If, as outlined above, one were to interpret the 'foreigner problem' faced by the Japanese state at the beginning of the 1990s as revolving around, first, the policy response to new entry of foreign workers, and second, the legal treatment of foreign long-term residents of Japan, then—apart from its unique historical origins—the debate is comparable to that seen in the countries of western Europe such as France and Germany.

In Japan, however, these two points are debated as separate issues, and there is not always adequate debate about the relationship between the two. Thinking about it in concrete terms, the introduction of foreign workers is fraught with danger unless the social and legal treatment of the existing foreign long-term residents can be improved. This is because it is clear from the experience of western Europe that the introduction of foreign workers will lead to a certain percentage settling, even if the initial period of residence is restricted. It is therefore necessary to make social and legal preparations based on that assumption. Admission of foreign workers without such preparations is both irresponsible on the part of the receiving state and also unfortunate for the foreign workers.

If one were to link the two points of the debate and add in the historical origins, this could be said to be a question of the Japanese state's 'standing as a state' in international society. The 'new' foreigner problem could well become an issue relating to the international responsibility of the 'economic superpower' Japan in a world epitomized by the now borderless movement of labour and waves of immigration from South to North and also from East to West. The 'old' foreigner problem, on the other hand, constitutes that part of the issue that questions how Japan will resolve its responsibility for past history in a form acceptable to the people of Asia.

The purpose of this chapter is to discuss the problematic nature of contemporary Japanese society using the subject-matter of the issue of foreign workers—an issue that has been one of the most important for Japanese society since the second half of the 1980s. We will begin by clarifying the position of foreigners in terms of the modern nation state and legislation. On the verge of the twenty-first century, international society is being forced to revise the traditional 'relationship between foreigners and nation states and legislation'.

Direct treatment of our main theme of the issue of foreign workers in contemporary Japanese society follows, with a focus on the December 1989 revisions to the Immigration Law and the new developments in the situation since then, before the whole discussion is drawn together.[15]

II. Legal Typology of Admission of Foreign Workers

1. Foreigners, states, and legislation

It goes without saying that there is no such thing as 'the general foreigner'. Foreigners exist because Japanese exist and Germans exist. In other words, the legal concept of *foreigner* has arisen because of the establishment of the modern nation state and the system of citizenship.[16]

The relationship between the modern nation state and its people is generally said to be that of loyalty and protection, the state having the exclusive right of control over its constituent citizens. Membership of a state is shown by citizenship and must be unique. Accordingly, the prevention of multiple citizenship and non-citizenship is a principle of international law. In Japan, too, when the citizenship law was revised in 1984, there was debate about how to handle dual citizenship, which inevitably became a possibility as a result of the adoption of the principle of recognizing both paternal and maternal lineage.[17] The reformed law took a traditional position, providing a mechanism for resolving dual citizenship by establishing a system for selection of citizenship. The requirement to renounce one's previous citizenship when taking on new citizenship is a general principle of the citizenship legislation of many countries.[18]

A state's exclusive right of control over its citizens, on the one hand, is the foundation for the state's right and responsibility to protect its citizens but, on the other hand, leads to the logic that the protection of foreigners falls outside that right and responsibility. Rather, because foreigners come under the exclusive right of control of another state, meddling protection might be construed as interference beyond one's own jurisdiction. For example, before unification, West Germany maintained the practice of deeming East German citizens 'German nationals' and instantly treated as one of its own citizens any citizen of East Germany who entered a West German embassy or consulate abroad or entered West German territory. Needless to say, East Germany protested that this was an invasion of the East German state's right of control over its constituents.[19] This attitude on the part of West Germany created a huge flow of people from East to West (the so-called immigrants or *Übersiedler*), and was one of the causes of the collapse of East Germany.

It is generally accepted in international law and in the laws of each country relating to foreigners that whether or not to permit entry and residence of a foreigner is a matter for the sovereign prerogative of the state and that the foreigner has absolutely no claim in the matter. According to the German state law scholar Josef Isensee, a decision of a state relating to entry is a 'decision as to who belongs to a territory' and therefore falls under the discretion of the state in the same way as does a decision on a change of nationality, which is a 'choice of who belongs to a state'.[20]

Decisions of a state relating to entry and residence of foreigners are limited by the constraints set up by that state itself. German basic law, for example, specifies that protection is guaranteed to foreigners suffering political persecution. Should, therefore, a victim of political persecution seek entry and be found to meet the requirements, Germany has the obligation to allow entry (i.e., those with the right to protection have the right to demand entry).

Another constraint is the framework of international law. A state may be subject to special restrictions regarding its treatment of foreigners by bilateral agreements, multilateral agreements, or agreements of international organizations. In addition, even though there may not be concrete agreements, international consensus on human rights standards is also a factor in restraining the behaviour of states. Japan has not ratified important international agreements on the treatment of foreigners such as the International Convention on the Elimination of All Forms of Racism (adopted by the United Nations General Assembly in 1965 and brought into effect in 1969) and the 1975 International Labour Organization Convention 143 (Convention on the Promotion of Equality of Opportunity and Conditions for Migrant and Immigrant Workers in Adverse Circumstances).[21] More recently, the International Convention on the Protection of Rights of All Migrant Workers and Members of their Families was adopted by the United Nations General Assembly on 8 December 1990. This convention, which consists of a preamble and ninety-three articles in nine sections, contains wide-ranging prescriptions on the human rights of foreign workers and their families. The twenty-eight articles of section three relate to foreigners regardless of the legality of their entry and residence and, in addition, the twenty-one articles of section 4 relate to cases of legal entry and residence. If the Japanese state is going to make noises about its international responsibility, it must first and foremost seriously consider these international standards in the debate on human rights.[22]

In the past one Ministry of Justice bureaucrat caused a scandal by referring to the discretionary right of the state in relation to the entry and residence of foreigners in the following manner:

[The treatment of foreigners] is totally up to the discretion of the Japanese government. In terms of the principles of international law, we can do with them as we please. The only thing restricting the Japanese government is agreements with particular countries. The only area in which the discretionary rights of the Japanese government are limited is the treatment of people who have been given special promises about the conditions of their entry, continued residence or any other matter, by virtue of something like a commerce and navigation treaty with Japan, and people who have been promised certain conditions by the normalisation treaty between Japan and Korea.[23]

This way of putting it is rhetoric designed to reinforce the point, but it is merely iterating the traditional legal argument noted above. Nowhere in this turn of phrase, however, can one discern a sense of respect for the human rights of foreigners. Moreover, the discretion of the state with regard to the acceptance of foreigners by no means includes the freedom to do whatever one likes with foreigners who are allowed in. As a general rule, foreigners who enter and reside with permission should enjoy basic human rights under the constitutional order of the country and should receive the same legal protection as the nationals of that country.[24]

2. Legal typology of admission of foreign workers

In cases where states do allow the entry and residence of foreigners, the ways in which this is done vary from country to country.[25] First, there is the distinction between admitting foreigners as immigrants and not doing so. Admitting foreigners as immigrants implies admission of foreigners from the start as 'future citizens'. In this sense, the United States of America, and also Canada, Australia, and some South American countries, are 'immigrant nations'. In contrast, Japan and Germany are non-immigrant nations. I will expound this further below. France has admitted immigrants in the past as part of its population policy, but at the moment it cannot be counted among the immigrant nations.[26]

Immigrant nations, of course, forge societies of mixed race and ethnicity. This is not necessarily to say that such societies are always open societies, for the type of immigrants who are admitted is at the discretion of the admitting country, and it is possible that selection by race and/or ethnicity will occur. Australia's abandonment of the White Australia Policy came ultimately with the 1972 revision of the Immigration Act (and the adoption of multiculturalism through a non-discriminatory immigration policy.[27] In the United States, the 1921 and 1924 Immigration Acts adopted an immigration policy of extreme, racial discrimination. The latter is known as the Japanese exclusion law. It was not until the 1965 revision of the Immigration Act that the racially discriminatory nature of United States immigration law disappeared.[28]

The second distinction is in the system of acquisition of citizenship. The two major principles in this area are the birthplace principle (*jus soli*) and the lineage principle (*jus sanguinis*). Immigrant nations use the birthplace principle, whereas non-immigrant nations generally use the lineage principle. In the former, territorial communality is thought to underpin national identity. In the latter, in contrast, the reproduction of national identity is thought to occur through blood ties. Japan and Germany have citizenship laws based almost purely on the lineage principle, but in French citizenship law the birthplace factor has played a big role since the French Revolution,[29] with the result that the number of 'pure French' in terms of lineage is few, and it is said that one-third of all French today have foreign blood in their parents' or grandparents' generation.[30]

The third distinction is in the form of administration of foreigners. In this area the division is between immigration control and residence control. The former is generally employed by immigrant nations such as the United States of America. Since it is modelled on America's, Japan's administration of foreigners is of the immigration control type. Foreigners' status during their stay, including whether or not they are permitted to work, is determined in one step at the time of entry. In Japan, residence status based on the Immigration Law is the absolute foundation for a foreigner's legal status. In contrast to this, residence control involves initially permitting foreigners to enter, and then administering foreigners in the country through the dual system of residence permits and work permits (or business permits in the case of the self-employed). Both Germany and France have a two-step type of residence control.

In terms of the above three distinctions, the admission of foreigners can be categorized into two major types: type A, which admits immigrants, applies the birthplace principle, and has immigration control; and type B, which does not admit immigrants, applies the lineage principle, and has residence control. The respective epitomes of each type are America and Germany, but the German legal system on this point is changing. We could even characterize the former as an immigrant nation type and the latter as a non-immigrant nation type. Japan should also be classed as a type B state, but in that it employs an immigration control system taken from America, it is not a 'pure' type.

In the American system there is strict differentiation of foreigners at the point of entry between those admitted as immigrants and those admitted as non-immigrants.[31] Entry visas are divided into non-immigrant visas and immigrant visas (or green cards) with the latter being subject to closer scrutiny. There is a legal quota per year for the issuing of immigrant visas, or in other words the acceptance of immigrants. On the other hand, there is no quantitative quota for non-immigrants (i.e., there is no limit on the number of non-immigrant visas issued). In this way immigrants and non-immigrants are strictly distinct categories, and as a rule it is not permitted for a person who has entered as a non-immigrant to become an immigrant. Those who have been permitted entry as immigrants are able to acquire citizenship by five years of law-abiding residence and meeting certain other conditions.

The Japanese Immigration Law has followed in the footsteps of only the non-immigrant visa section of the American system.[32] The Immigration Law also contains provision for permanent residence status, but this does not correspond to the American immigrant visa. This point has been reconfirmed with the recent revision of the Immigration Law. The new law deleted clause 4, paragraphs 5 and 6 of the old law, which included 'permanent residence' as an entry category, on the basis that they might 'lead to the misunderstanding that Japan admits immigrants', even though the thrust of the provision had always been that Japan does not admit foreigners anyway. In other words, it is considered quite impossible to allow a foreigner permanent residence from the start.[33]

There was no debate of this point in the parliamentary deliberations, but in 'Gaikokujin Rodosha Mondai—Kakushocho oi ni Kataru' (Ministries and Agencies Speak Out on the Issue of Foreign Workers) on page 10 of *Kokusai Jinryu* (The Immigration Newsmagazine) of March 1990, the following interesting exchange took place between the interviewer, Kamei Yasuyoshi, Director of the Japan Immigration Association and Yamazaki Tetsuo, Chief of the Immigration Bureau of the Ministry of Justice. Kamei posited that 'from my point of view the problem appeared to be the deletion of the section referring to permission of permanent residence at the time of entry. It is understandable in this age in which tightening up on immigration is happening even in America, but this means that the Immigration Law has closed off the option of immigration, which is the source of problems in human exchanges.' 'That's not true', countered Yamazaki. 'The revision of the Immigration Law tidied up the methods for taking in foreigners. [With the exception of intra-company transferees, people who enter Japan with a working visa] . . . are not limited to having to return home when their visa expires after a number of years . . . For a certain number of selected people integration is possible. The foreign population of Japan is less than 1 per cent of the total, so it is all right to continue to admit this type of people and have them ultimately reside permanently. The reason that permanent residence at the time of entry was removed in the revision is that we will not allow in as immigrants from the start unskilled workers with nothing but the clothes on their backs. They have never been allowed in up till now either.'

In America, which does admit immigrants, it is impossible for a non-immigrant to have permanent resident status, but in Japan, which admits foreigners only as non-immigrants (temporary residents), to 'ultimately reside permanently' is sanctioned. The same is true in Germany.

3. Type B states—non-immigrant nations and the concept of nationality

In contrast to type A states—immigrant nation-type states that forge societies of mixed race and ethnicity—type B states forge societies of pure race and ethnicity based on lineage principles. In such societies, the concept of being a national, or of national identity itself, greatly depends on the characteristic of belonging to a common ethnic and cultural community. There is little sense of a conscious common ownership of political ideals. In this regard the French concept of nationality is often adduced as diametrically opposed to that of Germany.[34] The ideals of the French Revolution and Republic or of American democracy give a political ideological basis for the concept of nationality. In the same vein, socialist states are states that provide the people with the clearest conscious political prescriptions. It is perhaps not surprising that the breakdown of the prescriptive nature of socialism has produced 'ethnic' eruptions.

In racially and ethnically pure societies there is no conscious differentiation between the legal concept of a nation's citizens and the sociological and cultural concept of ethnic group. Japan ratified the International Bill of Human Rights in 1979. Under the terms of Article 40 of Convention B (The Interational Convention on Civil and Political Rights), signatory nations are required to report to the Human Rights Commission on the domestic human rights situation. The first report of the Japanese government in 1980 stated that 'there are no ethnic minorities in Japan'. Criticism of Prime Minister Nakasone's 1986 statement (that Japan is an ethnically homogeneous nation) provided the opportunity in the second report in 1987 for recognition of the existence of the 24,000 Ainu people, but the existence as an ethnic minority of the 150,000 Koreans who had taken Japanese citizenship was ignored. It was as if the Koreans who had become 'Japanese citizens' were no longer ethnically Korean. Putting it another way, you could say that, in the legal sense, taking on Japanese citizenship was considered, even demanded, to be an act of becoming Japanese in body as well as soul. It is precisely for this reason that in response the Korean residents of Japan cannot but feel that taking Japanese citizenship is 'denying oneself' and 'betraying one's countrymen and women'.[35]

Barriers to recognition of naturalization on the one hand and psychological resistance on the part of foreign long-term residents to naturalization on the other are phenomena common to lineage-based non-immigrant nations such as Japan and Germany. In these nations, therefore, if foreign long-term residents are to be integrated, the importance of citizenship must be minimal-ized, equality between foreigners and nationals sought, and the option of naturalization simplified.[36]

III. The Foreign Worker Problem in Contemporary Japan

1. The position of work by foreigners in terms of Japan's immigration control

Work by foreigners in Japan is regulated by the Immigration Control and Refugee Recognition Act. This law was revised in December 1989 and the revision executed in June 1990 in response to the 'foreign worker problem' that developed suddenly in the late 1980s.

The basic system relating to the work of foreigners did not change follow-ing the revision of the law. A foreigner's length of stay and activities during that stay are determined by the residence status granted at the time of entry. Residence statuses are enumerated in a number of categories and within these there are those that have no restrictions on activities, such as 'permanent resid-ence', but residence statuses that allow work are limited. Where work is not incorporated into the residence status, work is not permitted, in which case undertaking work is seen as an activity outside status (i.e., illegal work).

Now, based on the idea that 'the admission of foreigners who have special-ist skills or expertise be expanded', the new law involved a complete review of the eighteen existing residence statuses. Ten new statuses were added to bring the total number to twenty-eight.[37] The new statuses for work entail-ing specialist skills or expertise were legal and accounting services, medical services, researcher, instructor, and specialist in humanities and international services, while for those entailing skills or knowledge in the natural sciences, a 'engineer' residence status was included. This, however, was an expansion of the old law's 4–1–12 status. A new status of 'intra-company transferee' was added in response to corporate 'internationalization'.[38]

Neither the new nor the old law contained a category of residence status for admitting so-called unskilled workers. However, the enumeration of resi-dence statuses leads to a lack of flexibility in terms of the administration of immigration control, so to retain flexibility the old law prescribed a special status that was bestowed at the discretion of the Minister of Justice (residence status 4–1–16–3 under the old law). This was able to perform a 'catch-all' function, so work by foreigners that could not be permitted under a separate status (including, therefore, unskilled work) became possible upon the grant-ing of the Minister of Justice's special status. However, an operating policy was determined for situations in which a foreigner was permitted to work with this special status; namely, that the foreigner be 'a person possessing specialist knowledge or particular skills or expertise who could not be replaced with a Japanese person'.[39] For example, in 1982, a foreigner's 'sensitivity' was recognized as irreplaceable and Seibu department store's application to employ foreigners was granted.[40] Moreover, in the former law, this special residence status was also used in situations where foreign students who had graduated from a Japanese university started work in a Japanese corporation. Under the new law such cases are able to be covered by the newly established statuses.[41] Furthermore, the new law also retains the general catch-all status ('designated activities' residence status, under which activities are specified by the Minister of Justice for individual foreigners), but, as previously, the operation of this status excludes unskilled workers.

Japan's immigration control system thus excludes unskilled workers in terms of its operation but does not totally block their entry in an inherent systematic way. Not giving working status to unskilled workers is a matter of policy selection. To date this has been decided at government level. The early development was that when cabinet decisions were made on the first, second, and third Fundamental Employment Policy Plans (on 14 March 1967, 30 January 1973, and 18 June 1976, respectively) verbal assent was given to the Minister of Labour's statement that 'the entry of unskilled workers will not, in principle, be permitted'.[42]

More recently, cabinet decisions were reached in the Economic Committee's Five Year Economic Management Plan of May 1988 and the Employment Committee's 6th Fundamental Employment Policy Plan of June 1988, 'to move toward admitting as far as possible foreigners with specialist skills and expertise and to endeavour to clarify the system'. This was, of course, based on the assumption that unskilled workers would not be admitted.

In addition to increasing the admission of foreigners to the extent indicated above, one of the basic aims of the latest revision of the Immigration Law was a crack-down on illegal foreign workers.[43] Because of the awareness that employers of illegal foreign workers and brokers 'are an attractive force which brings in foreigners who intend to work illegally', the new law established the crime of 'facilitating illegal work' to deal with these people (in clause 73, paragraph 2 of the law). Under this provision:

1. persons who cause foreigners to undertake illegal work activity in relation to business activities (the law reads 'in relation to business activities', so it is not limited to employers. Businesses owned by foreigners and businesses in which foreigners work as employees are also covered);

2. persons who place foreign workers under their management for the purpose of having them work illegally; and

3. persons who professionally mediate in relation to actions which cause foreigners to undertake illegal work activity or actions under 2 above;

are subject to a sentence of up to three years and a fine of up to 2 million yen.

The facilitation of illegal work is a newly established crime but the illegal work activities of foreign workers themselves have been a crime since before the law was revised. The new law clarified the provision of the former law, which had activities outside status as the general object of punishment, to render 'activities which constitute operating a business for income and/or activities for which remuneration is received' as the object of punishment. 'Persons clearly deemed to have engaged solely in such activities' are subject to a sentence of imprisonment of up to three years and/or a fine of up to 300,000 yen, while in cases in which such activity is not undertaken 'solely' (cases in which illegal work activities are undertaken alongside activities permitted by the foreigner's residence status, e.g., doing part-time work without obtaining permission), the punishment was to be a sentence of imprisonment for up to one year and/or a fine of up to 200,000 yen. (In the latter case the law before revision read 'a sentence of imprisonment for up to six months', so the punishment has been increased.) Moreover, foreign workers who have engaged in illegal work activities may be deported from Japan under clause 24 of the Immigration Law.

However, in the drafting process and deliberations on the bill, the point that received particular attention was that 'not admitting or not legalizing unskilled foreign workers in spite of the domestic need for them is causing an increase in illegal workers. Tightening up on illegal work without addressing this assumption will lead to the unlawful employment of foreigners going underground and further exacerbation of the problem of the human rights of foreign workers.'[44] This point of view, however, was not held by the majority and the revised law was passed as conceived by the Ministry of Justice. During parliamentary deliberations, the Socialist Party's Shimizu Sumiko highlighted commentary on the revised bill, *Nyukanho Kaiseian—Fuhoshurojochozai no Kento* (The Proposed Amendment to the Immigration Law—Review of the Crime of Facilitating Illegal Work), by Public Prosecutor Kurata Yasuji (an officer of the Criminal Affairs Bureau of the Ministry of Justice attached to the Immigration Bureau), and homed in on the fact that the Immigration Bureau's kind of perspective on illegal foreign workers lacked any sense of human rights.[45] However, in the end only the Communist Party opposed the revised bill. Taking the stance of 'allowing in principle the international movement of workers', the Communist Party 'strongly urged the reform of the government's harsh attitude of shutting out foreign "unskilled" workers'. (This was the counter argument of Ando Iwao in the House of Representatives Committee on Judicial Affairs.)[46] In this sense the Communist Party was the clearest advocate of an 'open country' policy.

The government and an overwhelming majority of the parliament thus determined Japan's national policy on foreign workers, namely that of expanding the admission of foreigners for work involving specialist skills or knowledge but preventing the influx of unskilled workers with harsh penalties (i.e., a policy of discriminatory admission). The question, however, is what sort of situation has developed and what problems are evident behind this façade.

2. The utilization of the lineage principle—the use of those of Japanese descent

The revised law established 'long-term resident' as a new category of residence status. Like permanent residence status, this category has no restrictions on activities (i.e., a holder is free to work), but unlike permanent residence status, which has no time limit, a fixed length of stay is specified. As a general provision that gives the Minister of Justice discretionary powers, the law stipulates that holders are 'persons whom the Minister of Justice permits to reside for a fixed length of stay, in consideration of particular factors', but Ministry of Justice ordinances do specify concrete examples (in Ministry of Justice ordinance No. 132 of 1990).

These provide for responding to cases in relation to Indo-Chinese refugees, Vietnamese, and Korean and Taiwanese residents of Japan, as well as for handling the descendants of emigrants of Japanese descent. In concrete terms these were:

1. the children of any person born to a Japanese (the situation of second generation emigrants, and 'any person born a child of Japanese', i.e., situations in which either parent has divested themselves of Japanese citizenship), and

2. the grandchildren of any person who had once been domiciled in Japan proper as a Japanese citizen, and who was born the child of a Japanese (the situation of third generation emigrants, with the requirement that the person's grandfather was born in Japan the child of a Japanese).

The length of stay for these people was specified as either three years, one year, or six months.

Before the law was revised, these people were able to enter the country and work freely on the Minister of Justice's special residence status 4–1–16–3 (known as invitational visas, and for which Japanese relatives took responsibility). Moreover, both before and after the revision, descendants of emigrants of Japanese descent (second generation emigrants who failed to indicate a desire to retain citizenship and lost their Japanese citizenship) entered Japan and worked with a residence status of 'spouse or child of a Japanese'. It seemed often to be the case that initial entry was on a tourist visa, with a change of residence status being made after the family register had been sorted out. After the law was revised, the process was streamlined, whereby the emigrant would apply in his own country of residence, while relatives in Japan would apply simultaneously to the Immigration Bureau for a 'Certificate of Approval of Residence Status', which was forwarded to the applicant.

These residence statuses were, of course, designed to make 'homecoming' visits to Japan by descendants of Japanese who have resettled overseas more convenient. On the basis that in cases where the homecoming was long-term, it was conceivable that the person would work, no restrictions were placed on activities. Comparing this treatment to that of other foreigners, one may see what amounts to preferential treatment, or perhaps even discrimination, on account of lineage.[47] In the view of the Ministries of Justice and Foreign Affairs, such preferential treatment is widely recognized internationally up until the third generation of migrants. However, the fact that South American emigrants of Japanese descent were being used as a pool of unskilled labour had already been pointed out before the law was revised.[48] This system is at present being allowed to function as a loophole behind the façade that has prevented unskilled workers from entering Japan.

It is well known in Toyota City that there are many Brazilians working with Toyota subcontractors. In the whole of Aichi prefecture, there were 5,280 as at the end of June 1990, a tenfold increase over the previous year. An executive of one subcontractor that manufactures components explained that 'they look the same and they were originally Japanese. There is little difference in their culture and customs, and no feeling of awkwardness such as there is with Asians. But above all, it's legal.'[49] A mediation system for the procurement of this labour already exists. In São Paulo, Brazil, there are 130 businesses that mediate for workers of Japanese descent, and that have linked up with Japanese personnel agencies to establish channels for sending workers to subcontractors. There are reckoned to be 1.15 million Brazilians of Japanese descent,[50] and the number of visas issued by the Japanese consulate in São Paulo rose dramatically from 6,800 in 1988 to 18,300 in 1989 and reached 26,000 in just the first six months of 1990. There is reported to be a shortage of labour in the Japanese community in Brazil and there are increasing expressions of discontent from non-Japanese Brazilians about the 'inequitable treatment' of the Japanese government (i.e., in light of the fact that all are Brazilians working away from home).

In November 1989 the Immigration Bureau through its Tokyo, Osaka, Nagoya, and Sendai bureaus conducted a survey of 59 companies employing or utilizing Japanese Brazilians in their businesses.[51] 415 people at 38 businesses were interviewed. Of the 415, 81 had Japanese citizenship and held permanent residence permits in Brazil or Peru, 284 had Brazilian citizenship, and 37 were Peruvian citizens. The opinion of the Immigration Bureau regarding their reasons for coming to Japan was that 'many intended to work, and when these were combined with those who work while visiting relatives, we could say that nearly all of them came to Japan in order to work'. Nearly all employers were involved in subcontracting to some extent, with many being subcontractors for items such as automobile components. In many cases the workers had borrowed their travel expenses in advance from the company (rather than a mediating agent), but there were no particular problems with

TABLE 3.1. Number of Brazilians entering Japan

Year	Number of people
1986	13,434
1987	12,126
1988	16,789
1989	29,241
1990	67,303

working conditions. Employers wished to see the continuation and expansion of employment,[52] with subcontractors experiencing labour shortages expressing a strong demand for diligent Brazilian workers. As for the Brazilians, those of Japanese citizenship holding permanent residence permits in Brazil return there within two years rather than forfeit their permit by staying abroad for more than two years, while others intend to remain for two to three years or permanently. Given the results of the survey, the Immigration Bureau was already aware of the fact that a 'loophole' existed and that the trend was leading to its enlargement.

According to immigration statistics, a total (including both first-time entries and re-entries) of 3,504,470 foreigners entered Japan in 1990, a 17.4 per cent increase over the previous year's 2,985,764. The number of Brazilians entering Japan increased most rapidly (a 130.2 per cent increase between 1989 and 1990). A breakdown by country between 1985 and 1990 is shown in Table 3.2.

Of these, what proportion are of Japanese descent is impossible to ascertain, but a breakdown of 1990 first-time entrants from Brazil by residence status shows that many were short-term stays, such as for sightseeing (although, as noted above, it is possible that a change of residence status occurs later), 7,545 came as 'spouses of Japanese, etc.' (the highest figure of any country), and 1,777 were long-term residents (second to China).

A Ministry of Foreign Affairs Immigration Affairs officer (for emigration from Japan) suggested the following about 'homecoming work' by South American emigrants:

The descendants of emigrants to South America cannot be categorized as 'foreigners' because of their lineage. The world trend is toward treating those carrying the blood of one's own country the same as nationals of one's own country to the third generation. The descendants of those who have succeeded in the country in which they settled are the ones who come, so there is little likelihood of their settling in Japan— this is the difference between them and other Asians. As far as the Ministry of Foreign Affairs, which allows emigration, is concerned, it would in fact be a problem if they were to return and settle. It would be contrary to emigration policy. In any case, so long as there is a need in Japan and in the country of origin for homecoming work by descendants of South American emigrants, it is the role of bureaucrats to make that as easy as possible.[53]

The fact that 'homecoming workers' are a most apt source of temporary labour when there is demand pressure for unskilled labour is well attested by this comment. The existence of a 'supply push factor' overseas is, of course, accelerating the trend.[54] The issue of workers of Japanese descent has thus already taken its place in labour policy. The January 1991 report of the Ministry of Labour Employment Security Bureau's Section for Employment of Foreigners—*Gaikokujin Rodosha ga Rodomen ni Oyobosu Eikyo nado ni Kansuru Kenkyukai Hokokusho ni tsuite: Keizai Seicho to Rodoryoku Jukyu, Shakaiteki Kosuto Oyobi Kokusaikyoryoku no Shiten kara* (On the Report of the Working Party on the Influence of Foreign Workers on Labour: from the Perspective of Economic Growth and the Labour Market, Social Costs, and International Co-operation)—stated that the short-term issues at present are illegal work and 'the need to look at ensuring there are suitable employment channels for workers of Japanese descent'.[55] Moreover, in the Employment Security Bureau's May report—*Heisei Sannendo no Koyo no Mitoshi to Shokugyo Antei Gyosei no Juten Shisaku: Nenji Koyo Keikaku* (The Employment Outlook and Key Policies of Employment Security Administration for Fiscal 1991: Annual Employment Plan)—its entry on 'Enhancement of Employment Policy in the Face of Internationalization: e.g., the Response to the Problem of Foreign Workers', specified that in addition to the preparation of a framework for the admission of foreign workers, appropriate work be obtained for second generation Japanese and others. Ensuring that their employment is appropriate does not imply that these people should be excluded from work, but rather that the regulation and prosecution of malevolent players such as brokers should proceed, and the existence of appropriate working conditions should be ensured. The report indicated that the following concrete steps would be taken:[56]

We will open an employment consultation office with close links to the Industrial Employment Security Center for workers of Japanese descent in Tokyo, and provide an employment consultation and introduction service which takes into consideration the characteristics of those of Japanese descent, e.g., using Portuguese interpreters. We will also, in addition to supplying labour related information to Brazil, start a study group on employment control for corporations wishing to employ people of Japanese descent, as a way of addressing the suitability of their employment.

In this way the 'appropriate' use of 'homecoming workers' was to proceed, buttressed by the concept of a racially and ethnically pure society based on lineage.[57]

The number of new arrivals from Brazil increased further in 1991 to 96,337. Since then the number has fallen slightly in the wake of the arrival of the recession following the collapse of Japan's economic boom (to 81,495 in 1992, 70,719 in 1993, and 72,236 in 1994), but it is still higher than the 1990 figure.

As at June 1994, the number of Brazilians registered as foreigners in Japan was 154,762, third only to Koreans and Chinese. More and more homecoming workers are settling in Japan. We could argue that there is a need for a new response in the 'hidden policy' of relying on 'homecoming workers' for temporary labour.

3. The utilization of the idea that 'letting foreigners learn = assistance to developing nations': the use of trainees

'Trainee' residence status under the new law is granted for 'activities involving acquisition of skills, expertise or knowledge in public or private institutions in Japan', a slightly revised continuation of the former law's 4–1–6–2 residence status for 'persons intending to acquire industrial skills or expertise in public or private institutions in Japan'. With the deletion of 'industrial', training at administrative institutions and self-governing bodies was permitted. However, the issue is, of course, industrial training.

The essence of 'training' activities is 'learning' and in this sense it is the same as for 'college student' or 'pre-college student' residence statuses. 'Training' is 'learning' at institutions other than education institutions. 'Work' status is not included in 'learning' status. Accordingly, in cases in which a training allowance is paid to a trainee receiving practical training in a corporation, should the money provided exceed actual expenses (travel, living expenses, etc.) and amount to remuneration, the employer is open to the charge of facilitating illegal work and the trainee will be punished and/or deported for illegal work activity.[58]

The point is that this sort of training system is not being taken at face value in the community. The distinction between practical training and work is very vague and the fact that corporations who were short-staffed utilized foreign workers in the guise of trainees was an openly acknowledged reality. In August 1989 the Ministry of Justice Immigration Bureau released data on the results of a survey conducted from April 1988.[59] According to the data, of the 40 companies and 547 trainees surveyed, only 5 companies were judged overall by the Bureau to 'have no particular problems'. In the remaining cases, there were suspicions that labour shortages were being overcome; 68 trainees were not permitted to renew their residence status and 13 were given deportation orders on the grounds that they were engaged in activities outside their status.

The admission of trainees, for the most part, occurs as one aspect of the Japanese government's official development assistance. About 70 per cent of trainees are admitted with some form of involvement by public institutions. However, in the remainder of cases the government has not had an adequate handle on the training situation.[60] Given the circumstances, the

TABLE 3.2. Number of first-time entrants to Japan on trainee visas (1985–90)

Year	Number of entrants (and breakdown by country)
1985	13,987 (China 2,877; South Korea 1,604; Thailand 1,233)
1986	14,388 (China 2,848; South Korea 2,336; Indonesia 1,114)
1987	17,081 (South Korea 2,800; China 2,688; Thailand 2,428)
1988	23,432 (Thailand 4,708; China 3,840; South Korea; 3,343)
1989	29,489 (Thailand 4,502; South Korea 4,125; Philippines 3,974)
1990	37,566 (China 7,624; Thailand 5,075; South Korea 4,485)

Ministry of Justice worked out a policy for ensuring the appropriateness of traineeships, establishing 'pre-entry screening standards for foreign trainees' in April 1989.[61]

During deliberations on the revision of the law, the issues of whether the grey zone between training and work would really disappear and whether traineeships would not in fact become a loophole for the utilization of unskilled workers were repeatedly raised. In response to this, the Ministry of Justice declared its intention to expand the scope for the acceptance of trainees after properly distinguishing between the two.[62] The Ministry of Labour responded in similar style that it would 'act so as to ensure the implementation of appropriate training in line with the essential purpose of training'.[63] Kato Toshiyuki, who appeared before the House of Representatives Committee on Judicial Affairs as a trade union representative, introduced the concept that 'training kills three birds with one stone'. His essential criticism of the training situation was that, whereas training worthy of the name should involve huge intake costs, the fact that corporations were supposedly 'for the sake of global goodwill . . . proactively volunteering for training' raised the question of whether or not it was in fact because 'there was profit in it'.[64] On the other hand, Masuda Masaichi, director of Nikkeiren (Japan Federation of Employers' Associations), emphasized in his testimony Japan's need, as an advanced economy, to promote the intake of technical trainees for the purpose of economic assistance (i.e., technology transfer) to developing nations, as long as caution was exercised in the liberalization of human resources.[65]

However, what of the number and general situation of trainees as a whole? Table 3.2 shows the increase, between 1985 and 1990, in the number of people entering Japan with trainee residence status.[66]

According to a survey of 2,104 listed companies and about 4,000 companies with between 30 and 299 staff conducted by the Ministry of Labour in July 1990,[67] of the 2,718 companies that returned valid responses, 273 (or 10 per cent) were taking in foreign trainees. The average intake per company was 16.8 trainees. A breakdown of those taking in trainees by industry type showed manufacturing (electrical machinery and appliances) at 20.2 per cent, followed by finance and insurance at 19.1 per cent, and manufacturing (transport machinery and appliances) and utilities at 15.8 per cent. Three to six months was the most common training period (25.2 per cent), followed by six months to less than one year (23.1 per cent), one year to less than two years (22.7 per cent), and one month to less than three months (16.8 per cent). Further, in 48.7 per cent of corporations, on-the-job training (as distinct from class-room training) accounted for more than 65 per cent of total training time, with 23.8 per cent of corporations in the 50–65 per cent range. The very real difficulty in distinguishing between work and training is evident. The Ministry of Justice's standard (in the above-mentioned pre-entry screening standards for foreign trainees) is that no more than two-thirds of training time is to consist of on-the-job training. In the problematic area of training expenses, total monthly expenses per person (excluding supervisor costs and facilities costs borne by the trainee) saw 150,000 to 200,000 yen the most common at 30.8 per cent, followed by less than 100,000 yen (17.7 per cent), 100,000 to 150,000 yen (16.5 per cent), and 250,000 to 300,000 yen (13.9 per cent).

There were, however, many complaints on the part of small and medium-size enterprises, which have the most severe labour shortages, about securing trainees. If we accept as a premiss the reasonable argument that 'training should actually cost money', then it does not stand to reason that anybody would want trainees, but in reality this is not the case. The Ministry of Justice took a step that fitted with 'reality'. The 'standards regarding training' established by a ministerial ordinance of 1 June 1990 pursuant to clause 7, paragraph 1, sub-paragraph 2 of the revised Immigration Law stipulated certain requirements regarding the institutions able to offer training, which included practical training, but where the institution was the state, a local municipal body, or in other 'cases specified by notification of the Minister of Justice', these standards were not to apply. The subsequent 'Ministerial Notification Regarding Training' of 9 August 1990 prescribed Chambers of Commerce and Industry, Commerce and Industry Associations, and small and medium-size enterprise groups as exceptions to the standards, with the aim being 'to expand ways for domestic small and medium size enterprises to be involved in training programmes'.[68] The proviso, however, was that they were required to operate the training programmes with financial and other assistance from, and under the guidance of, national and/or local municipal bodies.

In cases in which practical training was included, additional requirements were that there be no possibility that the trainees did work, and that the business organization inspect the training situation at least once every three months and report to the head of the regional immigration bureau. In any event, however, it is beyond doubt that this step was intended to open up more possibilities for small and medium-size enterprises to secure trainees.

There has already been a response from small and medium-size enterprise groups to the notification of the Minister of Justice. For example, the KSD Homeikai (with a membership of about 1.5 million), which is run autonomously by members of the *Zaidan Hojin—Chusho Kigyo Keieisha Saigai Hosho Jigyodan* (Small and Medium-Size Enterprise Managers' Disaster Compensation Fund) (KSD), has established an 'association' for the intake of foreign trainees as a non-profit entity under the jurisdiction of the Ministry of Labour, and is pushing ahead with a plan to delegate training to member corporations of the association.[69] The idea is that funding for the operation of the association would come from employers and corporate members. A 'language training centre' capable of accommodating 2,000 people would be established in Japan, and, after liaising with participating countries, trainees would be accepted, given three months of language training, and then sent to corporations. Training in the corporations would consist of three months of classroom training and two years and six months of on-the-job training. The association would levy 'training expenses' from corporations and pay trainees a 'training allowance'. The cost of travel to Japan and housing would be borne by the corporation, while the association would make regular deductions from the training allowance to cover the cost of return travel. The question is what the return would be for the economic burden of paying into the 'association' and then paying 'training expenses' in order to get a trainee. The role of the 'association' is coming perilously close to that of a 'personnel agency'.

4. From training to employment-establishment of the technical intern training programme

In the 1990s the number of trainees admitted to Japan has risen as shown in Table 3.3.

TABLE 3.3. Number of first time entrants to Japan on trainee visas (1991–93)

Year	Number of entrants (and breakdown by country)
1991	43,649 (China 10,668; Thailand 6,290; South Korea 4,439)
1992	43,627 (China 15,054; Thailand 5,385; South Korea 3,717)
1993	39,795 (China 15,688; Thailand 4,075; Indonesia 3,433)

The use of trainees entered a new phase in late June 1991 when it was reported that agreement about post-training work had been reached between the four ministries of Labour, Justice, Foreign Affairs, and International Trade and Industry.[70] According to the report, 'the agreement will allow trainees to switch to a "specified activities" residence status and work for about one year after one year's training. The proviso is that this will be limited to trainees and corporations who undertake training under the guidance of the "foreigner training association" (a working title of an organization to be set up in October 1991)'. Indeed in March 1988 the Ministry of Labour Employment Security

Bureau's *Report by the Working Group on the Foreign Worker Problem* had already canvassed the possibility of post-training work.[71]

This idea was promptly incorporated, as the 'Technical Intern Training Programme', into the December 1991 *Second Report on Administrative Reform Focusing on the Lifestyle of the People and Responses to Internationalization* of the Ad Hoc Administrative Reform Council.

Based on this, the government decided to look into the establishment of a new training system in its 1993 Administrative Reform Framework (to be decided on 28 December 1992), and in the 1993 Administrative Reform Framework of December of the following year, it decided to introduce a Technical Intern Training Programme. In light of this decision, the Communication Council of Ministries and Agencies Related to the Foreign Worker Issue (comprising seventeen ministries and agencies including the Ministries of Justice, Finance, Labour, and International Trade and Industry, and the Economic Planning and National Policy Agencies) agreed in March 1993 to a 'Basic Framework for a Technical Intern Training Programme', which began in April that year.

The content of the 'basic framework' was essentially the same as that reported in June 1991. The intent of the Technical Intern Training Programme was explained as 'a training programme in the broad sense of cooperation in the development of personnel responsible for the economic development of developing countries'. 'Technical internships' are internships where foreign trainees use the skills acquired as trainees to work as interns in the corporation (or institution) where they trained, in an employment relationship. In short, it amounts to nothing other than permitting work on the condition that training has occurred.

The combined period of the training and the technical internship may not exceed two years. The matter of a new residence status being set up to cover the period of the internship is to be looked at, but for the moment this is to be covered by the residence status of 'special activities'. Interns' families are not permitted to come to Japan during the period of the internship, and it is expected that, in order to guarantee that interns return to their home countries, certain steps will be taken to ensure that preparations for returning home are in place, such as supervision by the corporation through the provision of accommodation facilities, a departure reporting system, and regular payments into a travel expense account by the corporation. Moreover, the Japan International Training Co-operation Organization, which was established in October 1991, has been active in arranging the Technical Intern Training Programme.[72]

The number of technical interns between the beginning of the programme in August 1993 and June 1994 is reported to be about 1,700, including trainees who have indicated their desire to become technical interns (see *Kokusai Jinryu* (The Immigration Newsmagazine), February 1995, pp. 2 f.). On the question of how many interns are to be admitted, the explanation of the 'basic framework' mentioned above indicated that 'no admission quota will be set at the moment, but relevant ministries and agencies will consult about how to limit admissions in light of the situation following implementation'. At present the number of interns is not large and the Ministry of Justice is publicizing and actively promoting its use. The special coverage in the February 1995 edition of *Kokusai Jinryu* (The Immigration Newsmagazine) was titled 'Let's Promote Technical Internships', and carried an article by the Policy Section of the Ministry of Justice Immigration Bureau headed, 'Toward Expansion of the Technical Intern Training Programme' (see pp. 16–17). In any case, we can say that the Technical Intern Training Programme is in direct approval, through systematic assistance, of the situation of corporations that have utilized trainees as labour.

The above issues require further monitoring. The least that can be said is that, should the intake of foreign workers proceed on the condition of one year's training in accordance with the above-mentioned programme, it will be viewed by future generations as having happened because of short-term labour market vested interests without the consensus of the people, particularly through an act of parliament after thorough debate, and without a clear response strategy for the social and human issues that arise from immigration. The intake quota will essentially be determined by the demand of the Japanese labour market (there will, of course, be political negotiations with participating countries). Here once again we will see the principle of 'economic growth' taking precedence on the pretext of fulfilling our international obligations 'as a developed economy . . . for the sake of global friendship'.

IV. Restating the Problem

Although, throughout 1988, caution had been the predominant attitude of the business world, in 1989 a stream of proposals for the admission of 'unskilled' foreign workers came from various business organizations.[73] While this was a response that was linked to the revision of the Immigration Law, it was also arguably a very forward-looking one.

In January 1989 the *Kansai Keizai Doyukai* (Kansai Association of Business Executives) announced its 'secondment centre concept' in its *Gaikokujin Rodosha Mondai e no Teigen* (Statement on the Foreign Worker Problem).[74]

In March 1989, in its *Korekara no Gaikokujin Koyo no Arikata ni Tsuite* (On the Future of Employment of Foreign Workers), the *Keizai Doyukai* (Association of Business Executives) proposed the idea of a system of 'practical training programmes'.[75]

The 'foreign workers skill formation system' suggested by the Tokyo Chamber of Commerce and Industry in December 1989 contained the ambitious objective of setting up a single joint government and private sector entity for the introduction of foreign workers into Japan.[76]

The above three proposals focused on admitting organizations, but in April 1990 the Kansai Keizai Rengokai (Kansai Business Association) was more direct when it called for the introduction of a 'work permit system' in *Gaikokujin Rodosha Ukeire Mondai ni Tsuite* (On the Issue of Admission of Foreign Workers).[77] The 'employment permit system' which the Ministry of Labour had already put forward in 1988 had been harshly criticized by management as 'discriminating between employers' because it granted permits to employers to employ foreigners.[78] Work permits, in contrast, would be granted to foreign workers by the Minister of Labour with restriction on the employer, the region, and the type of work, and with a limit of a one-year period with no more than two renewals.

What these proposals have in common, however, is the fact that interest is concentrated on the system up to the point of getting foreign workers into the employing corporations, while there is scant attention paid to the broader social and human context of admission. Perhaps this is inevitable since they are proposals from business organizations, all of which have vested interests in employment. As an issue for Japanese society, however, and hackneyed though the expression may be, 'it is human beings, not labour power' that come. They will become our neighbours, and our local citizens, and perhaps even settle and become Japan's 'citizens of tomorrow'. Are we to argue that when a foreigner's period of employment is over he or she is to be packed up and bundled off home? Each of these proposals fails to give sufficiently thorough consideration to this matter, and even were they to do so, they would only lead to the expansion of the causes of illegal work—the very thing the Ministry of Justice is intent on eradicating.

The Economic Planning Agency's *Gaikokujin Rodosha to Keizaishakai no Shinro* (Foreign Workers and Directions for the Economy and Society) is outstanding among government policy papers on the method of admission of foreign workers because, unlike 'incoming worker control' approaches such as those in the above concepts, it proposes an 'integrative' type of approach.[79] It suggests, in other words, that foreign workers be admitted as 'permanent citizens'. The report does take the position, however, that the shortage of untrained labour is due to 'overall cyclical demand factors' and that to make up this shortfall by bringing in foreign workers would be inappropriate as it would nurture and foster a two-tiered structure in the Japanese labour market. It therefore argues that since the recent internationalization of labour is to be understood not just as a quantitative expansion but also as a qualitative development, the integrative type of admission of foreign workers as general labour is vital.

Regardless of the debate over the pros and cons of the introduction to Japan of untrained workers, there is much to be said for the 'integration' type of concept. The German experience has already shown well the difficulty of the 'incoming worker control' type of system. Discussion of the development of an integrative type of system in the paper mentioned above does not cover the issues of political participation (the right to political activity and electoral rights) and a naturalization system. In the European experience, these issues have been unavoidable in the integration of foreign workers. The biggest mistake of the paper is that, although it does call for an integrative type of approach, it pays no attention whatsoever to the issue of the Korean residents of Japan (the foreigners who are permanent citizens in Japanese society) and the issue of their 'coexistence' (the paper argues that 'coexistence' is equivalent to integration—see p. 87 of the paper) with Japanese nationals. If we are to speak of 'internationalization at home' and 'a Japan that coexists with the world' (p. 113 of the same paper), all the more reason why we must examine this experience of history. This is where the ability of the Japanese state and Japanese society to 'coexist' with foreigners comes under question.

The 'Proposals for Improvement in the Treatment of Korean Residents of Japan' mentioned in section I of this chapter shows the interests common to foreign workers who are accepted into a country in an integrated way (i.e., 'the foreign permanent citizens of the future'). We should note its main points.

On the whole, within the parameter of the official government position that 'unskilled workers will not be admitted', loopholes in policy are being created as required. In the business world, the prevailing position is increasingly that 'they'll eventually be admitted', while public opinion is also becoming more tolerant of illegal work and support for the admission of foreign workers grows as time passes.[80] The conditions are ripe for their introduction by default, or, dare I say, 'incrementalist development without a fundamental decision'. The trend of the times is predominantly 'the economy'. It is difficult to shut the door when demand equals supply. Rather, if we do that, we will not escape the censure of, to twist a popular expression, 'one nation economicism'. The problem is that developing a bandaid policy of loophole admission muddies the issue and will sow the seeds of trouble for the future. It is time we made up our mind to admit 'coexistent citizens', wrap up our history as a 'monoethnic society', and begin the preparations for forming an 'open society'.[81] Doing so could be the first step towards creating the new essence of Japanese society, but, given the above, that will not be an easy task.

4

Economic Co-operation in Place of Historical Remorse: Japanese Post-War Settlements with China, Russia, and Korea in the Context of the Cold War*

WADA HARUKI

I. Introduction

On 2 September 1948, at the end of a three-week visit to Japan, Chang Jun, a former prime minister of the Republic of China, made an appeal to the Japanese public.[1] He welcomed the fact that Japan was following the GHQ's directives to establish a new order based on democratic principles. However Chang Jun warned that 'while it is a simple task to bring about revolutionary changes to tangible systems and laws, intangible morals and psyches are not easily altered'. He concluded that 'Japan needs to undergo an moral revolution (*shiso kakumei*) and to build a new national psyche'. Chang Jun urged the Japanese public to reflect deeply on the mistakes of the pre-war period and the results of those mistakes while bringing about moral and psychological changes to the nation.

One year later, in September 1949, sinologist Takeuchi Yoshimi wrote that no one in Japan had responded to Chang Jun's message. 'Today Chang Jun's very visit to Japan has been forgotten. But I remember Chang Jun's warnings with a heavy heart,' he lamented.[2] 'I believe that Chang Jun's calls for "moral revolution and a new national psyche" are a criticism of the fundamentals of Japanese culture, and that they accurately reflect the general opinion of the Chinese,' stated Takeuchi. Initially Chang Jun's high status in the Chinese Nationalist government caused Japanese newspapers to pay particular attention to his statement. On the other hand, the Japanese communist newspaper *Akahata* (*Red Flag*) decided that, as Chang Jun belonged to the Kuomintang and had fought against Mao Tse Tung, his opinion was not representative of the Chinese people. Takeuchi sharply criticized both the ordinary newspapers and *Akahata* for having failed to grasp the soul of the Chinese people.[3]

* Translated by Nicolette Hillyer.

However, just one month after Takeuchi wrote the above critique, Mao Tse Tung proclaimed the formation of the People's Republic of China from atop Tiananmen Gate in Beijing, and the Nationalist government, together with its vanquished troops, began to flee to Taiwan. This political upheaval completely upstaged Chang Jun's appeal to the people of Japan and his comments disappeared from public memory.

In 1945, Japan accepted the Potsdam Proclamation and surrendered to the United States, Great Britain, China, and the Soviet Union. Japan proper was occupied exclusively by American troops. Furthermore, the United States single-handedly guided the Japanese government, oversaw the dismantlement of the Japanese army, and set the nation on the path to democracy.

The advent of the Cold War and escalating incidents of internal strife in Asia encouraged the United States to rapidly bolster Japan as a bulwark against communism in the region. At the height of the Korean War, America drew up a peace treaty with Japan that was designed to work in conjunction with the USA–Japan Security Treaty.

The peace treaty, signed at San Francisco in September 1951, reflected the aims of the United States and never forced Japan to accept responsibility for the war.[4] The preamble to the treaty failed even to mention the historical past. However, the treaty clause dealing with territorial issues was exacting, providing for Korean independence, and the renunciation of Taiwan, southern Sakhalin, and the Kuril Islands, and it was agreed that Okinawa would be placed under the mandate and provisional management of the United States. Former Japanese mandated territories were also placed under US control. Neither China nor the Soviet Union were amonged the allied signatories at San Francisco. However, the United States and Britain forced Japan to renounce its claims on these disputed territories, which were occupied *de facto* by the Republic of China and the Soviet Union. Japan had strong hopes that the islands of Shikotan and Habomai would be counted as part of Hokkaido and would not have to be handed over to the Soviets with the Kurils. Although America and Britain agreed to this, it was not mentioned in the peace treaty.

In exchange, reparations were considerably reduced. Article 14 (a) of the peace treaty outlined Japan's responsibilities for reparations for the damage and suffering it had caused during the war but also acknowledged that the resources of Japan were, at that time, not sufficient to make complete reparations. As a result, the first clause states that, at the request of countries that suffered from Japanese actions during the war, compensation should only take the form of services of the Japanese people in production to be rendered. The second clause stated that all goods belonging to the Japanese government or its citizens found within the boundaries of the allied nations were to be confiscated and disposed of by the Allies. Finally, Article 14 (b) declared that, with the exception of the above two cases, the Allies should waive all reparations. In that respect the treaty was remarkably lenient toward Japan. It is no wonder that Prime Minister Yoshida Shigeru stated that the treaty 'does not contain any punitive or retaliatory clauses', 'it is not a treaty of vengeance, but an instrument of reconciliation', and we are 'happy to accept . . . this fair and generous treaty'.

In all, forty-nine countries, including Japan, signed the San Francisco Treaty. Of these nations, the key signatories to the treaty were six western nations and five South-East Asian nations. However, only the western nations accepted the treaty as the final solution.

South-East Asian nations, which had suffered under occupation by Japanese troops and had seen their countries turned into battlegrounds, were never satisfied with the treaty's stipulations regarding reparations. Indonesia refused to ratify the treaty. The Philippines stated that it, too, would be unable to ratify the treaty without an agreement on reparation. Burma was extremely unhappy with the treaty and refused even to attend the peace conference. Japan was forced to begin negotiations with each of the disgruntled countries separately.

China, the third signatory to the Potsdam Proclamation, was unable even to attend the peace conference due to the split between the communist-controlled mainland and the Nationalist government, which had fled to Taiwan after the civil war. As Great Britain recognized the Beijing government, the United States could not bestow upon the Republic of China the right to represent China at the conference. Under heavy pressure from the United States, Japan decided to begin talks to establish diplomatic relations with the Republic of China. At the same time, the Soviet Union, the fourth signatory to the Potsdam Proclamation, boycotted signing the treaty, although it attended the peace conference. Naturally, Japan needed to negotiate a peace treaty with the Soviet Union as well. Finally, Japan also needed to atone for its period of colonial rule over Korea and to negotiate to establish diplomatic relations with independent Korea. However, the peninsula had split into the Republic of Korea and the Democratic People's Republic of Korea. Once again, the United States intervened, so that Japan began talks with the Republic of Korea. Thus, the San Francisco Treaty only set in order relations with the United States, Great Britain, and other western powers while relations with the Soviet Union, Korea, China, and South-East Asian nations needed to be dealt with further in separate negotiations.

As relations with the United States were of the utmost importance to Japan in the post-war period, Japan looked constantly to her protector, America, for guidance and made efforts to please it. The manner in which Japan undertook diplomatic negotiations with countries not dealt with under the San Francisco Treaty displays clearly the kind of relationship that it wished to establish with the rest of the world other than America. These negotiations therefore may shed a new light on another face of post-war Japan toward its neighbours.

This chapter does not deal with relations between Japan and the South-East Asian states, but focuses on the manner in which Japan undertook negotiations to establish diplomatic relations with China, the Soviet Union, and Korea.

II. The Sino–Japanese Peace Treaty

Despite criticism from Great Britain and Yoshida Shigeru's personal mis-givings, John Foster Dulles forced Japan to promise that it would commence negotiations for a peace treaty with the Chinese Nationalist government, as documented in Hosoya Chihiro's research. Yoshida foresaw the possibility of a split between the Soviet Union and the People's Republic of China and planned to make overtures toward the latter in the future. For that reason he had hoped to avoid concluding a peace treaty with the Republic of China. However, on 10 December 1951 while visiting Japan, Dulles warned that if Japan were not to make advances toward the Nationalist China it might not be possible for the US Senate to ratify the San Francisco Treaty. He gave Yoshida the draft of a letter to be sent to the United States government, stat-ing that Japan was ready to conclude a treaty with the Chinese Nationalist government. Yoshida obeyed and sent a copy of the letter dated 24 December to the US government.[5]

Dulles's heavy-handed tactics were guided by US political designs to sup-port the Nationalist government on Taiwan by forcing Japan to recognize them as the legitimate rulers of China. Naturally, these ambitions were shared by the Nationalist government itself.

Having decided to commence negotiations with the Nationalists, Yoshida placed one of his relatives, Kawada Isao, in command of the talks. Kawada had acted as the Minister of Finance on the eve of the Pacific War, from September 1940 to September 1941. In the last year of the war he had held the position of president of the Taiwan Colonization Company.[6] The Chinese Nationalist government was disappointed by Japan's choice. It had initially planned to place Chang Jun in charge of the talks. When Kawada's appoint-ment was announced, however, Chang was replaced in the negotiations by Yeh Kung Ch'ao, Minister of Foreign Affairs.[7]

The first official conference began in Taipei on 20 February, 1952. The opening speeches given by representatives of the Nationalist government and the Japanese government made it clear that there were fundamental differ-ences between them. Yeh Kung Ch'ao quoted Chiang Kai Shek's words of September 1949 when he spoke of 'the importance of being benevolent when we feel revengeful'. Yeh quoted Chiang Kai Shek once more. 'China is not looking for revenge against Japan. Because we believe that without peace in East Asia there will be no world peace . . .', said Yeh in Chiang Kai Shek's words of June 1951. Yeh avoided directly mentioning the issue of the Japanese invasion and only alluded to it, saying 'We have lived in the world where peoples were violated and menaced by invasion over and over again. Therefore we believe if we do not work together to strengthen our relationship . . . there will be no peace.'[8]

Kawada replied as follows:

We sincerely regret (*ikantosuru* in Japanese) that in recent years there occurred frequently unfortunate (*fukona* in Japanese) incidents between Japan and China and ultimately led to a state of war, against the true intention of the two peoples who desired peace from the bottom of their hearts. Upon the termination of the war, however, Generalissimo Chiang Kai Shek proclaimed throughout the world a most generous attitude towards our country. Our people were not only profoundly impressed by this but also given a cause for serious self-examination (*hansei* in Japanese). To these Government officials and people of China who at that time followed the intention of your President and took magnanimous and kindly measures toward the Japanese residents, I wish to express sincere gratitude on behalf of my Government and people. As regards the lofty morality of your President, we believe that the best way to reciprocate it is, in the long run, that we make the greatest possible contribution to the over-all recovery and prosperity of Asia and specially East Asia, and thus expedite its stabilization.[9]

Kawada's 'regret' about the 'unfortunate' past presents a characteristic prototype of the Japanese understanding of historical events. It does not show any remorse on Japan's part for its role as aggressor in the war. At the same time, Kawada's speech indicated that Japan intended to follow a non-political, economic path. It also indicated that Japan was not willing to support the Chinese Nationalist government's anti-communist stance.

At the first conference, the Chinese Nationalist government submitted its own draft of a peace treaty to the Japanese. This version was couched within the framework of the San Francisco Treaty, and consisted of twenty-two articles. Its preamble did not include any direct references to the war. Article 12 (a) discussed reparation as follows:

It is recognized that Japan should pay reparations to the Republic of China and Allied Powers for the damage and suffering caused by it during the war. Nevertheless, it is also recognized that the present day resources of Japan are not sufficient, if it is to maintain a viable economy, to make complete reparation for all such damage and suffering and at the same time meet its other obligations. Therefore (1) Japan will promptly enter into negotiations with the Republic of China with a view to assisting to compensate the latter for the cost of repairing the damage done, by making available the services of the Japanese people in production, salvaging and other work for the Republic of China.[10]

This requirement was copied almost exactly from Article 14 of the San Francisco Treaty and places Chinese Nationalist requirements for reparation in the form of services on a par with those from other allied countries.

However, Japan was displeased with the Chinese draft. Kawada conveyed Japan's reaction to Yeh at the Second Official Conference:

It is notable that the provisions of your draft, following as they do the example of the San Francisco Treaty, inevitably take the form of unilaterally imposing obligations upon us. Therefore, if those restrictive provisions of the San Francisco Treaty which are applicable to the defeated country are included in the present treaty in large numbers, it is certain that our people will find it contrary to their expectations and will be greatly disappointed. Frankly speaking, as you know, there are among our people those who do not fully favor the present treaty negotiation. Therefore I hope you will understand that it is necessary to give the contents of the treaty such form as will not arouse our national feelings in so far as possible.[11]

Kawada appeared not to believe that the Sino–Japanese Peace Treaty was a treaty between a winner and a loser. Rejecting the duty of reparation in the name of the feelings of the Japanese, he obviously paid no thought to the feelings of the Chinese. That is why he could make the following comments:

Even if a treaty of reconciliation is concluded between the Governments of the two countries, not only would it be most regrettable if there should remain a seed of ill feeling between the two peoples, but also would it obstruct the satisfactory execution of the treaty if it were to convey an undesirable impression that the treaty is the one between the two Governments but not between the two peoples.[12]

Perhaps prepared for such an outburst, Yeh Kung Ch'ao argued strongly against Kawada:

The relations between China and Japan have in the past few decades been marred by two wars and many unfortunate incidents. Indeed, from the Mukden Incident of September 18, 1931 to V-J day, the Chinese people, particularly those in our Northeastern provinces, were made the hopeless victims of continuous Japanese militarist aggression. The long years of war with Japan have so depleted China's resources and eaten into her vitals that at the close of hostilities she was left with more will than power to resist the onrushing tide of Red aggression. The war with Japan has, indeed, cost us dearly.[13]

'Had it not been for the devastations brought by the war, the Chinese mainland could still be in our hands', was the political stance taken by the Nationalist government in Taiwan. However the Nationalists were not the only group to criticize Japan for its invasion. Yeh commented about the structure of the treaty draft as follows:

True to the spirit of magnanimity and reconciliation which China has adopted towards Japan since V-J Day, we have, of our volition, chosen to follow the spirit of the San Francisco Treaty . . . The draft treaty which we have prepared is, in spirit and substance, largely based upon the San Francisco Treaty. We have not, for instance, patterned the preamble of our draft treaty on the conventional type of preamble for a peace treaty with an account of the origins of, and responsibility for, the state of war which is to be terminated. I hope that in further discussion you will take note of this spirit of goodwill and reconciliation.[14]

It seems that Japan did not listen to this plea to the end. A reading began that day of the Chinese draft treaty, and the Japanese delegates handed over their first draft, consisting of six articles. The preamble was even more simple than the Chinese version. Article 1 of the treaty confirmed that the war had been concluded. Article 2 called for co-operation in keeping with the principles of the United Nations constitution, 'in particular to promote the welfare of both nations by fostering a spirit of friendly co-operation in the area of economics'. Article 3 confirmed that Japan had relinquished rights over Taiwan and the Pescadores and promised 'to resolve rapidly' issues concerning goods and claims that Japan and the Japanese had in Taiwan, and that the Republic of China and the inhabitants of Taiwan and the Pescadores had in Japan.[15] Not surprisingly, the treaty made no mention of reparations of any kind.

The Chinese insisted that negotiations should be based on the Chinese draft. Kawada accepted that the treaty should be known as the 'Peace Treaty', but the Japanese were not prepared to accept the inclusion of any clauses dealing with reparations. In order to solve this stand-off, on 5 March the Japanese government took the unusual step of dispatching the Chief of the Asian Affairs Bureau from the Ministry of Foreign Affairs, Wajima Eiji, to Taiwan to set up a separate channel for negotiations behind the scenes. As a result of discussions between Wajima and Kawada based on the Ministry's new draft, a Japanese second treaty draft was presented to Yeh on 12 March.[16] The declassified version contains an omission. It is likely that the omitted section of the draft read that China would abandon the right to press for indemnity paid in services. Japan's intention was to force China to relinquish mention of reparations of any kind. Wajima explained the Japanese government's position in discussions with the American Ambassador Rankine:

The question of reparations is a domestic political issue for the Chinese and also, is an emotionally serious problem for the Japanese. We are now negotiating a treaty, the political aim of which is to enhance friendly feelings between Japan and China. However if reparations are included in the treaty, its major goal will be destroyed. Reparation in services in particular is not feasible without capital and material backing. I stressed that it is not suitable for the Chinese Nationalist government to insist stubbornly on conditions that cannot be fulfilled, simply to use as propaganda.[17]

At the time, Japan had just announced that it would provide reparations, in services only, to the Philippines and Indonesia. There is no doubt that Japan was taking advantage of the Chinese Nationalist government's weak position to single it out for separate treatment. Speaking for Japan, Wajima emphasized that 'we have already made concessions on 16 points' and 'we thought the negotiations were finished'.[18] On 14 March, Wajima paid a visit to Chang Jun. Wajima made the following comments to Chang Jun, who had initially raised the issue of reparations:

China should not take advantage of the clause regarding reparation in the San Francisco Treaty. Did not the Nationalist Chinese government let Dulles know that it would not press for reparations?

When Chang Jun argued that it was not acceptable that only the Chinese relinquish claims for reparation, the Japanese negotiators adopted a very impudent tone. Wajima stated that:

As Article 14 of the San Francisco Treaty is in actual fact unworkable, it is better for China to take to heart the magnanimous attitude of its Generalissimo at the end of the war. The citizens of Japan would certainly welcome that. We would like the Nationalist government of China not to keep rigidly to the concept of reparation, but to adjust to the aims of Article 2 of our draft (original plan).[19]

Article 2 of the Japanese draft dealt with economic co-operation. Chang Jun was at a loss how to handle Japan's uncompromising stance.

On 15 March Kawada met with Chang Jun and stressed that Japan was not prepared to make any concessions on the issue of reparations. Chang Jun repeated his statement of the day before but added, 'it might be possible, only to fix general principles of reparation in the text of the treaty and to exchange notes that payment will be suspended for an extended period', hinting at a method of reaching a compromise.[20] This scheme was discussed on 17 March in a meeting between Kawada and Yeh. According to the official chronology of negotiations, Yeh proposed that Kawada accept the Chinese draft regarding reparation, and exchange official notes saying that 'the issue of service indemnity is to be negotiated and resolved once the areas that had suffered the most were once again under the control of the Chinese government'. Kawada immediately rejected all of these proposals. According to Ishii Akira's research, the Chinese documentation indicates 'Kawada argued that the billions of dollars worth of Japanese assets left abandoned in China would more than suffice if they were counted toward reparation. He also suggested that the demands for reparation were not in character with the "lenient" attitude that your country has frequently expressed as being its aim in dealing with Japan.'[21] This was the Japanese rationale for the denial of the Chinese's right to reparations, whether they be Nationalist or Communist.

Japan's inflexible stance placed Yeh in a difficult predicament and on 19 March he said to Kawada at last:

In response to Prime Minister Yoshida's continued efforts, for the sake of the friendship between the people of China and Japan, I have decided to go against Chinese public opinion and suggest to the government that we voluntarily abandon the issue which the Japanese government has stressed the most, that of an indemnity paid in services.

He requested however that Japan agree to the Chinese treaty draft for all other clauses.[22] At this stage, the Chinese abandoned their own first draft and adopted the Japanese second draft. They presented their own second treaty draft to the Japanese negotiators on 20 March. The Chinese second draft did not include the indemnity issue in the main body of the treaty, but dealt with it in Protocol (d).

In extending to the Republic of China all the advantages it is obligated to extend to the other signatories of the San Francisco Treaty, Japan declares its recognition that it should pay reparation to the Republic of China for the damage and suffering caused by her during the war. The Republic of China, on the other hand, recognizes that the resources of Japan are not at the present time sufficient to make complete reparation for all such damage without endangering her national economy. In consideration of this recognition as a sign of magnanimity and good will towards the Japanese people, the Republic of China decides to accept all the rights and obligations stipulated in Article 14 of the San Francisco Treaty, and to waive the benefit of the services to be made available by Japan pursuant to subparagraph 1, paragraph (a) of that Article.[23]

Kawada immediately sent this second proposal by telex to Tokyo. On 25 March, in support of the proposal, he wrote, 'Despite the fact that our assertions, based on your guidance, have not been fully accepted, it should not be necessary to fight any more over unessential points. The time is now ripe to come to agreement'.[24]

Tokyo did not accept this. On 27 March, among demands that a great number of points be revised, Wajima wrote that 'it is difficult to agree with the points raised in the first half of the Chinese proposal' concerning the reparation issue. He requested that the treaty clauses requiring Japan to acknowledge its duty to recompense China and expressing China's acknowledgement of Japan's difficult situation be removed. Based on these new directives, Kawada submitted a third Japanese treaty draft on 28 March. Only the main section of this proposal, not including the Protocol, had been released to the public. Through his studies of the Taiwanese documentation, Ishii has shown the Japanese version of the Protocol to read as follows:

Based on the regulations of the San Francisco Peace Treaty, China has the right to receive the benefits of Article 14 (a) 2. In light of this and as a sign of magnanimity and goodwill toward the people of Japan, with the proviso that there are no further regulations to the contrary, by this treaty the Republic of China waives all claims to reparation arising from actions by Japan or its citizens to the Republic of China and its people.[25]

Yeh expressed extreme disappointment regarding this proposal. He stated that the draft was a retrograde step from Japan's second draft and that he would 'either have to ask Japan to reconsider or to admit that the negotiations have failed and give up'. He asked Kawada if 'there is a way to break this dead-lock'. Kawada reported that 'I explained the reason why there was no altern-ative left'.[26] Kawada met with Chang Jun on 29 March, at which time Chang criticized Japan more severely than at any earlier stage of the negotiations:

Recently the Japanese government seems to be looking down on the Nationalist government. In particular, they have been exploiting their advantageous position since the US Senate's ratification of the peace treaty to extend pressure on China. The atmos-phere in our government is becoming so tense that I am practically unable to act as troubleshooter. I would like to urge you to persuade the Japanese government to reconsider its position.[27]

On 2 April, Yeh sent a memo to the Japanese regarding their proposal in which he made the following comments about reparation:

It must be remembered that, of all the Allied Powers, the Republic of China fought the war against Japan the longest, incurred the heaviest damage, and her people suf-fered the most. It is therefore only fair that Japan should recognize her obligations to pay reparations to the Republic of China for the damage and suffering caused by Japan, an obligation Japan agreed to in the San Francisco Treaty. The Republic of China, on her part, would be willing to waive the benefit of services which Japan has promised to make available to the other Allied Powers whose territories were once occupied and damaged by Japanese Forces. In order to do so, the Republic of China must first be given an opportunity to accept the rights and obligations under Article 14 of the San Francisco Treaty. Such is the spirit that has guided the drafting at sub-paragraph (c) of paragraph one of the draft protocol. The Japanese version of the said subparagraph, fails to provide for the recognition by Japan of her obligation to pay reparation and attempts to deny China's position as one of the Allies. This is unacceptable to the Chinese Government.[28]

This memorandum was sent to the Japanese Ministry of Foreign Affairs, which chose to ignore it. After consultation with Prime Minister Yoshida, the head of the Asian Affairs Bureau and the head of the Treaty Bureau drafted new guidelines to pressure the Chinese into reaching an immediate agreement. Foreign Minister Okazaki was cautious by nature and received the Prime Minister's approval before sending new instructions by telex on 4 April:[29]

It seems that you are endeavoring to come to an agreement favourable to Japan on a number of problematic issues, including reparation, war crimes, and repatriation.

However I fear that it will be difficult to resolve the negotiations quickly given the repetitive nature of the current debate. Our government by no means intends to ignore the efforts you and the Chinese government have made to date, but we think we are obliged to leave all issues regarding mainland China to be resolved in future. At this stage the only way in which we can settle the negotiations is to concern ourselves solely with territories that are directly controlled by the Nationalist government.[30]

This sent a clear message of intimidation to the Chinese Nationalist government. The Chinese had no option but to give in. Arriving in Taiwan on 5 April, Wajima brought with him the Ministry of Foreign Affairs' new draft, which addressed the reparations issue in the Protocol as follows: 'As a sign of magnanimity and goodwill, the Republic of China waives all the reparation claims against Japan except those stipulated in Article 14 (a) 2 of the San Francisco Treaty.'[31] Kawada, however, believed that the language used in the Protocol was overstressing the point, and so changed the statement to one emphasizing that the Nationalist government was abandoning claims to indemnity paid in services. The third draft including this alteration was submitted to Yeh on 13 April:

As a sign of magnanimity and goodwill towards Japan, the Republic of China will voluntarily waive the benefit of the services to be made available by Japan pursuant to Article 14 (a) 1 of the San Francisco Treaty and the other benefits of this Article (a) except these related to (a) 2.[32]

The Chinese did not oppose this. However, they suggested that the Protocol simply state that China would relinquish service indemnity, and that the confirmation which Japan was requesting be dealt with in an exchange of official notes. The Chinese did not wish the fact that they were abandoning reparation claims to be too prominent.

The official notes to be exchanged were based on papers submitted by the Chinese on 14 March. The following text was decided on:

Japanese Delegate:
   It is my understanding that since the Republic of China has voluntarily waived the service compensation as stated in paragraph 1 (b) of the Protocol of the present Treaty, the only benefit that remains to be extended to her under Article 14 (a) of the San Francisco Treaty is Japan's external assets as stipulated in Article 14 (a) of the same Treaty. Is it so?

Chinese Delegate:
   Yes, it is.[33]

The Sino–Japanese Peace Treaty was signed on 28 April 1952. At the signing ceremony Kawada commented that 'The magnanimity of His Excellency the President of the Republic of China is simply manifested in the provisions which are of particular concern to our people', and the Japanese would remember the President's attitude gratefully. Kawada ended his speech by saying that the people of Japan would do their part for 'the solidarity of the peace-loving nations of the world'.[34] It is ironic that, despite flatly rejecting Chinese requests for reparations until the very end of the negotiations, Kawada wove a myth that Chiang Kai Shek was magnanimous enough to abandon all claims for reparation. For his part, Yeh concluded his speech with a quote from the Bible: 'Blessed are the peacemakers: for they shall be called the children of God.' It is not clear whether this was intended as irony directed at Japan, or whether it was a frank reflection of Yeh's innermost feelings.[35]

Japan took advantage of the Republic of China's difficult situation to force it to drop its claims for reparation. Considering that Prime Minister Yoshida foresaw negotiating with mainland China in the future, Japan's rigid stance with the Republic of China was perhaps a preliminary measure to force the mainland later also to abandon the reparation issue. Whatever the reason, Japan concluded the fifteen-year war with China by refusing to pay any reparations and with no signs of remorse or apology. This set the basic pattern for Japan's stance on diplomacy toward Asia in the years after the war.

Japan acknowledged that the Japanese assets that had been left behind in China were to be disposed of by China, in accordance with Article 14 of the San Francisco Treaty. However the treaty did not cover Japanese assets that had been abandoned in its former colony, Taiwan. Article 4 of the San Francisco Treaty set forth that Japanese assets and claims in the former Japanese colonies of Korea, Taiwan, the Kurils, South Sakhalin, and other mandated territories were to be dealt with individually by the administration of each particular region. Therefore edicts stating that Japanese public and private assets and claims that had been abandoned in Taiwan and assets and claims that authorities and citizens of the Republic of China had left in Japan needed to be dealt with separately were automatically set under Article 3 of the Sino–Japanese Peace Treaty. It is a mystery that the Chinese did not make more of an issue of Japanese assets in Taiwan, considering the firm stance they took on reparation.

The Japanese government valued Japanese assets in Taiwan at $32 billion. On the other hand, the claims, assets in Japan, government bonds, wages owed to civil servants, and allowances for bereaved families that Taiwan claimed from Japan only amounted to several hundred million dollars. Therefore, if the claim rights had been mutually settled, Taiwan would most likely have been liable for vast sums in the form of 'reverse reparations'. The Japanese government repeatedly requested that this topic be included in the negotiations with the Chinese Nationalist government, but as the Nationalist government had limited financial resources, it consistently refused to discuss the matter. This strengthened the Japanese resolve not to respond to Taiwanese claims for war damages. The Japanese government's viewpoint is summed up as follows: 'I have explained that as long as we are unable to discuss the mutual settlement of Article Three of the treaty, we cannot settle the Taiwanese claims, even though we are sympathetic towards them.'[36]

The Sino–Japanese Peace Treaty was ratified by the Japanese House of Representatives on 7 June 1952. It was supported by the Liberal party and the Progressive party, and opposed by the Socialist party, the Communist party, and the Labour-Farmer party. The treaty was presented to the House of Councillors on 5 September and was ratified by 103 votes to 38. The Socialist party, the Communist party, and Labour-Farmer party were against signing an agreement with the Chinese Nationalist government in exile, wishing to conclude an agreement with the People's Republic of China. No party paid any attention to the fact that Japan had refused to pay reparations to the Chinese.[37]

III. The Soviet–Japanese Negotiations—The Development of the Northern Territories Issue

As the Soviet Union had not been party to the San Francisco Treaty, Japan was faced with the task of concluding a separate peace treaty with the Soviets. Once a peace treaty was concluded, the status of the representatives of the Soviet Union who were stationed in Tokyo as one of the victors in the war would become problematic. The Soviet Union had interned a number of Japanese prisoners sentenced guilty of offences under Russian domestic law in 1949. But Yoshida had decided not to commence negotiations for a peace treaty with the Soviets. On 25 January 1952, he responded to a question from the House of Representatives by saying:

As long as the Sino–Soviet Treaty of Friendship exists and the Soviets continue to disturb law and order of our country by supporting the Japanese Communist Party, as long as they continue occupying Shikotan and Habomai without returning them to us, we will not be able to conclude a peace treaty with them.[38]

Yoshida's policies were based on strengthening Japan's ties with the United States. He believed that if peace were made with the Soviets and their embassy's activities were legalized, this would only encourage further anti-American activities of the Japanese Communist party.

The House of Representatives' resolution of 31 July 1952 clearly illustrates that at the time the peace treaty came into effect, unresolved territorial issues included the return of Okinawa and the Ogasawaras (Bonins) as well as 'the islands of Shikotan and Habomais'.[39] However, as long as Japan could not expect the United States to return Okinawa, it restricted its reaction toward the Soviet retention of Shikotan and Habomais to verbal criticism. In this respect, Japan's reaction to the territorial problem was in keeping with its general stance toward both the United States and the Soviet Union.

While Japan and the United States agreed that there were merits in not negotiating with the Soviet Union for a peace treaty and in not establishing diplomatic relations, the United States had, in fact, used the San Francisco Treaty as a vehicle to harbour clauses prejudicial to a peace treaty between Japan and the Soviet Union. Article 26 of the San Francisco Peace Treaty stated that Japan should be prepared to conclude a bilateral treaty of peace with nations that were not signatories to the San Francisco Treaty on 'the same, or substantially the same terms as are provided for in the present Treaty'. Furthermore, it stipulated that if non-signatories to the Treaty received greater advantages than those provided by the Treaty, the same advantages were to be extended to countries that had signed the Treaty. However the Treaty also stated that Japan was only bound to this obligation for a period of three years after the San Francisco Treaty came into effect. Thus if negotiations between Japan and the Soviet Union did not commence for three years, Japan would be under no obligation to extend to the Soviets the same conditions as those contained in the San Francisco Treaty. Moreover, if it seemed that Japan was going to have to make even greater concessions, America would be able to intervene directly.[40]

After peace was declared and Japan became an independent nation again, administrative purges came to an end and major politicians were reinstated. This led to a rise in nationalist tendencies, and Yoshida's policies came under criticism. Hatoyama Ichiro (Prime Minister 1954–6) was the champion of a new platform composed of two points:

(1) the creation of Self-Defence Armed Forces by the abolition of Article 9 of the Constitution; and
(2) a peace treaty with the Soviet Union.

If Japan was to follow an independent line from the United States with its own armed forces, it was also imperative that it improve relations with the Soviets and the People's Republic of China. A copy still exists today of the basic plan to commence negotiations between Japan and the USSR that Sugihara Arata, the brains behind Hatoyama's foreign policy who was later to become the head of the Ministry of Defence in the Hatoyama cabinet, sent on 12 February 1954 to Hatoyama.[41] This document notes that the negotiations were 'only expected to include attainable goals' including '(1) the release and return of prisoners detained as war criminals, (2) banning damaging propaganda, and (3) consent to Japanese fishing in the international waters of the north seas'. Territorial problems over Shikotan and Habomai were dealt with as follows:

(1) Japan asserts its territorial rights to those islands and does not acknowledge Soviet claims, (2) Japan emphasizes that those islands be returned quickly and (3) if we are left no other option, then after confirming that our demands that the islands be

returned have been understood, we will set the same conditions as for Ogasawara and other islands . . . Regarding the Kurils and southern Sakhalin, (1) we should negotiate, determined to waive our territorial rights and (2) we should leave the belongings of these territories to future negotiations.

Finally, the plan requested that Japan should ask the Soviet Union 'not to exercise its right to refuse Japan membership of the United Nations'.

Sugihara concluded by stating that 'the aim of solving the territorial dispute should not be the primary condition for re-establishing diplomatic relations'. This plan sums up Hatoyama's stance on negotiations with the Soviets.

This was the sort of reasonable and conciliatory line on relations with the Soviets that Hatoyama developed. He replaced Yoshida as Prime Minister on 10 December 1954. Not surprisingly, this change alarmed the Americans. The US Department of State sent a lengthy note to the Soviets on 25 September 1954 protesting that a US military plane had been shot down two years before over Yuri Island (one of the Habomai Islands), and demanding compensation.[42] The note referred to the Soviet occupation of the Habomai Isles as a 'deliberate violation of the terms of the Japanese surrender'. It also stated that in the context of the San Francisco Peace Treaty and the Yalta Agreement, the geographical name 'Kuril Islands' 'does not include and it was not intended by the parties thereto to include, the Island of Yuri which is a part of the Habomai Islands'. America claimed that the Soviets had no rights over Habomai and Shikotan and that it was therefore unfair to impede Japan from asserting sovereignty over these islands and from defending these islands with the help of the United States. The real intention behind sending a letter of complaint about an incident that had occurred two years earlier is obvious. America clearly wished to constrain Hatoyama's moves by stressing that the Habomai Islands should be returned to Japan.

The United States apparently carried out many protest flights over Habomai after 1951. No doubt the plane shot down by the Soviets was simply the tip of the iceberg. Directly after this action, on 7 November 1954 another US Air Force plane flew over Habomai and was shot down by a Soviet plane.[43] The case was brought before the US National Security Council, and Dulles sent a memorandum to US President Eisenhower headed 'Sovereignty of the Habomai Islands'. It states, 'In the treaty Japan did renounce any interest in the Kurile Islands, but Japan and the United States deem that the Habomai Islands are not part of the Kuril Islands. This is also the Japanese view.' However, 'I do not know anything we can do to get the Russians out short of war.'[44]

At that time, the Hatoyama cabinet was already in power and the Soviet Foreign Minister had announced on 17 December that its government was ready to commence negotiations with Japan. A letter from the Soviet government was delivered to Hatoyama's residence by A. I. Domnitskii, the

Soviet trade representative stationed in Japan. Now Japan began to take steps toward opening negotiations. This caused the Yoshida group, which had been ousted from power, and the United States government to consider carefully a number of factors. Dulles decided that if Hatoyama commenced negotiations with the Soviets, 'the existence of US relations with the USSR precludes strong efforts to persuade Japan from establishing relations with the USSR', but he did not want the development of Russo–Japanese relations to cause America to suffer 'a major public diplomatic defeat prejudicial to basic US–Japan security alignment'. In order to avoid such a defeat, America drew attention to the fact that it supported Japanese sovereignty over Habomai and Shikotan, and tried to create new tensions between Japan and the Soviet Union.[45] It calculated that, as long as the Soviet Union was not prepared to concede on the territorial issue, Russo-Japanese negotiations would face a deadlock. It is likely that the Yoshida group followed a similar train of thought.

On 9 April 1955 the US government adopted NSC5516/1—'American Policy toward Japan'—which once again set down in writing that America's goals for Japan were to build 'a strong Japan, firmly allied with the United States', and 'a counterweight to Communist China'. The United States considered its stance on Russo-Japanese negotiations a means to help achieve these goals. Hence America decided that it would 'support Japan's claim against the Soviet Union for sovereignty over the Habomai Islands and Shikotan'; . . . and 'not concede the Soviet Union's claim to sovereignty over the Kuril Islands and southern Sakhalin'.[46]

This basic document provided a blueprint for the first comprehensive view of America's stance on the territorial issues, summarized in a memorandum written by William Sebald, the Deputy Assistant Secretary of State for Far Eastern Affairs, on 20 April.[47] The memorandum stated that it would be to the advantage of the USA 'to exploit the serious differences between Japan and the USSR . . . Japan wants Habomai and the Shikotan Islands on the theory that they are not part of the Kurils', but 'it is unlikely that the Soviets will agree to this'. The memorandum admitted that Japan might claim that, as it had not acquired the Kuril Islands by violence, the San Francisco Treaty clause stating that the islands must be abandoned was invalid, or that the words 'Kuril Islands' in the peace treaty referred to the northern Kurils only. America was prepared to support Japan's claims regarding Habomai and Shikotan. Furthermore, it believed that there were 'strong political reasons for encouraging Japan's claim to at least part of the Kurils'. According to the memorandum the Kurils were 'strategically important to the free world', hence, America should not give the Soviet occupation tacit approval. However, if the status quo were to change, there was a danger that this would invite change in the Ryukyu Islands and Taiwan as well. Therefore the memorandum advised that the United States 'offer no objection to efforts on the part of Japan to get all or part of the Kurils, either as a part of a deal whereby Japan might recognize a valid Soviet claim to South Sakhalin . . . or even on the basis of a Soviet recognition of Japan's residual sovereignty over all or part of the Kurils'.

Sebald instructed the US ambassador at Tokyo, John Allison, to convey the substance of this memorandum to the Japanese. On 28 April Allison wrote a special memorandum to present to Tani Masayuki, an adviser to the Ministry of Foreign Affairs.[48] Thus, the US government suggested on the eve of the negotiation to the Japanese Foreign Ministry that it might ask for more than Habomai and Shikotan in the coming negotiation with the Soviet Union.

Allison's long analysis of the Japanese position dated 1 June 1955 is very illuminating about the anxiety of the US side, which was hidden behind the above suggestion. He wrote as follows:

From the Soviet viewpoint, considerable impact on the Japanese is possible from proposals not calling for an immediate break in treaty ties with the US, but placing considerable strain on these ties and yet involving only minimum concession by the USSR. Such an approach could involve Soviet agreement to 'residual Japanese sover- eignty' to Habomai, Shikotan, and possibly the southern Kurils, the inclusion of Japan in a UN admission 'package', . . . plus a promise to restore the above territory simultaneously with the US return of the Bonins and Okinawa, provided that the restored territory is neutralized (no US bases), and provided that the time limit is set for the withdrawal of US Forces from Japan.'[49]

The Soviet–Japanese Peace Treaty negotiations began in London on 3 June 1955. Japan was represented by Matsumoto Shun'ichi, who had been the Vice-Minister of Foreign Affairs at the end of the war. The Soviet delegate was their Ambassador to London, Iakov Malik. Matsumoto carried with him the instructions that had been agreed to by Hatoyama's proxy, Sugihara Arata, and Foreign Minister Shigemitsu Mamoru's adviser, Tani Masayuki. The instructions read that the return of the Kurils and southern Sakhalin could be negotiated, but that Shikotan and Habomai must be recovered.[50] It is not clear what Foreign Minister Shigemitsu's actual views were, but mem- bers of the Yoshida group within the Japanese Foreign Ministry must have agreed that the return of Shikotan and Habomai should be insisted upon. They believed that if Matsumoto persevered on this point, the negotiations would be fruitless.

From the outset of the negotiations, Japan and the Soviet Union were at loggerheads as Japan declared that the negotiations were to cover southern Sakhalin, the Kurils, Habomai, and Shikotan, whereas the Soviets claimed that territorial disputes had already been settled. But, hoping to drive a wedge between Japan and the United States, Khrushchev decided to hand over Habomai and Shikotan to Japan. Malik informed Matsumoto of this deci- sion on 4 August. Matsumoto was overjoyed, but the Yoshida group and the United States were stunned by the news, and the Japanese Foreign Minister Shigemitsu, who was just about to visit the United States, was embarrassed.

Word of the Soviets' decision arrived in Japan by telex on 10 August and was kept top secret. At a Japanese Foreign Ministry Summit, which was held on or about 18 August, a new option was decided upon. The Foreign Ministry decided to demand that the Soviets return not two, but four islands, and that the question of the fate of southern Sakhalin and the northern Kurils should not be fixed by Japan and the Soviet Union alone, but should await a decision from an international conference. With this new option, Shigemitsu no doubt was planning to extend the negotiation period for slightly longer to see whether a better deal could be reached. However, the Yoshida group in the Foreign Ministry, headed by Teraoka Kohei, a counsellor of the European Department, wished to complicate the negotiations with those two conditions that were unacceptable to the Soviet Union in the hope of tripping up the Soviets by one means or another. This new option was intentionally leaked to the *Asahi Shimbun* (newspaper) and published on 20 August. The impression given in the news report was that Japan had dropped its claims for the return of southern Sakhalin and the entire Kurils and was claiming only four islands in order to hasten the negotiation process. Shigemitsu left for the United States on 23 August apparently without gaining Hatoyama's support for the new option. In London, Matsumoto was surprised to hear of the leak to the *Asahi Shimbun* and divulged to a reporter of Jiji Tsushin (Jiji Press Service) that the Soviet Union had conceded the return of two islands. This became front page news in Japan on 25 August in the *Mainichi Shimbun*. That same day, Tani, an adviser to the Foreign Ministry, paid a call on Hatoyama, explained to him the Ministry's new option and apparently gained his support for it. New instructions were sent by telex to London on 27 August.[51]

If this interpretation of events is correct, the Foreign Ministry must have kept Matsumoto's telex without informing Hatoyama, covered up the Soviet offer to return two islands, and decided to reject the Soviet offer and counter it with new demands for the return of four islands without consulting the Prime Minister, and then leaked the accomplished fact to the papers.

Matsumoto informed Malik of Japan's new proposal on 30 August. The Soviets were astonished. Malik flatly rejected Japan's counterproposal and on 6 September added another condition to the return of Habomai and Shikotan. He told Matsumoto that the islands must be demilitarized.[52] The negotiations broke down and were called off. Matsumoto decided to return to Japan on 15 September.

No documentation has been released regarding America's initial surprise at these developments. No August telegrams from Allison to the Department of State have been declassified as yet. A memo from Walter S. Robertson, the Assistant Secretary of State for Far Eastern Affairs, dated 18 September, indicated a sense of relief that the negotiations were interrupted, but expressed concern about future developments and 'information . . . that Hatoyama may be in a mood for compromise'.[53] German Chancellor Konrad Adenauer's visit to the Soviet Union suggested that Japan might be able to resume negotiations with the Soviets in the same line. On the same day, Robertson sent a telex to Allison, in Dulles's name, instructing the Ambassador to put more pressure on Japan. The telex stated that:

(1) under no circumstances should Japan recognize the Soviet occupation of the Kurils and southern Sakhalin, and that disposition of these territories should be left for future international decision;

(2) Japan should not acknowledge the Soviet proposal to ban third country warships from the Japan Sea; and

(3) the Soviet proposal for demilitarization of Habomai and Shikotan was a derogation of Japanese sovereignty over these islands.

Matsumoto arrived back in Japan on 1 October, and tried to convince Tokyo that the Soviet concession was final and that Japan should compromise. However, while he was still presenting his case, on 6 October the *Mainichi Shimbun* printed an article by Koizumi Shinzo, an educational adviser to the Crown Prince and a close friend of Yoshida.[54] It read, 'the Soviet Union is a robber reaping a profit out of a neighbour's fire—that is the opinion of the silent masses'. Koizumi claimed that the USSR entered the war 'to make a profit out of a fire' and that, given that it still had possession of plundered property, the USSR had no right to talk of peace.

That autumn, there were two major political mergers in Japan. In October, two Socialist parties unified and decided that one of the new party's main policy objective was to secure the return of Okinawa as well as 'to demand the return of Habomai, Shikotan, the Kurils and southern Sakhalin'.[55] Realistic methods of solving the territorial problems were suggested, such as concluding the state of war with the Soviets with a *modus vivendi* and continuing negotiations for a peace treaty. However, the Socialist party line on territorial issues was unrealistic as it did not recognize even the San Franscico Treaty or the results of the London negotiations. The opposition's unrealistic policies aided the Yoshida group. The Foreign Ministry's new option was adopted in the Memorandum of the Chairman of the Liberal Party's Foreign Policy Council on 22 October.[56] Hatoyama's objections were pushed aside and on 4 November, this line was incorporated into the policy programme for the merger of the Liberal and the Democratic parties.[57] When the Foreign Ministry call for the return of four islands became the platform of the new ruling party (LDP), the policy turned into a national aim. Matsumoto returned to London in January 1956, but the negotiations made no progress and were called off in March.

Soviet–Japanese negotiations were resumed when Foreign Minister Shigemitsu visited the Soviet Union in July 1956. Shigemitsu maintained that the USSR should return four islands and declared that, if the Soviets acknowledged this point, Japan would acknowledge that it had abandoned southern Sakhalin and the Kurils according to the San Francisco Treaty. However, the Soviet Union was still only prepared to return two islands. Eventually Shigemitsu decided to compromise and agree to the Soviet proposal for a peace treaty, agreeing that only two islands would be returned and recognizing the remaining islands as Soviet territory. However the Hatoyama goverment took into consideration the decision of the LDP and the swing in public opinion, and decided that this would not be acceptable. The negotiations broke down and Shigemitsu, who had proceeded to London, met with the US Secretary of State, Dulles, to explain his course of action. Dulles's reaction was extremely negative, as has been well documented. Shigemitsu met with Dulles on 19 August and told him that Japan had no option but to compromise and accept the Soviet proposal. Dulles responded that if Japan were to accept that the islands of Kunashiri and Etorofu were Soviet territory, the Soviet Union would gain more territory than outlined in the San Francisco Treaty, and if that were the case, America would enforce Article 26 of the treaty and occupy Okinawa indefinitely.[58]

Shigemitsu was shocked, but narrowly returned the play by enquiring of Dulles whether, if that were the case, America was prepared to take the initiative and organize an international conference to decide the future of the Kurils and the Ryukyu Islands.[59] Dulles's threat was leaked by Matsumoto to an accompanying reporter and was reported as a scoop in the 23 August edition of the *Sankei Shimbun*.[60] The report read as if a bomb exploded. This reaction caused America grave anxiety.

After Shigemitsu had failed to make any progress, Hatoyama took direct charge of the negotiations. Following Adenauer's example, he decided to set aside territorial problems for the time being, and to visit the Soviet Union himself in the hope of establishing diplomatic relations by a joint statement. Within the ranks of the LDP, there was a violent reaction against these moves, particularly from the Yoshida faction. The United States softened Dulles's threat and, while not taking responsibility for the breakdown in negotiations, tried to pressure Japan into not backing out of its claim for the return of four islands.[61] At that point, the American position rested upon the following three premises. First, the Department of State and the US Embassy in Tokyo considered that it would not be of benefit for America to organize an international conference as Shigemitsu had suggested.[62] Second, the Policy Studies Branch, Historical Division, of the Department of State reported that 'in most United States documents which deal with the subject, Kunashiri and Etorofu are recognized as being a part of the Kurils, and the Japanese Prime Minister speaking to the San Francisco conference, which was convened to sign the peace treaty, specifically referred to these two islands as being a part "of the southern Kurils" '.[63] Therefore, it could not support the Japanese government's claim that the islands of Kunashiri and Etorofu were not part of the Kurils, which had to be renounced under the San Francisco Treaty. Third, Admiral

Arthur Radford, Chairman of the Joint Chiefs of Staff, reported that Kunashiri and Etorofu were of strategic importance to the Soviets.[64] Therefore, the Soviet Union was never going to abandon those islands.

On 3 September, Robertson, Assistant Secretary of State, proposed that an *aide-memoire* should be sent to Japan regarding the Soviet–Japanese negotiations, starting from these three points.[65] He stated that Japan was not able to take a firm stand against the Soviets because of 'disunity and factional politics . . . If we cannot directly assist Japan in its negotiations, there may be steps which would strengthen our bonds with Japan by way of contrast with Soviet imperialism'. Robertson believed that the United States government needed to send a memorandum to that effect. An *aide-memoire* of this nature was handed over to the Japanese government on 7 September 1956 and was made public on 12 September.[66] The *memoire* stated that 'by virtue of the San Francisco Peace Treaty Japan does not have the right to determine the sovereignty over the territories renounced by it therein', and that, after careful examination of the historical facts, 'The United States has reached the conclusion that the islands of Etorofu and Kunashiri (along with Habomai Islands and Shikotan, which are a part of Hokkaido) have always been part of Japan proper and should in justice be acknowledged as under Japanese sovereignty.'

The Japanese government's claims were not consistent with the San Francisco Treaty, and it was not likely that the Soviet Union would comply with them. Robertson foresaw that, by encouraging Japan to persist with its claim for the return of four islands, Japanese antagonism against the Soviet Union would increase and America's ties with Japan would deepen. Obviously, this memo was intended to restrain Hatoyama and support the Yoshida faction, which believed in taking a firm anti-Soviet stance.

On 11 September, the day before the *aide-memoire* was made public, Yoshida attacked Hatoyama in an article published in the *Sankei Shimbun*, saying, 'What on earth does an inexperienced and sick Prime Minister wish to accomplish by initiating a visit to the Soviet Union, and making an adventurous move of inviting the Red Peril?' On 20 September the Yoshida faction of the LDP forced the party council to adopt a new resolution that called for the conclusion of a peace treaty that defined the immediate return of Habomai and Shikotan, and further negotiations for the return of Etorofu and Kunashiri.[67] The Yoshida faction intended these moves to block Hatoyama's visit to the Soviet Union.

However Hatoyama gained the support of the Socialist party, and Cabinet votes swung in favour of his trip to the Soviet Union. Taking into consideration the new party resolution, after arriving in Moscow, Hatoyama offered a version of the declaration with the help of the Minister of Agriculture Kono Ichiro, which defined the return of two islands, and stated that discussions regarding territorial issues should continue. Khrushchev responded to this offer and promised to return the two islands, but in a draft proposal, he laid down two prerequisites to handing over the territories. The two conditions were that a peace treaty would be signed and that Okinawa would be returned to Japan. Kono requested that the condition regarding Okinawa be omitted, to which Khrushchev agreed. However, Khrushchev requested that the words 'including territorial issues' be omitted from the regulation about negotiations for a peace treaty. Japan agreed to this request.[68]

On 16 October 1956, Japan and the Soviet Union signed a Joint Declaration and diplomatic relations were re-established between the two nations. At a meeting of the Diet to ratify the declaration, Hatoyama explained that it would still be possible to negotiate territorial issues. However, Shigemitsu noted in his diary that 'in reality, Peace Treaty negotiations over territorial issues ended with the return of Habomai and Shikotan'.[69] On 27 November, at a plenary session of the House of Representatives, 365 votes favoured ratification, and no votes were opposed, so the motion was passed. However, 71 members, including Yoshida Shigeru, Ikeda Hayato, Tanaka Kakuei, Ohira Masayoshi, and Suzuki Zenko of the LDP Yoshida faction, and Sato Eisaku, all future Japanese prime ministers, showed their opposition by not attending the session.[70]

Anti-American feeling grew within Japan at the end of January 1957, following the Girard incident, in which an American soldier shot and killed a Japanese peasant woman. This occurred just after the Soviet Embassy had been opened in Tokyo, and America became increasingly apprehensive.[71] America responded by intervening one last time in the Northern Territories dispute. On 23 May 1957, America sent a document to the Soviets demanding compensation for an incident which had occurred three years earlier, in which an American military aircraft was shot down over the Habomai Islands by a Soviet fighter plane. The document repeated that the Habomai Islands were Japanese territory and protested the Soviet occupation of the islands. However, it dared to propound new interpretations to the Yalta Agreement and the Treaty of San Francisco as follows:

And the phrase 'Kuril Islands' in those documents does not and was not intended to include the Habomai Islands, or Shikotan, or the Islands of Kunashiri and Etorofu which have always been part of Japan proper and should, therefore, in justice be acknowledged as under Japanese sovereignty.[72]

Throughout 1956, the US Department of State had never adopted the view of the Kuril Islands expressed in the above document, but now it was assumed without any evidence. The only conceivable reason for this abrupt change was the political strain that the USA–Japan relationship faced in 1957.

Under the Kishi cabinet, relations between Japan and the United States improved steadily from 1957, culminating in the new Japan–USA Security Pact, which was signed in 1960.[73] The rationalization and increasing stability of relations between Japan and America were not welcome developments for the Soviet Union. The Soviets hoped to see the anti-new-Japan-USA Security Pact movement grow. In January 1960, Soviet Foreign Minister Gromyko stated in a memorandum that all foreign troops would have to withdraw from Japanese soil as a condition for the return of Habomai and Shikotan. No doubt the main objective in sending this memorandum was to use Habomai and Shikotan as trump cards to heighten opposition to the new Security Pact.

Despite growing opposition to the Security Pact that year, Yoshida's successor, Ikeda Hayato, took over leadership of the government when the Kishi cabinet collapsed. Ikeda planned to double people's incomes, and once again concentrated the government's attention on economic matters. At the same time, the new cabinet reconsidered Japan's relationship with the Soviet Union in order to fortify US–Japanese relations, which had become shaky. This political repositioning was occasioned by Anastas Mikoyan's visit to Japan and a letter written by Khrushchev. In October 1961, Prime Minister Ikeda announced to the budget committee in the House of Representatives that 'Chishima, or the Kuril Islands . . . comprise 18 islands north of Uruppu Island.' He stated that Nishimura Kumao, Head of the Treaty Department of the Foreign Ministry, was 'mistaken' in his famous response, and that 'there is no such thing as the southern Kurils'.[74] On 6 October, Foreign Minister Kosaka Zentaro expressed these points as the official Japanese government position on the matter.[75] In a *Sankei Shimbun* article entitled 'Resolving the Northern Territories Dispute', on 11 October, former Prime Minister Yoshida supported Ikeda. Yoshida pretended to have said at the San Francisco Conference that 'the Kurils do not include the islands of Kunashiri and Etorofu, which were originally Japanese territory'. Yoshida defended Nishimura, and emphasized that the Northern Territories should be returned to Japan by saying, 'luckily, both Japan and America are of one mind on this issue. The people of Japan must try even harder to convince Russians that ours is the correct stance.' Prime Minister Ikeda expressed this point of view in a letter to the Russian leader Khrushchev:

It is a clear historical fact that the 'Kuril Islands', over which the Japanese government renounced its rights in the San Francisco Treaty, are comprised of the 18 islands north of Uruppu Island, and that Japan has not renounced all rights over Kunashiri and Etorofu, which were not originally part of the Kurils and have always been Japanese territories.[76]

Ikeda was the second in command after Yoshida at the San Francisco Peace Conference. Yoshida and Ikeda relied on the letter of the US Department of State (dated 23 May 1957) to help each other rewrite history in this manner.

On the other hand, after visiting Japan, Mikoyan apparently returned to the Soviet Union with the impression that the USA–Japan relationship could not be broken. After listening to Mikoyan, Khrushchev must have finally realized that there was no point in attaching additional conditions to the return of Habomai and Shikotan. For the Soviets, what was the point in handing over the islands, if the USA–Japan relationship could not be weakened? Khrushchev determined to declare that territorial issues had officially been solved, and he had no qualms in cancelling the promises made in 1956. In documents dated 29 September 1961, Khrushchev stated, 'territorial issues were resolved a long time ago as part of an international agreement. How can territory that does not belong to Japan be dealt with as part of territorial issues with Japan?'[77] It was not difficult for Khrushchev to break the promise outlined in ratified diplomatic documents. In this respect it can be said that the Northern Territories dispute finally was formulated in 1961.

Seen in their entirety, the negotiations between Japan and the Soviet Union make it clear that any active Soviet–Japanese relationship was blocked in order to strengthen the USA–Japan alliance during the Cold War. Covert methods, which pitted Japan and the Soviet Union against each other, were employed. This strategy was successful. The Northern Territories dispute itself was a vehicle. The absence of diplomacy between the Soviet Union and Japan for twenty-five years served to reinforce the USA–Japan relationship.

IV. Korean–Japanese Conference and the Japan–ROK Treaty[78]

Japan finally recognized Korean independence in the San Francisco Treaty, and then had to establish relations of state with independent Korea. This meant that Japan had to deal with the serious problem of how to settle thirty-six years of colonial rule over Korea. The peninsula had split into two states, the Republic of Korea (ROK) and the Democratic People's Republic of Korea, but American intervention meant that Japan naturally commenced negotiations with the former. The negotiations began at the same time as talks between Japan and the Republic of China, in February 1952. However, it took thirteen years to come to a compromise.

The Koreans had hoped to participate in the San Francisco Peace Treaty talks with Japan as one of the Allied Powers. However, Dulles refused this request on the grounds that Korea had not officially engaged in warfare against Japan, and said that America would represent Korean interests at the talks. None the less, some amendments were made to the Peace Treaty in response to Korean requests. The most significant of these was Article 4 (b), which determined that the disposal of Japanese public and private goods in Korea carried out by American troops, or in accordance with their orders, was to be recognized as legitimate. Goods in South Korea belonging to the Japanese state and private individuals were seized by the US military administration and handed over to Koreans. Japan was extremely dissatisfied with this.[79]

Preliminary talks between Japan and Korea began under American auspices on 20 October 1951 in a room at the GHQ Diplomatic Bureau in the presence of the American bureau chief, William Sebald. Korea was represented by its Ambassador to the United States, Yang Yu-chan, and Japan by the Vice-Minister of Foreign Affairs, Iguchi Sadao. At the opening of the meeting, Yang read aloud an opening address drafted by President Syng-man Rhee himself:

... [We] hope that peace will come to the Far East. Korea and Japan must now form good neighborly, friendly relations. Korea has never invaded Japan, but time and time again, Japan has invaded Korea and made it suffer. You are fully aware of Japan's vile behavior toward us. Massacre, torture, conscription, requisitioning and other violent and illegal acts have made the peace-loving people of Korea angry. However we will not have a grudge for the past. We hope that all problems will be solved and our countries will be able to start afresh. We are not asking for recompensation for what you have done in the past. Let us bury the hatchet.[80]

There is no record of Japan's response. However Yu Chin-oh, one of the Korean delegates, recollected in his memoirs that Chiba Hiroshi, a Japanese Foreign Ministry official, enquired, 'What does "let's bury the hatchet" actually mean?'[81]

In any event, at these preliminary talks both parties agreed that the actual negotiations should begin in February 1952. Yoshida's government foresaw no difficulties in forming ties with ROK, and was prepared to conclude negotiations by the time that the San Francisco Peace Treaty came into effect.[82] However, conversely, the Korean President Syng-man Rhee had no need to stabilize Korea's international standing by forming diplomatic ties with Japan, and, at that stage, was not willing to hurry toward an agreement.[83]

The first conference began in Tokyo on 15 February 1952. Japan's chief negotiator was Matsumoto Shun'ichi. On the Korean side, Yang Yu-chan stayed in his post as chief negotiator. The two parties clashed over the issue of compensation. The conflict centred on how Japan was supposed to 'recognize' the legitimacy of the US military administration's right to dispose of Japanese goods, as prescribed by Article 4 (b) of the San Francisco Treaty. Korea argued from the perspective that Japanese colonial rule over Korea had been illegal, and that Japanese goods accumulated during this period were all connected to the unlawful nature of the colonial rule. Therefore, Korea claimed that Japan had no rights to the goods after the US military administration's disposal of them. Japan flatly denied all of the above assertions and said that Japanese citizens had not lost their rights of possession over personal property. It stated that if Japanese goods had been sold, it would acknowledge the sale, but could claim the proceeds from the sale. This difference in opinions was fundamental and caused the first conference to break down on 21 April.[84]

Japan hoped to find a way out of the deadlock, and appointed Kubota Kan'ichiro to represent it at the second conference, which began on 15 April 1953. This time, some progress was made, and, after a break over the summer, the third conference commenced on 6 October. However, the third set of talks broke down on 15 October, following a statement by Kubota to the Claims Committee. Kubota's comment sparked various evaluations of Japanese colonial rule, which was the real issue at the heart of the claims dispute.

According to the Korean official source, the clash occurred as follows. The Koreans first stated that Japanese assets in Korea had been seized by the US military administration in accordance with its Ordinance 33. They said that Koreans had every right to claim for damages incurred under thirty-six years of Japanese rule, but that they would refrain from doing so. 'As a reflection of the above facts, we hope that Japan also will refrain from making claims.' In response, Kubota argued that Japan, too, had the right to claim for compensation, due to the fact that, over thirty-six years in Korea, Japan had turned bare mountains into green mountains, laid down railroads, vastly increased the number of rice paddies, and brought many benefits to the people of Korea. The Koreans responded that Kubota's statement was based on the premiss that if Korea had not been occupied by Japan, Koreans would have stayed in a deep sleep, but, in fact, had it not been for the invasion, Koreans doubtless would have built their own modern state. Kubota replied that his own research on diplomatic history showed that had the Japanese not occupied Korea, the peninsula would have been occupied by some other country and would have been left in a far more miserable state; to which Koreans asked, if that was the case, why did the Cairo Declaration write of 'Korea's state of slavery', and why did Japan accept the Cairo Declaration? Kubota rejected this line of questioning and said that the Cairo Declaration 'is nothing more than an expression of agitated mentality during the war'.[85] Kubota was not here expressing his personal opinion, but that of the Japanese government. At the conference on 21 October, the Korean negotiators summarized Kubota's statement in five points and demanded that he retract them. When Kubota refused to comply, the talks broke down.

The Japanese government announced that the cause of the breakdown 'had nothing to do with the topic under discussion', and criticized Korea by saying that 'a trivial, unofficial remark at a minor committee meeting' was 'deliberately distorted'. The editorial of the Asahi Shimbun supported the Japanese government's statement and repeated that it was a 'trivial remark'.[86] Both the Socialist parties of Japan said that the breakdown was caused by Syng-man Rhee's 'xenophobic dictatorship'. As Korea's representative stated, the Japan–Korea conferences should be based upon the premiss of 'letting bygones be bygones and that Japan was sorry for its past actions'. While some Japanese thought it only natural that the Koreans insist that there was 'no room for concession' on this principle, their opinion did not come to the fore in Japan.[87]

For the next four years, Japan and Korea were unable to recommence the conferences. During that time, the United States attempted to persuade Syng-man Rhee to resolve the dispute, but with no success.[88] However, on 13 December 1957, America sent a memorandum regarding the disputed claims to the governments of both nations, and took an assertive role to try to hasten an agreement. In the same vein as documents dated 29 April 1952 that were sent to the US Ambassador in Korea, the memorandum stated that the US Department of State was of the opinion that 'the Japanese have been stripped of all rights, authority, and interests concerning property under the jurisdiction of the Republic of Korea' and that, 'in America's opinion, it is not possible for Japan to make any valid claims over property or interests of that nature'. America also offered the following piece of advice. It stated that the writers of the Peace Treaty 'assumed that in respect of the special agreements referred to in Article 4 (a), the countries directly concerned will probably take into consideration the fact that Japanese goods in Korea had already reverted to Korean control. In this manner, the disposal (of property and interests) relates to these special agreements. Therefore, special agreements between Korea and Japan must define the degree of nullification of Korean demands on Japan, according to the fact that the Korean government accepted Japanese assets in Korea.'[89]

In other words, as Japan could not lay claims to its former Korean assets, America advised Korea to restrain itself in making claims on Japan. American intervention meant that on 31 December 1957, after the Foreign Minister Fujiyama Aiichiro and Ambassador Kim Yu-taek retracted Kubota's statement and Japanese claims on assets in Korea, the two nations reached an agreement to recommence talks.[90]

The new fourth conference began on 15 April 1958 and continued until April 1960. It was cut short by the revolution that toppled Syng-man Rhee in April. The fifth conference, which commenced on 25 October, was broken off on 15 May 1961 because of the military *coup d'état* led by Pak Chong-hui. During this time, debate continued over eight claims made by Korea, but as Japan constantly refused to accept Korean demands, little progress was made. However, after the military coup, discussions between Japan and Korea suddenly blossomed under Pak's military rule. The thaw in relations was no doubt assisted by the fact that economic aid from Japan was indispensable to attain the Korean military government's goal of national economic growth. American pressure also played a role. In the end, a settlement was reached in which Korea relinquished claims on Japan in exchange for economic assistance. The secret agreement was concluded over two meetings in October and November 1962 between the head of the Korean Central Intelligence Agency, Kim Jong-pil, and the Japanese Foreign Minister, Ohira Masayoshi. At the meetings, memos were exchanged providing that $300 million would be provided unconditionally, $200 million would be lent at low interest, and $300 million would be lent by private credit associations.[91]

The relative value of these amounts becomes apparent when compared with reparation settlements reached with South-East Asian nations. Burma, for example, was paid $200 million in reparation and economic aid as part of a peace treaty signed on 5 November 1954. However, the peace treaty included a promise to reconsider the amount of reparations. Negotiations recommenced after 1959, and an agreement, signed on 29 March 1963, affirmed that a further $140 million would be given unconditionally, and $30 million in conventional loans.[92] In total, Burma received $340 million in unconditional funds and reparation. Shortly afterwards, on 9 May 1956, Japan signed a reparation agreement with the Philippines which stated that, over a twenty-year period, the Philippines was to receive $550 million in services and payments.[93] Indonesia and Japan signed a peace treaty and reparations agreement on 20 January 1958 awarding Indonesia $223 million in services and payments. Indonesia was also given a $400 million loan.[94] In comparison with these reparation agreements, the $300 million given to Korea in unconditional funds was a smaller sum than reparations to the Philippines or Burma.

After the sixth session of the Japan–Korea Conference, which lasted from 1961 until 1964, a compromise was finally reached at the seventh session, which commenced on 3 December 1964. Korea's chief representative at the seventh session was Kim Dong-jo, and Japan's was Takasugi Shin'ichi. Discussions at the seventh conference focused on the basic format of the agreement. Whereas Korea asserted that a treaty focusing on the fundamentals of the Korea–Japan relationship should be signed, Japan wanted the agreement to take the form of a joint declaration. In this instance, the Korean plan prevailed. Korea maintained that the preamble to the treaty should mention mistakes made under Japanese imperialism, but this was opposed by Japan, and Korea was forced to abandon this point. In the main body of the treaty, opinion was divided over the validity of the annexation treaty, and the issue of jurisdiction of the ROK.

Korea claimed that the annexation treaty, which was concluded on 22 August 1910, was 'null and void' from the outset. Japan, on the other hand, claimed that the annexation treaty was valid until the Republic of Korea came into existence, which caused the treaty to 'become null and void'. In other words, Japan claimed that Japanese rule over Korea was legitimate, and based on a valid treaty. The issue over Korean jurisdiction referred to Japanese demands that the peace treaty should include clear statements that ROK jurisdiction was confined to the southern half of the peninsula. Kim Dong-jo enlisted the help of Kishi Nobusuke, the former Japanese Prime Minister, who was able to persuade Japan to retract this demand. The ROK government demanded that the treaty include stipulations that it was the sole legitimate power in the peninsula. Japan suggested that a statement of this nature should be modified by adding, 'as clearly stated in the United Nations General Assembly Resolution 195 (3)'. This resolution stated that the legitimacy of the

ROK government was underpinned by free elections, which had been carried out in southern Korea under the observance of a UN Special Committee, and that the ROK government was the only government of this kind in the Korean peninsula. Japan referred to the resolution in order to emphasize once again that ROK jurisdiction was limited to southern Korea. The discussions reached a stalemate on these points.[95]

The Japanese Foreign Minister Shiina Etsusaburo had planned to visit Korea on 17 February 1965, but an agreement had still not been reached on the above two issues by this date. Shiina's arrival speech in Seoul was the subject of careful consideration by Japan and Korea. Japan wanted Shiina to reiterate the statement made by the former Foreign Minister Kosaka Zentaro on his visit to Korea, that 'our relationship in the past has been regrettable'. Kim Dong-jo said that the Korean people would not be satisfied with this, and demanded that an apology be made. Kim requested that Maeda Toshikazu, the former head of the Foreign Ministry's North-East Asian division, who was stationed in Seoul at the time, explain this to the Japanese government. As a result, Shiina read aloud the following statement upon arrival at Kimpo airport. 'I would like to express sincere regret (*ikan*) and deep remorse (*hansei*) that there has been an unfortunate period in the long history between our two nations.'[96] In fact, Japan did not feel remorseful about its period of colonial rule over Korea, which is why the term 'remorse' is combined with 'regret' (*ikan*) about an 'unfortunate (*fukona*) period' . However, the very fact that the word 'remorse' (*hansei*) was used helped to patch up relations with Korea to some extent.

At a meeting between Shiina and Lee Dong-won, the Korean Foreign Minister, on 18 February, Korea suggested that the two countries could reach a compromise on the issue of the validity of the former annexation treaty, by adding the word 'already' to the Korean draft. This enabled both parties to interpret the treaty as it suited them. Kim Dong-jo wrote that the nature of the compromise could be summed up by saying that 'if you put it in your nose it is a nose ring, if you put it in your ear it is an earring'. Shiina accepted the compromise. The final text of Article 2 of the treaty was, 'It is confirmed that all treaties or agreements concluded between the Empire of Japan and the Empire of Korea on or before August 22, 1910 are already null and void.'

At a meeting with Shiina on August 19, Lee Dong-won agreed to compromise and modify Article 3 in the treaty, that stated that the ROK was the only lawful government in the peninsula, by adding a reference to the UN General Assembly Resolution. Finally, the problem was overcome by using an adjectival phrase in the Japanese translation to read 'which was specified in the resolution 195 (III) of the United Nations General Assembly Resolution' and an adverbial phrase in the Korean translation to read 'as you see it specified in the resolution'.[97] Once again, both parties were able to interpret the text to suit their needs. The final text of Article 3 was, 'It is confirmed that the Government of the Republic of Korea is the only lawful Government in Korea as specified in the Resolution 195 (III) of the United Nations General Assembly.'

On 20 February, the basic draft of the treaty was initialled, and a joint communiqué was issued. Part of the communiqué stated that 'Lee, the Minister of the Korean Foreign Department, explained about the anti-Japanese sentiment in Korea which had stemmed from the unfortunate relationship between the two nations in the past. Shiina, the Japanese Foreign Minister, taking note of Lee's statement, expressed deep remorse, admitting that such a state of relations in the past is regrettable.'[98] Once again, this awkward use of 'remorse' is still based on the premiss that Japanese colonial rule over Korea was legal.

The Japan–ROK Treaty was formally concluded on 22 June 1965 in Tokyo. At the same time 'an agreement to settle issues over Japanese and Korean property, claims rights, and economic cooperation' was signed. Article One of this agreement dealt with Japanese aid, as agreed in the memo between Ohira and Kim. Article 2 confirmed that issues arising from claims made by both countries, including those covered by Article 4 (a) of the San Francisco Treaty, had been 'finally and completely resolved'.

In comparison with the Sino–Japanese Peace Treaty of 1952, only a slight change in Japan's stance was won by the Korean government's thirteen-year struggle. Japan was obliged to express remorse over historical events and to give Korea economic assistance. However, the changes were not substantial. Japan did not change its basic assumption that its colonial rule over Korea had been legal. When the Diet met to ratify the treaty, Prime Minister Sato Eisaku defended the 1910 Annexation Treaty, saying, 'There has been a lot of misunderstanding about this, but insofar as it was a treaty, it goes without saying that both parties fully expressed their opinions and concluded it from an equal footing. Therefore these treaties were valid.'[99] Such utterances made by the Japanese Prime Minister meant that Korean criticism of the Japanese could not but remain intact. Furthermore, as economic assistance from Japan took effect and the Korean economy began to grow, criticism of Japan increased.

V. The Post-war Settlements in Perspective

After losing hope for a victory in the Vietnam War, America took steps toward reaching a reconciliation with Beijing. On 15 September 1971, President Richard Nixon announced that he would visit Beijing the following year. The Japanese government, stunned by this change, was unable to respond straightaway. However, the following year in February, after Nixon had visited China, the Tanaka cabinet began to work toward establishing diplomatic ties with People's Republic of China.

Beijing's stance on the normalization of Sino-Japanese relations was voiced in a joint declaration made by the Federation of Parliamentarians for the Restablishment of Sino-Japanese Diplomatic Relations and the China–Japan Friendship Society. The declaration lists three fundamental principles: that the People's Republic of China is the sole legitimate Chinese government; that Taiwan is Chinese territory; and that the Japan–Taiwan Treaty (Sino-Japanese Peace Treaty of 1952) is illegal and invalid and should be abolished.[100] When Takeiri Yoshikatsu, the Chairman of the Komei party, visited China in August 1972 and met with Premier Chou En-lai, China elaborated on these points. Chou En-lai stated that the two nations should make a joint statement, or declaration, establishing diplomatic relations and stating their intention to conclude a peace treaty. He also stated that the USA–Japan Security Treaty and the dispute over the possession of the Senkaku islands should not be a hindrance, and that 'for the sake of goodwill between China and Japan, China is prepared to waive reparation claims for the Japanese invasion and the lengthy state of war'.[101] The Japanese government was extremely pleased.

On 9 September 1972, the Japanese government sent Furui Yoshimi, Tagawa Seiichi, and Matsumoto Shun'ichi to China under the pretext of exchanging memoranda on trade negotiations. While in China, they handed over a document about the points that Japan wanted to include in a joint declaration. The declaration was to include five points: formal conclusion of the war; acknowledgement that the People's Republic of China was the sole legitimate government; recognition that Taiwan was a part of China; Chinese renunciation of all reparation claims from Japan; and notice of the establishment of diplomatic relations. The Chinese agreed to the contents after they were told that the Japanese Foreign Minister would announce that the Japan–Taiwan treaty was no longer valid.[102]

On 25 September 1972 Prime Minister Tanaka Kakuei arrived in Beijing, together with Foreign Minister Ohira. At a function that evening, Premier Chou En-lai made the following speech:

From 1894 for half a century the people of China suffered dreadful misfortune under the Japanese militarists' invasion of China, and the people of Japan also experienced great losses. There is a Chinese saying, 'Do not forget the mistakes of the past, so that you can learn from them for the future.' We must learn from our experiences and take this lesson to heart.[103]

Prime Minister Tanaka replied:

Regrettably, for the past few decades, China and Japan's relationship has passed through an unfortunate period. During that time Japan caused the people of China much inconvenience (*gomeiwaku*), for which I would like to express deep remorse once more.[104]

The gap between the two statements was enormous.[105]

The Chinese demanded full Japanese recognition of the historical facts. In the end, the joint statement stated that 'Japan feels responsible for the enormous damage it has inflicted on the people of China through war in the past, and expresses deep remorse for this'.[106] Finally, twenty-seven years after the end of the war, this one sentence was the first apology that Japan made to a victim nation. Only the People's Republic of China could have forced Japan to acknowledge this fact.

However, the Japanese Ministry of Foreign Affairs requested that the statement should not conflict with the Sino-Japanese Peace Treaty of 1952, and opposed mention of 'the conclusion of the state of war'. Chou En-lai accepted that the phrase be changed to read 'the end of an abnormal state of affairs'. Furthermore, the Japanese Ministry of Foreign Affairs was opposed to the expression that the 'rights of reparation claims will be waived' in the statement, on the grounds that it had been already been covered in the Sino-Japanese treaty. Once again China conceded, and the document was changed to read 'war reparation claims will be waived'.[107]

In fine, some changes were brought about in the Japanese government's attitude, but they were by no means comprehensive ones. The Republic of China had earlier waived reparations because it was forced to do so by Japan, which had refused to admit responsibility for the war of aggression. Had Japan admitted responsibility for the war and apologized, it should have offered to pay reparations. Also, if the People's Republic of China had abandoned claims for reparation, Japan should have accepted this gratefully and responded to the Chinese decision with efforts of its own. However, Japan's only thought was that economic aid was the appropriate response to every situation.

The Japan–China Treaty of Peace and Friendship was signed on 12 August 1978, and Japan began to supply China with economic aid from around that time. In 1979, Ohira visited China and promised the Chinese a loan of $150 million. However, the funds were not accompanied by any concrete reflections on the history of Japan's invasions.

In this respect, it is not coincidental that in 1982, ten years after diplomatic relations between China and Japan had been established, problems arose over the distortion of historical events in Japanese school history textbooks. Amid a barrage of criticism from China and Korea, on 26 August Miyazawa Kiichi, the Chief Cabinet Secretary, conveyed the government's opinion on the issue in an official statement:

The government and the people of Japan are fully aware that the actions of our country have caused Asian nations, including China and Korea, and their peoples much suffering and damage in the past. We now follow the path of peace based on remorse and a determination that such actions will never be repeated.[108]

In suggesting that, for the thirty-seven years since the end of the war, Japan had been guided by this attitude, the statement was misrepresenting history. However, if read as an expression of Japan's future intentions, the statement makes sense. Still, Miyazawa went on to mention the 1965 Japan–Korea Joint Communiqué, and the 1972 Sino-Japanese Joint Statement, stating that 'Japan's remorse and determination, which I mentioned earlier, remain unchanged today'. This means that Miyazawa refused to recognize any difference between Japan's stance in 1965 and that taken in 1972.

Although Japan expressed remorse and apologized for its war of aggression against China, it made no efforts to back up its words with concrete actions, and it believed that economic aid alone would suffice to atone for its past deeds. Meanwhile, Japan's belief that the colonization of Korea was legal meant that it did not consider an apology to be necessary. However, in recent years this issue has provoked increasingly fierce criticism from Korea. Generally speaking, the new wave of criticism toward past Japanese actions started after the end of the Vietnam War in 1975.

From the criticism of Emperor Hirohito's speech, made when President Chon Du-huan of Korea visited Japan in 1984, and that of Emperor Akihito's speech, made when President Ro Tae-woo visited Japan in 1990, it is clear that this issue remains unresolved. Japan's relationship with China has also been tense since the 1985 visit to Yasukuni Shrine by various high-ranking Japanese politicians. The lack of progress on these issues has been thrown into sharp relief by other developments, such as the fact that *perestroika* and new thinking with regard to diplomacy have brought the Cold War to an end, so that the Age of World Wars now seems remote. Finally, in 1991, Japan commenced negotiations with North Korea (the Democratic People's Republic of Korea) to normalize diplomatic relations. At the same time, moves to gain compensation have been initiated by people in China and Korea who suffered because of the war with Japan and who were ignored afterward, including the so-called 'comfort women'.

On the other hand, the end of the Cold War and the Age of World Wars has meant that there is no longer a need to block a Russo-Japanese relationship in order to strengthen ties between Japan and the United States. However, the Northern Territories problem remains unresolved, leaving Japan at an impasse. Though the United States and Russia are friends, the onerous heritage of the Cold War still binding Japan and Russia continues. Now is the time for Japan to play a more independent role in north-east Asian international politics. Japan must re-examine the origins of the territorial dispute and find a way that would make a solution to the problem possible.

Fifty years after the end of the Second World War, Japan in the mid-1990s has had to confront the meaning of the past, in front of the critical eyes of its Asian neighbours. Whether the Japanese have managed to meet this test or not will have to be left for further studies. But it is obvious that Japan has neither passed through a 'moral revolution' nor acquired a 'new national psyche' as indicated by Chang Jun in 1948. Nevertheless, Japan in 1995 may be showing some signs of change with the Diet resolution of historical remorse, the Prime Minister's statement of 15 August, and the establishment of the Asian Women's fund for former 'comfort women'.

PART II

Domestic Issues

5

The Feminization of the Labour Market*

OSAWA MARI

I. Introduction

In this essay, I would like to articulate the following ideas: (1) Japan's extremely high economic growth springs out of the society's distinctive 'corporate-centred nature' (*kigyo chushin shakai*); and (2) the most fundamental and vital element of this corporate-centred society is a patriarchal system that controls women's labour both in the workplace and in the home.

Of these two points, the first is not my own original idea, as I will explain below. It is in fact one of the main themes of the multi-disciplinary research project on 'Contemporary Japanese Society' (*Gendai Nihon Shakai*) conducted by the Institute of Social Science (ISS), University of Tokyo, in 1986–91, for which this essay has been written. The notion of Japanese society as a corporate-centred society also has recently been shared by an increasingly larger segment of the general public. In contrast, the second point (the role of patriarchy) is rather new and produces a sense of unease, if not discomfort, especially among male scholars in the social sciences. In fact, even the assertion that the investigation of women's labour is an important prerequisite for rendering clear the fundamental structure of Japanese society still does not fit easily within the dominant paradigm of social science inquiry in Japan. The reason is that Japanese social science until recently, particularly in the field of economics, has developed by ignoring women. To borrow an expression from German feminist Claudia von Werlhof, women are the 'blind spot' of the social sciences.[1] This fact is expressed in archetypal fashion in the ISS's theories of 'corporate-centred society'.

II. Women as the Blind Spot in Social Science

According to the '*Joron: Gendai Nihon Shakai no Kozo to Tokushusei*' (The Structure and Characteristics of Contemporary Japanese Society: Introduction), hereafter known as the Introduction, to volume i, *Problems and Perspectives* (*Kadai to Shikaku*), of the ISS's seven-volume series *Contemporary Japanese Society*,

---

* Translated by Kirsten McIvor.

Japan, in its meteoric rise as an economic power during the first post-war period of marked economic growth, and after the oil crisis in 1973, embodies the 'universal nature' of modern capitalism, the major characteristic of which is this very type of rapid growth. The phenomenon of Japanese economic advancement, however, has brought not only prosperity, but a host of problems viewed by many as the penalty paid for its rapidity.

In searching for the basis of this growth, the Introduction explains, our attention is drawn inevitably to the 'unique structure' of Japanese society, the reason being that problems such as *karoshi* (death from overwork), excessively long working hours, confusion in the education system, and the disintegration of the family unit are all related to this distinctive social structure. One of the two major elements of Japan's remarkable growth is 'companyism', or corporate-centred society. The other is the international framework under which Japan is subordinate politically and militarily to the United States. Only the first element, however, has its origins within Japan itself.[2]

As noted in the Introduction, any study of 'companyism' would benefit from reference not only to the work of Baba Hiroji, but also to that of Watanabe Osamu. Here I would like to examine Baba's paper *'Gendai Sekai to Nihon Kaisha Shugi'* (Japanese Companyism and the Contemporary World) and Watanabe's book *'Yutaka na shakai' Nihon no Kozo* (The Structure of Japan, an 'Affluent Society').[3]

The phenomenon of 'companyism' dates back to Japan's first post-war period of rapid economic growth, and became truly established, perhaps even accelerating, in periods of slower, but steady, growth. In its narrowest sense, the term refers to the immense power that corporations have to integrate employees into the company culture. Baba emphasizes the strong sense of belonging that company employees feel, while Watanabe prefers to focus on the incredible power that management wields over the lives of workers.

With regard to the actual substance of companyism, Baba describes it as 'a subtle combination of capitalistic competition and communal or socialistic relationships'. Why communal or socialistic? One reason is that the power of owners to control business is so weak that it is difficult to find more than a handful of large-scale capitalists in Japan; another is the lack of differences in wages and job content within individual companies. In other words, employees are not 'alienated' as in 'classical capitalist labour relationships', but 'actively participate in management'. In Japanese companies, authoritarian practices and differences in rank are not obvious on the surface. Therefore, workers may voice their opinions freely on such matters as wage structures and management, and opportunities for promotion are available at every level of the organization.[4]

In contrast to Baba, Watanabe places emphasis not so much on 'participation' as on the ceaseless 'competition' between employees. The Japanese company system, he argues, is not in fact 'communal or socialistic' but an excellent example of 'bourgeois capitalism'. Watanabe believes this business culture based on companyism to be of a 'democratic' nature. Of course, for the small minority who refuse to participate in the fierce competition, the ensuing punishment may include physical violence, but for those who faithfully toe the company line, promotion is always a possibility if deemed appropriate after evaluation by management. Differences in status between blue- and white-collar workers no longer exist, with promotion a possibility for all loyal employees, so in this sense the system is indeed of a 'democratic nature'. Employees do not obey the company rules purely because they are forced to do so, Watanabe maintains, but voluntarily in hope of advancement.[5]

In this way, according to Baba, workers voluntarily develop their own productive capacity for the company, making companyism 'the most efficient method of increasing production in the history of mankind'.[6] However, according to Watanabe, in the high-growth period of the 1960s, this companyism or corporate-centred society really only covered regular employees of large private enterprises. It was after the 1973 oil crisis and the ensuing low-growth period that 'efficiency and competition' also severely affected workers in small and medium-sized companies via the subcontracting and *keiretsu* (corporate group) system. Rationalization and privatization brought pressure to bear even on the public sector.[7] Moreover, the effects came to influence the organization of labour unions, politics, education, and family, and defined the structure of contemporary Japanese society. This societal structure is the essence of the companyism or corporate-centred society in its broader sense.

How is this phenomenon of companyism, peculiar to Japan, related to a number of problems also peculiar to Japan? Baba contends that overdevelopment of productive capacity and excessive dominance of competition have drained Japanese society. These effects may be observed within the company itself, where there is not only discrimination against non-company-employees, and deliberate isolation of those who are too individualistic, but also cases of loyal employees dying from overwork. Even excluding the extreme of *karoshi*, we find that the world view of the loyal majority becomes frighteningly narrow. Knowledge of society, the state, the world at large, and even matters close to home is sacrificed in a preoccupation with the company, and the relentless race for efficiency produces employees who have lost the ability to think anything long-term. Companyism also drains the local community outside of the company, leaving it a hollow shell, because the people who form the nucleus of the community expend all their energy at work, leaving no time for local affairs. The phenomenon of *tanshin funin* whereby workers are transferred away from their families also contributes to this weakening of community ties.[8]

The theory of companyism leaves us in no doubt as to the suffocating nature of Japanese society, dominated as it is by competition and the drive for efficiency. There is, however, one glaring omission in both Baba's paper and that of Watanabe: the fact that even though women comprise half the members of society, and 40 per cent of the workforce, their presence is barely acknowledged.

Perhaps I am being a little hasty in concluding that women are virtually non-existent in these discussions. Could, one wonders, Baba and Watanabe be including women in their categories of 'workers' and 'employees'? Unfortunately, the evidence proves otherwise. While, as Baba states,[9] the companyism theory is based on the concepts of Japanese management and Japanese-type industrial relations, it is common knowledge that the so-called 'three divine treasures' (sanshu no jingi) of Japanese industrial relations—lifetime employment, the seniority system, and company unions—are only relevant when discussing the regular male employees of large corporations. Sumiya Mikio, then president of the Japan Institute of Labour, suggested in 1984 that a comprehensive theory of industrial relations should be devised to include small and medium-sized enterprises and women.[10] A study of Sumiya's reconstructed theory of industrial relations will show, however, that he has not succeeded in incorporating women comprehensively at all.

Sumiya proposed that the 'three divine treasures' of Japanese industrial relations be replaced by 'gradated', 'humanistic', and 'individual attributional' relationships. These concepts actually tie in very well with the theory of companyism. A gradated relationship in the context of industrial relations means one in which labour and management are side by side on a continuum of authority, rather than polarized at top and bottom of a vertical hierarchy of power. Humanistic describes a state whereby personal relationships form the basis of labour-management contact, making the company a type of communal body. Sumiya also uses the term 'the company as family' (keiei kazoku shugi) to describe this communal body, calling attention to Japanese tradition whereby the village existed as a geographically based community in conjunction with the kinship-based community of blood relations. Finally, individual attributional means that, just as workers' salaries are not determined so much by their actual job as by a set of individual attributes such as gender, education, age, experience, and length of service, so is the overall employment relationship. Among these various attributes, Sumiya points out that 'discrimination based on gender is the most influential'.[11]

He does not, however, explain the reasoning behind this statement. Nor does he elucidate on how the attribute of 'being a woman' interacts with the other two of his revised sacred treasures, or whether it stands on its own apart from them. This is despite the fact that it is very easy to imagine the type of gender-based differences in position and roles within the traditional Japanese home and village community. In any case, Sumiya's call to include women in theories of Japanese industrial relations has been largely ignored by researchers, and even today, important studies of women's labour, such as that of Takenaka Emiko, have not been incorporated into industrial relations theory.[12]

This problem is not confined to industrial relations research. Nakanishi Yo, for example, demonstrated that, from the time of the British classical economists, through Marx, to the neoclassicists, the field of economics has failed to incorporate the family into its analytical structure. According to Nakanishi, both Marx and the object of his criticism, J. S. Mill, viewed modern society as being made up of 'individuals'; these individuals, in fact, being the adult males at the head of each family.[13] It is thus not surprising that this kind of social science has ignored issues of the structure of families' internal distribution of goods and services. First and foremost, it seems to be women who have been deliberately ignored. The analytical perspective that equates the individual with the patriarch ignores the role of women within the family by treating the husband as the single representative of the family. Moreover, by regarding only the individual *qua* patriarch as society's essential unit, it ignores the existence and role of women not just in the family but in all areas of society.

The German Marxist feminist von Werlhof, following in the footsteps of Rosa Luxemburg, argues strongly that, by ignoring women, the field of economics is seriously flawed, not just in terms of wage theory but also in its interpretation of history, i.e., the understanding of the international division of labour between 'core' and 'peripheral' states.[14] How, then, does this exclusion of women relate to understanding contemporary Japanese society? In focusing on women's labour, what characteristics of Japanese society come to light? This chapter is an endeavour to deal with the issue of corporate-centred society or companyism in a straightforward manner, and to unlock the secret of how it was propagated and solidified in the 1980s, by focusing on women's work both at work and in the home.

III. Women's Labour in Modern-Day Japan

In this section, I would like to provide an overview of women's labour in Japan in the 1980s, and its role in the accumulation of capital, drawing primarily on comparisons with 'advanced' western nations, and occasionally with South Korea.[15]

First, it is important to grasp the distinction between paid and unpaid labour, and to understand the meaning of gender division of labour. Here I will make reference to the *Somucho* (Management and Co-ordination Agency) *Survey on Time Use and Leisure Activities (Shakai seikatsu Kihon Chosa)*, a survey of the daily activities of citizens 15 years of age and over, which has been conducted every five years since 1976. In these surveys, activities essential to physiological survival, such as eating and sleeping, are classified as primary activities, while those activities seen as obligatory duties for the maintenance of society such as paid work, commuting, housework, childrearing, shopping, schooling, and commuting to school, etc., are secondary activities. Tertiary activities consist of free time and leisure activities. Secondary activities may be interpreted as the total of social labour. At the time of the 1986 survey, 57.1 per cent of all social labour in Japan consisted of paid labour, 28.5 per cent of housework, childcare, and shopping, while the remainder covered commuting to school and work, and attending classes. Sixty-five per cent of paid labour was carried out by males, and 35 per cent by females, while over 93 per cent of unpaid labour was that of women. Males contributed no more than 6 per cent of unpaid labour.[16]

Even if there were no differences in hourly wage rates between men and women, this division of labour according to gender would still lead to a sizeable gap in income between the sexes. In actual fact, women only earn 50 per cent or at the most 60 per cent of the hourly wage rate of men. Thus, despite performing over half of the social labour in Japan, they earn only 20–5 per cent of the total wage income.

1. Paid labour

Participation

The first thing to note, regarding the participation of women in the labour force, is the low percentage of women who are actually employees. Only in the latter half of the 1960s did this group account for over 50 per cent of the female labour force, and even in 1990 it was no more than 72.3 per cent; 10.7 per cent of working women were self-employed, while the remaining 16.7 per cent were family workers (family relations of self-employed workers, who help out in the family business). In contrast, 80.8 per cent of males are paid employees, a figure not particularly low by international standards. (The figures for male self-employed and family workers are 16.3 per cent and 2.5 per cent respectively.) Comparing these figures with other countries, we find that in 1987 over 90 per cent of working women in Britain, the United States, and Canada were paid employees, while in France and the then West Germany the figure was over 85 per cent. The nations most comparable with Japan in terms of the percentage of employees among working women are Italy and Spain: it must be remembered, however, that both these countries have a large number of self-employed women, as opposed to female family workers. With the exception of Spain, in all these countries the percentage of employees among working women is greater than that among working men. Incidentally, a look at the situation in South Korea shows that the figures for women in paid employment, self-employed, and family workers were 55.3 per cent, 19.3 per cent, and 25.5 per cent respectively, while those for men were 61.8 per cent, 35.4 per cent, and 2.8 per cent.

These figures do not prove, however, that Japanese women are 'lagging' in their participation in the workforce as employees. Statistical resources are insufficient to conduct a direct comparison of the situation before and after the Second World War; however, any investigation of the employment situation of Japanese women before Japan went to war against China in 1930, which was to spark a conflict of some fifteen years, will show that women constituted over half of factory employees, and if we include the immense number of women who did textile piece-work in their homes, and domestic servants, the inescapable conclusion is that, before 1930, Japan's labour force of paid employees was overwhelmingly female. Since the war, the percentage of women employees in the paid labour force has risen again, albeit slowly, from 22 per cent in 1945[17] to 37.9 per cent in 1990. During that time, again with the late 1960s as the turning point, the nature of the female workforce has also changed. Originally consisting mainly of young and single women, the female paid labour force came in the late 1960s to be dominated by middle-aged and older, married women.

A graph of the labour force participation of Japanese women by age shows a bi-modal, M-shaped curve, with peaks in the 20s and 40s, only in Japan, and a lesser degree in the UK. This pattern of employment was formed around 1965 in Japan. Previously, the greatest number of female participants in the labour force had been aged 20–4, with a steady decline after 24, but after 1965 the proportion of working women in the 25–34 age group declined, and this combined with a rise in employment among middle-aged and older women to produce an M-shaped curve. The proportion of working women in the 25–34 age group continued to drop until 1975, since which it has begun to rise again. However, a concurrent rise in employment among women in the peak age groups has resulted in the shape of the curve remaining the same, with no likely change in the near future. The year 1975, directly after the oil shock, was the year that Japan recorded its lowest ever average female labour force participation rate.

The male–female wage gap

Once again I shall draw attention to the discrepancy between the wages paid to men and and those paid to women. The fact that the gap between the two has widened since the latter half of the 1970s cannot be viewed lightly, nor the fact that this widening coincides with the rise of the corporate-centred society. According to the Ministry of Labour's *Monthly Labour Survey* (*Maitsuki Kinro Tokei Chosa*), female wages in 1960 were 42.8 per cent of those of males. During the following period of rapid economic growth this gap shrank, with women's wage levels at 50.9 per cent of men's in 1970, and 56.2 per cent in 1978. Since 1978, however, the gap has been widening again, with women's wages in 1990 standing at 49.6 per cent of those of men (calculated on the basis of average monthly earnings for both full-time and part-time employees in workplaces with thirty or more workers).

In another survey conducted by the Ministry of Labour, the *Basic Survey on Wage Structure* (Chingin kozo kihon tokei chosa), which dealt with full-time workers in companies employing ten or more people, the wage gap was demonstrated to have shrunk in the first half of the 1970s, and remained at approximately the same level until 1985, since when it has closed further, women's wages being 57.1 per cent of those of men in 1990 (monthly regular earnings including pay for overtime).

These two types of survey also show that the increase in the gender-based wage gap is due largely to the increase in part-time workers in the labour force,[18] an issue I will address later. This situation invites comparison with that of the United States and Europe, where the wage gap has remained stable or has decreased slightly. However, the lack of data available makes it unwise to indulge in oversimplified comparisons between countries.[19]

The wage gap explained above is generally understood as being the product of either pure sex discrimination, or differences in productivity between men and women. In other words, differences able to be explained by viewing the worker as human capital and taking into account factors such as education, work experience, and size of company are termed 'reasonable' differences while remaining differences in men and women's wages, i.e., what cannot be explained, are seen as straight-out prejudice, or sex discrimination. It soon becomes obvious, however, that this analysis is far from convincing. The idea that factors such as education and length of employment are totally separable from gender is overly mechanistic and contradicts what anyone with common sense would observe. It is widely accepted, in fact, that the gender gap needs to be examined holistically, and that its major cause lies in the gender division and the segregation of men and women into different occupations.[20]

Here I would like to deviate from the main argument and examine the work of Ishikawa Tsuneo, who, in criticism of the theory of a pure wage gap as it relates to the difference in wages between companies of different sizes, studied male workers in the manufacturing sector.

Ishikawa disagreed with the theory that, once factors such as education, age, and length of employment are controlled, any remaining differences in wages are purely the result of company size, arguing that 'differences in length of experience in a company must be considered a result of difference in company size'.[21]

The fact that length of employment among people of the same age differs according to company size (the tendency being for people to be employed longer in large corporations) points to difference in length and intensity of job training according to the scale of the enterprise. Thus, part of the difference in wages calculated to be a result of differing lengths of employment must be seen as a true difference arising from variation in educational opportunities available to workers of equal calibre, over which they have no control.[21a]

Ishikawa emphasizes, therefore, that in considering wage differences one must note the type of job training, and the relevant system of labour management. Koike Kazuo also demonstrates this. Koike's work is of interest because his writings provide an important basis for Baba's theory of companyism.

Koike compared differences in wages in Japan with those Britain, France, and West Germany in the early 1970s. He found that, particularly for over the age of 30, the gap was very marked in Japan, making the overall wage gap greater in Japan than any of the other countries surveyed. This gender gap is not a result of the level of women's wages, but men's: in Japan, the age-related salary curve is steep for both white- and blue-collar male workers.[22]

This ties in with Koike's theory that male blue-collar workers in large Japanese corporations are undergoing 'white-collarization'. Advancement of workers' intellectual skills through broad-based on-the-job training does not only provide the basis for white-collarization, Koike claims; it is also the underlying factor in the efficiency of Japanese companies. What, then, of skill formation among female workers?

Segregation in its narrow sense

Let us return to the question of job segregation. Compared to other advanced industrial nations, the indices measuring job segregation in Japan are extremely low, as may be seen in Tables 5.1 and 5.2. I believe that this fact is one of the most important characteristics of job segregation in Japan. These figures are based on ILO statistics, and it should be noted that they use the total labour force as a base. The low level of these indices, however, does not correspond to a low level of job segregation itself, or mean that there is a high level of equality between males and females. In fact these WE indices (named after the OECD report *Women and Employment*) show nothing more than the relative measure of the number of women in every industry or occupation (the CFR, or coefficients of female representation, determined by dividing the proportion of women in each field by the proportion of women among all workers), from which 1 is subtracted to obtain an absolute number (known

TABLE 5.1. Occupational data, WE index[a]

(%)

	1970	1977	1978	1979	1980	1981	1982	1983
Canada	53.4[b]		49.9	49.5	46.9	46.7	44.6	40.9
W. Germany	41.8		44.0		44.1		44.2	
Japan	30.6	28.9	28.4	28.6	28.6	27.5	27.5	
United States	47.5	51.1	50.1	49.4	48.4	47.4	46.5	

Notes: (a) Calculated at the ISCO one-digit level
          (b) For 1971

Source: OECD, *The Integration of Women into the Economy*, Paris: OECD 1985: Table II.1

TABLE 5.2. Industrial sector data, WE index[a]

(%)

	1970	1976	1977	1978	1979	1980	1981
Canada	40.3[b]	39.0	39.0	38.9	37.9	37.0	36.4
W. Germany	35.2	35.6	35.3	35.0	35.2	35.0	36.3
Japan	22.3	23.5	23.4	23.1	23.2	22.7	22.0
United Kingdom	39.0	40.8	40.3	40.4	40.6	40.9	41.2

Notes: (a) Calculated at the ISCO one-digit level
(b) For 1975

Source: OECD, op. cit., 1985: Table II.3

as the 'deviation'), which is then adjusted to a weighted average. The weighting is based on the relative number of workers in each industry or occupation. For reference, according to the OECD, the formula of the WE index is as follows:

$$\sum_{i=1}^{k} \left(\frac{N_{fi}/N_i}{N_f/N} - 1 \right) \times \frac{N_i}{N} \times 100\%, \text{ and } CFR_i = \frac{N_{fi}/N_i}{N_f/N}$$

It may also be written as $\sum_{i=1}^{k} \left(\frac{N_{fi}}{N_f} - \frac{N_i}{N} \right) \times 100\%$ and thus can be seen as the

sum of the difference between the female share of each employment category and the total share of each category without respect for sign; of which

N_{fi} is the number of women in employment category i,
N_i is the number of persons in employment category i,
N_f is the number of women in total employment,
N is the total number of persons in employment,
k is the number of employment categories.[23]

Figures 5.1 and 5.2 are graphical representations of the segregation index I devised, as broken down into its constituent elements in accordance with the foregoing formula with the vertical axis showing the incidence of women in each category and the horizontal axis showing each classification's share in the total working population or in total employment. In these figures, the segregation index is equal to the sum of the dotted and the shadowed areas. By comparing the segregation indices for Japan with those for other countries on the basis of these figures, we can tentatively pinpoint the factors which seem to be primarily responsible for keeping the segregation index of Japan lower than that of other countries.

Figures 5.1 (*a*), (*b*), and (*c*) show the segregation indices by occupation for the United States, West Germany, and Japan in the mid-1980s. From the Figure 5.1 diagrams, we may see that the Japanese segregation index is low

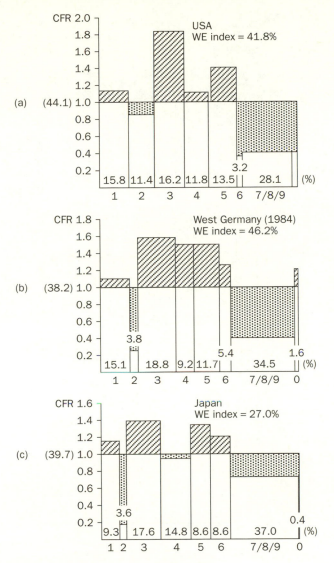

FIG. 5.1-a,b,c Gender segregation by occupations, 1985

Note: The occupations are defined according to the *International Standard Classification of Occupations (ISCO)*.

   (1) Professional, technical and related workers
   (2) Administrative and managerial workers
   (3) Clerical and related workers
   (4) Sales workers
   (5) Service workers
   (6) Agriculture, animal husbandry and forestry workers, fishermen, and hunters
   (7/8/9) Production and related workers, transport equipment operators, and labourers
   (0) Workers not classified by occupation

Source: ILO, *Yearbook of Labour Statistics*, 1986, Table 2B

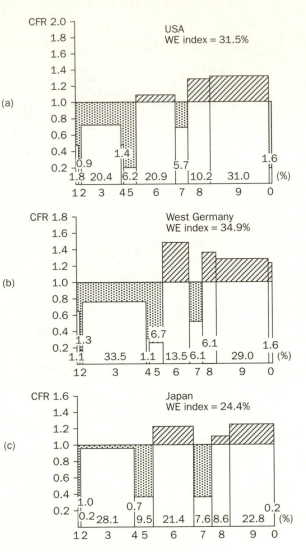

FIG. 5.2.-a,b,c Gender segregation by industries, 1986 (Employees)

Note: The industries are defined according to the *International Standard Industrial Classification (ISIC)*.
  (1) Agriculture, hunting, forestry, and fishing
  (2) Mining and quarrying
  (3) Manufacturing
  (4) Electricity, gas, and water
  (5) Construction
  (6) Wholesale and retail trade, restaurants, and hotels
  (7) Transport, storage, and communication
  (8) Financing, insurance, real estate, and business services
  (9) Community social and personal services
  (0) Other

Source: ILO, *Yearbook of Labour Statistics*, 1987.
          Figure constructed by the author from Table 2A in Yearbook. The sum of the area of the dotted and
          diagonal-line sections is equal to the segregation indices.

because (1) even though the relative share of total workers in production, transportation, and manual labour (groups 7/8/9) is high, in these areas the deviation from 1 is not large, i.e., the CFR is not especially low; and (2) in the second-largest sector, clerical workers (group 3), which accounts for the largest proportion of female workers, the CFR is not especially high.

Figures 5.2 (a), (b), and (c), on the other hand, show the industrial segregation of employees (i.e., excluding self-employed and family workers). From the figures, we can see that the Japanese workplace segregation index is low, because: (1) Japanese women's CFR in manufacturing is close to 1; and (2) the relative size of the service sector is small and the CFR in services is not particularly high. The general view of women's entrance into the ranks of paid employees is one of tandem development with the rise of the service industry and white-collarization about which, it appears, we should have serious reservations.

The situation regarding job segregation in Japan cannot be easily grasped by looking only at the broad classifications of industry and occupation. Rather, what should be examined are differences in company size, job types, and grades within individual organizations, and categories of employment.

Differences in company size

Company size is important in Japan because it is one of the major factors contributing to differences in remuneration, and in Japan 55 per cent of female employees are concentrated in small businesses (those with ninety-nine employees or less). The percentage of males in small companies is 45 per cent, and neither of these figures has altered significantly since 1965.

Koike, furthermore, made some international comparisons of company-size-based wage differences, finding that, in 1972, Japan's figures were close to those of Italy, the country in the EC showing the greatest discrepancy between wages in companies of differing size. Between 1954 and 1970 the gap in wages narrowed dramatically, he points out, but has remained much the same since then. For some reason, however, Koike confined his study to the wages of male manual labourers in the manufacturing sector: therefore, within the overall context of a stabilization of the wage gap, the decrease in the gap between the wages of workers in their 40s from the late 1970s on applies only to men. In addition, the reason given by Koike for this narrowing of the wage gap between workers in different size companies is that the number of workers with intellectual skills increasing in small and medium-sized companies as well as large ones which again applies only to men.[24]

A study of statistics published in the Basic Survey on Wage Structure concerning the age and education level of workers shows that, since the late 1970s, the wage gap between companies of differing sizes has been slowly growing. Furthermore, as shown in Figure 5.3, this difference is greater with regard to

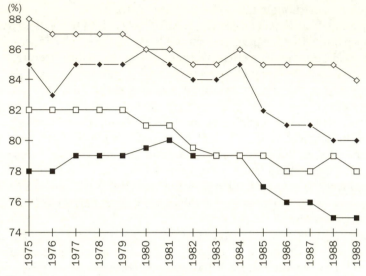

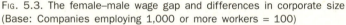

FIG. 5.3. The female–male wage gap and differences in corporate size
(Base: Companies employing 1,000 or more workers = 100)

Note: Average monthly earnings, excluding over-time pay, of full-time employees in private sector
—◇— Male employees of medium-sized companies employing 100–999 persons
—◆— Female employees of medium-sized companies employing 100–999 persons
—□— Male employees of small companies employing 10–99 persons
—■— Female employees of small companies employing 10–99 persons

Source: Rodosho (Ministry of Labour), *Chingin kozo kihon tokei chosa* (The Basic Survey on Wage Structure)

female than male workers. In the early 1980s, the wage gap for males according to company size widened a fraction compared to the late 1970s, resulting
in an equal difference in wages between both males and females of different
sized companies. In the late 1980s, however, the gap widened again for women,
making it once more greater for them than for their male colleagues.

The phenomenon of wage gaps between employees in different sized companies may be observed among female as well as male workers. However,
research in the field is constantly frustrated by dead ends, i.e., a lack of data
available on women. In *Labour Conditions of Women* (*Fujin Rodo no Jitsujo*),
published by the Ministry of Labour, company-size-based wage differences
are barely mentioned, and in the 'White Paper on Labour' (*Rodo Hakusho*),
the only data on the subject are concerned with men.

Segregation within companies

Now let us move on to segregation by job category and grade within individual companies. As Kumazawa Makoto pointed out, since half-way through
the period of rapid economic growth in Japan, a 'qualification-based' (*shikaku*)

or 'job-ability based' (*shokuno bunrui*) system has taken hold, and under this system full-time female employees have been pushed into repetitive subsidiary tasks paying low wages, with little chance of those wages increasing. Not only this, but the desire to continue in paid employment for long periods is discouraged, and the phenomenon of women leaving the company after a relatively short period has in fact become built into the system. In his study of the qualifications of workers at Toshiba in 1973, and at Nanajunana Bank in 1976, Kumazawa confirmed that women are forced into low-level positions, remaining concentrated at the lowest part of a pyramid-like employment structure where promotion is blocked. Takenaka Emiko demonstrated the same tendency at S Bank and C Precision Machinery Manufacturing in 1970, as shown in the basic wage curves based on job ability at these companies.[25]

This system provides the foundation for the smooth functioning of Japan's merit-based labour management structure. The high turnover rate of women, who remain at the lower levels of the employment ladder, is precisely what enables 'loyal' male employees to be promoted. In another study Kumazawa argues that the 'community' within large Japanese steel companies is nothing more than a community of full-time (male) workers engaged in the mutual struggle for promotion.[26] Women are excluded from this competition from the very beginning, and remain as outsiders, ensuring that competition between male employees does not become so intense as to destroy this supposed sense of 'community'. Later, I will elaborate on this point, drawing on the example of the microelectronic technological innovation at Hitachi. In workplaces with very few women, temporary workers or outside workers (those employed by subcontractors but actually working in the larger company's factory) fill the same roles.

Admittedly, there has been a slight increase in promotion opportunities for women in recent years, but the positive effect of this has been negated by the increasing employment of women in categories other than permanent full-time ones.

The gender gap in employment categories

The gender gap in employment categories is related to the gender-based wage gap and the company size-based wage gap. As I discussed in detail in another paper[27] problems surrounding the definition of part-time workers, and their actual working conditions make the situation in Japan even more peculiar. First, since the 1970s the proportion of official 'part-time workers' (*tanjikan koyosha*, or persons working no more than 35 hours per week) has gradually increased, and this is essentially due to the increasing proportion of women part-time workers. While the percentage of men working part-time was consistently 5–6 per cent to the end of the 1980s, the same proportion for women came to exceed 27 per cent in non-agricultural work (the percentage of all part-time workers comprised by women was 72.4 per cent in 1988 and 68.6 per cent in 1990). Moreover, the definitions of 'regular employees', 'part-timers', 'temporary workers', and others are decided by companies themselves without regard to the actual number of days or hours worked. Data from a 1987 survey reveal that just 60.6 per cent of women employees are regular employees, while the proportion of part-timers and temporary workers has risen to 31.7 per cent. This is in contrast to male percentages of 83.2 per cent regular and 4 per cent part-time/temporary workers. Seventy per cent of all regular workers are men, and 82 per cent of all part-time workers are women. These data make clear that the number of persons who are called 'part-timers' or 'temporary workers' far exceeds the actual number of part-timers who work less than 35 hours per week.

In the '1990 Comprehensive Survey of the Condition of Part-Time Workers' by the Ministry of Labour, the most recent and comprehensive study of part-time workers in Japan, the main criterion for defining 'part-time workers' is that they are 'treated as so-called part-timers' and not as regular employees. The reason the study did not define part-time work simply by the length of work hours was because past surveys indicated that many workers are called 'part-timers' and treated as such even though they are working virtually full-time. These workers, who are often called 'full-time part-timers', or 'pseudo-part-timers', have been categorized as 'Part-timer B' in the 1990 survey. As for the results of the 1990 survey, 1,200,000, or 20 per cent, of the 5,840,000 'so called part-timers' were grouped as 'Part-timer B', of whom 710,000 were female.[28]

Table 5.3 shows the working conditions of 'so-called part-timers' according to gender and group (710,000 student part-timers are subtracted here). The first thing we notice is the long work-week of Japan's 'part-time' workers. Not many have two days off a week and overtime is customary, not an exception to the rule. Considering that work hours of part-time workers in the EU countries seems to be about 20 hours a week, even Japan's 'Part-timer A' group appears 'overworked' to be called 'part-time'. Second, Japan's part-time workers are very poorly paid compared to regular employees. According to the annual Wage Census, the average fixed wage for female full-time workers in 1990 was 175,000 yen per month, which amounts to 988.7 yen per hour, while the average hourly wage of female part-time workers was 712 yen. In some European countries and Australia, the hourly wage rates of part-time workers are as much as 80 per cent and sometimes over 100 per cent of those of full-time workers. Thus, part-time employment in Japan is characterized not only by long working hours, but also by low wage rates.

The third remarkable thing in Table 5.3 is that wage rates for group B are not higher than group A, even though work hours for the former are about equal in length to those of regular employees. Theoretically, the fixed costs, such as those for recruitment, training, and social security, are higher

Table 5.3. Working conditions of 'part-timers' by gender and group (student part-timers excluded)

		Female		Male	
		A	B	A	B
Number of workdays per week	(days)	5.2	5.6	5.0	5.6
Designated work hours per week	(hours)	28.7	42.8	26.3	43.1
Designated work hours per day	(hours)	5.7	7.7	5.5	7.8
Ratio of overtime workers	(%)	21.3	42.1	20.2	45.1
and average hours of their overtime					
for Sept. 1990	(hours)	8.8	10.1	13.2	18.9
Average of real work hours for year					
1989	(hours)	1285.3	1806.0	1200.9	1965.7

Workers' ratio according to form of payment (%), and average wage according to form of payment

by the hour	(%)	87.7	56.0	59.2	26.8
	yen	669.0	663.0	1015.0	790.0
by the day	(%)	6.0	26.0	18.0	35.0
	yen	6640.0	6734.0	7434.0	7565.0
by the month	(%)	4.7	17.1	16.8	36.2
	1000 yen	100.0	142.0	116.0	198.0

Source: Rodosho (Ministry of Labour), *Heisei 2-nen paatotaima no jittai* (*The Actual Situation of Part-time Workers in 1990, A Report of a Comprehensive Survey on Part-time Workers*), Tokyo, Finance Ministry Press, 1992.

per working hour for short-hour workers, so it is said that it is economically rational for there to be lower pay even for equal work. But the figures in Table 5.3 belie such a theory. An econometric study done by Nagase Nobuko based on a different survey to find the wage function for women in Japan indicates that short-hour workers (those who work less than 35 hours a week) have higher wage rates than those who work longer hours with the same attributes (levels of education, skill, length of service, etc.).[29] Nagase has also found that female part-timers B in the 1990 Comprehensive Survey were hardly more internalized than female part-timers A.[30]

The theory that there is rationality in the pay being lower for workers working shorter hours is thus not corroborated in the Japanese context.

Rather, Japanese part-time workers are paid lower wages and deprived of fringe benefits not because they work shorter hours, but precisely because they are 'treated' as 'part-time workers' regardless of their work hours. In other words, my present hypothesis is that it is more realistic to consider 'part-timer' as a 'status'. It is mostly through an increase in the number of this kind of female part-timers that the feminization of employment in Japan has been taking place.

It may be argued that the feminization of employment mainly through employment of women as part-time workers is by no means a phenomenon limited to Japan, but is shared by other advanced countries as well. To probe into this question, let us look at Table 5.4, which compares the situation of part-time workers in major countries. The number of female employees increased significantly in the period from 1979 to 1986 in countries such as Canada, the United States, Japan, and Italy. In the countries other than Japan, the increase in female employees was mostly accounted for by increases in the number of full-time employees. In stark contrast, Japan in the same period saw a 10 per cent increase in female employees, but as much as two-thirds of that increase was accounted for by part-time workers. It seems safe to say that this is what makes the feminization of employment in Japan so peculiar. One thing we must keep in mind here is that the definition of a part-time worker, as explained in the footnote to the table, differs from one country to the next; and that the definition for Japan adopted here is more restrictive both than that used in other countries and than the several altern-ative definitions used in Japan.

Then, what sort of effects has the Equal Employment Opportunity Law had on the peculiarly Japanese feminization of employment? According to Hanami Tadashi, chairman of the Central Labour Standards Council, private companies are taking an increasingly greater interest in differentiating their workers into two distinctive groups to use them more effectively. One group consists of a small number of efficient, core workers (male), and the other consists of a 'large number of peripheral workers who can be readily replaced'. 'It is obvious', Hanami concludes, 'that women and immigrant workers are expected to constitute the latter group. The gist of the problem is that laws such as the Equal Employment Opportunity Law fit in perfectly with this design'.[31] In other words, the law is tailored to the patriarchal corporate-centred society.

Subcontracting and segregation

Gender-based job discrimination plays a vital role in the world-famous efficiency of Japanese corporations, a fact which becomes even more evident when we include the subcontracting system in our investigation. The theory of companyism states that 'the longevity of business relationships' is the driving force behind increased production; subcontracting, however, does not receive the same attention. Despite this omission it is common knowledge that, particularly in the automobile and electronics industries, a pyramid-like structure exists which is comprised of countless layers of subcontractors, the bottom level of this hierarchy consisting of piecework done in the home. Large numbers of family workers who represent 17 per cent of Japanese working

TABLE 5.4. A comparison of part-time workers in major countries: their share in the total working population, women's share in part-time workers, and female part-time workers' share in women workers* (%)

	Male and female part-time workers as % of total working population				Female part-time workers as % of total female working population			
	1973	1979	1983	1986	1973	1979	1983	1986
USA	14.0	14.4	14.4		23.8	24.1	23.3	
		16.8	18.4	17.4		26.7	28.1	26.4
Britain	16.0	16.4	19.1	21.2	39.1	39.0	42.4	44.9
Italy	6.4	5.3	4.6	5.3	14.0	10.6	9.4	10.1
Canada	10.6	12.5	15.4	15.6	20.3	23.3	26.2	25.9
W. Germany	10.1	11.4	12.6	12.3	24.4	27.6	30.0	28.4
Japan	7.9	9.6	10.5	11.7	17.3	18.4	21.1	22.8
France	7.2	8.2	9.7	11.7	14.7	17.0	20.1	23.1

	Women's share in part-time workers				Percentage breakdown of increments in female employment in 1975–86 by part-timers and full-time employees		
	1973	1979	1983	1986	Part-time	Full-time	Total
USA	68.4	63.8	70.3				
		67.8	66.8	66.5	4.5	13.8	18.3
Britain	90.9	92.8	89.6	88.5	6.4	−5.3	1.1
Italy	58.3	61.4	64.8	61.6	0.3	7.2	7.5
Canada	69.5	72.1	71.3	71.2	8.7	15.0	23.7
W. Germany	89.0	91.6	91.9	89.8	8.4	−7.4	1.0
Japan	60.9	64.5	70.7	70.0	6.7	3.3	10.0
France	77.9	82.0	84.6	83.0	7.1	−2.6	4.5

Note: * A part-time worker is defined as follows in different countries

USA: A person who at the time of the survey was working less than 35 hours a week of his/her own will, not for economic reasons.

Britain: A person who considers himself/herself a part-time worker (or a person who is called such).

Italy: A person who works shorter hours than the normal working hours.

Canada: A person who normally works less than 30 hours a week (but the definition excludes those who identify themselves as full-timers even if they work less than 30 hours a week).

West Germany: A person who considers himself/herself a part-time worker (or a person who is called such).

Japan: A person who at the time of the survey was working less than 35 hours a week (but the definition excludes those who were on leave of absence).

France: A person who considers himself/herself a part-time worker, or who works less than 30 hours a week.

Source: Rodosho Fujinkyoku (Ministry of Labour Women's Bureau), *Fujin rodo no jitsujo* (The Labour Conditions of Women) [1987: Attached Table 107; 1988: Attached Table 112].

women (12 per cent in the non-agricultural sector) work for very small sub-contractors at the bottom of this pyramid.[32]

In the early 1980s, two detailed investigations of technological innovation in the microelectronics industry concluded that subcontracting and gender-based job segregation are two major factors in Japan's international competitiveness, an extremely significant finding. The first of these investigations, conducted by the Chuo University Institute of Economics, studied automobile part subcontractors in the city of Ueda and its surrounds, in Nagano Prefecture, examining also the lifestyle and working conditions of their main source of labour, the local agricultural communities. The researchers concluded, in the published report entitled *ME Gijutsu Kakushinka no Shitauke Kogyo to Noson Henbo* (Subcontracting Industries and Social Change of Rural Districts as a Result of ME Innovation), that, taking into account the wage differences between companies of various sizes, location (urban or rural), gender, and employment categories, housewives in rural communities come out the worst off of any group, and the system which enables these women to be mobilized in large numbers is truly 'the foundation of Japan's superior international competitiveness in strategic industries'.[33] For a closer look at this system of employment, let us examine the example of one operation, that of a brake assembly subcontractor.

The Aoki works of N. Industries, located in the village of Aoki near Ueda, in Nagano Prefecture, is a small operation manufacturing aluminium alloy brakes and cylinders, and employing fifty workers, of whom thirty-seven are women. At the time of the study, between 1983 and 1985, the average age of female employees was 44–5 years, all were farmer's wives living within walking distance of the workplace, and all received between 4,500 and 6,000 yen a day in wages, the average being 5,000 yen. Of the thirteen males, four, including the factory manager, were in management positions, and the daily wage of the men on the shop floor was 6,000 yen. Daily attendance at work was high at 96 per cent for all employees. The work involved operating several machines with cycle times of 15 and 35 seconds in a 'multi-task assembly system'. At the company's main assembly works, it was noted, 'these tasks are performed by men, but at the Aoki branch, they are mainly the responsibility of women, excluding the night shift'. The report paints a picture of these women engaged in this precision work as follows: 'Middle-aged and older farm housewives covered in oil carried out the thirty second production cycle repeatedly, moving between the machines and flicking switches with not a second to spare—an amazing sight.'[34] One wonders how the 'intellectual skill' theory would evaluate their performance.

It is not only women actually employed by subcontractors who play an important role, but also those seen to be at the bottom of the pile, family workers. As is demonstrated by the example of a machinery alloys maker, also located in Aoki, a considerable number of the very small businesses at the bottom end of the subcontracting chain are also involved in farming, meaning that the women engaged in agricultural labour for their families are also the mainstays of these subcontracting operations. It became clear during the investigation that subcontractors and their families are often forced to work long hours, sometimes until late at night, to meet the strict demands for prompt delivery for which the automobile industry is known. Unfortunately the report omits to give details of the gender of these family workers and whether or not they are paid for their labour.[35]

The 'Japanese model' and segregation

On the other hand, an investigation of the increasing use of microelectronics at Hitachi, *FA Kara CIM we: Hitachi no Jirei Kenkyu* (From FA to CIM: A Case Study of Hitachi), conducted by Tokunaga Shigeyoshi and Sugimoto Noriyuki, questions the working conditions which form the foundation of the 'Japanese model' that has received much acclaim from business leaders and governments in other 'advanced' nations. The 'Japanese model' describes the system by which regular employees are guaranteed work, industrial relations run smoothly, and technological innovation is carried out on an ongoing basis, enabling Japanese industry to remain extremely competitive in the international marketplace.

In Tokunaga's summary however, co-written by Nomura Masami, the authors point out that guaranteed employment for regular staff (who are also union members) is only made possible by (1) adjusting the amount of work done within the company by adjusting subcontractual relationships; (2) employing and laying off non-regular staff where necessary; and (3) employing young women as regular workers.[36] This last condition refers not only to the fact that young women are used as buffers in the labour market, i.e., employers choose whether or not to replace them when they leave, according to the business climate, but, as I will demonstrate, the fact that the presence of these women enables men to avoid repetitive, de-humanizing tasks.

According to chapter 6 on the Hitachi Tokai VTR plant (written by Mawatari Shoken and Hirachi Ichiro), factory automation divides types of job into three categories: highly skilled factory automation jobs, less-skilled factory automation jobs, and simple assembly and inspection jobs. This was the situation when the 'Y-meka' assembly line was introduced at the Tokai plant. The Y-meka assembly line was a fully automated line developed in 1985 with the aim of giving Hitachi an edge over its competitors in the race to produce the first VCR priced at under 100,000 yen. The previous 'U-meka' line had employed 35 workers, while the Y-meka needed only 22 (18 when fully completed), and eliminated the need for 130 workers previously employed by subcontractors. A study of the line shortly after it came into production showed that of 15 workers, 11 were male, all of whom were engaged in PM (preventive maintenance). Two of the women were engaged in hand assembly, and the remaining two in quality control.

The preventive maintenance men were responsible for the operation and maintenance of the machinery, and were divided into low-, mid-, and high-level grades according to the difficulty of the work. Low-level maintenance men, of whom there were eight, were responsible for several work stations each, observing everyday operation and responding to any temporary problems. Their work also included some simple programming. Mid-level maintenance men, of whom there were two, were each responsible for half the assembly line, cooperating with the low-level maintenance men to carry out large-scale maintenance work (including improvements in the workplace, operation, and production processes), and the development of new programmes. The remaining maintenance worker, the most skilled, was responsible for the entire line, carrying out similar tasks to production engineers, programming work, and major overhauls/maintenance of equipment. He was not involved in the day-to-day operation of the line.

Under these circumstances a polarization between low-level and high-level factory automation jobs would be expected to occur. However, in an effort to avoid creating a rigid hierarchy, job descriptions were made broad and overlapping, enabling the low-level maintenance workers to obtain the skills necessary for promotion.

In contrast, the four women on the assembly line, all of whom were 20 years old, were, at Grade 4, among the lowest-ranking workers in the factory. The hand assembly workers were wedged in between robots, carrying out simple repetitive assembly tasks at a high speed dictated by them. The quality control work required using the human senses of sight and touch to perform the same precise movements over and over. When one considers that at the time the plant was producing almost 200,000 VCRs per month, it is not difficult to see why even the personnel management described these women's work as 'using human beings as machines' and 'difficult to endure'.[37]

With regard to the full-time male employees in factory automation jobs, even though the work at the lower levels was 'not that difficult', the company recognized the possibility that workers would be alienated and dissatisfied if the jobs were too rigidly stratified, so every effort was made to avoid this occurring. Ways were devised to minimize differences and divisions among the male employees, and from the lower levels up they were encouraged to be 'independent'. All this served to intensify further the rigid job stratification between men and women at the plant. Female workers were not given the opportunity to develop skills or branch out into other types of work.

This type of system does not only exist at Hitachi, but is the usual way in which large Japanese corporations carry out the 'allocation of educational opportunities' or 'intellectual skill formation' in their labour force. At any rate, the type of hand assembly and quality control work said to be 'impossible for one person to carry out for any length of time' is allocated only to women, and without any 'special allowances or consideration in terms of job grading'. The reason given for this is that apparently 'because the vast majority of women are employed only for a relatively short period, the labour unions have never paid them much attention'.[38]

Even assuming that union officials at Hitachi had no interest in the advancement of female employees, what about female union members themselves? Did they have no demands whatsoever? This of course, was not the case. As Nomura explains in chapter 8 of the same work, according to a survey conducted among employees by the Hitachi union in 1984, which asked their opinions on how the union should respond to the increasing automation of factories made possible by microelectronics, both males and females saw 'health and injury issues' as the union's first priority (each person was allowed to make two choices); interestingly however, only 33 per cent of males gave this answer, as opposed to 56.9 per cent of females. Number two priority for women was 'fair distribution, and expansion, of educational opportunities' (32.8 per cent), while in marked contrast, this issue did not even feature in the top five concerns of male employees.[39] While expressing concern about damage to their health caused by the repetitive nature of their work at the 'coal face' of factory automation, these young women were also clearly pinning their hopes for advancement on opportunities for acquiring skills and training. One cannot help but conclude that the relatively short period of employment of women is not a problem that business finds itself faced with over which it has no control, but rather a situation created by companies which allocate women the most boring, soul-destroying work, and alleviated in no way by unions which refuse to listen to the demands of their female members.

We know, of course, that women's working lives do not end with that 'short period' during their youth. Within ten years of leaving work to raise a family, many will return to the workforce as part-time employees in small companies. Rates of pay for these women, generally without skills or training, frequently fall below the legal minimum wage, and though the work is often of a repetitive nature, it can be extremely intensive, as described in the case of the N. Industries Aoki plant. After a number of job changes and the eventual acquiring of a certain level of skill at their work, these women are then forced to leave in order to take care of their elderly parents, or those of their husband, and eventually the husband himself.

2. Unpaid labour: some examples from Tokyo

At this point I feel it is time we moved on to the topic of family life. As previously observed, the companyism or corporate-centred society produces 'a loyal majority of workers . . . whose field of vision becomes extremely narrow'; however I believe the word 'male' should be added to this statement. As a survey of women in management positions makes clear, even high-ranking women in large corporations do not escape the extra burden of housework.[40] Even if a woman's field of vision becomes too narrow to include 'global and national issues', she cannot become so involved with the company that she loses touch with the details of everyday life. In contrast, men are able to devote themselves body and soul to the company only because they can leave all responsibility for the home to their wives, even that for their own personal daily needs. In the theory of the companyism, it is tacitly assumed that the 'wife' is not only responsible for raising the next generation of workers, i.e., the children, but that she will vicariously ensure the ongoing ability of her husband to perform at work.

'The new gender division of labour'

This role of 'wife' does not disappear with the 'entry of married women into the workplace' or the 'externalization of domestic work'. Rather what occurs is a 'new gender division of work', whereby the husband goes out to work, and the wife goes out to work and does the housework as well. This may be confirmed by examining the above-mentioned *Shakai Seikatsu Kihon Chosa* (Survey on Time Use and Leisure Activities) conducted by the Management and Coordination Agency.

Looking at nuclear families and distinguishing between households where wives work and those where they do not, we find that the hardest 'workers', i.e., those who spend the longest hours engaged in labour of some form or another, are wives in dual-income families, who spend over 10.5 hours per day performing 'secondary activities'. The next 'hardest workers' are husbands whose wives do not work outside the home, at just under 10 hours per day (1 hour and 12 minutes of which is commuting time), with husbands in dual-income households spending 9.5 hours (55 minutes of which is commuting).

With regard to an important 'primary activity', sleep, we may note that husbands whose wives work get the most, at 7 hours 39 minutes per night; while those whose wives do not get slightly less at 7 hours 34 minutes per night. In contrast, even wives who do not work outside the home obtain less sleep than their husbands, at 7 hours 14 minutes, while working wives get a mere 7 hours 7 minutes, a full half-hour less than their husbands. The amount of time husbands devote to housework each day is 8 minutes for men in dual-income households, and 7 for those whose wives do not work outside the home, so it would appear that having a spouse in outside employment has next to no impact on male shouldering of domestic chores. These figures are for 1986; sleep time decreased for all groups in comparison with 1981, and time spent engaged in secondary and tertiary activities increased for all groups (with the exception of secondary activities performed by working wives, which decreased by 6 minutes a day). Apart from these changes, all figures showed the same pattern in 1986 as they did five years earlier.

A look at the 1986 figures for how people spend their time on Sundays shows that, in families where both husband and wife work 35 or more hours per week, wives spent 7 hours and 17 minutes engaged in secondary activities, only just over three hours less than on weekdays, the reason being that housework, childcare, and shopping eat up 5 hours 22 minutes, almost 2 hours more than on weekdays. Husbands, it must be admitted, do engage in more housework on days off, however, at only 59 minutes, they still manage 8 hours 10 minutes of leisure time, over twice the amount they have on workdays. Their wives only enjoy 5 hours of spare time, and even then the time spent on primary activities such as sleeping is still 30 minutes less than their spouses.[41]

Perhaps we should clarify exactly what is meant by 'housework' in these surveys. No definition is given, so we must assume that 'housework' refers to the domestic tasks commonly thought of as such. But by whom? Are we to assume that men and women have the same ideas on the subject?

A survey entitled *Tomobataraki Kazoku/Sengyo Shufu Kazoku Hikaku Chosa* (Comparative Survey of Dual and Single Income Households) conducted in March 1989 by the Asahi Kasei Institute for Dual-Income Families is revealing. Three hundred and fifty households in the Tokyo metropolitan area were asked questions about the division of responsibility for thirty-four domestic chores in their homes, excluding the care of children and invalids. Survey results showed that even when the wife was engaged in full-time employment, she still shouldered 82 per cent of the responsibility for housework, as opposed to her husband's 5 per cent (other individuals and miscellaneous accounted for a further 4 per cent each), and if she worked part-time, the figure rose to 90 per cent, with her husband responsible for 4 per cent. If the wife did not work outside the home, her responsibility for housework rose further, to 93 per cent, her spouse's falling to 2 per cent.

Leaving aside this high level of wives' responsibility for chores, let us examine more closely the actual content of male housework. To our amazement we find that number one on the list of male responsibilities in the home is 'fetching the newspaper', number two is cleaning the extractor fan, and number three is polishing shoes (in households where the wife works part-time, two and three are interchanged), and if we exclude number one, the inclusion of which in the category of housework is dubious to say the least, the share of husbands falls by 1 per cent across all groups. Cleaning the extractor fan in the kitchen is without a doubt a worthy contribution, but a household which did this even once a month would be considered fanatically clean, and in fact this task, according to the same survey, is usually carried out only once or twice a year.[42]

A brief comparison with other countries

This situation is unique from an international perspective, though admittedly there is not much material available for comparison. One survey, entitled *Seikatsu Jikan no Kozo Bunseki* (An Study of Time Budget Structure), conducted in 1975 by Keizai Kikakucho (the Economic Planning Agency), and including some international comparisons, states that the Japanese pattern whereby 'working males sleep well, and housewives less than anyone' is opposite to the situation elsewhere. The 'Japanese' referred to here are the respondents to a survey conducted in the city of Matsuyama in 1972, and the international data are derived from surveys carried out between 1964 and 1966 by a group of mainly Hungarian researchers.[43] A more recent investigation, conducted by Ito Setsu and Amano Hiroko in the 1980s, surveyed the residents of Tama New Town in Tokyo, and, while admitting the difficulty of international comparisons, concluded that, because Japanese males spend so much less time on housework than their wives, 'gender roles are more inflexible in Japan than other countries'.[44]

Another survey, published by the Prime Minister's Office in 1982, and entitled *Fujin Mondai ni Kansuru Kokusai Hikaku Chosa* (An International Comparative Survey on Life and Attitudes of Women), focused on women in legal or common-law marriages in Japan, the Philippines, the United States, Sweden, West Germany, and Britain. Women were questioned on who was responsible in their homes for the following six domestic chores—cleaning, laundry, shopping, food preparation, clearing up after meals and washing dishes, and care of young children. In Japan wives were shown to be responsible for over 90 per cent of work in each of the main categories (for clearing up after meals the figure was 88.6 per cent, for care of children 75.6 per cent), well above the other countries surveyed, with the exception of the Philippines, where wives were found to be responsible for 87.4 per cent of the care of young children.

Another characteristic of the Japanese situation was the relatively small difference—10 per cent—between the responsibility for domestic chores of housewives and those employed full-time. Furthermore, it appears that in Japan, the younger the wife, the more housework she does. This is in stark contrast to other countries, where in general such chores are shared more evenly between younger partners, the exceptions being the Philippines and Britain, where young wives shoulder most of the responsibility for clearing up after meals, cleaning, and laundry.[45] In Japan, there is little difference in terms of domestic responsibilities between a young working wife and an elderly full-time housewife.

In 1990, the Asahi Kasei Institute for Dual-Income Families released a survey conducted among husbands and wives in dual-income households in Tokyo, New York, and London. A sample of around 100 households living in detached housing, and where the wife worked 25 hours a week or more, was surveyed in each city. The results, which have since been widely quoted, showed that while in London and New York husbands went to bed later and got up earlier than their wives, the opposite was true of Japanese men, who went to bed earlier and rose later in the morning than their wives. With regard to housework, Tokyo husbands shouldered only 6 per cent of the responsibility, compared to their equivalents in New York and London, who looked after 27 per cent and 23 per cent respectively of the domestic chores. Incidentally, these figures do not include the infamous 'fetching of the paper'. With the above advantage, it would be incredible indeed if Japanese men were not more efficient at work than those in Britain and the United States.

Looking at the working conditions of the women surveyed, on the other hand, we find that Tokyo women commute further, work longer hours and more days per week than women in the other countries surveyed, and yet their income as a percentage of total household income is lower. Really, then, Japanese women lose out on all counts. Incidentally household incomes in Tokyo are higher than London, but much lower than New York.[46] Women's share of household income in Japan is not low because their husbands' is high, but simply because their own rates of pay are so bad, particularly taking into account the number of hours they work.

The political economy of overwork

The long working hours of the Japanese recently became the focus of economic friction with other countries, and the government, labour, and management are all in agreement on the need for shortening them. Once again however, the emphasis is on male workers. Surely if there is a need to address the issue of overwork, attention should be given to wives in paid employment, who must also shoulder the burden of unpaid work, i.e., housework. Of course, if men's working habits do not change, neither can the situation of women, as has often been pointed out, so there is no doubt that men's working hours are indeed a problem. We cannot assume, however, that these long hours are the sole reason for the lack of housework done by males, or that they would help more if they had more time at home.

Let us suppose, for example, that in the early 1980s the standard number of working hours had been reduced to around 40 per week, which would have been quite a revolutionary change for Japan. The examples of Sweden and West Germany show us, however, that this is unlikely to result in a significant increase in the amount of housework performed by men. According to the aforementioned international comparison conducted by the Prime Minister's Office, West German women were second behind Japan in the four categories of cleaning, laundry, food preparation, and clearing up after meals; in contrast, Swedish women had the lowest rate of responsibility for shopping, food preparation, and clearing up of the six countries surveyed, and the rates for laundry and cleaning were also among the lowest. Only in the field of child-care did Swedish women appear in the top three countries, at 42 per cent after Japan's 75.6 per cent. It is a well-known fact that in Sweden women's participation in paid employment is of an extremely high level. West Germany, on the other hand, has one of the lowest rates of female participation in full-time paid employment in the western world, and one of the highest rates in part-time work, with a sizeable gap between male and female wages. Even there, however, a low rate of female responsibility for housework is recorded among young working couples.[47]

Other relevant data may be found in the report published in 1981 by the Tokyo Metropolitan Government's Life and Culture Bureau (Seikatsu Bunka Kyoku), entitled *Josei no Chii Shihyo ni kan Suru Chosa Hokokusho: Chukan Hokokusho* (An Index of the Position of Women: A Mid-term Report). The survey investigated the actual and ideal distribution of time expended on household affairs, work, leisure, and society at large, according to stage of life. Men, it was discovered, were eager to decrease the amount of energy they expended on work, but showed little inclination to increase the amount of time spent on activities in the home.[48] The results of another survey, con-ducted by the National Institute of Employment and Vocational research (Koyoshokugyo Sogo Kenkyusho) in 1985, among couples with children in kindergartens and nursery schools in the Shinjuku, Itabashi, Setagaya, and Shinagawa wards of Tokyo, are also of great interest.

This report, entitled *Josei no Shokuba Shinshutsu to Kazoku Kino no Henka ni Kansuru Chosa Kenkyu Hokokusho: Zoku* (An Investigation of Changes in the Function of the Family Unit in Relation to Women's Participation in the Work-force: Continued) and published in 1986, revealed that even in Japan, where males take responsibility for next to no housework, in the case where a wife works full-time for a government office, her burden of the domestic duties is remarkably low. It should be noted that respondents in this category worked longer hours and more days per week than full-time female employees in the private sector. Husbands who were themselves government employees showed a high rate of participation in housework. The report gives the rea-sons for this phenomenon as follows: 'In addition to conditions which make this situation possible (i.e., time at home), the fact that sex discrimination at work was absent as a rule instills in husbands a flexible sense of work roles.'[49]

After extensive research on the subject of job segregation, Sylvia Walby concluded that 'a better job can improve a woman's bargaining position over the domestic division of labour'.[50] Women who for the time being do not do paid work or whose hourly wages are low end up having to do all the house-work as unpaid labour. With this kind of assistance from his wife, in the end it becomes possible, indeed necessary, for the husband to devote himself entirely to the *kaisha*. With respect to household finances, this choice is 'rational' in three different senses: (1) it efficiently maintains and increases wage income; (2) it saves the monetary cost of housework, namely by avoiding paying for expensive housekeeping services or ready-made items; and (3) it minimizes the opportunity costs of housework (in other words, the amount of employment time and thus wages the household would have to give up in order to do housework).

In sum, the bias towards women performing unpaid labour within the household and women's low workplace status—low hourly wage, exhaustion, and alienation from intense, rote, supplementary labour—mutually reinforce each other. This kind of gender-based segregation is extremely rigid and unyielding in Japan. And Japan's gender-based segregation is the material basis for the worsening of international tensions through the economy's excessive competitiveness, and the basis also for the incessant defacement of both humanity and nature within Japan.

IV. The Corporate-Centred Society and the 'Patriarchy'

How is the gender-based segregation described above related to the essential characteristics of the companyism or corporate-centred society? As mentioned in the second section of this paper, one of the reasons Baba describes companyism as 'a subtle combination of capitalistic competition and communal or socialistic relationships' is the relative lack of differences and divisions within companies, i.e., the fact that vertical differences in rank are not immediately obvious. Watanabe's view is that this system has caused a breakdown in the social barriers previously present among workers of differing ranks, and that companies have a 'democratic character' since advancement within the company is possible for all loyal employees.

But where do female employees appear in this picture? How are we to understand the differential treatment, the massive barriers that even regular female employees face in this Japanese corporate-centred society where class differences and barriers of social status are not supposed to exist? I find it difficult to call a corporate-centred society that has its basis in gender segregation capitalistic, as Watanabe does, at least to the extent that we are not here to redefine the concept of capitalism.

In contrast, Baba's argument, which identifies non-capitalistic relationships within the corporate-centred society, is latently consistent with recent feminist theories of 'public patriarchy'.

Patriarchy has within Japanese social science contexts come to be linked to the pre-war *ie* (household) system. It is frequently thought of as nothing more than a relic that was bundled off to history museums by defeat in war and the new post-war Constitution. This is one reason why feminist theories of patriarchy cause great feelings of unease, especially among male Japanese social scientists.[51] However, as Ueno Chizuko documents, the feminist concept of patriarchy does not refer to a feudal, pre-modern system of relationships, but to the oppression of women and control of them by men, a central principle of modern industrial society. Ueno defines this concept as 'a power relationship whereby the norms of society, and authority, are distributed unevenly based on gender and age'. This relationship is not only one of psychological domination and oppression, but, Ueno emphasizes, has a 'material basis' which is found in the exploitation of housework as 'unpaid labour'. For this reason, patriarchy can also be defined as 'the appropriation of women's labour by men'.[52]

The concept of patriarchy forms an essential part of any discussion of women's employment because, according to Ueno, the reasons why 'labour necessary for the production and sustaining of the lives of others'—in other words, domestic labour—is delegated almost exclusively to women cannot be explained by capitalist principles. Ueno further argues that, while patriarchy is typically seen to function within the family, gender oppression is not in fact confined to the family, but may occur between men and women in couples, male and female relations, and, in a broader societal context, between 'males' as one stratum and 'females' as another. While urging us to understand this relationship, however, Ueno confines her own analysis largely to the family unit.[53]

In contrast, Heidi Hartmann and Sylvia Walby have recently argued that the centre of gravity of the patriarchal system has shifted in modern times from the family to the public sphere—to employment, social policy, and the police.[54] Without a doubt, the 'communal relationships' of the corporate-centred society, a society of which gender discrimination is the base, are power relationships whereby material possessions and authority are distributed unevenly according to gender and age. Rather than viewing these relationships as socialist because there are few divisions by class, it would be more accurate to extend the argument of Sumiya and emphasize their *ie*-like, in other words, their patriarchal, nature.

On the other hand, however, I find myself unable to agree entirely with Walby's theory in which she contrasts private patriarchy in the nineteenth century with public patriarchy in the twentieth, because I believe that not only contemporary Japan's corporate-centred society, but also the organization of labour within companies at the time of their origin, were essentially patriarchal.

As Mori Tateshi explained in his work *Koyo Kankei no Seisei* (*The Formation of the Employment Relationship*), even in the birthplace of capitalism, Britain, employment relations were never really of a bourgeois nature. Marx explained the concept of class division as follows: in a modern society composed (one would expect) of free and equal citizens, capitalists and workers would have equally powerful bargaining positions. In reality, however, this equality is in name only, and the relationship is rendered unequal by exploitation via the production process. This inequality in turn leads to class conflict. However,

Mori points out, the capitalist's right to command the production process, which facilitates exploitation, cannot develop from 'contracts based on the free will of equal participants'. Because modern economics has developed with this notion of contracts as its foundation, Mori adds, 'employment relationships, which occupy an important place in economic activity, have not been paid enough attention'.[55]

Mori demonstrated, by analysing a large number of precedents and legal texts, that employment relationships are relationships based on status, in which employers give orders and employees follow them, and that the authority of an employer derives from the authority of a man over his wife, children, and servants and the division of domestic labour which the male, as father, husband, or patriarch, enjoyed in earlier times. It is this theory of employment relationships, he argues, which best explains the development of organizational structures and bureaucracy in management, and of industrial relations conducted on a collective basis, but unfortunately Mori's analysis does not extend to these matters, nor to the problem of gender segregation.

Nevertheless, I would like to expand on Mori's valuable work, and state my belief that the authority that companies exercise over their employees is in fact 'patriarchy' in its original form, and, this being the case, it should hardly surprise us that women occupy a low rung on the employment ladder.

It is not, in other words, that women are forced by the private patriarchy system to carry the burden of household responsibilities, or that this system alone restricts them to, at best, second-class employment. As the French materialist feminist Christine Delphy emphasizes, the material foundation of women's oppression is their role as unpaid workers in the home, but, as she adds, the systematic discrimination women encounter in paid employment is, conversely, a factor which drives them into that kind of disadvantageous marriage system.[56] Women turn to marriage because they have little choice, and once in the matrimonial state, the burden of housework as unpaid labour is forced upon them, leaving them in an even more disadvantageous position.

In this way the patrarchal system controls women's sexuality as well as their role in the labour market. It would not be an exaggeration to say that, apart from a handful of élite women, marriage is rarely a union based on 'the free will of equal participants'. Thus, despite the overdevelopment of commodity economy, it is this kind of 'communalistic relationship' that sustains the family in Japan, even if only, in some cases, the outward appearance of it.

A glance at the financial circumstances of women bringing up children on their own will confirm the extent to which Japanese women are pressured into marriage. As Hayashi Chiyo demonstrated in her analysis of the 1988 *Nendo Zenkoku Boshi Setai to Jittai Chosa Kekka no Gaiyo* (*Summary Report of the National Survey on Female-Headed Household, 1988*) (Ministry of Health and Welfare, Bureau for Children and the Home), the average income in 1987 for a family with a mother as the sole parent was 2,020,000 yen after tax. A closer analysis of the statistics reveals that the average for households headed by separated or divorced women was 1,850,000 yen, while that of widows was 2,420,000 yen. At the time of the survey, an average household received an average income of 5,130,000 yen, three times that of a household headed by a separated or divorced woman. Even if the figures are calculated to take into account income per capita in each type of household, the latter type of family still has an income less than 40 per cent of the average. Eighty per cent of those women in the divorced or separated category live in rental accommodation, and 75 per cent have never received maintenance from their former husbands.[57]

Under these circumstances, it is easy to imagine how even a slight deterioration in a mother's health could lead to disaster, as witnessed in the shocking death from starvation in January 1987 of a woman in the Shiroishi ward of Sapporo, a tragedy which occurred at a time when Japan was being proclaimed the most affluent it had ever been.

In that same year and month of January 1987, the Ministry of Health and Welfare published its 'White Paper' for 1986, boasting that 'since the War, our nation has shown unprecedented progress, becoming one of the world's major economic powers, producing a tenth of the world's GNP . . . in the field of social welfare also, as an advanced welfare state we must pursue our policies from an international standpoint.' This was the first time Japan had announced itself to be an 'advanced nation' in the field of welfare.[58] The welfare authority of Sapporo were aware of the desperate circumstances of the mother; despite this they were unable to prevent her horrific death, nor were they found culpable.[59] One cannot but marvel at the fact that, if this incident had occurred in late nineteenth-century Britain, under the jurisdiction of the Poor Laws, rather than in the 'advanced welfare state' of Japan in the 1980s, the authorities responsible would not have escaped criminal prosecution so easily.[60] This woman's case was no one-off incident, but a reflection on the structure of modern Japanese society, and should be recognized as such by all those involved in the social sciences.

6

The Ageing Society, the Family, and Social Policy*

HARADA SUMITAKA

I. The Themes and the Perspective of Analysis

1. *The themes*

(1) The ageing of the population and contemporary Japanese society

According to a demographic estimate as of 1 October 1994, the number of people aged 65 or above in Japan increased from the preceding year's figure by 680,000 to 17,580,000, to account for 14.1 per cent of the national population (Table 6.1). The ratio still remained lower than those in western European countries, but was higher than those in the United States and Canada. Moreover, given the recent declining trend in the birth rate, the share of over-65s in Japanese population forecast is bound to become the world's highest within less than a decade.

In view of the fact that this ratio exceeded the 7 per cent mark only as recently as 1970, the country is ageing at an exceptionally fast speed. Elderly people in the latter stage of ageing (aged 75 or above), who are in need of special considerations from the standpoint of social security policy (unless otherwise specified, the expression 'social security policy' is used in a broad sense here and elsewhere in this chapter to include social welfare measures), are also increasing their share in the population (see Table 6.1). There is no denying that this ageing phenomenon is among the most prominent factors that characterize Japanese society today, and will impart far-reaching effects to that society in the future.

The ageing of society, on the one hand, was brought about as a direct consequence of the extension of life span and the continuing decline in the birth rate, but these two factors, in their turn, are an important manifestation of the profound social changes that have taken place during the three-decade-long process of Japan's rise to an 'affluent society'. The exceptionally high

---

* Translated by Moriya Fumiaki.

TABLE 6.1. The ageing of the population: real and forecast changes in main indices of population changes, 1920–2020

Year	Total population (million persons)	People of 65 or older as % of total population	People of 75 or older as % of total population	Rate of marriages per 1,000 persons	Rate of divorces per 1,000 persons	Total fertility rate	Average life expectancy for males	Average life expectancy for females
1920	56.0	5.3	1.3	9.8	0.99	5.24	50.06[a]	53.96[a]
1950	84.1	4.9	1.3	8.6	1.01	3.65	58.00	61.50
1955	90.1	5.3	1.5	8.0	0.84	2.37	63.60	67.75
1960	94.3	5.7	1.7	9.3	0.74	2.00	65.32	70.19
1965	99.2	6.3	1.9	9.7	0.79	2.14	67.74	72.92
1970	104.7	7.1	2.1	10.0	0.93	2.13	69.31	74.66
1975	111.9	7.9	2.5	8.5	1.07	1.91	71.73	76.89
1980	117.1	9.1	3.1	6.7	1.22	1.75	73.35	78.76
1985	121.1	10.3	3.9	6.1	1.39	1.76	74.78	80.48
1990	123.6	12.0	4.8	5.9	1.28	1.54	75.92	81.90
1991	124.0	12.6	5.0	6.0	1.37	1.53	76.11	82.11
1992	124.5	13.1	5.2	6.1	1.45	1.50	76.09	82.22
1993	124.8	13.5	5.4	6.4	1.52	1.46	76.25	82.51
1994	125.0	14.1	5.5	6.3	1.57	1.5	76.57	82.98
1995	125.5	14.5	5.7					
2000	127.4	17.0	6.9					
2005	129.3	19.1	8.5					
2010	130.4	21.3	10.0					
2015	130.0	24.1	11.2					
2020	128.3	25.5	12.5					

[a] The figures are for 1947.

Sources: The figures of population for years up to 1990 are from the Prime Minister's Office Statistics Bureau, *Kokusei Chosa* (National Census), those for 1991–4 are from id., 'Kakunen no Suikei Jinko' (Estimated Population for Each Year), and those for 1995 and after are from the Ministry of Health and Welfare Institute of Population Problems, 'Nihon no Shorai Jinko Suikei' (Forecasts of Japanese Population in the Future: The Median Values Forecast as of September 1992).

Average life expectancy (at birth) is based on Koseisho Daijin Kambo Tokei Johobu (Statistical Information Department, Minister's Secretariat, Ministry of Health and Welfare). 'Kanzen Seimeihyo' (Comprehensive Table of Life Expectancy: Up till 1990), and 'Kan'i Seimeihyo' (Summary Table of Life Expectancy). The other indices of population statistics are based on id., 'Jinko Dotai Tokei' (Population Movement Statistics).

speed of ageing, then, is closely related to the dazzlingly fast speed of economic expansion that has characterized Japanese society since the end of the Second World War.

On the other hand, this same fact is now making serious demands on Japanese society's ability to 'readjust its overall social fabric' and better to accommodate the progress of ageing. Following the launching of a government plan to 'reassess the welfare programmes' in the post-oil-crisis years of the mid-1970s, this challenging task gradually moved to one of the focal points in the government's policy agenda. In 1986, the government adopted the 'Guideline on Measures for Dealing with the Ageing of the Population'. The 'Guideline of Measures' defines the policy agenda in a long-range perspective, and stresses the need to transform and restructure the existing socio-economic system in its entirety into one 'more befitting the era when the span of human life extends to 80 years'. Identified as being most important of all the measures is, naturally enough, the measure to 'restructure the social security system', including social welfare programmes.[1] The way in which these policy measures are going to be put into effect will determine to significant degrees what features Japanese society will take on in the years to come.

(2) Changes in the family and social security in present-day Japan

If the ageing of society is one facet of the profound social changes mentioned above, the family in post-war Japan has also undergone a profound transformation that is no less significant than it. In addition to some aspects of this transformation that are described in Table 6.1—i.e., the declining marriage rate and the increasing divorce rate, and the continuous decline in the total fertility rate—the family in Japan has been subjected to a number of other changes that affected the family in the West, including the rapid decrease in family size (Table 6.2). These changes are at once the product of the socio-economic developments of post-war Japanese society, and a peculiar and important determinant of what will become of the society in the years to come.

It is important to take note, on the one hand, that the transformation of the family in Japan basically has much in common with the profound transformation that the families in the western countries had experienced earlier. The transformation of the family in the West, which is far more extensive and profound than that in Japan, unfolded in close correlation with a number of factors, including the western societies' rise to 'affluent urban societies' on the basis of their economic growth, the accompanying changes in their social structures and employment patterns, and the maturing of the social institutions of these societies to the extent of characterizing them as welfare states. Similar correlations among pertinent factors are at work in Japan, if

TABLE 6.2. Changes in family composition (in terms of ordinary households^a), 1920–90

	1920	1955	1965	1975	1985	1990
Nuclear families (%)	54.0	60.6	62.6	64.0	62.6	61.8
Extended families (million)						
Families consisting of lineal relatives	approx. 31 }	32.6	24.3	22.0 }	19.7 }	17.8 }
Families consisting of other relatives	approx. 8 }	2.9	5.0			
Families including non-relatives		0.5	0.3	0.2	0.2	0.2
Single-person families (million)	6.6	3.4	7.9	13.6	17.5	20.2
Total (actual number in million families)	1,112	1,740	2,329	3,127	3,648	3,919
Total (%)	100.0	100.0	100.0	100.0	100.0	100.0
Average family size (persons)		4.97	4.05	3.44	3.23	2.99

^a An 'ordinary household' means a group of persons living in an ordinary house, or a single person keeping a house of his/her own, but excludes those living in a lodging house, a dormitory, a social facility, and the like. As such the table's coverage is slightly different from the one based on the concept 'general households' adopted by the 'Kosei Gyosei Kiso Chosa' (A Fundamental Survey for the Administration of the Welfare), the concept that includes those excluded from this table. But the present table seems to be more appropriate for tracing the changes in family composition of ordinary families.

Sources: Tabulated on the basis of a table given in Yuzawa Yasuhiko, *Zusetsu: Gendai Nihon no Kazoku Mondai* (A Graphical Explanation of Family Problems in Contemporary Japan) (Nihon Hoso Kyokai, 1987), 7, and data given in the 1994 edition of *Kokumin Seikatsu Hakusho* (White Paper on National Life), 72 and 380. The two data sources depend for the 1920 figures on Toda Teizo 'Kazoku Kosei' (Family Composition), and for the figures of 1955 and after on the Prime Minister's Office Statistical Bureau, 'Kokusei Chosa' (National Census).

only in a more restrained manner. It is highly plausible, then, that a similar transformation of the family, even though it appears to be unfolding only to a limited extent at present, can start to unfold on a much fuller scale in the near future.

On the other hand, it is also important to note that the family, embedded as it is in a specific way in present-day Japanese society, occupies a distinct place and performs a distinct role in it. The interaction between the family and Japanese society at large may be summed up as follows: the family, with features of its own and its relative stability, has constituted an indispensable part of the social structure that has sustained the country's extraordinary growth potential. This fact is manifested before all else in the characteristics underlying the relationships between the social roles to be played by the family on the one hand, and the way social security programmes operate in Japan, on the other.

For instance, the traditional ideology regarded childcare and support and the caring of aged parents as basic responsibilities of the family. It was very common for three generations of direct blood relatives to live under one roof. These factors, coupled with the relative stability of family relations, founded upon the rigid division of labour between the sexes in family life and at the workplace, had the effect of narrowing the problems to be covered by social security. This explains why Japan, unlike many advanced countries of the West, has failed to formulate *a system of family policies in the narrow sense, which is devoted to the protection and reinforcement of the family itself.*[2] Not only that, as the government proceeded with its effort to 'reassess the welfare programmes' from the mid-1970s onwards, a renewed emphasis was placed on *the role of the family (especially the role of women in the family), as the main source of support for the livelihood of the elderly.* It was argued that the existence of three-generation families living together should be regarded as 'latent property of Japanese welfare', and that these families should be revitalized and strengthened as the basis for social security. Both the 1986 'Guideline of Measures' and the 1986 edition of the *White Paper on Welfare* with its call for 'restructuring the social security system' subscribed to this view.

A political tenet like this might also be regarded as constituting a part of a family policy understood in the broad sense. But its purpose is significantly different from that of the family policy defined in the narrow sense referred to above. This is because *the family policy understood in the broad sense* is aimed primarily at making the best possible use of the family's potential to support and take care of aged parents as a means of minimizing as much as possible the increases in social security outlays. The reason why the government has been able to feel contented with only trying to improve and upgrade the country's social security system to the level that could at best qualify Japan as a 'medium-ranked welfare state', but not further,[3] is basically ascribable to the specific locus and role assigned to the family.

(3) The family under transformation with the ageing of society and the family policy

The policy orientation described above, however, has recently been forced to undergo modifications and revamping, as the very two phenomena that the family policy is expected to deal with are growing to far more serious proportions. One is the ageing of the population, which is advancing at a pace beyond anyone's expectations, and the other is the transformation of the family, which, too, is picking up speed.

To begin with, the accelerated ageing of the population is bringing into focus the sheer inadequacy of the nursing arrangements available for the aged who must depend on someone else for their care. Previously, as noted already, the government had adopted the policy of making the family bear much of the burdens for the care of the aged, while limiting itself to supporting the family's nursing efforts directly and indirectly. As a consequence of this, and as the government itself admits, aged people's needs for nursing are addressed far less properly than their needs for other social services, such as the right to receive pension benefits and medical social security. Recently, however, the increasing number of elderly people in need of nursing and the expanding duration of nursing have saddled the family with far greater burdens. At the same time, the transformations of the family—the decreasing size of average households; the increase in the number of aged people living alone or aged couples living alone; the ageing of the caretakers themselves; and the growing participation in the workforce by women with spouses, who used to be the caretakers of the ageing parents—have seriously weakened the family's ability to take care of the elderly. As a result, it has become unrealistic to assume that the pre-existing arrangements would keep on functioning as they used to.

From around 1990, therefore, a growing understanding began to be shared by government officials in charge of social security policy that they should take a hard look at the wisdom of counting on the family to serve as a safety net for the elderly, and start looking instead into ways of reorienting health, medical, and welfare services for them.

As to the accelerated transformation of the family, on the other hand, the precipitating drop in the total fertility rate that began in 1989 has commanded much attention, because, if this trend is to continue for some time, it will accelerate the ageing of the population still further and produce profound and far-reaching effects on social and economic life. Consequently, some shift is also taking place in the government's attitude concerning the basic orientation of its family policy. For instance, the 1990 edition of the *White Paper on Welfare* took note of the declining birth rate, and pointed to the need to 'establish a more comprehensive family policy, which pays attention to the decay in the various functions of families and households, and aims at reinforcing and strengthening these functions'. Establishing such a comprehensive policy to cope with the declining birth rate, the *White Paper* emphasized, 'will be *pivotal for social security in the future*' (on p. 104). This line of argument has been pursued with added intensity in the subsequent reorientation of the family policy.[4]

Thus, in the ongoing discussion on policy planning concerning the family and the elderly, there is clearly a shift of emphasis away from that in 1986. But how this is likely to be translated into concrete policy measures is a moot point. The future prospects of social security policy in relation to the family remain clouded.

2. The analytical perspective

In an earlier study, the author attempted to trace the transformations of the family itself, and the changes in its locus and social functions in contemporary Japan, as looked at primarily in connection with the developments in the social security policy, in the period since the 'reassessment of the welfare programmes' got under way in the mid-1970s.[5] Following the oil crisis, three factors with profound bearing upon the family emerged at once, overlapping with each other: serious cutbacks on social security outlays as a means of coping with the slowed growth of the economy; the emergence of the ageing of the population as a serious problem; and the continuing trend toward transformations of the family. The author's concern in that study was to assess how *the family policy in relation to the social security policy* was trying to perceive the family and its social roles, and to what extent such a perception was tenable and justifiable.

The perspective adopted in the earlier work seems to be still valid enough to be retained in this chapter, too, as its first basic perspective. This is because the question of how to perceive the locus of the family and its role in an ageing society can be essentially reduced to the following question: How best could the family—the arena for intergenerational reproduction of labour power—be properly situated in the socio-economic system of Japan in the future, and subsumed into the system as its part, while letting it shoulder a proper share of the burden to support and care for the ageing generation?

None the less, since the purpose of this chapter is to examine this same problem by identifying it as one of the basic factors characterizing present-day Japanese society, it is necessary for us to adopt an additional perspective as well. It is the perspective of trying to answer the following question: Why is it that the ageing of the population and the transformations of the family —despite being social changes universal to contemporary advanced capitalist countries—are manifesting themselves in present-day Japan as problems of far greater significance than elsewhere, and with their unique features? To address this question from a historical perspective means to shed light on the social structure of Japan underpinning its exceptionally high growth potential in close reference to *the locus and role assigned to the family in the society*. Besides, to question what will become of the locus and role assigned to the family seems to have much in common with inquiring into what will become of the characteristic features of contemporary Japanese society, dictated as it is by the logic of *companyism*.

In what follows, the author will try to examine the major issues identified above concerning the ageing of the population, the family, and social security. The author will do so mainly from the standpoint of taking critical stock of the relevant policy measures having been proposed or implemented.[6]

II. Transformations of the Family and Developments of Social Security Policy

1. *The family-should-support-itself principle and social security*

At the outset, the author would like to state briefly his understanding of the reasons why the relationship between social security and the family can become an important issue in advanced capitalist countries today.

(1) The family-should-support-itself principle and its decline

The modern family, or the family in capitalist society since the modern era, is a fundamental group founded upon affection, which, in its capacity as a constituent element of a social system, is expected to perform two economic functions voluntarily. One is to secure a certain level of living standards for its members, and the other is to secure the reproduction of labour power, the function which the market cannot fulfil by itself. The family performs these economic functions through its interplay with the market economy external to itself; but the law governing the unity among members of the family is qualitatively different from the law governing the market economy. As such, the family, in terms of its economic functions, too, manifests itself as a community with characteristics of its own.

Therefore, in fulfilling its economic functions, the family is expected by society to live by the principle demanding that the family should support itself—that the costs and domestic labour necessary for the fulfilment of its functions ought to be expended by its own members through co-operation among themselves. Such a relationship of mutual help and co-operation among members of the family, which is assumed to involve no remuneration, translates into a norm that governs the behaviour of individuals at the mental level, obliging them to partake in this relationship voluntarily. At the level of state law, moreover, this relationship is institutionalized by civil codes in many countries in the form of provisions that hold family members responsible for supporting the livelihood of each other within certain limits.

However, so long as each family has to confront the external market economy on its own, the 'family-should-support-itself' principle in reality only works to certain limits, but never fully. For one thing, real families are neither equal nor homogeneous in terms of both the amount of burden of self-help each shoulders and the ability to face up to such burdens. For another, it is unavoidable that illness, accidents, death, and a host of other factors can render some families incapable of supporting themselves, making the provision of some form of public support essential. In rural communities of the past, safety nets of collective support were provided by kinship or social groups; but present-day society has no such community-based safety nets to turn to. Only the state and other public bodies can be expected to step in from outside to provide support to families in difficulty.

This is why the state came to implement various measures whereby it takes over part of the responsibilities of families in distress, and lightens their burdens by offering support. The emergence of social security measures early on that were aimed at relieving the poor or preventing families from becoming poorer was the first form of public support in this direction. Also, some western European countries, in the aftermath of the First World War, began to implement measures of protection and assistance aimed at the family, many of them as part of their population maintenance policies. These formed one origin of the family policy in the narrow sense.

Furthermore, as the rapid economic growth process after the Second World War brought into place affluent urban societies and transformed the family at an accelerated pace, the family's self-help ability was shaken on a far wider scale than ever before. Included among major changes in factors affecting the family that have taken place as a result of economic growth are: a quantitative increase in the responsibility of the family that has resulted from the general rise in living standards, and from the increased requirements for labour power reproduction; a widening of the inequality in burdens to be borne by different families; and an increase in the number of women with spouses entering the workforce and women's ability to be economically more independent. Underlying the last factor are a number of developments such as: the trend toward longer years of education received by women; changes in their life-cycles brought about by increased life expectancy and the decrease in the number of children they give birth to; and the lightening of housework by the diffusion of household electric appliances.

The changes that the family itself has undergone include: an increase in the number of households of the employed; a decrease in the number of three-generation households, coupled with increases in the numbers of nuclear families and single-person households; a narrowing of the family's self-supporting ability due to the decreased family size; an increase in the number of double-income families, with its attendant problem of women being overburdened doing 'double shifts', which has shaken the division of labour between the sexes, and has even resulted in an increased number of divorces; an increased diversification of lifestyles, and an increased externalization of housework (including childcare), which have increasingly blurred the difference between unremunerated domestic labour and services purchased on the market.

These changes have affected all the advanced countries, though to varying extents. The trend toward a lower birth rate, and the propagation of the view that perceives the family not as a unit of secure livelihood and parenting but rather as a place where one can get emotional satisfactions, have also emerged as a joint product of the interaction among the various factors mentioned above.

(2) Implications of social security and family policy

Our foregoing observations mean that the family of today, unless supported by various public and social measures, is no longer able to perform the various functions it was originally expected to. The welfare states of western Europe have developed in response to this very challenge. It is not far-fetched to say that one primary purpose of these welfare states has been to enable the family system mentioned above to keep functioning properly, by giving assistance to the family on a more extensive and profound scale. It is then natural that social security policy in western European countries has been developed to include, as one of its supporting pillars, a family policy in the narrow sense, one aimed specifically at protecting and assisting the family itself.

The experience of these countries up till today, however, seems to suggest that the accomplishments of the welfare states are not necessarily the same as what they were originally intended for. The development of the welfare state and the family policy in these countries, on the one hand, has subjected the family to public interference and concern to an significant extent, encouraging directly or indirectly the imposition of the judicial ideal type of the modern family on the actual family. On the other hand, in effect it has, rather, promoted the family's transformation to such an extent as to arouse strong voices calling for a reassessment of the very question of what the state's relationship with the family should be. To give one illustration of how such strong voices are gaining influence lately, the legislators themselves begin to approve that the principle of 'neutrality' should govern the state's interference with, and legal restrictions on, the family.[7] Should this principle be accepted, the desirable family policy in the future will be to accept as given and irrevocable the transformations of the family in present-day society, and also recognize the desires and rights of individuals to self-determination regarding the family, thinking about what the state might be able to do for the family and, for that matter, for individuals.

The situation in Japan cuts a sharp contrast to this. It is true that Japan has undergone some changes apparently similar to those experienced by western European countries, such as the transformations of the family and the corresponding improvements in social security programmes. But its family policy, as looked at in relation to social security, has, from the outset, been different in both content and orientation. Moreover, the judicial ideal type of the modern family upheld by Japanese family law as part of its Civil Code seems to prevent family policy in Japan from developing into a new direction.

As should be clear from our foregoing observations, this difference is ascribable to the difference between Japan and European countries in the way the 'family-should-support-itself principle' is conceptualized, including the extent of the coverage of the 'family', and is put to work in reality. This is because the extent to which the provision of social assistance to the family is actually carried out as a socially and publicly justifiable act of the state can vary from one country to the next depending on the financial resources available, and on the concept of 'the family's self-help' prevailing in the society concerned. We will start our concrete analysis of the situation in Japan by looking into this point.

2. The family as conceptualized by the post-war Civil Code, and the two-layered self-help principle

(1) Dual implications of the family's private responsibility to support its members

The Family Law (both its Books on Kinship and Inheritance) of the Japanese Civil Code was established after the Second World War in 1947, abrogating the pre-war Family Law of 1898 with its prescriptions about the *ie* or 'household' system (see note 8). Established in accordance with the ideal of upholding the dignity of individuals and essential equality between the sexes in family life, as proclaimed by the Constitution of 1946 in Article 24, the new Family Law was very progressive, at least as a matter of formality, by the international standards of the time. This explains to a large extent why most of the provisions of the law are still in effect today. However, as regards the family's support responsibility, the question of close relevance to the self-help principle, the law has the following characteristic features.

On the one hand, the Family Law identifies a small, modern family consisting of a married couple and a minor child (or children) as the ideal type of family, in which the husband and the wife are obliged to help each other in bringing up the child(ren), providing for the costs of living, and maintaining the common life (Articles 752, 760, 818, and 820). This obligation is usually called the '*livelihood maintenance obligation*', and is understood to mean *the relationship in which a couple must be united to maintain a joint livelihood by sharing with each other whatever they have, and collaborating with each other*. Needless to say, this obligation is central to the legal prescriptions on the family's self-help principle.

On the other hand, the Family Law also provides for the responsibility not simply of persons of a direct lineal relation and brothers and sisters, but also of relatives within the third degree of relationship by blood or marriage, to support each other (Article 887). It also stipulates that 'lineal relatives, and collateral relatives living together should support each other' (Article 730). This extensive support obligation, which constitutes another facet of the family's self-help principle, is commonly called the *'livelihood assistance obligation'*.

It should be noted, however, that, in the actual application of the civil law, this extensive support obligation has been interpreted as secondary. It is considered secondary in the sense that *if a person is in need of support, and if there is anybody among his/her relatives noted above who has enough means to spare after sustaining his/her own livelihood, this relative should be held responsible for supporting the person in need*. And, legally speaking, the responsibility of offspring to support and take care of their aged parents falls under this 'livelihood assistance obligation'.

The practice of breaking down the members of a broadly defined family into different family groups, and assigning to different groups livelihood assistance obligations of varying nature and degree, is no means specific to Japan alone. The French Civil Code, for instance, does not simply provide for the support obligation among a married couple; it also holds persons of a direct lineal relation and those of a direct marital relation (a son-in-law or daughter-in-law and parents-in-law) responsible for supporting each other, though to different extents. However, one defining feature of the 'livelihood assistance obligations' among lineal and collateral relatives stipulated by the Japanese Civil Code was—as evident from the heated debate during the post-war legislative process—retained as a vestige from the pre-war 'household' system, as a means of encouraging the post-war family to continue perceiving the obligation for the caring for the aged essentially as a 'household' matter.[8] In actual society, too, the perception that children should naturally bear the responsibility to take care of their parents in old age has persisted strongly, as noted already. Because of this fact, the post-war Family Law is often said to have 'two guiding spirits', the modern and progressive view that identifies a small family as being desirable, on the one hand, and the more traditional concept of the extended family, on the other. According to the terminology adopted here, the family in Japan is governed by the 'two-layered self-help principle'.

(2) The Family's livelihood-securing functions and the role played by the post-war Family law

As a matter of fact, because it was equipped with the two guiding spirits, upon its establishment, the post-war Family Law was able to perform peculiarly important roles as socio-economic upheavals subsequently unfolded.

First, prescriptions of the law that derived from its identification of a modern, small family as ideal (including the system of equalized inheritance) played a role conducive to the process whereby a large number of young workers with high educational backgrounds and unconstrained by the 'household' system participated in the labour market, moved to the urban areas, and formed their nuclear families there.

Second, within those nuclear families, a division of labour between the husband and the wife took roots over again in close combination with a division of labour between the sexes that was established in the workplace during the course of Japan's high economic growth centred on its heavy and chemical industries. The development of the two forms of division of labour between the sexes produced two mutually reinforcing effects: on the one hand, the husband as the breadwinner, assisted by the wife as the caretaker of domestic affairs, was induced to work long hours, devoting himself to the prosperity of the company he worked for; and on the other, the nuclear family of the worker was ensured a degree of relative stability. The Family Law, with its proclamation of equality between the couple only in theory, indirectly helped in the process by which the Japanese-style modern small family was incorporated into the industrial society of post-war Japan as one of its underpinning structural bases.

Third, the self-help principle of the extended family played a considerably important role in holding the family, often the three-generation family living under one roof, responsible for privately supporting and taking care of the elderly. This arrangement was followed not simply as a matter of practice. It also had the backing of laws such as the Daily Life Security Law of 1950 (with its stipulations that the eligibility to public assistance be judged on a household-by-household basis, and that relatives should assume primary responsibility to support persons in need) and the Law for the Welfare of the Aged of 1963 (which instituted a scheme for charging part of the costs of welfare services for aged persons to those with support responsibility).

3. Transformations of the family and developments of social security policy during the high economic growth period

(1) Economic growth and transformations of the family

Subsequently, however, as the effects of the economy's rapid growth began to be felt throughout the society, the family's self-supporting ability began to flag. Most of the important changes concerning the family noted already were apparent by the end of the 1960s. Let us cite some relevant data.

To begin with, there was a change in family composition (see Table 6.2). Nuclear families increased phenomenally, if somewhat less so as a percentage of the total families, but in urban areas these became the most popular form

TABLE 6.3. The employment pattern of women with spouses, and their share in female employees, 1960–93

(% and (1,000 persons))

	1960	1965	1970	1975	1980	1985	1990	1993
A. Women's labour force participation rate	54.5	50.6	49.9	45.7	47.6	48.7	50.1	50.3 [26,810]
B. Employment pattern of married women								
Total job holders	46.6	48.0	48.0	44.7	48.5	50.2	52.0	52.2 [16,470]
Employed	8.8	14.1	18.3	21.3	26.1	29.6	33.9	35.7 [11,640]
Self-employed	9.6	11.8	14.7	13.4	14.5	14.0	5.9	5.5 [1,680]
Working in family businesses							12.2	10.7 [3,130]
Agriculture and forestry[a]	28	22.2	14.9	9.9	7.9	6.5	–*	–
C. Breakdown of female employees	[1962]							
Unmarried	55.2	50.3	48.3	38.0	32.5	31.3	32.7	32.8 [6,550]
With spouses	32.7	38.6	41.4	51.3	57.4	59.2	58.2	57.8 [11,540]
Widowed or divorced	12.0	11.1	10.3	10.8	10.0	9.6	9.1	9.4 [1,870]
Total	100.0	100.0	100.0	100.0	100.0	100.0	100.0	100.0 [19,970]

[a] 'Agriculture and forestry' as a job category has disappeared from statistics lately.

Source: Ministry of Labour Women's Bureau (ed.), Fujin Rodo no Jitsujo (The Actual Situation of Female Labour), 1989 and 1994 editions.

of the family for an employed worker. The 'modern, small family', which had been envisioned no more than as a sort of 'judicial ideal type' at the time of the post-war reform, took shape in reality as a nuclear family. In contrast, three-generation families continued to decrease as percentages of the total families. On the rapid increase lately instead are single-person families.

As a result of these changes, coupled with the declining birth rate, the average family size plummeted from 4.97 persons in 1955 to 3.69 in 1970, 3.33 in 1980, and 2.99 in 1990. Given the fact that the figure remained virtually stable around 5.0 persons from 1920 to 1955, the shrinkage of family size was drastic.

The family's life structure, too, underwent rapid changes:

1. households headed by employed workers continued to increase (increasing their share of the total households from 54.6 per cent in 1960 to 61.4 per cent in 1989);

2. as these households typically took the form of the nuclear family, the family's structure and functions became even more simplified;

3. in a related development, the traditional kinship groups and neighbourhood communities, were dissolved;

4. in tandem with these changes, the propagation of the urban lifestyle based on mass production and mass consumption accelerated the 'externalization' of family life; and

5. worthy of special attention was the change in the employment pattern of women, especially those with spouses.

Let us have a closer look at the last point (Table 6.3).

The labour force participation rate for women as a whole was on the decrease trend up till 1975, and so was the rate for women with spouses. But this decrease was due to the fact that the number of women (especially those with spouses) employed in agriculture was decreasing far more rapidly than could be made up for by an increase in the number of women employees (Table 6.3, A and B). It should be noted that the labour force participation rate, as employee, for women with spouses was steadily increasing as early as in the 1960s (Table 6.3, B), and their share in all the female employees exceeded the 50 per cent mark in 1975 (Table 6.3, C). Already in the 1960s, the number of dual-earner families headed by employed male workers was gradually on the increase, in parallel with the ongoing changes in family size, pattern, and life structure.

Against the backdrop of these changes, the family's weakening ability with regard to childcare, housework, and the support to aged parents, as well as conflicts over various choices for family life, began to assume increasingly serious proportions. Symbolic of the changes was that, as divorces began to increase gradually at the time, the number of cases where the wife took

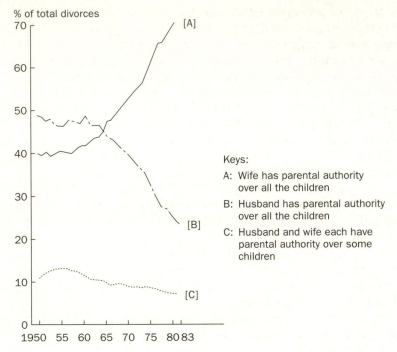

% of total divorces

Keys:

A: Wife has parental authority
over all the children

B: Husband has parental authority
over all the children

C: Husband and wife each have
parental authority over some
children

Fɪɢ. 6.1. Parental authority after divorce

Note: Only the divorce cases involving infant children are taken into account.

Source: Ministry of Health and Welfare Statistics and Information Department (ed.), *Rikon Tokei: Jinko Dotai Tokei Tokushu Hokoku* (Statistics on Divorces: A Special Report on Population Movement Statistics), (Kosei Tokei Kyokai, 1984), 24.

charge of the children began to increase sharply from around 1965 (Figure 6.1). The last fact was significant because it pointed not only to the growing potential for women to become economically independent, but also to the rapidly waning restraints imposed on the wife by the husband's 'house'.[9]

(2) Characteristics of family policy until the late 1960s

During the 1960s, government policy documents began to take heed of 'the emergence of new family problems', emphasizing the need to devise and implement measures for reinforcing the family. In the area of social security, several new developments were already in the making under the impact of high economic growth, the most notable development being the establishment in 1961 of a universal pension scheme and a universal health insurance plan. And the new awareness of the need to reinforce the family added a further impetus to these ongoing developments. However, some words must be said about the framework within which the need to reinforce the family was perceived.

First, policy documents of this period, while accepting the transformations of the family concomitant with economic growth as unavoidable, interpreted the 'new family problems' as originating from transitional functional failures and conflicts faced by the new family in the process of its consolidation. In other words, it was assumed that a variety of family problems that were at the focus of public discussion (such as changes in the social consciousness about the responsibility to support one's aged parents and in the husband-and-wife relationship, and issues having to do with the increase in double-income families, such as the questions of how to rear and discipline children) would be overcome before long, by helping the nuclear family 'discover' a new order of family life. Thus, in the words of a 1967 recommendation of the Council on Family Life Problems,[10] social security and other public policy measures were expected to perform a role of *indirectly helping the family so that it could overcome* its 'transitional functional failures' *with less difficulty than otherwise*, but this role should be basically limited to helping 'the efforts of those directly involved in family life . . . by providing them with proper clues and guidelines'.

Second, during this period, difficulties faced by families and individuals left out of the economic prosperity (such as aged persons, widows, female-headed families, and families with disabled members) became the focus of public attention, and a series of laws for providing financial support to these individuals and families began to be legislated; but as to the question of how their welfare needs, other than their income security, should be met, the government continued to give priority to helping the family gain greater stability and become self-supporting. It was argued that 'no protective measures can match the power of co-operation generated by human relationships within the family' (the policy recommendation referred to in note 10).

Third, the social security policy, while founded upon its view of the family, was given a role as a supporting pillar for economic growth. For instance, a policy document announced in 1966 by the Council on National Life, a consultative body to the Prime Minister, under the title 'The Image of People's Lives in the Future', argued that social security outlays would have economic effects, and should be characterized as social costs for economic growth. The 'Socioeconomic Development Plan' announced by the government in 1967 also declared an important task expected of future improvements in social security measures, in addition to coping with changes in the practice of mutual support among family members and other social practices. This task was one of assisting in the smooth promotion of structural readjustments necessitated by the economy as it gains in efficiency, or in the prevention or mitigation of possible friction that will accompany such structural readjustments. In other words, in designing improvements in social security programmes in order to deal with the transformations of the family and neighbourhood communities, the government was bent on making such improvements primarily as part of policy instruments for sustaining continued economic growth.

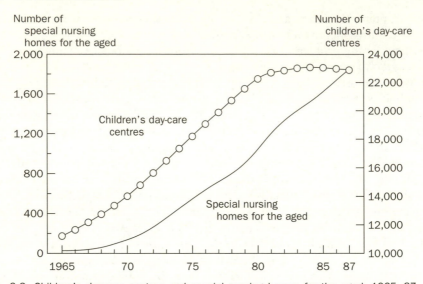

Fɪɢ. 6.2. Children's day-care centres and special nursing homes for the aged, 1965–87

Source: Ministry of Health and Welfare, *Kosei Hakusho* (White Paper on Welfare), 1988 edition, 12, based on the same ministry's Statistics and Information Department, 'Shakai Fukushi Shisetsu Chosa' (A Survey on Social Welfare Facilities).

Fourth, another feature of social security policy related to the preceding three was that the policy makers depended heavily on the roles to be played by the family. This attitude of the policy makers was evident in the way they perceived 'the new family problems', as noted in the first point above, but it also dictated their approaches to other problems as well. Let us cite some examples:

1. In explaining why an increasing number of families were having difficulties in supporting aged parents, the Council on Family Life Problems in its recommendation referred to above (note 10) simply reasoned that 'changes in society are so excessive . . . that knowhow is not yet established which will enable aged parents and younger couples to cooperate and support each other in ways best suited to their age differential and their economic capabilities'.

2. The Socio-economic Development Plan mentioned above asserted that the role of women in the new family should be, above all else, to adapt themselves to the new trend in consumption life, enrich their knowledge and ability to become wise and rational caretakers of household affairs, and to safeguard their children's health and educate them properly.

3. As to the increase in the number of married women holding jobs, the tendency for these women to be overburdened with multiple tasks was taken note of, and an call was made for the improvement in their working conditions, with children's day care centers gradually increasing in number. But all

the measures implemented on behalf of working women with spouses were premised on the philosophy that these women ought to perform their dual responsibilities at home and at workplaces harmoniously.

This means that the economic policy and social security policy at the time were able to take advantage of the family's two self-help principles. Put differently, the friction and ripples that affected the lives of ordinary people as an inevitable consequence of social upheavals under the high economic growth were, in the end, left to the care of the family.

(3) The achievements of social security policy and family policy during the high economic growth period

(i) The Social Security System and 'the First Year of Welfare': As the economic boom continued until 1973, the transformations of the family proceeded apace, producing ever greater effects. On the other hand, the period from the late 1960s to the early 1970s saw outbursts of a host of negative side-effects of the high growth. These included: the spiral increase in consumer prices fuelled by growth-promoting policies; growing qualms felt by ordinary people in designing their future life-courses, as they faced soaring prices, changing lifestyles, and prolonged life-cycles; the growing contrast between over-populated cities and depopulated countryside; the intensifiction of land (housing) and housing problems; and a host of industrial pollution problems. Indeed, all the basic conditions and problems that characterize the life structure in contemporary Japan appeared on the scene during this period.

The government, in its effort to deal with these developments, devised and/or implemented a series of social security programmes in the period from May 1970 (when the Sato cabinet announced the 'New Socio-economic Development Plan') until February 1973 (when the Tanaka cabinet announced the 'Fundamental Plan for the Economy and Society'). Included among the new measures that were put into effect in rapid succession were: (a) the establishment in 1972 of a free medical care program for the aged; (b) a 1973 revision of the health-care insurance system that raised benefit levels for dependants, and introduced a subsidy programme for exceptionally expensive medical treatment; (c) a series of improvements in the pension system (including the introduction in 1973 of a price-indexation scheme); (d) the establishment in 1971 of a universal programme for children's allowance, which had been called for for many years; (e) a 1974 revision of the employment insurance programme; (f) improvements in 1973–5 of the contents of the benefits paid under the public assistance programme for people in need; and (g) announcements of proposals on the improvement of social welfare services.[11]

The Fundamental Plan for the Economy and Society of 1973, subtitled 'For a Vital Welfare Society', was appraised as having marked the 'first year of welfare' in Japan. Identifying the betterment of various social security programmes as one of the most urgent tasks to be fulfilled, the plan offered a detailed list of specific measures that the government was planning to implement by 1977. And many of these measures were actually put into effect.

As a consequence, social security outlays as a percentage of total government expenditures, which were a little over 16 per cent in 1970–2, increased sharply to 20.6 per cent in 1975, and 22.1 per cent in 1976. It should be admitted that, as it turned out, the Fundamental Plan's two-point 'guiding philosophy'—the need to drastically reorient the socio-economic policy from the one in pursuit of economic efficiency and economic growth, on the one hand, and the need to 'distribute the fruits of economic growth to all the strata of society, and redress the uneven distribution of wealth and other forms of inequality', on the other—was not a castle in the air.

(ii) Changes in the Perception of the Family: Naturally, the policy ideas with these new features were accompanied by certain changes in the basic perception of the family. For instance, the New Socio-economic Development Plan of 1970 argued that the betterment of social security was indispensable for mitigating social conflicts and tensions that were resulting from the accelerating ageing of the population, the accelerating increase in the number of nuclear families, the decrease in the number of children, changes in the employment structure, and other factors; it also emphasized that, in taking the actual steps toward this end, special consideration should be paid to the aged and the physically disabled, who tend to be left out of economic development. This perception was further elaborated by several government organs, and, in particular, the Council on National Life in its November 1970 report, *Guidelines for Improvements in Human Environments*. The new perception about the family may be characterized as follows, when looked at in connection with the betterment of social security.

First, the *Guidelines* took note of the fact that nuclear families were becoming increasingly vulnerable and unstable in dealing with various difficulties which they are bound to face, and were in fact having difficulties even in raising children. It then characterized the problems faced by the family as constituting part of the 'havoc wrought on the social environments' by an advanced industrial society. At the same time, the *Guidelines* claimed that, precisely because of such a social situation, the family is expected to play an increasingly important role as a mental resort for individuals. It went on to assert that 'the contemporary family, . . . increasingly dependent as it is on society, cannot be expected to solve all the problems by itself', and that, as such, it should receive greater social support. In other words, the *Guidelines* argued for improving social security programmes, so that these could directly underpin the very basis of the nuclear family.

Second, a strong concern was expressed about the question of how to deal with the needs felt by aged persons. The needs related to factors such as the children's decreasing sense of responsibility to support their aged parents, an increase in the number of households composed only of aged persons in the depopulated areas, the decline in the authority or the significance of aged people in families, and aged people's alienation from the workplace and neighbourhood communities. These problems, too, were perceived to be part of the 'havoc wrought on the social environments', which was the flip side of the increase in the number of nuclear families. Then, the *Guidelines* took note of the woeful lags in the public and private adaptation to these situations. Not simply the measures for assuring free medical care for aged persons and improvements in pension benefits, but also those for raising public assistance levels and social welfare benefits to be discussed in the subsequent two paragraphs, were reflective of this perception. Policy makers seem to have reached a decision at this stage that income security for the aged ought to be basically financed by public funds.[12]

Third, another new development in the perception of family problems was that improvements in livelihood assistance levels and social welfare programmes were pursued. On the one hand, the former measure mirrored the fact that aged people and disabled persons emerged as the major targets for livelihood assistance, because the years of the economic boom had virtually done away with the issue of destitution faced by people capable of working (Table 6.4). The betterment of income security measures was meant to help support those households which are unable to keep functioning normally. On the other hand, the latter efforts at improving social welfare programmes meant that the support offered to families having members with specific problems would be expanded and enriched accordingly.

Fourth, the formation of new communities was proclaimed as a new challenge, in close connection with all the three points noted above. The intent was to face up to the reality in which the family must depend increasingly on a neighbourhood community as it grows smaller in size, while the traditional community was being dissolved, and to do so by forming a new type of community which would be founded upon a new sense of social solidarity. A new awareness of the need for community care of the aged and disabled also came on the scene.

(4) The betterment of social security: its logic and limitations

Having characteristics such as those pointed out above, the social security measures designed in the early 1970s may be interpreted as having been meant, at least to a certain extent, to bring Japan closer to the welfare state on the European model, even if gradually. These policy measures saw the family as

TABLE 6.4. Households receiving livelihood assistance by type of households (monthly average), 1960–93

	Total households receiving livelihood assistance (=100%)	Household type (%)				Persons covered by livelihood assistance (1,000 persons)
		Households consisting only of aged persons	Female-headed households	With sick, wounded, or disabled members	Other households	
1960	574,000*	21.5	13.3	–	–	–
1965*	644,000	22.9	13.7	29.4	34.0	1,599
1970	658,000	31.4	10.3	35.9	22.4	1,344
1975	708,000	34.3	9.5	46.1	10.2	1,349
1980	747,000	32.6	12.6	43.5	11.3	1,427
1985	781,000	32.5	14.4	43.6	9.5	1,431
1990	624,000	39.3	11.7	41.1	7.9	1,015
1993	586,000	43.3	9.3	39.9	7.5	883

(For 1960, the figure 65.2 spans the "With sick, wounded, or disabled members" and "Other households" columns.)

Note: Of the total households consisting only of aged persons in 1990, as many as 85% were single-person households.

Sources: Tabulated on the basis of Kosei Hakusho, various annual editions. However, asterisks indicate figures taken from Seikatsu Hogo 30-nenshi (A 30-Year History of Livelihood Assistance Programmes), 430.

worthy of receiving public and social support. And the expenses for these measures were underwritten by the expectation that high-growth economy would continue, despite a certain degree of policy reorientation implied by these measures.

None the less, the ultimate purpose of the economic policy at the time was, first and foremost, 'growth', and not 'welfare'. In fact, the two economic plans referred to above were drawn within the framework of a grand design for continued economic growth that was set by the Second Comprehensive National Development Plan of 1969. The basic philosophy governing the social security programmes remained the same as the one that had prevailed throughout the high economic growth period. Improvements in social security had been viewed essentially as costs necessary for dealing with the social transformations that would inevitably take place in the course of economic growth, and doing so in ways to allow the economy to grow further. These costs were assumed to be financed with ease as the government budget would expand, keeping pace with the economy's expansion.

The idea of social support to the family, too, was a far cry from what is required of a family policy in the narrow sense. This was partly due to the demographic forecast. While the ageing of the population was already being anticipated, it was believed that the productive population, aged 15 to 65, would remain large enough to support the aged population for an extended period. Another plausible reason was that policy makers seem to have continued to expect that the family would keep performing the important role it had throughout the high growth period.

Let us cite some pieces of evidence that would corroborate the last point:

1. The policy documents referred to above, in their comments on the status and roles of women with spouses, only saw the reduction in their domestic labour as giving them longer leisure time, without mentioning any specific problems they were faced with.

2. On the issue of increasing labour force participation by these women, too, these documents emphasized the importance of childrearing by mothers at home, while making only a peripheral call for the building and expansion of day-care centres. In other words, policy makers seem to have been of the opinion that the two forms of division of labour between the sexes would continue to function smoothly.

3. The children's allowance programme, despite having been introduced with much fanfare, failed to show much improvement.

4. Measures planned and/or implemented for the sake of the aged in need of care focused before all else on improvement and expansion of public welfare institutions for institutional care (typically, special nursing homes for the aged). Although the need for home care and community care began to be voiced, the policy documents failed to say anything specific about the role

that the family was to perform for the aged. The basic attitude of policy makers was that the number of the aged in need of care was still limited, and that the burden of caring for them was often being borne by their families.[13] The building of nursing institutions to accommodate those who had nobody to take care of them at home took second place in their minds.

5. While it is true that efforts to improve social welfare services began to be made during the period under consideration, such efforts were very limited in extent.[14]

Then we might be able to conclude that the social security policy of 'the first year of welfare' did not make a radical departure from the earlier one. After all, it was meant to assist in sustaining the economic boom, by simply trying to redress the maldistribution of the wealth within the means left unused for the promotion of economic growth. At least in theory, the family was perceived as worthy of being supported publicly and socially, but in practice, the support that was offered was conceived within the narrow framework described above, and, moreover, with a tacit assumption that the family would live by the two-layered principle that it should be self-supportive. This was precisely why the plans for improvements in social security measures that were launched in the early 1970s failed easily when the economy plunged into a deep recession in the wake of the oil crisis, only to be replaced by a call for a wholesale reassessment of welfare as a means of redressing the government's budget deficit in the era of slowed economic growth.

III. Social Security and Family Policies after the 'Reassessment of the Welfare'

1. Reorientation of social security and family policies

Developments concerning the social security policy since the emergence of the argument calling for a radical reassessment of the welfare can be broken down into three phases: the latter half of the 1970s; much of the 1980s; and the period from the late 1980s to date.

(1) The emergence of the argument for 'Japanese-style welfare society' and a reassessment of the family's role

Phase one covered the second half of the 1970s, when efforts were made to redefine the priority of the social security policy, and to readjust and streamline those various programmes under the pressure of the stretched financial ability of the government. The intent was to help the government avoid being burdened with the mushrooming social security outlays which it would inevitably have to shoulder had the policy proposals launched in the early

1970s been put into effect to the letter. As early as in 1978–9, a new blueprint was prepared that called for establishing *a Japanese-style welfare society and distinct from the welfare states of the western European model*. To begin with, an 'Economic Plan for the First Half of the Fifth Decade of Showa', which was adopted in 1976 by the Miki cabinet to deal with the economic crunch after the oil crisis, redefined *the direction to be pursued by social security policies*. The Plan asserted that not all the efforts to improve the public welfare should be expended solely by the government, but the roles to be played by individuals, the family, and business, as well as mutual aid based on a social and communal sense of solidarity, were no less important. It proposed to reinforce the functions of the family, and to count on communities and the family as the major vehicle for raising the level of welfare. This policy reorientation was echoed and promoted further by the Liberal Democratic party's 'Action Programme for 1978', and by the 1978 edition of the *White Paper on Welfare*. The LDP's policy document emphasized that, in order to avoid repeating the 'errors' suffered by the welfare states of the western European type, Japan ought to reject pork-barrel welfare programmes, and ask the programmes' beneficiaries instead to carry greater burdens in accordance with the spirit of self-help. The *White Paper* echoed the same theme, pointing out that the existence of three-generation families in Japan at a higher rate than in other advanced countries—or what it called 'latent property for the welfare in Japan'—was an invaluable asset that should be harnessed and put to good account. This policy direction was further refined by the LDP's 'Action Programme for 1979', with its call to 'give greater role to the family, and build a Japanese-style welfare society', and by the LDP Political Affairs Research Committee's policy document announced in June 1979, entitled 'Guidelines on Measures for Improving the Family Base'.

The expression 'Japanese-style' was meant to connote the sense of emphasizing the self-help by individuals, and the roles played by firms and neighbourhood communities, but its most important implication was that the family should perform the roles which traditional values had assigned to it, including the role in taking care of aged parents. For instance, the LDP's Action Programme for 1979 praised, in addition to the spirit of self-help, the 'communal sense of the family . . . which is a laudable custom of Japan', and the fact that nearly 80 per cent of aged people are living with their families. The LDP document asserted that 'Japanese-style welfare society' would be 'a fair and vital welfare society which should be built on the base of these advantages in combination with appropriate public welfare programmes'.

This was why the same document simultaneously called for the betterment of the family base. It was essential, the party declared, to arouse public awareness that the family should assume primary responsibility to support aged parents and to rear children, and thereby 'to make the family more competent to make up for the defects in the economic and social institutions'.

On the other hand, the use of the expression 'welfare society' instead of 'welfare state' reflected the orientation of the new social security policy which proposed to improve the public well-being by depending not only upon state-financed social security programmes, but also, and increasingly, upon the self-help efforts of each private citizen, the solidarity between the family and the neighbourhood community, and corporate-sponsored in-house welfare programmes. In that sense, the two expressions 'Japanese-style' and 'welfare society' were inseparably related to each other.

The same idea was endorsed by the 'New Seven-Year Plan for the Economy and Society' in 1979. The Seven-Year Plan tacitly expected the family to perform the above-mentioned roles, as it defined its purpose as follows: 'Having caught up with the advanced countries of the West, Japan in plotting the future course of development for its economy and society should stop turning to these countries for an ideal model, . . . but should choose and discover a uniquely Japanese model that would be driven by the creative energy of a society of a free-market economy, in which social security would be underpinned by individuals' self-help efforts, and the solidarity within the family and neighbourhood or local communities, with an efficient government performing a secondary role of providing appropriate public welfare benefits on a selective basis—that is to say, Japan should aim at realizing what might be called a new welfare society of the Japanese-type.' On the issue of fiscal outlays for social security programmes, the Plan declared that the old practices of government finance and administration during the high-growth period should be subjected to a wholesale reassessment in accordance with a three-point principle:

1. carry out social security programmes effectively and on a priority basis;
2. correct inequalities among different programmes; and
3. balance the levels of benefits and partial contributions to be made by the beneficiaries.

The government actually launched efforts to curb the growth rate of social security outlays beginning with its budget for Fiscal Year 1980.

In a word, the reorientation of the social security policy explained above represented beyond doubt a choice to put economic growth over and above welfare, and, as such, put the family to test in shouldering more of the burden for safeguarding the welfare.

(2) The Report of the Ad Hoc Council on the Administrative Reform, and the adoption of the 'Guideline on Measures for Dealing with the Ageing of the Population'

Phase two of a radical reassessment of the welfare began with the establishment in December 1980 of the Second Ad Hoc Council on the Administrative

Reform, an advisory body to the Prime Minister, for the purpose of finding ways of rebuilding government finances without tax increases. (Shorty before this, the government's proposal to introduce a general consumption tax had been severely criticized in the 1980 general elections and had been withdrawn.) Phase two lasted until the end of the 1980s.

In a series of its reports, the Ad Hoc Council clearly identified social security programmes as an important target for public parsimony. For instance, the Council's final report of March 1983 argued that while 'the welfare benefit levels guaranteed to those truly in need of support ought to be maintained, it is essential that the government pay as much respect as possible to the people's efforts to be independent and help themselves, and their sense of responsibility, . . . and refrain from excessive interference that could harm these efforts'. Social security programmes should, therefore, 'be limited to a minimum level so as to allow a full play for unrestrained private activities'. The proposal found its way into the economic plan announced by the Nakasone cabinet in August 1983, entitled 'The Prospect and Guideline for the Economy and Society of the 1980s', with its stated purpose of giving 'vitality to the economy and society'. The Prospect and Guideline inherited the three-point principle from the New Seven-Year Plan of 1979, and proclaimed an intention to 'overhaul and renovate social security programmes' along the lines explained above.[15] There is no denying that promoting the social security policy in this direction was to swim with the neo-liberalist or neo-conservative tide as seen in the developed industrial countries around the world, with its orientation toward a smaller government.

It was within this framework that the family's role and position relative to social security were subjected to a comprehensive review at the level of national policy. The Ad Hoc Council emphasized in its final report that a 'more efficient government' would require the maintenance and further development of 'the peculiarly Japanese practice of allowing the family, the community, and businesses to perform extensive roles'. The Prospect and Guideline listed the 'improvements in the environmental factors concerning the family' as one of the important items on the policy agenda along with the 'adjustment and reforms of social security programmes', and identified the measures to be implemented for this purpose. Worthy of special attention were some new shifts in emphasis:

1. unlike the earlier policy documents, the Prospect and Guideline refrained from making direct reference to the traditional or peculiarly Japanese family, but instead discussed policy measures in more general terms to include those aimed at nuclear families; and

2. it placed greater emphasis than did its earlier counterparts on the need to strengthen 'organic solidarity' between the family and the neighbourhood or local community.

The 1983 edition of the *White Paper on National Life*, which was dubbed the 'first *White Paper* on the Family', made a comprehensive analysis of the current reality of the family, identifying what measures for improving the family base should be implemented in line with the newly proposed family policy.

Another important development was the emergence of the rapid ageing of the population as a policy issue having extremely important implications for the efforts of the government to restrain the expansion in social security outlays and maintain the vitality of the economy and society. That was why the Prospect and Guideline called for the 'establishment of a new system adapted to the life-style in the age of an 80-year life expectancy', specifically, 'a comprehensive arrangement whereby people, feeling secure about their lives by means of employment, social security, and asset formation, can live more decently in the family, the community, the workplace, and other arenas of their lives'. The intent was to reorganize and reformulate various policy measures in a comprehensive manner and well in advance of the ageing of the population's getting into fuller swing.

On the issue, three successive reports were compiled in 1986. The last document, entitled the 'Guideline on Measures for Dealing with the Ageing of the Population', and adopted by the Cabinet in June the same year, was meant to define such a policy on more concrete terms, and to lay out specific policy measures. The basic intent of these policy proposals, summed up shortly, was to build a 'new economic and social system' which could accommodate a social factor quite new to Japan, i.e., the ageing population, without allowing it to hinder the growth potential of the economy. Not surprisingly, the existing social security scheme was regarded as one of the existing schemes that needed to be overhauled drastically.

The redefinition of policy priorities such as this rendered the image of the family envisioned by policies of the state quite different from what it once used to be. Whereas previously the family had been regarded as the object of support by social security programmes, it was now perceived as a means of facilitating the cutbacks on social security expenditures, or even as an important pillar safeguarding the social security and welfare of the country.

(3) The emergency of a new policy trend

Phase three of the development of Japan's welfare in a new direction covers the period from the late 1980s, when the social security policy took a new turn as described above (in I-1(3)). But, before dealing with the new trends in the family policy in Phase three, let us sum up the implications of the policy changes in Phases one and two.

2. Main tasks faced by the family policy and the orientation of policy measures

As noted in I-2, the period under review saw the simultaneous emergence of three factors concerning the family in an overlapping way: the adoption by the government of a policy to restrain increase in social security outlays, the emergence of the ageing of the population and its attendant problems, and the continuing transformations of the family and its increasing vulnerability. These new factors challenged policy makers with a question of how best they should realign family policy in relation to social security. The main questions that were at issue, and the essential features of the policy measures that were actually adopted to deal with them, might be summarized as follows.

(1) The family as the linchpin of the ageing society

The ageing of the population inevitably called for improvements of social security and social welfare measures, not only so as to guarantee a certain level of living conditions to aged people but also to deal with the increase in the number of those in need of care. The provision of nursing and care for aged people would require the securing and training of human power, and thus could not be solved by means of income security measures alone. Yet, given its determination to put a lid on the growth rate of social security outlays, the government would never be able to afford to address the question mainly by expanding the publicly funded support. Consequently, policy makers called upon the aged to support themselves as much as possible, on the one hand, while re-evaluating the role the family was performing in privately support-ing and nursing aged parents, calling this role Japan's 'latent property for welfare'. Underlying this re-evaluation of the family's role was the fact that as recently as the mid-1980s, as many as 90 per cent of aged people living at home and suffering from immobility and/or senile dementia were taken care of by family members with whom they were living, and more than 80 per cent of these caretakers were women (i.e., the wife of an aged man, and the daughter-in-law and daughters of aged parent(s)) (see the 1987 edition of the White Paper on Welfare, pp. 41, 51).

The expression 'latent property', when it began to be used in support of the argument for a Japanese-style welfare society, had conservative connota-tions. The White Paper on the Family of 1983 referred to above still retained some traces of this perception, when it said that the situation of the family 'where the transition from the system of a family composed of direct lineal relatives to one of a genuine nuclear family [had] not yet been completed . . . [was] on the whole, much preferable to the way the state of things stood in the West', and emphasized the need to reinforce such a 'family in Japan' (pp. 243, 251).

By the mid-1980s, however, the importance of the family had been redefined in more progressive terms. It was now asserted that while an individual aged person's spirit of independence and self-help was most fundamental, the family closest to him/her should be expected to offer primary support and assistance to him/her in accordance with the spirit of mutual help. More specifically, the 1986 edition of the *White Paper on Welfare* argued that, in order to restructure the social security system, a proper division of labour should be established among 'self-help, mutual help, and public help'. Elaborating on this principle, the *White Paper* underlined that 'a healthy society should be equipped with a three-layered mechanism of help. Forming the base is the individual's effort to be independent and self-supportive, then come the support provided by the family and neighbourhood community, and on top of these the public sector provides additional support' (pp. 33–4). By that time it had become a commonly accepted practice to differentiate the providers of social security services into the formal sector and the informal sector, and to perceive that those portions of services left uncovered by the primary services provided by the former sector should be offered mainly by the latter sector. In this perception, the family was identified as the nucleus of the informal sector.

As a matter of fact, the 1986 *White Paper* also argued that in order to facilitate 'efficient administration of the social security system, . . . it is essential to redraw a division of labour between public and private services, . . . redefine the appropriate extent and levels of benefits to be covered by social security programmes' (pp. 34–5). Similarly, the 1987 edition of the *White Paper on Welfare*, in its detailed discussion of the need to secure caretakers for the aged, took note that 'many share[d] a strong willingness to take care of or nurse aged parents at home, should conditions permit', and argued that it would be necessary to 're-evaluate and help improve the functions of the family as a supply source of informal caretakers' (pp. 39, 41). Thus, the family's function as a self-supportive safety net was conceived, at the level of a policy blueprint, as constituting a part of the 'welfare supplying system' in a broad sense.

(2) Measures for strengthening the family as a provider of welfare service

Yet, the family in reality had grown smaller and weaker than it used to be. In order to enable the family to perform its newly assigned role, some measures had to be devised to strengthen and augment its waning capacity. Main measures implemented to this end were as follows.

One group of measures that received much emphasis between the late 1970s and the mid-1980s was aimed at strengthening the family base. It was considered important to assess properly the social value of domestic labour and, especially, the role performed by a full-time housewife (or one having a part-time job). While keeping unchanged the existing division of labour between the sexes within the family, the housewife was to be held mainly responsible for the nursing of her husband or the aged parents of her husband. The measures that were actually devised and put into effect along this line of thinking included: an upward revision in the spouse's legally guaranteed portion of the inheritance as part of the 1980 revision of the Civil Code;[16] a special tax relief on the income earned from a part-time job (introduced in 1984); a guarantee of a basic pension for the unemployed wife of a wage-worker (1985); and the granting of the spouse's special deductions from a donation tax and income tax (1985 and 1987). Also included in this category of measures were: the granting of a special tax credit to an income earner who lives with and supports aged parent[s] (1984); and the launching of subsidies to individuals who build or remodel houses so that they can live with, or live next door to, their aged parents.

A second set of measures was implemented in the areas of health, medical care, and welfare services to help improve the care and nursing of aged persons living at home. It is very true that the family with its decaying self-supportive ability would not perform its expected role as a provider of welfare services unless it could receive some outside support that would help lessen its burden. The idea that the family should be shored up by the surrounding community, which had been proposed as early as the first half of the 1970s, began to take shape in the latter half of the 1980s in the policy objective of providing new forms of social services for those being nursed at home. The policy blueprint announced in October 1988, called the 'Vision of Welfare' (see Table 6.8 in IV-1 below), presented an overview of the measures grouped under the second category that had been put into effect by the end of phase two, along with policy targets to be attained in the years to come.

The third set of measures, implemented since the mid-1980s, was aimed at improving the working conditions for women, especially those with spouses. The trend toward greater labour force participation by women with spouses (Table 6.3 and Figure 6.3) was expected to intensify further in keeping pace with major changes taking place in the industrial structure. Then it was necessary to implement the measures that would enable working women with spouses better to reconcile their willingness to continue holding jobs and their need to fulfil family responsibilities. These measures included: the establishment of the Equal Employment Opportunity Law and the Law Governing Personnel Agencies Dispatching Temporary Workers (1985); revisions in the Labour Standards Law that relaxed the regulations on women's working conditions; and measures encouraging private firms to improve or establish programmes for childcare leave, re-employment of women in their middle age, and nursing care leave for their aged parents.

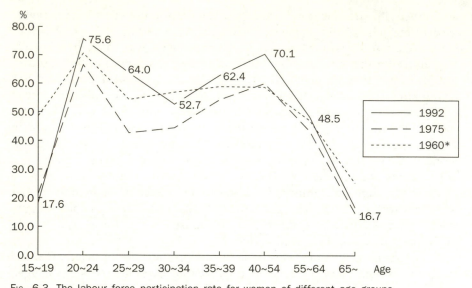

FIG. 6.3. The labour force participation rate for women of different age groups

Note: It should be kept in mind that, as shown in Table 6.3, the graph for 1960 reflects the relatively high percentages of women who were engaged in agriculture.

Sources: Somucho Tokeikyoku (Statistics Bureau, Management and Coordination Agency), 'Rodoryoku Chosa' (A Survey on Labour Force), reproduced in Koseisho Daijin Kambo Seisakuka (Policy Division, Minister's Secretariat, Ministry of Health and Welfare) (ed.), *21-seiki Fukushi Bijon* (A Vision of Welfare in the Twenty-First Century) (Daiichi Hoki, 1994), 96.

(3) A more comprehensive response to family problems of an ageing society

These measures of support to the family by themselves, however, would never be enough to stem the transformations of the family. If so, a more comprehensive plan to deal with family problems would have to be devised, taking into account that the family could bear the burden of supporting the aged only to a limited extent. And hammered out to meet just such a necessity was the 'Guideline on Measures for Dealing with the Ageing of the Population'. The Guideline adopted by the cabinet in 1986 had the following features.

First, the Guideline emphasized that the aged themselves in the future ought to exert greater efforts to be more independent and self-supportive by building up and making better use of their own assets, continuing to work for longer years, and increasing their subscriptions to personal pension programmes. In line with this view, subsequent editions of the *White Paper on Welfare* identified the 'new, model image of an aged person' for the future as one who, even if afflicted by some illness, would be basically affluent and healthy enough to continue working or pursuing other forms of social participation, and proposed the restructuring of various social security pro-grammes premissed on this image.

Second, at the level of concrete policy measures, too, the early consolida-tion of an 'employment and income security system' that would help the aged to be more independent and self-supportive was regarded as a first-order issue that would reduce the relative burden of public income security programmes. Specific measures implemented to this end included:

1. reform of the pension system in 1985, aimed partly at *preventing a possible bankruptcy of pension finances* in the future;
2. preparation for raising the minimum age for eligibility to a pension to 65;
3. measures to encourage a larger number of private employers to adopt the system of retirement at 60, and to adopt various means of enabling their employees to continue working up to the age of 65;
4. measures for the propagation of corporate-administered employee pension plans and personal pension plans; and
5. measures for encouraging people to build assets to provide for their old age.

Third, with regard to various welfare services, the Guideline emphasized the need to expand their provision on a commercial basis, by charging for services that were hitherto free and encouraging private bodies to under-take these. This shift in emphasis accorded with the effort to 'diversify the providers of services', and was also linked to the idea of encouraging efficient handling of individual assets as a guarantee for one's old age. Taking this as given, the Guideline further proposed that individuals, families, neighbour-hood communities, volunteers, private firms, and welfare institutions of both the public and private sectors should play their roles in an extensive variety of combinations.

Looking at these factors, it becomes clear that the question at issue was calling for a 'drastic remodelling of the socio-economic system'. This meant that the social security policy had to be synthesized more closely with policies in the related areas such as the employment and housing policies, and the family policy, too, had to be subjected to a rethinking from a similar perspective.

(4) Several latent problems

The increased 'synthesization' among various programmes concerning the family has some advantages of allowing these programmes to deal with vary-ing needs of aged people and their families with greater flexibility. At the same time, however, this has several problems as discussed below.

First, the basic philosophy that informed the developments in the policy measures examined in (1) to (3) was oriented toward something different from the concept of the family policy understood in a narrow sense. More specifically, the idea of depending on the family to perform the role as a provider of welfare services was basic to all these developments and derived from the sense of necessity to restrain the growth of social security outlays.

For instance, the measures in support of the family were aimed primarily at maintaining the role the family had traditionally performed in the caring of aged parents. This means that the shouldering of the burden by the family and the measures in support of that family had to always stand in an ambivalent relationship. To be sure, the call for enriching the 'support to those who are helping aged people in need of care' has been advocated lately in countries of western Europe. It must be kept in mind, however, that the implications of this view are quite different from those of the similar view in Japan.

Second, the move to synthesize among various policies is also laden with one serious problem. The synthesization can possibly obscure the definition of the role which publicly and socially financed social security programmes are supposed to perform, and let the problems which these programmes are meant to address disperse and disappear into the general task of restructuring the socio-economic system.

Third, the foregoing two points, and the view that regards the family as responsible for 'offering primary support and assistance to individuals', can work together to obscure the difference and relationship between public and private support, making it easier for the state to mobilize and depend primarily on the 'family's role as a provider of welfare services'. Indeed, a policy system such as this calls upon the family, first, to offer human power for the care and nursing of aged parents, and, should it fail to do so fully, to purchase the necessary welfare services by paying for the costs not only out of the assets held by the aged person, but also out of the children's incomes. Thus, it must be kept in mind that, when the concept of 'normalization' is referred to in Japan, it would often be attended with the meaning of a means of reducing financial burdens of the government.

Against the backdrop of these developments in the social security policy, some new currents in academic discussions are emerging in various fields of the social sciences. In the area of law, some arguments are being advanced that the difference between the two legal concepts of civil law, i.e., the life maintenance responsibility and the livelihood assistance responsibility, should be redefined, and that the children's responsibility to support and nurse their aged parents should be reinforced in clearer terms. In the field of sociology, there is a current of thought that expands on the general definition of the family—i.e., the family is a primary group in pursuit of the welfare sustained by mental unity—and to invoke and paraphrase it for use as a theoretical justification for the assumed role of the family as a provider of welfare services. There are also recent arguments by economists that regard the family as part of an 'insurance mechanism', and highly appraise the extended family, or 'modified extended family' (whose members live close to each other, if not together), as an invaluable 'resource' for social security. Thus, the theme of what might be called a 'contemporary realignment of the self-support principle of the family' has begun to emerge as a focal point of attention of both policy makers and some academics.

However, there was lying latent behind these new developments the question of whether the actual family could carry out such a demand satisfactorily. The question takes on an especially risky proportion if one takes into account the possibility that the new policy orientation examined above would have the effect of more fully subjecting the family to the market mechanism, thereby making the traditional sense of the norm of support and care for aged parents weaker and weaker in the long run. This is exactly why a leading sociologist sounded an alarm about the advent of these new developments as early as in 1983, pointing out that 'the family today is no longer the "latent property for welfare in Japan", as the country [has] already eaten itself out of this property'.[17]

IV. Present Developments in the Family Policy and its Future Prospect

The new policy reorientation discussed above has actually been forced to undergo yet another new series of revisions and amendments since around 1990, as mentioned in I-1(3). While the ageing of society has proceeded at a pace far faster than expected, the question of the family's actual role has surfaced rapidly with the precipitating drop in the birth rate. In this section, we will discuss the developments in the family policy at the present stage, i.e., phase three, dealing first with problems having to do with countermeasures for the welfare of the aged, and then with problems involved in the efforts to establish a 'comprehensive family policy'.

1. The family and trends in countermeasures for the welfare of the aged

(1) The family and the present state of care for the aged

In 1993 there was an estimated total of some 2 million aged people who were in need of care (or 11.8 per cent of all people over 65), of whom approximately 900,000 were bed-ridden (including those suffering from both immobility and senile dementia), some 100,000 suffering from senile dementia and in need of care, and another million suffering from other forms of weakness.[18]

TABLE 6.5. Main caretakers of the bed-ridden elderly living at home

	Number of caretakers (000s)	Percentage breakdown	Female (%)	Male (%)
Total number of caretakers	289	100.0	85.9	14.1
Caretakers living with the aged	248	86.0	85.3	14.7
Spouse		27.9	79.4	20.6
Child		20.6	70.3	29.7
Child's spouse		33.4	99.0	1.0
Other relatives, and non-relatives		4.0	89.8	10.8
Caretakers living apart from the aged	41	14.0	89.3	10.7
Relatives		5.7	93.7	6.3
Non-relatives		8.4	87.5	12.5

Source: Tabulated on the basis of Koseisho Daijin Kambo Tokei Johobu (Statistical Information Department, Minister's Secretariat, Ministry of Health and Welfare), *Kokumin Seikatsu Kiso Chosa* (A Fundamental Survey on National Life) (1992), table 133, pp. 190–81.

These numbers are bound to increase in the future, in keeping with the ageing of the population.

At present, more than half of the aged people in need of care are being nursed at home by their families, and more than 60 per cent of the social costs of their nursing (totalling approximately ¥3,500 billion) was estimated to have been borne by the family in 1993.[19] Of the main caretakers for the immobile aged people living at home, 86 per cent live with them, and as many as 85 per cent of these caretakers are women (Table 6.5). Broken down by family relationship, more than 80 per cent of the caretakers are the spouses, children, and the spouses of children—who are virtually the same as the wives, daughters, and the wives of sons, respectively. In particular, the fact that the wives of sons living with the aged account for one-third of the main caretakers shows that the traditional family relations are still subsisting firmly. What is more, not only aged people in need of care, but also the caretakers themselves are ageing; caretakers in their 50s account for 27.5 per cent of all the caretakers at home, those in their 60s 27.0 per cent, and those in their 70s 22.0 per cent. On the other hand, the development in medical technology extends the duration over which the aged are nursed, with the result that 26.8 per cent of the bed-ridden remain immobile for one to three years, and 47.3 per cent for more than three years (see source of Table 6.5).

Consequently, as the findings of various surveys have revealed, the mental and physical burden shouldered by family members, especially female members, is growing much heavier than it used to be years ago. The mere fact that as many as 81,000 people, of whom 90 per cent are women (according to the Management and Co-ordination Agency's 1992 'Fundamental Survey on the Employment Structure'), quit their jobs per year in order to take care of aged family members is indicative enough of how the situation has grown to abnormal proportions. Stories of exhausted female family members refusing to take care of the aged or maltreating the aged begin to make newspaper headlines. None the less, the absolute amount of public services offered to relieve the burden of the family is far smaller than necessary, as the government itself admits (see also note 19).

Furthermore, three-generation households continue to decrease (Table 6.6), households composed only of aged couples or single aged people are increasing rapidly, or the percentage of the aged people living with their offspring decreases (Tables 6.6 and 6.7), and the labour force participation rate for married women is continuing to increase, while the sense of responsibility to support aged parents is waning.[20] Another development worthy of mention is that the divorce rate has begun to rise again lately, and especially that the number of divorces by couples in middle and advanced age is growing phenomenally as a percentage of the total.

These developments show that it is impossible to depend on the family to continue performing an important role in the nursing of the aged in the years to come. This is why a recent poll found that 90 per cent of the respondents have anxieties about their lives in old age, and approximately 50 per cent of them cite as the major cause of their anxieties the apprehension about the possibility that either they or their spouses may become in need of care.[21] Little wonder that the necessity of emergency countermeasures has come to be felt increasingly keenly.

(2) The '10-Year Strategy for the Promotion of the Health and Welfare of the Aged' and the reform of eight welfare-related laws

Efforts to devise emergency countermeasures began with the adoption in December 1989 of the '10-Year Strategy for the Promotion of the Health and Welfare of the Aged' to replace the 'Vision of Welfare', which was announced in October 1988. Having been compiled in the wake of the introduction in April 1989 of the 3 per cent consumption tax under the pretext of securing enough funds for social security and social welfare programmes, the 10-Year Strategy, as the government claimed, marked the beginning of a new era for social security policy.

Indeed, the Vision of Welfare still took a basic tone heavily dictated by the policy orientation that was adopted in 1986, and thus it suppressed the target figures to significant levels (Table 6.8, column B). In contrast, the 10-Year Strategy shifted away from this orientation to a certain extent, adopting a new slogan of building 'a service provisioning system which will make appropriate and high-quality services available to anybody, anytime, with ease and free of anxiety'. Even though it inherited the idea that aged persons should be taken care of and receive welfare services in their homes as much as possible,

TABLE 6.6. Aged people and family composition (%)

	Household with people over 65 (=100%)	Household composed of a single aged person	Household of an aged married couple			Three-generation household	Household of aged parent(s) and unmarried child(ren)	Other forms of household	Actual no. of households (1,000)
			Total	One of the couple is below 65	Both of the couple are over 65				
1972	100.0	8.1	11.3	-	-	55.8	24.8		6,578
1975	100.0	8.6	13.1	-	-	54.4	9.6	14.4	7,113
1980	100.0	10.7	16.2	[7.7]	[8.5]	50.1	10.5	12.5	8,495
1985	100.0	12.0	19.1	[8.5]	[10.6]	45.9	10.8	12.2	9,400
1990	100.0	14.9	21.4	[8.4]	[12.9]	39.5	11.8	12.4	10,816
1992	100.0	15.7	22.8	[8.4]	[14.3]	36.6	12.1	12.8	11,884*
Actual number in 1992	11,884	1,865	2,706	1,002	1,704	4,348	1,439	1,527	11,884*
% breakdown:									
Urban area	100.0	16.8	24.5	-	-	33.3	13.3	12.1	8,604
Countryside	100.0	12.7	18.3	-	-	45.3	8.9	14.7	3,280

Note: As of 1992, the households with persons of over 65 accounted for 28.8% of the total (ordinary) households.

Source: Koseisho Daijin Kambo Tokei Johobu (Statistical Information Department, Minister's Secretariat, Ministry of Health and Welfare) (ed.), Kokumin Seikatsu Kiso Chosa (Fundamental Survey on National Life) (1992) i. 148 and 153.

TABLE 6.7. Aged people over 65, broken down by patterns of living (%)

| Year | Total (%) | Living alone | Couple living alone | Living with a child or children | | | Living with other relatives | Living with non-relatives | Actual no. of people over 65 |
				Total	Living with the child's family	Living with unmarried child(ren)			
1980	100.0	8.5	19.6	69.0	52.5	16.5	2.8	0.2	10,799
1985	100.0	9.3	23.0	64.6	47.9	16.7	2.8	0.2	12,111
1990	100.0	11.2	25.7	59.7	41.9	17.8	3.3	0.2	14,453
1992	100.0	11.7	27.6	57.1	38.7	18.4	3.4	0.3	15,986

Source: The same as the source for Table 6.6, p. 151.

TABLE 6.8. The targets of the 'Vision of Welfare' and the '10-Year Strategy for Welfare of the Aged'

	(A) Actual figures, end of FY 1989	(B) Target to be attained by around FY2000, set by 'Vision of the Welfare' (Oct. 1988)	(C) Target to be attained by FY1999, specified by the '10-Year Strategy' (Dec. 1989)	(D) Target to be attained by FY1999, set after the December 1994 re-examination	(E) Actual figures as of end of FY1993	(F) Number available in 1999 per 1,000 people over 65 (3)
1. Emergency countermeasures for welfare of the aged living at home						
Home helper	31,405 persons	50,000 persons	100,000 persons	170,000 persons	69,000 persons	7.8 persons
Short stay	4,274 beds	50,000 beds	50,000 beds	For 60,000 persons	For 22,000 persons	2.77 beds
Day service centre	1,080 units	10,000 units including small-sized centers	10,000 units including small-sized centers	17,000 units	3,453 units	0.78 units
Support centre for the aged being cared for at home (1a)	–	–	10,000 units	10,000 units	1,238 units	0.46 units
Visiting care station for the aged (1b)	–	–	–	5,000 units	658 units	0.23 units
Home helper station	–	–	–	10,000 units	–	0.46 units
2. Urgent expansion and improvement of facilities						
special nursing home for the aged	162,019 beds	} A total of 500,000 beds	240,000 beds	For 290,000 persons	For 210,000 persons	13.4 beds
Health care facilities for the aged	27,811 beds		280,000 beds	280,000 beds	For 90,000 persons	12.9 beds
Care house (1c)	200 persons	–	100,000 persons	100,000 persons	For 6,853 persons	4.6 persons
Life and welfare centre for the aged in sparsely populated area (1d)	–	–	400 units	400 units	135 units	–
3. Training and securing of caretakers						
House-mother and attendant (2)	–	–	–	200,000 persons	74,343 persons	9.2 persons
Nurse (2)	–	–	–	100,000 persons	?	4.6 persons
Occupational therapist and physiotherapist (2)	–	–	–	15,000 persons	1,355 persons	0.69 persons

Notes and sources:

1. 1c began to be established in FY1989, 1a and 1d in FY1990, and 1b in FY1992. 1d is a small, multi-purpose facility established in a sparsely populated area, for supporting the care of aged people living at home, providing residential care, and providing opportunities for socializing to aged people of the area.

2. The actual number of housemothers and attendants as of the end of FY1993 has been calculated on the basis of a table on 'Number of Employees of Social Welfare Facilities' in *Kosei Hakusho* (White Paper on Welfare), 1995 edition, 333. However, the number of nurses has been unidentifiable.

3. Based on median forecast values for the year 2000 presented in the Ministry of Health and Welfare Population Problems Institute, 'Nihon no Shorai Jinko' (Forecasts of Japanese Population in the Future), which reports on its forecast as of September 1992.

the 10-Year Strategy proposed to improve drastically the ways in which these services are to be provided and delivered. It thus set the target figures at levels considerably higher than those of the Vision of Welfare, and proposed to build a wider variety of facilities (Table 6.8, column C). Looked at side by side with the arguments presented in policy documents that were compiled as the basis for the 10-Year Strategy, the Strategy's orientation can be characterized as follows.

First, there was a growing awareness that it was becoming increasingly difficult to continue to hold the family responsible for the care and nursing of aged people. Thus the 1989 edition of the *White Paper on Welfare* (published in March 1990) emphasized the need to 'pay closer attention to the quality of the life of aged people in need of care', and to 'take a new approach to the question of care for the elderly by the family'. More specifically, two new policy orientations were put forth:

1. to reorient priorities from 'care for the elderly by the family members without the support of home services' to 'caretaking by the family which makes proper use of home services'; and
2. with regard to aged people who are in need of care and who are living alone, or living alone as a couple, to provide them also with 'improved home services which would enable them to live in their homes as long as possible'.

These orientations specified the target figures of home helpers, support centres for aged people being cared for at home, and 'care houses,' in Table 6.8, column C.

Second, as for the provision of health and welfare services, a new policy was adopted to bring both welfare programmes for aged people at home and those accommodated in institutions under the unified authority of municipal governments (see note 1). The June 1990 reform of the eight laws related to welfare, including the Law for the Welfare of the Aged, was meant to hold municipal governments primarily responsible for working out 'health and welfare plans for the aged', and to change institutional arrangements accordingly. Unquestionably, it should be more desirable to have health and welfare services for the aged provided by municipal governments, which are much closer to local residents, than by government agencies, so long as this does not entail the reduction or shirking of the responsibility on the part of the national government. In this sense, Japan has at last become equipped with a rudimentary institutional set-up necessary for implementing a new form of social welfare programmes as 'a community-based, comprehensive, systematic, and multiple-layered endeavour'.

Third, however, this new orientation was premissed on the understanding that the development of private-sector welfare services should be further encouraged to perform greater roles as important suppliers of the services. In fact, the 10-Year Strategy expected that one-third (or ¥2,000 billion) of the total expenses necessary would be forthcoming in the form of private investment. The 1989 edition of the *White Paper on Welfare*, too, devoted a new section on a discussion of 'Sound Nurturing of Private Welfare Services'. In addition, emphasis was placed on the roles to be played in realization of 'community-based welfare' by other organizations, including public corporations for community welfare with investment by municipal governments, non-profit organizations of local residents, and volunteer groups. The 1991 edition of the *White Paper on Welfare*, for instance, featured a lengthy analysis on the theme of 'An Expanding Variety of Agents of Welfare'. With the needs for expansion and improvement of nursing services growing urgent and keener, the task of realizing an 'adequate and effective division of labour between the public and the private' has come to be pursued in a more clearly defined and more concrete form than previously.

(3) Recent developments in the social welfare policy for the aged: measures for care for the aged and state responsibility

It is clear from the discussion in the preceding section that the question of how to strike a proper balance between the first and second policy orientations and the third one is one of the focal points for future welfare policy for the aged. And when we review the recent developments in the welfare programmes, we cannot but take note that several new issues have emerged that call for careful assessment. This is because, while recent policy discussions on the theme are paying greater attention to the urgent necessity of implementing proper measures that can address the problems involved in the nursing of aged people, on the one hand, these same discussions are concerned more and more about the question of how to relieve the national government of its financial burden to underwrite the programmes for the aged, by letting the population bear greater burdens, on the other. Let us see how the situation stands now, by referring to some of the major policy documents and concrete programmes.

(i) To begin with, the Advisory Council on the Social Security System's Committee on the Future Image of Social Security, in its 'First Report' of February 1993, addressed directly the question of a proper division of labour between the public and private sectors. The report pointed out that given the inescapable likelihood that the 'financial resources for financing social security [would] be subjected to severer constraints', it was inevitable to redefine the sphere of responsibility of publicly administered social security programmes more narrowly than previously, both in terms of the variety and contents of individual programmes, and in terms of the financial burden. Meticulously examining the existing relationships between 'the responsibilities of public bodies and individuals or the family', and 'undertakings of the government and those of private businesses', the report underlined very straightforwardly the need to hold individuals responsible for being more independent and for shouldering proper portions of the financial burdens, the need to hold the family responsible for the rearing of children and the nursing of aged parents to a certain extent, and the need to utilize a diversity of privately administered services more actively. The report also emphasized that social security was only a part of the safety net sustaining the social and economic life of the population.

Although these arguments were an extension of the pre-existing policy objective, the report pointed out more explicitly the need to 'redefine the sphere of responsibility of social security in relation to various other components of the safety net' so as to cope with the severer financial restraints.

(ii) This was followed in September 1993 by the announcement of a 'Report of the Round Table Conference on the Basic Orientation of Programmes for the Aged'. On the one hand, this document postulated a 'new image of the aged' as 'people who differ widely from each other in terms of physical strength, insight and self-respect, and economic means'. On the basis of this perception, it emphasized the need to build a system which would enable the aged to continue working up to around 70 years of age. On the other, it made a number of proposals for the 'remodelling of various programmes and schemes for nursing services and other related issues'. More specifically, the document proposed that:

1. the services be made more universal and general in view of the 'growing risks involved in the nursing of the aged';

2. a great variety of services be provided to 'support the self-help efforts of the aged';

3. arrangements be made to enable users to select the type of facilities and the contents of services and enter contracts arranging for these;

4. home services and institutional services be brought into closer combination with each other;

5. commercial services be put to greater use so as to meet varying needs of the users and to render the delivery of services more efficient;

6. the burdens borne by persons nursed at home and those receiving institutional care be more equalized;

7. arrangements be introduced allowing beneficiaries to pay for the costs of the services, and arrangements guaranteeing nursing care to individuals who put up their property as a collateral;

8. a national consensus be formed regarding the greater burdens to be borne by the population as a whole as social security costs increase, and about how these burdens should be shared; and

9. the need to cultivate local residents' sense of participation in social welfare.

(iii) Subsequently, in March 1994, a comprehensive report entitled 'The Vision of Welfare in the Twenty-First Century: In Preparation for an Ageing Society with a Smaller Number of Children' was compiled by a round table meeting convened by the Minister of Welfare, and was presented to the cabinet meeting. Included among the main contentions of the document were the following:

1. emphasizing the need to change the social security system into one which would attach importance to welfare programmes in support of nursing for the aged and rearing of children, it proposed to change the distribution of social security benefits among the pension, medical care, and welfare programmes from the existing relative ratios of 5 : 4 : 1 to 5 : 3 : 2;

2. presenting a few scenarios of the relationship between benefits and contributions in the population, it asserted that 'Japan should strive to establish a welfare society of its own which can strike a balance between appropriate benefits and appropriate charges through a proper combination between public and private services.' Further, it proposed a basic rule for any increments in benefits in excess of the economic growth rate 'to be borne and shared both by the tax payers and the payers of insurance premiums and by the beneficiaries'; and

3. it called for a reassessment of the pension system and improvements in the efficiency of health and medical care services, while presenting a number of concrete proposals for improvements in the support services for nursing of the aged and rearing of children.

The basic tone of the report was that of the 'Guideline on Measures for Dealing with the Ageing of Population' of 1986 (which still remains in effect as the overall principle) and the first report mentioned above. In fact, the report, too, assumed that 'affluent and vigorous aged persons' with enough incomes and assets would increase, proposed to establish 'a multiple-layered welfare structure that appropriately combines self-help, mutual help, and public help systems', and asserted that social security should be sustained by four major pillars, i.e., the public sector which should deal with the basic needs, the private sector which should supply support through market mechanisms, activities of locally based non-profit organizations, and welfare services provided by private firms to their employees.

Thus, the primary object of the report was to emphasize point (2) and the first half of point (3) mentioned above, namely, to justify restraining public social security benefits as much as possible and letting people bear greater burdens. As a matter of fact, the government subsequently implemented a series of measures for putting lids on social security outlays, in particular outlays for health and medical care, and in November 1994 it revised the pension system, increasing the premiums for old-age pensions, and raising the minimum age for eligibility to receive pensions to 65 beginning in 2005. As for the proposed increase in the share of welfare outlays in the total social security outlays mentioned in point (1), too, we may be sure that this increase will be financed mostly by slashing the health and medical care outlays.

It should be noted, however, that the report claimed its emphasis on the need to improve nursing services (point (1) and the latter half of point (3)) to be its important selling point, and proposed specifically:

1. that the target figures postulated by the 10-Year Strategy be overhauled and revised upward;
2. that a new system for the nursing of the aged be established;
3. that a wide range of human resources needed for nursing be secured and trained; and
4. that a law requiring employers to adopt a system of leave for nursing care of the aged should be legislated.

Proposals 1 and 3 were put into effect in December 1994 (Table 6.8, column D). Proposal 4 calling for legislation about a system of nursing care leave, too, was put into effect—though not in a fully satisfactory manner as will be pointed out below—in two stages, first in June 1994 through the legislation of a Revised Working Hours Law for public employees, and then in June 1995 through the legislation concerning a system of nursing care leave for private sector employees.

As for proposal 2, the report, following the footsteps of the 'Report of the Round Table Conference on the Basic Orientation of Programmes for the Aged' mentioned in (ii) above, specified five basic features with which the new nursing system should be equipped: first, the system should be able to supply medical care, welfare, and other services in a comprehensive and co-ordinated manner; second, it should allow its users to choose freely from among alternative combinations of services; third, it should make possible 'sound competition among various suppliers of services'; fourth, it should be such a system that the 'increasing costs of nursing of the aged are borne equitably by the entire population'; and fifth, it should also be able to attain an equality between the costs borne by individuals being taken care of at their homes and those receiving institutional care.

(iv) The idea of the new nursing system advocated by proposal 2 found its way into, and was further elaborated by, two other policy documents, namely, the 'Second Report' of the Advisory Council on the Social Security System's Committee on the Future Image of Social Security compiled in September 1994, and the 'Report of the Study Group on the Support System for the Nursing and Self-Reliance of the Elderly', which was compiled in December the same year. These documents made it clear that the proposed new nursing system was aimed before all else at establishing a compulsory and general nursing insurance scheme. In particular, the latter document went to great lengths offering very detailed and systematic descriptions of the proposed new system. Its argument went as follows in essence: in trying to face up to the urgent task of 'establishing a system of nursing security', the existing pro- grammes would not function because of strained budgets and other prob- lems; on the other hand, the need for nursing services in support of the efforts of the aged to become as independent as possible would grow keener. Given this state of things, it would be advantageous, from the standpoint of secur- ing the financial source, and from that of facilitating early establishment of the new nursing system described above, to start from the perception that the 'risk involved in the nursing of the aged' was growing universal, and to introduce, on the basis of this perception, a new social insurance system as a means of 'mutual help based on social solidarity'.

To be sure, with a basic financial source secured by the introduction of a compulsory nursing insurance scheme, it would become possible to shorten the time required for launching a new nursing service system. It would also be true, as the 'Report of the Study Group' declared, that running the nurs- ing service system as a form of social insurance programme would make it easier to charge the users the exact costs needed for supplying the services of their own choice, and would facilitate the nurturing and participation of a wide variety of service suppliers, including private businesses. This partly explains why the Study Group's report was able to uphold a lofty ideal of establishing a nursing security system, and lay out the concrete way by which the lofty idea could be put into reality.

On the other hand, however, this arrangement for nursing security would force the population to bear greater burdens. At the same time, as the Study Group's report pointed out, the role of the public bodies would be limited mainly to that of 'institutionalizing the nursing service system, and supervi- sing its proper operation'. In this sense, the most prominent feature of the new system would be its orientation toward limiting the role and respon- sibility of the public bodies within certain boundaries, and toward letting the population as a whole bear greater financial burdens.

The state of things discussed above shows where the argument for redefining a division of labour between the public and private sectors, which has been advanced since the 1980s, stands as of today. And deliberation has been undertaken since February 1995 by the Council on the Health of the Aged to work out a concrete plan to introduce a nursing insurance system beginning in 1997.

Problems for the family

On appearance, the foregoing developments suggest that policy measures in support of aged persons in need of care are being reinforced quite significantly compared with the policy measures of a very restraining nature that have been pursued in the late 1980s. It should be kept in mind, however, that even if the nursing services were to be improved in the direction as examined in (3) above, the family would still be left with a number of serious problems concerning the nursing of aged persons.

First, there is a question of whether the policy targets now pursued are sufficient or not, when we take into account the forthcoming transformations of the family. As a matter of fact, if regarded in terms of the rate of availability per aged person, the target figures of various facilities proposed by the 10-Year Strategy (see Table 6.8, column F) remain at a low level. What is more, given the slow progress in the implementation of the health and welfare plans for the aged by municipal governments, or the insufficient financial outlays the national government is planning to make for these plans, there is much doubt whether these targets can be attained. This is why the 'Report of the Study Group' referred to above had to forecast that 45 per cent of the social costs of nursing would still be borne by the family in the year 2000.

Second, the new system of leave for the nursing of the aged is not of much help. In particular, the system, as proposed for application to private sector employees beginning in April 1999, is far from adequate, because it provides that, for an aged person constantly in need of care, only one member of the family can take a leave of absence (basically unpaid) for up to three months only once, by filing an application two weeks in advance. With regard to the introduction of a nursing insurance scheme, too, there is a great likelihood that this can give rise to a number of new problems:

1. What should be the fair standards for assessing whether or not, and how seriously, an aged person is in need of care, and what particular services he/she is entitled to receive?;

2. Conversely, can there be a possibility that a person in need of care is denied medical service?;

3. Assuming that the benefits are paid to cover the costs of nursing at home, what should be the adequate benefits to be paid?;

4. Is there any possibility that the coverage of the public nursing insurance scheme can be narrowed so as not to interfere with private nursing insurance policies which have already been marketed?

It is also important to keep in mind that these new programmes are conceived to be merely supplementary to the caring by the family, and that, depending on the way they are implemented, they can have the effect of solidifying the practice of the nursing of the aged by the family.

Third and moreover, there is a growing tendency among nursing services, both public and private, to implement fee-based services, or to raise the fees still further. The introduction of a nursing insurance programme and the arrangement for asking the users to bear proper portions of the costs for their services can add fuel to this tendency and make it more universal. This is why the Study Group's report made concrete suggestions about procedures for collecting fees, in particular with regard to low-income users, from out of the inheritance left by them, or in advance from their pension benefits.

This means that even if multiple arrangements for nursing services were installed, those burdens on the aged and the family which have been pointed out in III-2 (4) will remain unsolved. And it is easy to speculate that so long as this problem is left untended, the switch from free nursing to fee-based nursing will discriminate against persons of low-income strata. Generally speaking, the willingness of persons of low- and high-income strata to avail themselves of welfare services is inversely proportional to and markedly affected by whether the services are free or fee-based. It is highly plausible, therefore, that families of low-income strata will tend to refrain from purchasing services, and depend more on the nursing services provided by family members.

If these problems are to be solved in preparation for the further ageing of society, it seems essential to take radical stock of the basic philosophy dictating the social security policy, i.e., the philosophy which asserts that the care and nursing of aged parents by the family constitutes part of unpaid domestic labour, which, by its very nature, must be carried out in accordance with the principle of self-help by the family.[22] So long as this perception underpins the social security policy, it will be a long time before we begin to see any significant change in the view that nursing services for the aged ought to be provided for pay, according to the discretionary decision of the public authorities which have been shouldering portions of the family's burdens.

To put it differently, this means that the task of 'contemporary reassessment of the self-support principle of the Japanese family' should be conceptualized and undertaken in a way radically different from what has been pursued at the level of policy planning, as examined, in particular, in III-2 (4) above. In fact, a view has lately been gaining influence among scholars of law that asserts that, since the care and nursing of aged persons involve tremendous burdens, and since such burdens cannot be imposed on specific individuals by force of law, the actual deeds of caring for and nursing aged parents should be differentiated from the question of paying for the costs of the nursing services, and be regarded as falling beyond the scope of children's responsibility to support their aged parents. Even though this argument may sound drastic or eccentric, it is not without some objective grounds. Indeed, as we will examine below, there is yet another new policy orientation that is emerging lately which attests, even if indirectly, to the importance of reassessing the family's self-help responsibility.

2. The family and a new orientation of the family policy

In fact, the decreasing birth rate in the last years reveals that the family in Japan is in serious trouble. Not only is it suffering from the deterioration of its ability to take care of aged parents, but it is also becoming less and less viable as a self-supporting unit for the intergenerational reproduction of labour power. As pointed out in I-1 (3), the question of how to cope with the 'growing trend toward a smaller number of children per family at a time when the ageing of population is accelerating' presents itself as a 'policy issue of top priority no less important than the question of dealing with the ageing of population' (the 1995 edition of the *White Paper on Welfare*, p. 207). In order to support the family in a situation like this, it is essential to devise and implement policy measures having orientations and characteristics different from those of the existing ones. In this sense, the emergence of the new policy issue is posing a serious question to the existing family policy.

The question as it is perceived, and the measures being proposed

To begin with, the recent decrease in the birth rate is ascribed primarily to the increase in the percentage of unmarried women consequent upon the increase in the number of women who get married later in life,[23] and also the declining fertility rate among the recently married couples. These factors, moreover, are usually explained in terms of the increased labour force participation rate for women and the increased economic independence of women, the growing sense of apprehension on the part of women about the physical and psychological burdens of domestic labour, childrearing, and education of children, and the deep-rooted cultures that uphold the division of labour between the sexes both at home and in workplaces. Put strongly, the declining birth rate may be taken as an unconscious or tacit resistance against society by the family, which has been forced to bear various burdens to sustain the country's economic growth—and especially by women, many of whom, while holding jobs of their own, have been doing a large portion of the domestic work to sustain the 'self-support principle of the family'. As a matter of fact, the total fertility rate for a working woman is significantly lower than that for a non-working woman, e.g., 0.60 as against 2.96 in 1990. Given this fact, any meaningful countermeasures to the dropping birth rate can only be worked out on the basis of a thorough-going reassessment of the locus and role the family occupies in contemporary society.

The policy plans that have been proposed since 1989 seem to have taken such nature of the problem into account, and have been aimed at working out 'comprehensive' countermeasures covering a wide range of problem areas such as child day care, employment, housing, and education. For instance, a policy document was announced in December 1994 under the title of 'On the Basic Orientation of the Future Programmes in Support of Parenting', or otherwise known as the 'Angel Plan', giving a list of priority measures which should be implemented in a period of ten years or so, centred around the following five basic precepts:

   1. that support should be provided to help make parenting and occupational life compatible with each other;

   2. that parenting within the family should be supported;

   3. that housing and living environments should be improved to cater better to the needs of parenting;

   4. that education should be made less straining and grinding; and

   5. that the costs of education should be reduced.

The idea emphasized by this document, that 'for the purpose of putting a brake on the growing tendency for the family to have a smaller number of children, it is essential that the costs of parenting be regarded as part of social overhead costs to be shared jointly in order to raise the next generation of the population', has been echoed by a number of other similar documents.[24]

In the implementation of concrete measures in line with this document, emphasis has been placed on those related to point (1) above, including: (*a*) in addition to the establishment in May 1991 of the Law for Childcare Leave, which provides for an unpaid leave of a maximum of one year following childbirth, measures have been devised to encourage employers to employ women seeking chances for re-employment, and to adopt more flexible working hours; and (*b*) measures for dealing with diversifying demands for the nursing of children, including newborn babies and school age children in after-school hours, have been identified as important means of helping mitigate the burdens of parenting, in combination with efforts to make local environments more amicable to the rearing of children through the March 1994 revision of the Children's Allowance Law. Measures having to do with points (2) and (5) above include the following: (*c*) a change was made in April 1995, to exempt an employee for the duration of a childcare leave from the payment of his/her contribution to the social insurance premium, and a one-off allowance for childbirth was increased in October 1994.

Parallel with these measures: (*d*) the government has gradually made efforts to encourage people to review and change the division of labour between the sexes both at home and in workplaces, and to shorten the actual working hours for both men and women as a prerequisite for the improvement of conditions of the parenting. However, these measures leave much to be desired. Furthermore, there is still no knowing how the government is trying to resolve the education and housing problems, which have close bearing upon the rearing of children.

Problems left to be solved

Therefore, if it is really necessary to reverse the declining trend in the birth rate at all, it is essential that the family be provided with a greater amount of support and in a more comprehensive manner than has been the case previously. Comprehensive support programmes of this nature, if actually put into effect, may mark the beginning of the formation in Japan of family policy in the narrow sense. Before this becomes a reality, however, there are a number of problems that need to be solved.

First, making a pledge that the burden of childcare will be lightened, while counting upon the family to continue performing a central role in the nursing of aged parents, is clearly inconsistent, and is incompatible with the life-cycle of the majority of women today.

Second, a number of policy documents emphatically have asserted that 'a marriage and childcare are part of private matters closely related to the value and the lifestyle of individuals, matters which the government should refrain from directly stepping into'.[24] The lifestyle chosen by a couple, and the way a couple make arrangements between their occupational life and distribution of domestic responsibility, can vary from one specific family to the next, and the social security system ought to be neutral on the choice made by each family, but the context in which the need for such neutrality is emphasized is open to question. More specifically, the need for the government to refrain from stepping into private matters seems to be cited often for the purpose of confining public programmes in support of childcare only to those efforts aimed at 'preparing the environments which can facilitate sound nurturing of children'.[25] This is in stark contrast to the argument presented by policy documents in connection with the support to be provided to the family to help it perform another responsibility, the nursing of aged persons.

Third, concrete measures meant to support the family's role in the rearing of children, just like those in support of the family's role in the nursing of aged persons, count very heavily upon services to be provided by a multiple-layered structure, in which 'the family performs the central role, and firms and communities also share the responsibility, with the national and local governments devising programmes necessary for supporting the efforts of the family, firms, and communities' (the 1995 edition of the *White Paper on Welfare*, p. 207). Firms are expected to play especially significant roles, not simply by improving the working conditions for women employees with parenting responsibilities, but also by establishing in-house day-care centres. In the same vein, great emphasis is placed on the need to nurture private day-care services which can flexibly cope with the increasingly diversified needs for nursery care.

Fourth, the argument that 'the costs of parenting should be regarded as part of social overhead costs to be shared jointly in order to raise the next generation of the population', mentioned above, remains too ambiguous and needs to be defined more clearly. It is giving rise to a debate as to how the costs to be borne by society should be differentiated from the costs which the family ought to bear in payment for the benefits accruing to the children or the parents. The ambiguity may derive in part from the fact that policy makers are still unable to assess the extent of the effects which the decreasing number of children per family is likely to produce on the society at large. However, it is the very fact that the policy orientations about the support and the nursing of aged persons have had to shift their emphasis from arrangements that would hold the family primarily responsible, to those that would be sustained primarily by public and social responsibility. In that case, the arrival of the era with a smaller number of children per family is sure to make the question of intergenerational support one of the main focal points of attention for the social security policy. If so, it is essential that the idea of social sharing of the burden of childcare be presented in a more clearly defined way. Only when the endeavour of giving birth to and nurturing children is perceived as the endeavour of bringing up the next generation of bearers of social security costs can the idea of reinforcing public and social support to the family undertaking this endeavour become truly justifiable.[26]

This means that a part of the responsibility of the intergenerational reproduction of labour power, which the family has been supposed to bear by the self-support principle, should be borne publicly and socially to prepare for the future. Indeed, the self-support principle of the family needs to be reassessed with regard to the rearing of children, as well as the care and nursing of aged persons.

If family policy in the new sense described above is to be established in earnest, the very way that Japanese society operates today, including its public finance, economy, labour, firms, communities, and the family, must be subjected to radical scrutiny. And the question of what can be the appropriate form of the division of labour between the sexes in each of the arenas of life cannot but be raised. What is at issue is whether Japanese society can really reorient itself by doing away with its traditional and excessive preoccupation with economic efficiency, and start reforming itself in such a way that the recent buzz word 'decent life' ceases to be a hollow promise and becomes, instead, the reality that governs the everyday life of ordinary individuals.

3. Concluding remarks

To sum up the foregoing discussion, social security and family policies in Japan today are bound to deal simultaneously with two tasks that are contradictory to each other in nature and content. One is the task of establishing a public or social system for nursing security for the sake of aged people in need of care, thereby lightening the burden of caring for aged parents borne by the family. The other is the task of lightening the family's burden of childcare through the implementation of a comprehensive family policy, thereby reinforcing the function the family performs in intergenerational reproduction of labour power. Actual policies have begun to deal with these tasks with increasing sincerity, but, judging from the perspective of the 'contemporary reassessment of the family's self-help principle', the policy measures being implemented still leave much to be desired. Let us conclude by commenting on the questionable way in which the interrelationship between the two tasks is perceived by the policy measures.

Since these tasks look similar in appearance, because both are supposed to deal with social security needs that derive from deterioration in the family's functions, they are often considered to be of the same nature by policy makers. In fact, policy documents today try to link the two as closely as possible and at the same level, as exemplified by the Minister of Welfare's introduction to the *Vision of Welfare in the Twenty-First Century*, which emphasized the need to reconstruct the social security system into one 'that attaches importance to welfare services for caring for the aged and for parenting'.

In substance, however, the two tasks are clearly different in nature and content. Whereas the former task is oriented toward freeing the family from the burden of taking care of aged parents to some degree, the latter is oriented toward reinforcing the family's function as the social unit that produces and nurtures children. When characterized in terms of their relationship with the family's self-help principle, the former is aimed at loosening or moderating the binding effects that the principle has over the broadly conceived family in Japan (in legal terms, this means to lighten the family's 'livelihood assistance obligation'). The latter is aimed at reinforcing the binding power of the principle within the small family which would take various forms (in legal terms, this means to strengthen the family's 'livelihood maintenance obligation'). When compared in terms of the objects to be dealt with, the two are radically different: nursing security for the aged can be interpreted as an arrangement for social and public support to be offered to independent citizens/individuals as and when they come in need of care. But in offering support for childbirth and parenting, the society has no choice but to depend on the family and devise and implement programmes in support of the family.

Thus, the social security policy, with its inclination to deal with the two tasks at the same level, is open to serious critique. One might naturally suspect that its hidden intent must be to conceptualize the former task in as close association as possible with the family's role, and to retain and make the maximum use of the family's self-help principle for the care of the aged in the future. If this was indeed the case, one must say that the basic orientation of the broadly defined family policy that was set forth in the 1980s has not yet undergone any profound change.

Given, however, the fact that the family has grown incompetent to the extent of needing substantial support even for its parenting activities, it is becoming increasingly clear how illogical and untenable it is to keep expecting the family to bear the burden of caring for the aged. The social security policy and the family policy have been assured of a choice of relatively wide-ranging alternative policy measures because the family, characterized by the distinct consciousness and structure, has continued to perform as an

important safety net against various pressures produced by rapid and profound social changes, while being made increasingly fragile by the same social
changes.[27] However, the family's role as a safety net is now rapidly on the
wane. A 'contemporary reassessment of the family's self-help principle' must
be carried out, by taking full account of this fact, and by properly differentiating between the two tasks with their intrinsically different characteristics. The
social security policy in Japan, including its family policy components, is facing the very serious question of how best it can define the family's functions
in the rapidly ageing society, how best it can redefine the scope of its self-
help ability, and how best it can design social security measures suitable for
the twenty-first century.

7

The Problem of Land Use and Land Prices*

INAMOTO YONOSUKE

I. The Land Problem

1. The essential 'land problem' concept

Until the present, the 'land problem' has been distinguished from other social and economic problems by the relatively clear definition of its essential framework. It is characterized by a sharp distinction between agricultural use and urban use, and with respect to both, there can be little doubt that the core of the problem is in the social system or structures surrounding each type of use. In recent years, concerns have arisen over the conditions which underpin land use, with effects on the environment and upon conservation of national land. The rising prominence of such concerns in debates over the land problem marks a shift in the focus of the debate, but the *essence* of the land problem as one of centring on land use has not changed.

With respect to agricultural land use, attention originally focused upon the protection of cultivation from the landowner. Even if this shifts to economic questions such as rents and the burden of improvements to the land, the important issue that must still be addressed is the comprehensive land use problem of agriculture and village communities. How best to provide social and structural (*seido-teki*) assurances of land use—and are those assurances, in fact, being provided? The essence of the problem is still the same.

With respect to urban land use, important aspects of the land problem extend beyond that of ownership and use as between private persons, to include the relationship between public and private use, the space required for social amenities (including infrastructure), and the planning restrictions and compulsory purchase mechanisms that support them. These are problems of *land use*, and may be classed together under the heading of urban problems generally.

Recent concerns over conservation and the environment are reflected in an awareness of the limits and conditions that have meant that the impact on the environment of agrarian and urban development, and the conversion of

* Translated by Frank Bennett.

land from agricultural to urban use, has proceeded to a certain level in limited regions of the country.

Thus, the land problem is fundamentally one of land use and its impacts on the social and environmental system. It has come to be discussed in the context of the preservation or promotion of land use, its rationalization and evaluation, the balancing of societal benefits and burdens. In the future, too, these efforts will undoubtedly continue at both the academic and administrative levels.

The preceding description applies more or less equally to attitudes toward the land problem in western Europe as well. In point of fact, this description very closely tracks an answer given recently by a well-informed French observer to a general question about the nature of the French *problèmes fonciers*. Addressing the question, they clearly felt that the land problem was one of land use. They stated that, although the land problem would no doubt grow increasingly important over time, it was a problem that could be resolved, and indeed perhaps *had been* resolved. 'The land problem as one of land use' both expresses the difficulties of this pressing issue, and provides a methodological framework for its resolution. I would now like to turn to a general discussion of 'modern Japanese society and the land problem', using the land problem in modern Europe as a comparative backdrop.

2. The land problem as one of land price

The land problem has been the object of academic research in Japan since the pre-war period. The focus in this field for much of this period has been on agrarian landlord-tenant relations, and the impact which the preservation of these relations in agrarian communities had upon the nation's political and economic structure. The actual land system in Japan differs greatly from that in western European states, but there were attempts, at least, to compare the land problem between Japan and Europe.

The land problem became an object of administrative attention and a focal point for public opinion after the war, particularly since the first half of the 1960s. The land issue was perceived to be a composite of two things. One was the persistence of housing problems in the period of economic and industrial recovery following the war—the so-called 'land and housing problem'. The other was the 'land price problem', signalled first by the explosive rise in land values between 1959 and 1961.[1] As the rising cost of land came to affect the supply of housing by the public sector, forcing increasing reliance on privately financed housing development and construction, interest in the land problem broadened from issues of land use to encompass the working of the market in land, and its impact on prices.

After this initial surge, prices rose more or less continuously, but there were fluctuations until the time of the oil shock. As we shall see, the price rises at this time affected not only industrial property, but commercial and residential land as well. Residential property, in particular, rose sharply against the previous year; in the three major urban centres, the increase ran above 30 per cent consecutively for two years (1973 and 1974). Although wages and savings rates were increasing, this failed to keep up with the explosive increase in land prices. The cost of private housing rose, and a feeling arose that the increase in land prices was making the purchase of homes difficult. Price inflation from 1960 onwards triggered a new commonplace at this point: 'The land problem is the land price problem.'

In Japan after this period, the land problem was considered, more than anything else, one of land prices. Among the analysts, the most favoured position was that 'land prices should be reduced by increasing supply and relying on the market'. For example, one critic who had been a Minister of Construction said, in the summer of 1972:

The land problem, or the mechanism that determines prices, is related to supply and demand. Methods of providing a large supply of land, and of preventing speculation, these are the first premises for addressing this problem in Japan. And for this purpose, one must contemplate bold limitations on private ownership rights.[2]

This way of thinking fed the policy line, under the Nakasone administration, expressed in the slogans 'increasing domestic demand, relying on the power of the private sector, deregulation and limitation of private rights'.

The recent conception of the land problem as a land price problem may have been a product of the hard choices that were forced in the wake of the explosive rise in land prices. There was also a sense that the stabilization of land prices was necessary to a resolution of the more fundamental aspects of the land problem; we therefore cannot say that the identification of the land problem as a land price problem was entirely in error. All that is questioned here is the policies adopted to control and reduce land prices.

Two choices were theoretically possible. One was to impose controls on land prices and the use of land, and simultaneously to reduce demand through the strengthening of restrictions on use. The other was to ease restrictions on land use, provide incentives through the tax system, and thereby expand supply. The former was viewed with apprehension because, while it would restrict prices and lay a foundation for resolving the fundamental land problem (i.e., that of land use), it would entail further restrictions on the supply of housing through private-sector development projects. And this 'raised the question of how the economy as a whole should be managed'.

On the other hand, the latter approach could be expected to increase the supply of land, and thereby promote growth in the construction industry, but at the cost of making it even more difficult to solve the essential land problem once prices were brought under control.

This was clearly a choice between two evils, but in the event, from roughly 1980 to 1985, the government's policy on the land problem followed the latter course—reducing land prices through increased supply. Measures to deal with the essential land problem were therefore put off, and the government was criticized, inevitably, for making matters worse.[3]

Even so, the year-on-year growth in land prices slowed during this period. Although there had been a strong rise, particularly in residential land values from 1979 to 1981, from 1981 to 1986 the year-on-year increase slowed, falling as low as 1 per cent, for residential property in metropolitan Tokyo. As evidence of this stabilizing trend mounted, the need to address the other, land-use side of the land problem came to be discussed. One such example was the Report of the Land Problem Round Table (1982–3), which served as an advisory panel to the Land Bureau Director, National Land Agency:

To the present, the land problem has been conceived as one of prices; in other words, land policy has sometimes appeared to boil down to direct controls on land prices; but this will not lead to a fundamental resolution of the land problem. Land prices are determined by the market, in response to social and economic movements. Any attempt to control land prices themselves independently of the social and economic use to which land is put is not going to be effective. And it is inconceivable that such an approach will improve the quality of land use . . . Therefore, if land prices stabilize, this does not mean that the land problem had eased; rather, we should see this as presenting an opportunity to deal with the land use problem outlined above.[4]

Here we do see a recognition of the essential land problem, and an intention to take affirmative measures to deal with it—but this is premissed on the stabilization of land prices; the statement is a product of the land policy of that time. If further rise in prices should hit, a statement of this sort loses its underlying premiss, and its persuasive force is thereby weakened. As if to leave a parting impression of the Showa era, another round of land price inflation, led this time by commercial properties, hit in 1987–90.[5] This brought on a return to the frame of mind that had equated the land problem with land prices—a reversion to which there was little resistance.

3. Factors in the land problem

I will forgo a detailed review of the debate to which this latest round of land price inflation has given rise. The newspaper publishers and television companies have each repeatedly put on special programmes on this subject, gathering unprecedented efforts to shape public opinion. Their contribution has been an appropriate one. Here, I would like to examine the scope of the general public's understanding, through the media, of the land problem of 1989, and structure the argument of this essay around the questions that arise from that review.

The most direct and strongest journalistic interest was in the 'problem of the land market'—land prices, land transactions, speculation, finance, supply promotion through special tax incentives. Once again, and to a greater extent even than before, the public was ready to accept that the land problem equated to the problem of land prices. This article, in light of this fact, will begin its examination of the land problem with the land price issue.

The media then examined, from various perspectives, the structural factors which hindered the prevention of a further surge in prices. A common theme in special reports appearing in the newspapers is the defects, loopholes, and contradictions in land-use planning and the system for controlling changes in land use, as well as the ineffectual nature of the enforcement mechanisms meant to back up such controls. This is, of course, a problem of land use within the larger topic of 'urban problems', but I would like to raise it here in a narrow sense, as a problem of urban land use planning.

Third, as a result of the rise in land prices, great attention focused on the deterioration of housing quality in large urban areas. On top of the rise in housing prices, the stagnation in supply, and the recession in public housing projects, entrepreneurial developers sought to mingle residential and industrial use, with a consequent decline in the quality of living environments; the land problem became directly associated with the housing problem.

Fourth, the utility of land as an asset raised a new question of social fairness. Even if land speculation were excluded, the various ways in which land owners received income without effort came to be criticized, and there was talk of the need for 'social recovery of capital gain benefits'.

Fifth, as a source of consciousness about the land problem, the following was discussed: the preparation and disclosure of information concerning such issues as the cadastral data, the state of land ownership, use and change of land use, the practice of property transactions, transaction price, and especially each type of public land price standard or measure. The inadequacy of the information systems on which a resolution of the land problem relied was identified as one part of the land problem itself.

Finally, there is the problem of the conception of land ownership. When the special character of the land price problem in Japan is reviewed, and each of the points raised above has been argued to exhaustion, there remains the question of whether the way of thinking about ownership has something to do with this—whether, in other words, there is a distinctively Japanese concept of land ownership. This goes beyond generalization about the special nature of our nation's history and the peculiar character of its people; it is a phenomenon that should be taken as arising out of, or fostered by, the legal system that has developed in Japan since the Meiji era.

Below, I shall attempt to follow the outline just laid down in pursuit of the real face of the Land Problem of Heisei Year 1. This with one proviso; that the third point, concerning the housing problem is important not to the resolution of the land problem, but as an important problem in its own right; and as such, I will not treat it here in this essay.[6] Also, item five, the problem of land information, must await another occasion because of limitations on space.

II. The Land Price Problem

Long-term price movements in land at the national level since 1955 are shown in Figure 7.1. Five peaks occur, in 1961, 1970, 1973, 1980, and 1987. Among these, that of 1961 centred upon industrial properties, while that of 1973 was a sharp spur affecting all properties. None the less, both of these peaks followed shifts in Japan's GNP; the economic life of the populace perhaps most strikingly showed through in the land market. In any case, it may be said that we need not look to land policy or distinctive features of the market in land to

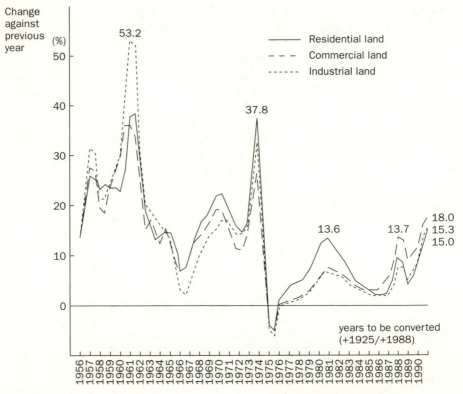

Fig. 7.1. Long-term movements in land price: rate of change year on year in the national urban land price index

Source: Nihon fudosan kenkyujo (zaidan hojin), Urban Land Price Index.

explain these particular fluctuations. Between these two spurs, we find a peak in 1970; but this was the controlled product of the tax reform introduced in 1969 to encourage a slow recovery from the 1966 depression in the property market. As will be discussed later, the expansion of supply and sustained high prices that this tax reform brought about should be the subject of critical review, but it did not produce a reaction among the public, and was soon forgotten in the explosive rise that set in in 1973.

Concerning price movements since 1975, a separate caution is called for. When the year-on-year rise in residential properties hit 13.6 per cent in 1980, this was not paralleled by a rise in GNP. The same can be said of the rise in 1987–8, led by commercial properties. We therefore cannot say that these rises simply reflected the economic position of the population in a straightforward and sensible way. We must look for other factors that fuelled the price inflation in this period. Behind the 1980 rise is the increase in the supply of land for the construction of condominiums, in turn brought on by the expansion of finance for private housing purchases by private lenders (7 trillion 411 billion 500 million yen in 1979). Despite the rise in condominium prices, the participation of the lending institutions further fuelled demand, and consequently further increases in prices.

While this rise of 1980 can be explained as an artificial product of an expansion of real demand, the 1987–8 rise is of a different character. It is now generally agreed that this exceptional rise was created by finance being directed, in a short period of time, at the major urban centres, by lending institutions—a phenomenon never before experienced. Banks, non-banks, and, through non-banks, the real estate houses and ordinary corporations to whom banks had ultimately provided finance, the unrestrained lending bubble that propelled these property acquisitions is well known. And behind that, as is also well known, was the 1985 Plaza Accord of the G5; the strong yen following the Accord shifted the financial markets away from the banking sector into the securities markets, causing the banks to seek new business, from customers who could provide ready security and had a need for finance.[7, 8]

1. Land prices and land tax

Contrary to the common expectation, the tax system has an indirect effect on land prices, and there are always difficulties in measuring its effect. Although there is a 'direct' connection in that rising land prices are followed by talk of tax reform, in actual debate on tax reform, there has been a tendency to avoid, rather than to embrace, the land problem as an immediate target of reform efforts. At least, until the government's Investigatory Committee on the Tax System of 1988,[9] self-restraint on the part of the tax system was its distinguishing feature.

None the less, taxation does have a direct effect upon transactions in the property market, where land prices are actually set; and as such, its effects on market activity can be clearly identified. Accordingly, those within and without industry brought pressure on the government and the Tax Committee, sometimes with success, to introduce tax reforms that would expand the property market.

However, although it is simple enough to speak of the relationship between the property market and the tax system, there are various ways in which the two interact. We can get a rough idea of what is involved by examining each of the three pillars of land taxation (transfer, holding, and capital gains tax) in turn.

Transfer (income) tax	Strengthening of tax on income from short-term (extremely short-term) transfers	Restriction of speculative transactions
	Transitory reduction of tax on profits from long-term transfers	Short-term promotion of land supply
	Uniform tax on profits from long-term transfers	Promotion of supply of land held long-term
	Separate taxation on profits of individuals	General easing of income tax, gentle promotion of supply
	Separate supplemental taxation of legal persons	Increasing the tax burden on legal persons, restricting demand by legal persons
	Special regulation on purchase of replacement properties	Promotion of supply, curbing of excessive demand
	Offset of profit and loss allowed	Curbing of widespread sharp rises in demand (real estate investment)
Holding Tax (Property Tax)	Exceptional strengthening of land holding tax rate	Expansion of supply, control of demand
	Taxation of agricultural lands at residential rates	Sales for alternative uses, promotion of development
Acquisition (Inheritance) Tax	Use of a rateable proportion of current land value as the value for calculating inheritance tax	Increasing the supply of land in areas of high land value, and indirectly expanding the corporate demand for land acquisitions

First let us examine taxation on transfer. There are various cases in which taxation of transfers can affect prices through its impact on the land market, but those with which we are concerned at a practical level are:

1. to sustain prices while expanding supply;

2. to stimulate, according to the content of the tax law, a large-scale transfer of land ownership from private individuals to corporations;

3. again according to the content of the tax law, to confuse the markets, creating excessive demand, and putting pressure on real demand and thereby bring about price inflation (for example, through a special regulation on the replacement of industrial and residential assets, city-centre land price levels lift land prices in outlying areas).

In the absence of additional measures to curb speculation, and on account of existing measures losing their effectiveness, speculation was enhanced in certain cases, but little more need be said about that.

If we look back over the course of events since the war in the light of these points, the 1969 tax reform was indeed a reform that calls to mind the over-all land problem—not merely the problem of prices. This is not because it exhibits a basic policy on resolving the problem, but rather precisely because it amplified the problem, and helped embed it in the structure of the nation's finances.

First of all, the pre-existing tax on 50 per cent or the full sum of income upon transfer was suspended for particular periods.[10] For properties acquired prior to 31 December 1968 and held for periods of more than five years, sep-arate tax bands of 10 per cent for 1970 and 1971, 15 per cent for 1972 and 1973, and 20 per cent for 1974 and 1975 were introduced. Other properties were taxed at 40 per cent of the net profit from the transaction. On the other hand, there was no change in the taxation of corporate landholdings.

What is the impact of this tax reform? First, by reducing tax rates on income from transfer of properties held over a long term, and imposing a stepped increase in taxation over time, sales of land held by individuals were increased. On the other hand, because no similar measures were introduced with respect to corporate land holdings, legal persons had no incentive to sell their own properties. On the contrary, corporations lined up to purchase the properties being disposed of by individuals, and had little resistance to such purchases, because there was no penalty, for corporations, for short-term profit-taking. In this way, the shifting of land ownership from individuals to corporations—an effect not anticipated by the reform—took place quickly and on a massive scale.

Another problem with the 1969 tax reform, as mentioned earlier, was that the expansion of supply was not linked to price restraint; rather, corporate demand for land expanded, including demand for residential properties, effectively stabilizing high prices, as noted above. Even after this hole in the tax fabric had become clear, a corrective could not be introduced immedi-ately; faced with the price rises of 1973, the response amounted only to the introduction of a separate supplemental tax of 20 per cent on profits from short-term corporate land holdings.[11]

In this way, one result of the 1969 tax reform was that corporations paid no special tax on profits from sales of land held short-term in the five years after the reform came into effect. There can be little doubt that this special favour bestowed on corporate land owners led to the build-up of appreciation in land acquired through new and replacement purchases, and owned by them over long periods.

2. Corporate land ownership

There are various advantages to holding land through a corporation. Because it is taxed at book value, the cost of keeping land is small, while it is a strong form of collateral for lending as it is appraised at current market value. Increases in value create internal build-up, but this is not taxed in any way. Furthermore, a corporate landowner does not suffer the burden of inheritance tax, and so can postpone the realization of internal build-up for long periods. In principle internal build-up is taxed as profit on sale or transfer, but, as outlined above, such profit was not made the object of special tax in the 1969 reform, and was limited to a tax on sales of land held short-term in the 1973 reform. And corporations with balance-sheet losses can set these against profits from the sale of land, thus avoiding corporate income tax on the transfer. That the advantages of corporate land ownership under this system 'increase the desire among corporations to hold land'[12] hardly needs to await a report from the Investigatory Committee on Taxation.

Corporate land ownership is more common in Japan than in other countries, reaching about 23 per cent of land subject to property tax nationwide. And at least in the nationwide figures, this is a figure that does not change greatly year on year. Even if corporate purchases of land increase because of financial conditions or changes in the tax system, these changes are confined to Osaka, Tokyo, and neighbouring urban areas; and in any event, such changes tend to centre on commercial properties. Tables 7.1 and 7.2 are based upon

TABLE 7.1. Transition in the proportion of corporate land acquisitions

	Tokyo	Chiba	Kanagawa	Saitama	Kyoto	Osaka	Hyogo	Nara
1982	25.8	25.0	22.0	23.5	17.6	16.4	14.9	15.2
1983	25.7	26.7	24.7	22.4	16.5	16.4	17.5	17.3
1984	27.3	27.3	23.6	23.5	19.0	14.6	18.3	15.3
1985	30.4	27.5	22.4	22.9	18.5	16.6	18.2	15.8
1986	39.1	32.2	28.3	28.8	23.7	19.6	20.8	14.8
1987	45.7	37.1	36.9	34.1	23.3	20.8	25.1	14.6
1988	35.4	27.4	21.0	25.1	21.3	21.5	20.6	17.8

Source: National Land Agency, Tochi Hoyu Ido Chosa (Land Holding and Land Transfer) and Tokyo City Government, Tokyo no Tochi, 1989 (Land in Tokyo 1989).

TABLE 7.2. Land transactions in four wards of metropolitan Tokyo (proportion)

Seller	Buyer 1984		1985		1986		1987		1988		1986/90
	Indiv.	Corp.	Indiv.	Corp.	Indiv.	Corp.	Indiv.	Corp.	Indiv.	Corp.	
Minato-ku											
Indiv.	9.1	33.6	9.1	29.7	4.8	30.6	7.3	40.7	7.8	32.8	
Corp.	6.6	47.1	7.6	38.9	2.5	53.8	4.0	45.8	5.2	46.1	
Area	225,096		356,653		403,981		311,083		229,163		1.8
Koto-ku											
Indiv.	9.8	10.0	13.4	11.0	10.1	14.9	7.9	14.7	13.7	16.7	
Corp.	2.1	31.9	4.1	47.8	4.4	46.9	2.7	34.4	5.2	37.7	
Area	478,819		428,156		455,753		516,890		236,696		1.0
Setagaya-ku											
Indiv.	31.1	28.3	29.9	29.7	21.1	18.4	21.0	39.0	30.5	26.4	
Corp.	18.0	20.0	16.7	19.0	27.5	30.1	11.6	25.0	12.9	16.8	
Area	650,558		784,848		980,964		824,616		515,982		1.5
Adachi-ku											
Indiv.	36.6	24.6	35.8	26.7	32.8	30.1	27.8	31.0	29.2	24.2	
Corp.	13.4	11.2	12.5	10.1	12.0	16.2	13.9	18.8	12.2	11.4	
Area	567,257		644,708		874,288		686,419		564,900		1.5
Total area	1,921,730		2,214,365		2,714,986		2,339,008		1,546,741		1.4

Source: Tokyo City Government: *Tokyo no Tochi*, 1989.

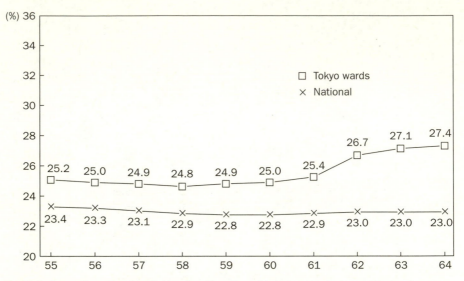

Fɪɢ. 7.2. Proportion of residential land, nationally and in Tokyo wards, owned by legal persons

Note: National figures show the proportion above the taxation boundary.

   Tokyo ward figures include properties below the taxation boundary as well.

Sources: Tokyo City Government, 'Land in Tokyo'; Local Government Ministry, 'Outline Report on the Value of Fixed Assets'.

partial figures, but do show the proportion of corporate land acquisitions in metropolitan Tokyo, and Minato Ward therein, in 1985–8. From Figure 7.2, one can see how the proportion of land owned by corporations increased in this period.

Figure 7.3 gives estimates of land transactions in 1989, derived from the 'Land Holding and Land Transfer Survey' done annually by the National Land Agency and other sources. If we accept these figures as reliable, we find that out of transactions worth 52 trillion yen, corporate traders acquired a net value of 13.5 trillion yen in land, while individuals sold off 17.6 trillion yen's worth. Likewise, if we look only at the value of purchases, against 20.1 trillion yen in purchases by individuals, we find 24.6 trillion by corporations. Comparing money lent toward purchase, we have the estimated figures of 9.7 trillion for individuals, 11.4 trillion for corporations.

Turning to the National Land Agency's 'Land Holding and Land Transfer Survey',[13] the breakdown of reasons given by corporations for land purchases was: 53.2 per cent for business use; 27.5 per cent for subsequent sale or trade; 2.2 per cent for investment purposes. However, 7.2 per cent of the properties bought and kept for business purposes are not in active use, and for 77.8 per cent of these properties there is no current plan for exploiting their potential. Of properties purchased for resale, 55.2 per cent do not have work

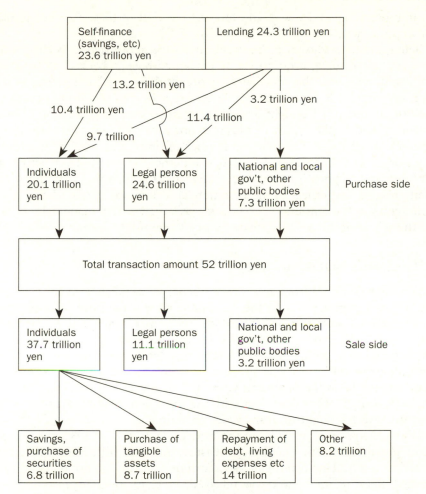

Fɪɢ. 7.3. Estimated capital flows involved in land transactions

Notes: 1. The categories listed beside the labels 'purchase side' and 'sale side' do *not* match those used in the Economic Planning Agency publication 'Kokumin Keizai Keisan'.

2. The total transaction amount is the sum of the 'purchase side' items listed in the figure.

3. The individual 'purchase side' items are derived from National Land Agency materials, including 'Kigyo no tochi no Shutoku Jokyo to ni Kansuru Chosa' and 'Tochi Hoyu ido Chosa'.

4. Sale side items are derived from National Land Agency materials, including the publication 'Tochi Hoyu ido Chosa'.

5. Lending institutions include governmental lending institutions.

6. The amount lent by lending institutions is derived from National Land Agency materials, including the publication 'Tochi Hoyu ido Chosa'.

7. The uses to which sale monies are put by individuals is derived from the National Land Agency publication 'Tochi Hoyu ido Chosa'. Note that 'repayment of debt' includes repayment of money originally borrowed from lending institutions.

Source: National Land Agency, 1990: Tochi no Doko ni Kansuru Nenji Hokoku, p. 98.

on improvements under way, and for 59.5 per cent of these there is no plan for improvements.

The general conclusion to be drawn from the above figures is that in the post-1987 price surge, acquisitions by corporate buyers, backed up by financial institutions, rose sharply; that a portion of these purchases went forward without any plan for use or for resale of the properties concerned (at least a majority of properties bought by real estate houses and construction firms as inventory had neither work in progress nor a development plan associated with them); and that a significant number of properties were held without any plan other than to await a further rise in the price of the land. This most recent round of price inflation was anticipated by financial institutions, real estate houses, and others in the commercial sector, was entered into projections, and was brought into existence; it was largely a man-made 'false boom' (in the words of the Ad Hoc Investigatory Committee's Interim Report).

3. Land price countermeasures

According to statistics from a survey by the Japan Real Estate Institute,[14] from the end of September 1990 to the same date in 1991, the price of commercial and residential properties in Tokyo fell by 1.3 per cent[15] and 6.0 per cent respectively, while prices in Osaka fell by 12.3 per cent and 16.4 per cent. At the national level, commercial properties rose by 0.2 per cent while residential properties fell by 0.3 per cent in the same year. A sharper drop over a matching period in the preceding years had not been recorded since the end of March in 1975. What caused this drop in the market? What sort of countermeasures were brought to bear by the government?

When the price surge had become noticeable, in July of 1987, the government put the problem of 'countermeasures for land prices and other land issues' to the Ad Hoc Investigatory Committee on the Promotion of Administrative Reform. An answer was received on 12 October of the same year in the form of the 'Report Concerning Current Land Prices etc.' (interim report), and based on that report the government issued the 'Outline for Emergency Land Countermeasures' (16 October 1987). Land price countermeasures (regularization of land transactions) were to be comprised of three elements: 'regulation of speculative land transactions'; 'guidance issued to property companies'; and 'guidance issued to financial institutions'. Concerning the regulation of transactions, the Outline called for 'directions to local authorities that [price] monitoring districts are to be designated, and the parcel size for which filings are required is to be elastically reduced', and that the way be paved for the designation of control districts, and that guidance issued to financial institutions include as central provisions references to 'a thoroughgoing exercise of self-restraint in financing speculative transactions', and 'the establishment of inspectoral organs within each financial institution'.

The Ad Hoc Committee handed down its final report, 'Report on Land Prices and Other Land Countermeasures', on 15 June 1988, after which the government issued its Comprehensive Outline on Land Countermeasures (28 June 1988). Reinforcing the government's line on land countermeasures was the report of the Basic Land Law Round Table (an advisory committee to the Minister of the National Land Agency), 'Concerning the Way of Thinking About the Basic Land Law' (23 December 1988); and subsequently the Basic Land Law (22 December 1989); and, based upon that Law, the report of the Investigatory Committee on Land Policy, 'Concerning the Course of Policy Following the Introduction of the Basic Land Law' (29 October 1990); and, following this report, 'Outline of a Comprehensive Motivating Policy on Land' (25 January 1991). Further, the Investigatory Committee on Taxation produced the 'Report on the Course of the Land Tax System' (30 October 1990), which spurred a sweeping change at the hands of the Liberal Democratic party's Committee on Tax, and the revision of several laws on inheritance tax and the enactment of the Land Price Tax Act.

This is sufficient chronology on land countermeasures; I would now like to concentrate on how the price problem was addressed. Simply stated, the immediate response was in the 'Outline of Emergency Land Counter-measures', while Section 4 of the Basic Land Law merely stated that 'Land shall not be the object of speculative transactions'. On this basis, a general review of land policy is under way, to avoid opening the door to another cycle of price inflation, and efforts are under way to show 'the government's aggressive stance' in the face of the land price problem, and to enlist the support of public opinion.

What do we make of the connection between the easing of land price inflation and the policies adopted to tackle it? On the evidence of oral interviews made to date, the decisive factor was the translation of 'self-restraint in lending against speculative land transactions' into the 'Comprehensive Regulation of Real Property Lending' under Ministry of Finance administrative guidance. 'Deflation' was a domino effect, as real estate houses which had continued purchase with loans found their finance dry up in the face of the Comprehensive Regulation, and found it necessary to sell off properties below their purchase cost in order to meet interest obligations (from an Osaka interviewee).

With respect to the regulation of speculative transactions in the narrow sense, there is no doubt that the Monitoring Districts intended to regulate small-scale transactions were quite effective. Yet many local authorities fixed the price above which registration was required rather high, in order to capture speculative transactions. This gave no means of controlling prices that had begun to deflate, however.

If the 1987–8 price surge was, as suggested above, anticipated by financial institutions, real estate houses, and others in the commercial sector, entered into their projections, and brought into existence by them, it is reasonable to bring the surge under control through administrative control upon financial institutions. The problem that arises is that, where the value of property before the surge had doubled in two years (residential properties in Tokyo), or risen by 250 per cent in three years (residential properties in Osaka), there are limits to how far restrictions on finance can be used to restore such properties to their original values. And insofar as the restrictions are a form of preventive medicine, a release in the restrictions can be expected to be followed by another rush on prices. The outlook is not bright for the future.

III. Problems of City Planning

1. The City Planning Law of 1968

It has been twenty full years since the City Planning Law (Law no. 100 of 1978) took the place of the City Planning Law of 1919 (Taisho 8, Law no. 36). It is an open question how much of a role city planning and city planning law with teeth can play in shaping the growth and development of a city. But we do yet have 'proper cities' in Japan, guided and managed by the new City Planning Law. Japan has had a taste of the difficulties in regulatory planning in the face of rapid change in the large cities and surrounding areas (both concentration and spread of population); but administration of city planning has not emerged from the stage of youthful experimentation. Under these circumstances, preparatory work for a reconsideration of Japan's city planning system, and for a reform of the law, has begun.

The old City Planning Law provided for urban facilities, urban development projects, and a system of zoning; provision was thus made for development projects and limitations on land use. The new law provided additionally for urbanization districts and urbanization control districts, within the zoning framework.[16] The new law also included improvements to each of the three core functions of the old law, with a particular view to consistency, but the introduction of urbanization and urbanization control districts ('line-drawing') was by far the most important reform introduced in the new law.

Before the new law was introduced, the Deliberation Council on Residential Land, in response to a question put to it (March 1967, 6th response), stated that there were to be four types of urban districts, consisting of: 'Existing Urban Districts' (districts either actually comprising urban districts, or neighbouring districts in the process of actually becoming such); 'Urbanizing Districts' (those that should, in course of time and according to plan become urban districts); 'Urbanization Control Districts' (those for which there is no plan for urbanization, and therefore a need for gradual urbanization to take place, to control or regulate urbanization for a period of time); 'Preservation

Districts' (those that should be protected as green areas, or on account of their being areas difficult to develop, or of special historical, cultural, or scenic interest). However, in the event, this was pared down to two district types in the legislative process. The four-category scheme had the attraction that, by distinguishing between Existing Urban Districts and Urbanizing Districts, a separate standard of development approval could be required in the latter; and distinguishing between Urbanization Control Districts and Preservation Districts would allow Urbanization Control Districts to be used as a flexible zone that could be urbanized gradually and in a planned way. Even today, there are those who cite these potential advantages with regret for their loss.

Against this, the two-category system does not have much flexibility. There is a clear, simple, man-made division between lands that are Urbanization Districts because they do not fall within the permit system for farmland conversion and are smaller than 1,000 square metres, and lands that, as Urbanization Control Districts, are doubly restricted, both barred from change in use and prohibited from development.

This type of line-drawing system had the following practical effects in the end. First, the Urbanization Districts came to include large tracts of agricultural land, the development of which could not be expected to take place within a ten-year period. Furthermore, as a direct effect of the line-drawing, land prices soared, and, in anticipation of further price rises, owners refrained from either selling the land or building on it. Where development did take place, the lag in development of urban infrastructure made urban sprawl unavoidable. With no tool to promote the residential development of agricultural land, apart from the tax system (i.e., a tax rate on agricultural land equivalent to that applicable to residential property), local government officials generally sought *not* to apply those provisions. These and other problems meant, in short, that, with Urbanization Districts, conversion of farmland to residential use was without restriction, and permits were almost completely unnecessary for development work. At the same time there was no *obligation* under the City Planning Law to proceed with conversion to residential land use. Land ownership was swathed in two or three layers of additional freedom. That this sort of regulatory air pocket developed in the name of city planning itself was in fact part of the problem.[17]

2. Euclidean zoning and maximum floor space

From pre-existing law, the new City Planning Law inherited four land-use zone types: the residential zone; the commercial zone; the quasi-industrial zone; and the industrial zone. Almost immediately after it was enacted, two more exclusive residential zones, a neighbourhood commercial zone, and an exclusive industrial zone were added (by the 1970 revision). This produced the same eight zoning types that are in use today. But the basic character of the zones—lack of refinement and affirmative effect—is much the same as under the old law. And the planning they represent is simply a matter of categorization, without an overarching master plan.[18]

However, if city planning is done by informing private property owners in a concrete way of the use and shape of buildings that they may construct, there is a need to divide the urban landscape into districts, and for each one to specify in detail the types of buildings that should be constructed in each. The city planning regimes of Germany and France are based on this kind of thinking, setting aside the 'building freedom' of owners, and creating a regulated city. In order to assure the reasonableness of such affirmative restrictions when imposed by local authorities, an overarching master plan is established, which is binding upon the local authority with planning powers.

Japan's system of zoning, apart from the fact that the districts are rather broadly defined, stops at *restricting* the types of buildings that may be constructed within the district, while giving basic recognition to the property owner's building freedom. Because of this, the 'free landowner' has the freedom to build—apart from the exceptional instance that violates a regulation—or not to build; and the flip side of his freedom to build whatever sort of structure he likes is that there is no means of knowing what sort of buildings or what sort of city will be constructed.

One more peculiar feature of Japan is that the maximum floorspace limit in each zone (*yosekiritsu*) is scrutinized more than the mellow, passive effect of zoning for use. Changes in this ratio have a direct effect upon property prices, and are the object of great interest. Such a system of land-use zoning and floor space restrictions, for all that it can restrict the overall volume of indoor space within a city and a somewhat structured set of incentives, cannot be used to shape a harmonious cityscape.

Finally, city planning that places the line-drawing districting system and the passive/restrictive approach of the land use and floor space zones at its centre suffers from a structural weakness, which readily becomes apparent when there is a change in external conditions. The planning system does not have within itself the means of resisting a loosening of regulations (on the contrary, it has a capacity for resisting a tightening of restrictions). Among the causes of the current round of price inflation, it must be said that there was a deep link with the policy of 'increasing domestic demand, relying on the power of private-sector, deregulation and limitation of private rights'[19] which has been pursued since 1975; and within this policy, the Nakasone administration carried out a remarkable deregulation of city planning. Because of limitations on space in this volume, I cannot go into detail in the text, but Table 7.3 shows the principal movements in this connection. From this figure, it should be clear that there was a progressive loosening of restrictions both with respect to the line-drawing districts and the land-use and floor space zones.[20]

Table 7.3. Major deregulation conducted by the Ministry of Construction

Month/year	Provision	Source	Description
July 1983	Redesignation of Type 1 Residential zones within the Number 7 Ringway as Type 2 Residential	Announcement of the 'Urban Countermeasures Promotion Committee' of the Ministry of Construction	City of Tokyo eliminates floorspace-to-plot-size ratio inspections for Type 1 Residential zones within the Number 7 Ringway; precise properties to be affected still under investigation at the time of the announcement.
July 1983	Reduction of minimum size requirements for approval of residential developments within Urbanization control Districts	Revision of the Implementing Regulations of the City Planning Act	Reduced from 20 hectares to 5 hectares; by April 1986, 47 cities and metropolitan areas had implemented the new regulations.
June 1983	Policy on provision for Outline Guidance relating to residential development etc	Circular of the Vice Minister	Acknowledgement of the excesses of Outline Guidance; by December 1984, 152 city and village administrations had revised their Outline Guidance.
Apr. 1984	Relaxation of height restrictions in Type 1 Residential zones	Circular of the Housing Bureau Director	Raised from 10 metres to 12 metres under certain conditions; aimed at increasing the supply of good-quality 3-storey housing.
Apr. 1984	Relaxation of the floorspace-to-plot-size restrictions along planned roads	Circular of the Housing Bureau Director	Relaxation of the floorspace-to-plot-size ratio under certain conditions for properties fronting on planned roads.
Apr. 1984	Establishment of the System for the Promotion of Excellent Redevelopment Construction Projects	Circular of the Vice Minister	Assistance to excellent private-sector redevelopment projects (greater than 1,000 m^2 in size); projects under way in 11 districts by March 1985.
Apr. 1984	Establishment of exceptional fiscal measures for asset exchanges in connection with excellent private-sector redevelopment projects	Circulars of the Urban Bureau Director and the Housing Bureau Director	Deferral of taxation of income from transfer relating to private-sector redevelopment projects specifically approved by the mayor.

Table 7.3. (cont'd)

Month/year	Provision	Source	Description
June 1984	Establishment of the System of Districts for Promotion of Redevelopment Projects	Circular of the Vice Minister	Assistance to excellent private-sector redevelopment projects; implemented in one district by March 1985.
June 1984	Relaxation of the requirements for raising the floorspace-to-plot-size ration in designated urban districts projects	Circular of the Urban Bureau Director	Approval of a 'premium' and right to transfer a floorspace-to-plot-size ratio under certain conditions.
Feb. 1985	Relaxation of the floorspace-to-plot-size ratio through application of a special scheme for buildings forming part of a single development	Circular of the Housing Bureau Director	Relaxation of the floorspace-to-plot-size ratio under certain conditions, where plots facing narrow streets and plots facing wide streets form part of a single development scheme.
Mar. 1985	Relaxation of restrictions on the disposition of residential land for new town development projects	Revision of the Implementing Regulations of the New Town Development Act	Approval of the transfer of newly created land to a private developer, attached with conditions relating to sale to the general public.
Dec. 1985	Rationalization and streamlining of the processing of development permits	Circular of the Construction Economic Bureau Director	Streamlining of the processing of development permits for land on which public facilities have been established.
Dec. 1985	Re-examination of Urbanization Districts and Control Districts	Circular of the Urban Bureau Director	The second re-examination of district boundaries draws to a close; necessary re-examination of land-use zones is carried out; determination and modification of floorspace-to-plot-size ratios and zoning classifications is examined.
Dec. 1985	Improved application of the Construction Standards Act with respect to promoting enhanced land use	Circular of the Housing Bureau Director	Response to the need for rights in airspace, through consolidated planning system and other measures.

TABLE 7.3. (cont'd)

Month/year	Provision	Source	Description
May 1986	Manual for the processing of development permits for large-scale development projects	Circular of the Construction Economic Bureau Director	Publication of standard time periods for processing each stage of applications, as a means of shortening the overall time required for processing.
Dec. 1986	Provision for improved use in 'Designated Urban Districts' projects and 'High-Rise Urban Districts'	Circular of the Urban Planning Section, Urban Bureau, Ministry of Construction	Raising of the upper limit of floorspace-to-plot-size ratio, and necessary changes to the requirements for transfer of floorspace-to-plot-size ratio on projects.
Dec. 1986	Revision of guideline permit requirements for the Consolidated Planning System	Circular of the Housing Bureau Director, Ministry of Construction	Increase in the floorspace-to-plot-size ratio 'premium'; affirmative appraisal of satisfactory public open land.
Jan. 1987	Re-examination of district boundaries	Circular of the Urban Bureau Director, Ministry of Construction	Flexible application of the line-drawing system to accord with actual local conditions (partial abolition of the line-drawing system).
Aug. 1987	Adjustment of the application of the development permit system to redevelopment works	Circular of the Construction Economics Bureau Director	In order to speed the development permit process, projects not accompanied by land reclamation works or establishment of public facilities are excluded from the class of development works.
Nov. 1987	Partial revision of the Construction Standards Act	Partial revision of the Construction Standards Act and of the accompanying Implementing Regulations	Relaxation of regulations on wooden structures; relaxation of restrictions on floorspace-to-plot-size ratio arising from the width of frontage roads, and relaxation of aerial setback restrictions.

Source: Planning Investigation Bureau, Mitsui Fudosan KK, *Collection of Real Estate Statistics (12th collection)*, 229.

3. District planning system

In 1980, a system of 'District Planning', based on a fundamentally different concept from the provisions of the 1968 City Planning Law, was introduced as the seventh city planning system. Under this system, in order to achieve rational land use in accord with the special character of individual districts, local authorities were to fix district plans after consultation with those with an interest in local land. The legislation provided for the independent determination of the distribution and size of public facilities, of green and forest areas to be preserved, and of the use, height, floor space area, building footprint area, lot size, and placement of walls. Apart from the general system of District Planning, which strengthened use restrictions in affected districts only, other such systems that have been introduced are 'Roadside Preparation Planning' (1980), 'Village Settlement Planning' (1987), 'Urban Redevelopment Planning' (1988), 'Intensive Use Residential District Planning' (1990),[21] and 'Floor Space Area According to Use District Planning' (1990). The last four in this list ease restrictions on use applying to particular zones.

The distinguishing feature of District Planning is that, in varying degrees, these are more detailed, and more aggressive urban planning regimes, that they are plans developed at the local level with the participation and co-operation of those with an interest in the land, and that they can override the provisions of otherwise applicable planning laws, and set up a separate planning regime that responds to the special character of the district. The establishment of this District Planning system marks the introduction of an element foreign to the Japanese city planning system, but if it should go beyond the experimental stage, spread widely, and find common usage as the normally applicable law, it would fill a need that Japan has had for detailed city planning. If this subsidiary planning carried out by city, ward, district, and village governments can be laid down under higher-level (master-plan) planning, there would be a great change in the character, role, and effect of city planning in Japan.[22] It also would become possible, institutionally, to leave behind the current faith in building freedom.

District Planning, with its merits, has been born within the context of the current City Planning Law, which inherited its essential character from the old law. We will watch eagerly to see the extent to which its future development can change the current system. On the other hand, one must also be on guard against taking backward steps, as through unprincipled use of the District Planning system (such as where principal services which a public authority is to provide are shifted to the private sector, and paid for by an increase in floor space limits under the Urban Redevelopment District Planning scheme).[23]

IV. Problems of Social Fairness

1. The utility of land as an asset

The only record of a year-on-year drop in land prices since the Second World War—apart from the current occasion, discussed above—was the year after the oil shock, in 1975. Nationwide residential land prices for March dropped by 5.7 per cent over the previous year. At that time, while real estate houses had a rising sense of danger, there was a prevailing feeling among property owners that 'the market had gone too high', and of relief that it had come to a head. If prices in 1972 are taken as 100, two years later they had reached 184. They fell in the third year to 173, but if we exclude those who bought in for short-term resale, this should not necessarily be viewed as loss. Afterward, residential properties in the Tokyo area reversed the downward trend, returning to 1974 levels before the 1980 price surge. Applying the same scale, the current price surge (1988) easily attained a level of 620.

It is already clear from this evidence of land price movements that land has performed better than other types of assets in the Japanese market. But particularly after experiencing the volatility of the theretofore rising stock market after October 1987, the idea that 'land is a sure bet to rise, and poses little risk' penetrated that much more deeply into the minds of investors. This is the so-called 'land myth'.[24]

Originally, within the real estate community, among those familiar with the speculative nature of real estate transactions, the land myth was not something to believe themselves, but rather something to have others believe. But after the market began to expand with the encouragement of financial institutions (as outlined above), real estate houses came themselves to believe, and rushed to borrow money for their own purchases. In other words, what might be termed the 'Speculative Land Myth' was fostered within the industry itself.

The land myth, founded as it is on the belief in the 'utility of land as an asset', may be distinguished from the Speculative Land Myth. Precisely speaking, this utility is anticipated price increase which is 'unearned by one's own labour or capital investment, but rather external conditions such as changes in population, industry, or social capital in the area'. Put another way, this is anticipation of 'price increase caused by long-term development of the area'.[25] To this, we may add the fact that the land myth is sweetened by the tax system, which has favoured land ownership over other forms of investment.[26]

2. The burden accompanying the benefits

When the land myth brought about 'unearned income due to external conditions', this income naturally fell to the owners of land (or those with an interest in it). People at large, targeting this profit, acquired land themselves and awaited the expected price increase. However, this profit (*a*) does not accrue to anyone without an interest in land, (*b*) does not result from any input by the land owner (such as labour or capital), but (*c*) is derived from the burden of social capital. If any one of these three points fails to achieve approval as being socially appropriate, the gain cannot be guaranteed to the landowner, and the land myth comes into dispute.

Under price inflation, public opinion proved quite sensitive on point (*a*); the widening gap between those with and those without land was perceived to be socially unfair. With respect to point (*c*), an opinion arose that those who had profited from the rise in land prices should return that profit to those third parties who had borne the burden. And with respect to (*b*), there was an opinion that, where an increase in price was due to investment by the land owner, that profit should naturally stay with him.

The 'Interim Report' of 1988 raised five basic points concerning land countermeasures, the fourth and fifth of which were that 'a portion of the profits from capital gain should be restored to society, and social fairness should be assured', and 'in accordance with the use and enjoyment of benefit from land, there should be a fair undertaking of commensurate social burdens'. In the legislative process behind the Basic Land Law, the 'Round Table Discussion on the Basic Land Law' reduced this to a single proposition, stating 'There must be an appropriate burden to accord with the benefit derived from land.' This entered the Basic Land Law in Section 5: 'When the value of land within the district where it is located rises due to the social and economic factors specified in Section 2, an appropriate burden commensurate with the profit derived from the increase in value shall be charged against those with an interest in the land concerned.' The gathering of the two propositions of the Ad Hoc Committee into one was done because, at the point of drafting the legislation, the relationship between the two was not perfectly clear, and in a legal provision, it was thought better to combine the two into a single governing provision.[27] This is a provision that wants further theoretical inquiry, including the question of the relationship between its elements.

3. Various forms of capital gain

Let us tentatively refer to the 'profit derived from the increase in value' referred to in Section 5 of the Basic Land Law as 'capital gain'[28] (in a broad sense). Price rises accompanying such profit can arise from various causes, and these need to be classified. The following four categories are the principal ones:

1. Appreciation of a specific district or area as a result of the provision of a specific public facility or set of facilities;

2. Appreciation resulting from the provision of basic services infrastructure or from ground-breaking development;

3. Appreciation resulting from a loosening of standards for building permits or other change in city planning restrictions;

4. Appreciation following improved savings due to a change in social and economic circumstances.

Among these, the recipients of benefit are limited in number in the case of (1), and it is possible to consult with the recipients concerning the recovery of benefits at the time the relevant public works are undertaken. In such a case, one can identify both the recipient and the amount of benefit received, and consider means of setting a precise amount for payment. By defraying expenses by such means, a portion of the benefit can be recovered.

In contrast, for (2), (3), and (4), the benefited land is wide in scope, and it is difficult to attach an obligation to compensate those bearing the burden by a discrete agreement. In a case under (2) which involves a ground-breaking development project, one can contemplate collecting against capital gain in advance to the extent necessary within and around the area of the development project, but in Japan there has been considerable resistance to advance payment against capital gain, and there are many practical and legal problems with this means of proceeding. For these reasons, the latter three categories of benefit must be left to a strong tax system.

4. Recovery of capital gains through inheritance tax

There is much discussion at present of securing social fairness by recovering a portion of capital gain through a tax on the income from the transfer of land. For example the 'Basic Report' of the 1990 Investigatory Committee on Taxation called for a strengthening of tax on long-term land transfers for both individual and corporate land owners, arguing that 'Land is an asset with a limited and public character, and where faced with an increase in value brought about by external factors such as public investment and the performance of the economy, requiring a higher contribution from the income resulting from transfer serves the needs of a fair distribution of the tax burden. Furthermore, from the standpoint of breaking down the land myth, controlling speculative transactions and reducing the utility of land as an asset is called for. An appropriate tax on the profit from the transfer of land would serve these needs.'[29] Thus, the taxation of gain from long-term transfer of property is founded upon the recovery of capital gain.

Accordingly, tax on gain from long-term transfers (after five years or more) was raised to 30 per cent for individuals (20 per cent or 25 per cent before the reform), and a supplemental tax of 10 per cent was introduced for corporate owners (applicable also to corporations showing a balance-sheet loss). The reasoning behind the system in place to that date had been that lenient tax treatment was appropriate because long-term land transfers have no speculative character, and contribute to land supply. This reform of the law marks a major change in this thinking. The intended effect of improving the recovery of capital gain through the tax system is to decrease the utility of land assets and regulate demand, but there is still a question over whether it is proper to legitimize private profit through capital gain in exchange for a tax increase of 5–10 per cent. One should probably view this as principally a move to increase the tax base, rationalized by reference to a recovery of capital gain; but to the extent that this doctrine is invoked in argument, the impact of consequent law reform on land policy must be taken seriously.

Until recently, as discussed above, the Reports of the Investigative Committee on Taxation have viewed the tax system as having a supplemental role, and have opposed resting land policy upon tax policy. However, in 1995, giving the enactment of the Basic Land Law as the reason, the Committee changed its stance, and stressed the importance of the role which taxation should play in land policy matters. And what the Committee came forward with, as a means of imposing 'burden commensurate with benefit' under Section 5 of the Basic Land Law, was the national Land Holding Tax.

With this new concept in taxation, an 'appropriate burden' was imposed against the internal build-up of capital gain owned by legal persons. But a direct tax against internal build-up was avoided; instead, both legal persons and individuals were taxed for the benefit of tenure. That is to say, regardless of their period of holding the property, a holding tax was charged each year. The government's Tax Committee applied an implicit rate of 'one per cent of any amount above half a billion yen'; but this was lightened considerably by the Liberal Democratic Party Committee on Tax, and although ultimately enacted as a land price tax, it had been thinned down to 'three-tenths of any amount above one billion yen'. The relationship between this new tax and the recovery of capital gain or Section 5 of the Basic Land Law is that, unlike an increase in tax on long-term transfers, it is direct. Rather than being aimed at increasing the tax base, it is a tax strategy aimed at the need for 'fairness of burden'. In terms of their weight, it is difficult to compare a tax of 10 per cent on transfer with a yearly tax of 0.3 per cent, but one cannot dispel the feeling that the latter presents a front of matching burden to benefit, while the former accomplishes the core goal of increasing the Treasury's share of revenue.

V. Problems Arising from the Conception of Land Ownership

1. The topology of land ownership in modern law

To this point, we have examined various debates, legislation, and adminitrative responses arising from the land price inflation that Japan has experienced in recent years. But to reappraise this problem in the context of Japanese society, it is necessary to consider the special characteristics which distinguish the concept of land ownership in Japan from that found in western European countries. We will begin with a look at the concept of land ownership in the modern era.

First, land is a creation of nature; even when it becomes the object of private ownership and control, it is different in character from goods which have been manufactured and consumed. Because land is not made by man, is not consumed by him, and cannot be moved, and because it can become the object of absolute and exclusive ownership when private rights in it are recognized, even if it is converted into a product, an autonomous market based on supply and demand cannot form around it.

The common legal view among traders in the pre-modern period recognized private ownership, as the product of an individual's efforts. A private capacity to control and dispose of this ownership was recognized, as one of the natural rights accruing, in this instance to producers;[30] but for land, which is not the product of man's efforts, this reasoning cannot apply, and a (natural) private right in land could therefore not be established through the power of such reasoning. Rather, such a right comes to be determined when the social contract is equated with law, as the content of the law is determined. And this is accomplished by analogy with other types of goods for which there is a natural logic to ownership and control.

Whenever the process of civil revolution has necessitated the dissolution of the feudalistic system of property ownership, the question of title has had to be settled. In whom would the original right of ownership in lands be created, and what would be the structure of the social system surrounding land use? In France, title was settled upon the farmers working the land, and the reasoning behind that decision was that legal ownership was the surest device offered by the law to guarantee a secure right to use of the land. This was the social contract that was struck with respect to land.

In this way, land ownership was granted to the actual occupant working the land, on the governing premiss that land should follow its use. Following a similar understanding, this notion carried through to the general theory of property, and both 'freedom' of property and its private ownership were guaranteed.

It is submitted that a similar historical process touching the recognition and assignment of private ownership rights in land underpins the concept of property ownership in the various western European countries. Land is owned for the purpose of its use, and for that reason the recipient of land took with it an obligation to make use of it. There was, further, a social concensus on what constituted appropriate use of land, and it was on this basis that city planning laws were established.

2. Distinguishing features of land ownership in Japan

In the early years of the Meiji era, as a consequence of the restoration of the registers to the Emperor (*hanseki hokan*, 1870) and the abolition of the feudal domains (*haihan chiken*, 1872), feudal rule came to an end, and *bushi* below the rank of *daimyo* lost the right to land tribute, taking in its stead stipendiary payments from the state. One of the reasons why this sweeping change was possible within a short period of time was the fact that the right to control over land enjoyed by the court noble (*kuge*) and the *daimyo* was not conceived as ownership; rather, tribute was paid by farmers on the premiss that the land itself was their own. According to Professor Shiro Ishii, the right to tribute, and the right of disposition applying to it, were conceived as nothing more robust than a payment from feudal superiors for the performance of duties.[31] Whether among the overlords or among the farmers, the sense that a piece of land was 'one's own' was weak at best.

With the abolition of feudalism, the right to tribute was transferred to the imperial government, then the right to tribute was redistributed by the government. The content and meaning of this new control to be exercised by the recipients of land had to be constructed. The farmers working the land continued to be obligated to pay tribute, but the government substituted a tax based upon land value for the one based upon crop yield that had existed previously. And by confirming both the individual liable for tax and the amount owed through the land tax reform of 1873, the government sought to firm up its tax base. Toward the end of the Tokugawa period, the feudal system gave rise to parasitic landlord–tenant relationships, which were gradually spreading at the time of the Meiji Restoration. One of the problems that had to be addressed in implementing the land reform was whether the land certificate, representing both title and the obligation to pay tax, should be issued to the tenant working the land, or to a landlord with no immediate involvement in the use of the land.[32] In Japan, the establishment of original rights in land was not done as a means of guaranteeing the use of land, but rather as a tax device. Landlords who received title to land in the land reform, by accumulating further lands from farmers during the Meiji era, established themselves as a distinct social class within Japanese society.

Under this parasitic form of control over land ownership the connection between ownership and use failed, and land ownership came to be viewed as the authority to collect rents, quite independently of its use. For this reason, the drafters of the Civil Code missed the premiss, in the early modern property systems that they adapted to Japan, that ownership exists for the purpose of putting land to use. That is to say, an absolute conception of ownership came to be associated with land in their thinking. Indeed, the concept that land ownership was accompanied by a duty to put it to use must have been difficult to grasp, in the presence of the controlling pattern of parasitic land ownership.

We also should note another turning point in the drafting process of the Civil Code that worked to aggravate further the opposition between use and ownership. This was the refusal, without convincing grounds, of the Review Committee on the Civil Code to accept a government proposal that buildings should be treated as part and parcel of the land on which they stood.[33] After this time, in Japan, and only in Japan, buildings have been treated as immoveable assets separate from the land on which they stand. And as a result of this, it became possible to occupy land under a form of land lease, while having outright ownership of a building standing upon the same parcel.

Compounding this error, the framers of the Civil Code mistakenly assumed that leases for the ownership of buildings would be entered into as real leases (*superficies*), rather than as mere contractual leases; what they missed was that in negotiations between prospective building owners and land owners, the contractual lease, with its relatively weak protection for the user/building owner, inevitably emerged as the dominant choice of the parties. In the minds of land owners, a conception spread that subordinate use of land matched the 'land lease', based upon a contractual lease only.

While there was some variation from region to region, generally speaking the urban landowners in the centre of the cities were former samurai and affluent merchants, while often those on the periphery were landlords who owned tenant lands. It is not hard to imagine how the concept of land ownership that became established with the parasitic landlords in villages was communicated to the cities. The land lease, within which the lessee is in a subordinate position to the land owner, is well suited to the position of bourgeois landowners.

The separation of land and buildings, to the extent that each could be held and transferred without reference to the other, had more than a minimal impact on the market for land. Vacant land is a ready-made product for the market, and came to be seen as the real asset of greatest value. The value of land with buildings attached, on the other hand, is lower than that of vacant land—the opposite of the case in western Europe. In short, in Japan, the value of land as a market item for sale is judged first on the basis of its vacant value, and if it is being used, this reduces the valuation figure. This general treatment applies equally to cases where the building and land are owned by different persons, and to those of unified ownership. The idea that land ownership exists for the promotion of land use has difficulty taking root in such soil.

3. Protection of the right to use, and the concept of land as an asset held in reserve

Land use through land lease gained protection with the Building Protection Act (1910) and the Land Lease Act (1922), legislation which brought an end to the dominant position of landlords. However, this legislation did not engender the sense among landlords of 'ownership for the purpose of productive use'.

In 1941, the requirement of 'appropriate reasons' for preventing an automatic renewal of building leases, and land leases as well, was introduced through a reform of the laws applicable to each interest. Introduced to stabilize tenures in preparation for war, this provision played a greater role in the peace that followed, as a tool for stabilizing and apportioning access to housing. Even more significant for the market today is the subsequent reluctance of land owners to grant land leases at all, given the uncertainty that possession would ever return to them. As a result of the appropriate reasons requirement, the land owners' conception of leasing relationships was confronted with the practical reality that land leases had become a form of quasi-permanent transfer. Although technically a form of lease, through the appropriate reasons standard the land lease came to proxy for ownership itself.

The land lease did survive as an actively granted interest for a time after the war, supported by the spirit of charity and mutual assistance in a time of hardship. But from about 1960 onward—with some variation between regions—with the advent of the custom of making payments to encourage abandonment of such properties and other similar customs, the number of such interests began to decline. Today, apart from some rather special districts of Japan, land leases are no longer granted in normal practice. The land lease, which had elevated a right of use to a status nearly equal to ownership itself, has by that very fact all but vanished from the market.[34]

On the other hand, the bottleneck that the strengthening of the tenants position created in the supply of land for lease did add a further level of analysis to the analysis of our concept of land ownership. When land which one does not need oneself is offered for lease, the underlying reason for leasing the land is, generally speaking, the income that can be gained thereby. The strengthening of tenants' rights may have reduced the amount of income that could be gained, but this was not incompatible with the thinking of landlords of this kind.

However, this legislation went hard against the attitudes of owners for whom the return of the property was more important than income, and they left the market. These are the owners who view land as something to be sold when one needs a block of capital. This is not the petty bourgeois view of land ownership that downplays the importance of securing income, but what might be called 'capital retentive land ownership' which carries capital in the form of land with a view of enjoying capital gain. If one takes this view of land ownership, one would naturally anticipate appreciation in value, and take a reserved view of leasing, development, and even sale as a consequence. This is not the attitude of the land investor during the bubble who insisted on rapid turnover; but this view is none the less in harmony with the land myth, insofar as it is a regressive, obstructive attitude standing in the way of proper land use.

Concerning the criticism that has been directed in recent years at the agricultural land that persists within the Urbanization Districts, if that criticism is directed at anything, it would be those parcels of agricultural land that cannot be explained in any way other that through the concept of 'capital retentive land ownership'. It is difficult for the long-term agricultural holding system (with its favourable treatment of lands within its scope) to dodge the criticism that, if they are seeking capital gain from the ultimate conversion of this land to housing, they should pay tax at housing rates.

A word should be mentioned about agricultural land use. Under the agricultural reform following the Second World War, the parasitic concept of land ownership became a thing of the past. A policy of owner cultivation was explicitly adopted, and small-scale farms on owned land began to appear. The idea of owner cultivation holds that 'agricultural land exists for cultivation, and ownership should therefore be in the farmer himself'. This parallels what we have described as the western European conception, under which land ownership is granted in order that the land be put to good use.

However, the main points of the policy of owner cultivation are, generally speaking: (1) to release land from absentee landlords and large-scale village landlords for the establishment of owner cultivation; and (2) to prevent a resurgence of tenancy relationships, to impose limits upon the acquisition of land by farmers over a certain scale, and to restrict the leasing of land through a permit system. But on top of these measures, (3) it is important to note that, for those lands which remained in the hands of landlords, the tenancies applying to them were given a degree of protection similar to that afforded outright ownership, with the regulatory restrictions that entailed. Because these provisions, developed to cover the 'surviving tenancies', would, under the law, cover new tenancies as well, land owners became reluctant to grant regular tenancies on any terms. The fact that land holdings did not increase in size through the spread of tenancies may be due, not to (2), above, but to (3).

Today, much urban land, including protected agricultural land, is not under cultivation. Much of this land has been abandoned to agriculture because there is no one to work it, or because it is not economically viable. But a proportion of such land has been abandoned because a 'capital retentive' conception of ownership has diluted interest in its use. Such cases have something in common with lands in the long-term agricultural holding system, mentioned above.

4. The land myth and the freedom of the owner

With the percolation of this concept of land as a reserve asset into social consciousness, the land myth struck in full force in the mid-1980s. Under the influence of this myth, speculative movements in the market—which actually conflicted with the myth itself—took place without attracting criticism, and land prices soared without regard to the real demand for land as a productive asset. The 'utility of land as an asset' and 'speculation benefit' derived from it were distinguished in the tax system, but it should be noted that the latter came to be permitted, as reinforced and supported by the former.

Let us consider this situation from the standpoint of the economic freedom of the land owner. In western Europe, firm regulation is imposed on land ownership; that freedom is quite restricted. The freedom that attaches in the abstract to ownership generally is not compromised, but this cannot be said of *land* ownership. Under city planning laws, denial of freedom to build is the norm.

In Japan, even if the full strength of the legal system is brought to bear, it is difficult to deny the general freedom of ownership attaching to land. The Urbanization Districts referred to above introduce two levels of freedom for agricultural land within them. This freedom also means the lack of a detailed master plan for urban infrastructure development and land use conversion; and one should understand the awkward position in which this puts land owners blessed with such freedom.

The freedom of land ownership is not limited simply to the freedom to decide whether or not to build, and what sorts of structures to build. The common assumption that increases in land value accrue to the land owner (i.e., as unearned capital gain) is a realization of this freedom, in the concept of land as an investment asset. The freedom of land ownership has been received with approval as market freedom by some economists, but it must be observed that to make market freedom work in this context, we must oppose a freedom that disregards both external burdens and the societal demand for the productive use of land.

For many years the freedom of land ownership—not necessarily travelling under this nomenclature—has been the target of critical evaluaton by legal scholars. This is due to the inevitable involvement of this issue in the question of when and to what extent ownership rights in land should be protected in the legal system of a capitalist society. The critical position is put by Professor Yozo Watanabe:

With respect to interests in land, we should put use, rather than ownership, in the central position. In the relationship between ownership and use, use should be given precedence. In the relations between land owners, and between users of land, we should consider the guarantee of the right to life as the principal human right in our thinking; the rights of enterprises should, on this analysis, be limited accordingly.

Although a reexamination of our property regime would be in the spirit of the current Constitution, with its primary concern over the protection of human rights, the historical development of property runs counter to this.[35]

In this analysis, the two propositions—the precedence of use over ownership and the precedence of property rights associated with a right to life over those which are not—are each connected to a larger context. The former is derived from a post-war study of English property law, showing that ownership was subordinated to use in the development of property law in the premodern period; the latter from Professor Watanabe's theory of constitutional interpretation.

The first proposition criticizes Japan's 'ownership first' ideology, which excludes users of land (as in the parasitic landlord–tenant relationship) or overlooks the importance of use (as in the view of land as a reserve of capital). It argues for the establishment of a property system that emphasizes the importance of use. This continues to be a supportable position, but it must now face the criticism that strong *rights* of use do not necessarily lead to enhanced use of land in practice (because the process of granting new rights of use comes to a halt, while existing rights of use become something close to ownership). Experience has taught that, however much one might recognize use as a right superior to ownership, one cannot throw off the yoke of ownership as a concept and an institution.

The second proposition holds that, when there are competing interests of ownership and use, that connected with a right to life (for example, use of a farm for production, or use of urban land for housing) should be given precedence. Insofar as this holds that regulation of land use must not violate the right to life, it warrants close attention today. However, even if we might argue for a land policy *informed by concepts of human rights*, it is not possible, *in the law* to take a single right to property and divide it into rights associated with the right to life and those which are not, to the end of giving preference to the former. There is also a question, unresolved in the civil revolution, of whether ownership is in fact a human right. Professor Watanabe goes to great efforts to avoid use of the term 'right-to-life land ownership', but this is what his view entails. In the *exercise* of property interests, there are cases which impinge upon the right to life, and cases which do not. Protecting one right against encroachment by the other is a question for human rights discourse.

At this point we find that there is a problem with the tonic of 'limiting private rights' which is invariably brought out at times of land price inflation. In recent discussion on this line, it has been asserted that 'In the interest of public welfare, the limitation of private rights and land ownership is unavoidable' (former Prime Minister Noboru Takeshita), and that 'We should carefully respect rights of land ownership while limiting [rights] of land use' (former

Prime Minister Kiichi Miyazawa). What is to be limited here is not use that interferes with the right to life, but rather use which does not contribute to the public welfare. It is not clear what constitutes the 'public welfare' in this context; we are left with a plea for the restriction of rights of use and the protection of ownership interests.[36] Perhaps the latter includes the freedom of land ownership discussed above.

5. Re-examining the concept of land ownership

In December of 1989, when the weakness of existing land policy was bared in the wake of the third and fourth waves of land price inflation, the Basic Land Law was enacted. Two or three cautions concerning this legislation are in order. The basic terms of this law are: (1) a statement concerning the idea or concept of land; and (2) a clarification of the basic policies which the state and local authorities should take with respect to land. As put by the Basic Land Law Round Table, this legislation makes a strong appeal (through administrative measures and the citizens' sense of duty) to 'reverse the unnatural sense of attachment that people feel to land'. Second, the details of concrete policy itself are not contained in this law; this is left for the government to determine through deliberation councils in applying the law. Third, in accordance with the conceptual framework and policies of the Law, laws are to be prepared, and various administrative organs are to move in accordance with the government's outline of land policy. At present, we are entering the third stage, but it must be said that it is hard to expect that a reasonable land policy will be constructed on the foundation of the Basic Land Law itself, and the process of implementing policy will doubtless take a great deal of time.

From a legislative perspective, the distinctive feature of the Basic Land Law is the introduction of a uniform awareness of land for the state, local authorities, citizens, and enterprises. The fact that the declaration of purpose, customarily stipulated in the first provision, is broken into subsequent provisions in the law perhaps reflects sensitivity to the terms of Article 29 of the Constitution.[37]

In the past, the first section of the Article, stating that 'The right to own or to hold property is inviolable', has been uniformly interpreted as a statement of fundamental principle, on which is premissed the second section, to wit 'Property rights shall be defined by law, in conformity with the public welfare'. On this view, rights of land ownership are property rights, and therefore clearly within the scope of this provision; land ownership cannot be infringed upon (Section 1), but where it impinges upon the public welfare, it can be limited by law as a special exception to the more general principle (Section 2).[38] Under this interpretation, when one seeks to impose public limitations on the right of land ownership, one must show that, in the absence of that public restriction, the public welfare would be damaged. There is need for care in restricting rights of land ownership in the land policy field, because there is strict control over new legislation through constitutional interpretation applied by the *hosei kyoku*. By means of Article 29, there is a possibility that the freedom of land ownership would effectively escape regulation.

Among the definitional provisions of the Basic Land Law (Sections 2–5), that which warrants closest attention is Section 2 concerning the precedence of public welfare. In the original government draft, this provision read, '. . . in the interest of public welfare, public restrictions shall be introduced which accord with its special needs'. This was revised by opposition parties to read, '. . . with respect to land, the public welfare shall have priority'.[39] By this provision on priority, the interpretation of Article 29 of the Constitition is changed. With respect to land, as opposed to other forms of property, the public welfare has priority, and related legislation must therefore affirmatively promote public welfare.

Basic Land Law section 3 (1) refers to a duty to make appropriate use of land, while 3 (2) refers to a duty to use land in accordance with public planning. These are legislative enactments of suggestions in the Ad Hoc Investigatory Committee, respectively section 1 of its Report (the obligation to use land), and section 3 (planned use of land).[40] Thus, the five sections of the Report, with the addition of prohibition of speculative transactions, have been incorporated, with necessary changes for legislative publication, into the definitional provisions of the Basic Land Law.

The question is the context within which two elements not set forth in the framework provisions of the Law—the expansion of public land ownership, and citizen participation—will be joined to the rest. One can only say that this is left dependent upon the future circumstances relating to the land problem.[41]

Finally, the question of social fairness now being discussed within the narrow context of the recovery of capital gain benefits should be widened to cover questions of land use more generally. At its most extreme this involves redistribution of land, but in recalling that the yoke of ownership cannot be shed, we should take a prudent view of such extremes. What is needed may be a reconsideration of self-reflective 'eternal land ownership'. Several pieces of legislation have been introduced which impose limitations on the physical space occupied by the ownership interest; but of limitations in time there are none.

For myself,[42] I would invite discussion of how the Japanese concept of ownership could be moved toward that of the Anglo-American leasehold, which might be characterized as an ownership interest limited in time. The Fixed Term Land Lease established under the new Land and Building Lease Act is one example of a lease interest limited in time; if this is afforded the full protection of a right in property, it could perhaps be developed into a right of use with the benefits of ownership.[43] One of the factors that has stemmed debate on this topic is the erroneous commonplace in legal study that takes the automatic renewal of land leases as a sign of their 'propertification'[44] I hope that further discussion and debate on this topic will lead to a deepened understanding.

Limitation of ownership rights in time is a legal device for distributing the benefits of physical occupation rationally and by a fair method. As such, we must beware of the danger that imperfections or distortions in the social system of distribution will introduce further injustice. To assure against this, our analysis must encompass a wider field than mere questions of legal technique.

Following what we have seen of land ownership in this short article, such a wider perspective could be expressed as a typology on four axes. First is the speculative concept of land ownership that arises from gain from purchase and resale. Second is the parasitic landlord's or market investor's attitude, under which there is a desire to acquire and hold an increasing area of land, with only a secondary interest in putting the land to use. Third, if we consider that against these there is a conception of ownership which is directed at actual use of the land, following the demands of the market, this leads us to the fourth: the consideration of an ownership interest that can be limited in time in response to the market.

This will be recognized as a hypothetical typology; it does not suggest that conceptions of property ownership in Japan have reached this stage. In actual fact, any one property owner in Japan will experience the conflicting pressures of all of the concepts of ownership discussed in this article. The ambivalent feelings of the members of farming communities when land they own has risen sharply in value, for example, are well known.

The attitudes toward property owners in present-day Japan are various. Whether the policies afoot today will succeed in replacing the keywords 'increasing domestic demand, relying on the power of the private sector, deregulation and limitation of private rights' with a new paradigm remains to be seen. However, there is no doubt that the social sciences have an important role to play in the resolution of these problems.

PART III

Facing the Post-Cold War/Post-Bubble World

8

Employment Relations after the Collapse of the Bubble Economy*

NITTA MICHIO

I. Introduction

The transformation, or disintegration, of Japanese employment practices has been the subject of intense debate. However, for as long as we fail to clarify the central issues, it is difficult to dismiss the impression that phrases like the 'mobile labour market' (*rodo shijo no ryudoka* or *koyo no ryudoka*) are being bandied about indiscriminately. One problem is that we often discuss this issue without establishing certain fundamentals, such as: (*a*) whether employment practices have really changed; (*b*) whether they may or may not change in the future; and (*c*) whether they should change. This chapter is limited to an exploration of the first of these questions. Based on a consideration of the evidence, we will consider how Japanese employment practices have or have not altered in the economic fluctuations that have occurred since the collapse of the so-called bubble.

While developing this argument the writer is forced to recognize two out-standing difficulties. First, large-scale economic change is still taking place. Indeed, as the instability of the foreign exchange markets continues to demonstrate, it is not obvious where structural change, which holds much longer term implications, is headed.[1] Consequently, reservations should be attached to the assumptions made by this argument, which is inevitably tentative.

Second, it is hard to reach a common understanding of what precisely Japanese employment practices and labour relations were in the past. Some might say that the particular characteristics of Japan's employment system and labour relations are to be found in the Japanese employment system, which is organized around life-time employment, seniority pay, and enterprise unions. However, if we consider carefully terms such as 'life-time employment', 'seniority pay', and 'enterprise unions', it is often difficult to understand what they really mean. Defining even 'life-time employment' is a rather complicated business. To begin with, few enterprises put their commitment to life-time employment, that is, the undertaking not to dismiss workers, in writing. This is true across a range of written agreements be it in worker contracts,

---

* Translated by Stephen Johnson.

employment regulations, or agreements with the workforce. Indeed, one would be hard pressed to find any examples.

It is not easy to establish a very basic understanding of whether Japanese enterprises dismiss workers. This is because through Japanese employment adjustment, when the need to reduce existing personnel is really pressing, it is common to call on employees to take voluntary severance or retirement. This applies most typically to big companies, whereas among small and medium-size enterprises large numbers of workers are simply dismissed. If we accept the argument that those who leave or retire when 'voluntary severance' is called choose to do so because of the increased lump sum that they receive on leaving their company, and that this, therefore, does not constitute forced dismissal, then it is possible to regard such practices as one more manifestation of life-time employment. In point of fact, it is the older individuals, who have higher pay costs, and those who perform badly in the workplace who tend to be on the receiving end of these measures, and it is said that they often have to resign because of the psychological pressure to which they are subjected in the workplace. If we see this as dismissal with compensation, then, on closer consideration, it might still be reasoned that there is no life-time employment in Japan. Rather, at best, these practices should be called 'long-term employment', in the sense that it is likely that workers will find and continue employment at one enterprise.

Finally, if we take a further look at what is actually involved in personnel policy, it seems that there are a variety of responses even among the largest companies. On the one hand, some companies elicit voluntary severance/retirement relatively easily, and fill the gaps in their workforce when economic conditions improve, keeping pace with these changes in economic conditions. In contrast, other enterprises avoid voluntary severance/retirement until the last possible moment and rely heavily instead on other methods to adjust their personnel.

Below, this chapter avoids getting involved in the abstract implications of life-time employment. Instead several of its fundamental aspects are investigated with a focus on the adjustment of employment and industrial relations after the collapse of the bubble.[2] The approach taken here draws out the particular characteristics of the current recession through a comparison of it with similar changes that took place during the two most serious recessions of the last twenty years. These were the recessions that followed the first oil shock and the extreme appreciation of the yen that accompanied the Plaza Accords.

II. Employment in Recessionary Japan through to the Collapse of the Bubble

1. Adjustment measures of labour input

It is possible to investigate the shifts in employment patterns within businesses using the *Survey of Labour Economic Trends* (*Rodo Keizai Doko Chosa*), which

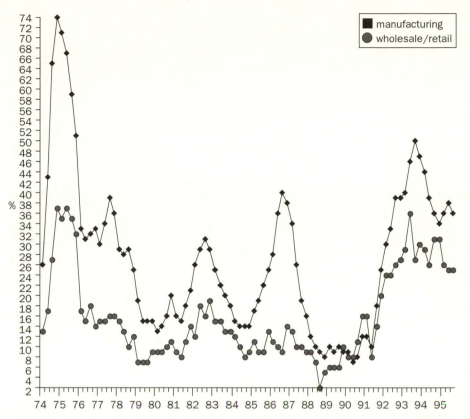

FIG. 8.1. Ratio of establishments that applied employment adjustments

takes data from 5,000 Japanese businesses that employ more than thirty non-temporary workers.

Figure 8.1 represents data divided into three-month blocks, from the time of the first oil shock to the period October–December in 1995. Businesses that tried to adjust their workforces (this includes such methods as restrictions on overtime, the secondment of personnel, voluntary severance/retirement, and redundancy) are categorized by industry.

From this figure it is clear that:

1. As the current recession has spread, employment adjustment has been taking place on a huge scale, second only to the economic down-turn that followed the first oil shock, which fell to its lowest point between April–June and July–September 1975. The current level of workforce adjustment has exceeded that which took place during the high yen recession (the trough in this recession was reached between October–December 1986 and January–February 1987), in terms of the amount of employment adjustment carried out within manufacturing, wholesaling, and the small retail industries.

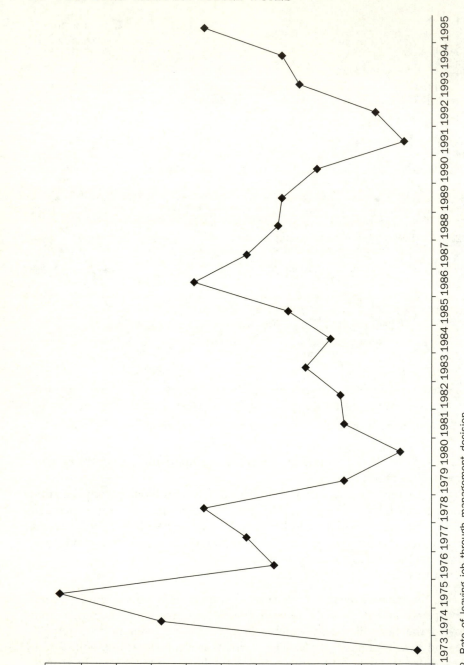

Fɪɢ. 8.2. Rate of leaving job through management decision

2. The lowest depths of the current recession appear to have been plumbed around October–December 1993 and also employment adjustment has been continued over a relatively long period.

Next, we should consider what is involved in the adjustment of employment and industrial relations in more detail. For the manufacturing industry—a sector that feels the influence of recessions particularly keenly—restrictions on overtime, redeployment of labour, secondment, cutbacks and suspension of year-round hiring, the rescheduling and increase of holidays, the failure to renew contracts, and the dismissal of temporary, seasonal, and part-time workers have all been more common in the current recession than they were in the high yen recession, although there are fewer instances now than there were in the first oil shock. However, the levels of voluntary severance, retirement, redundancy, and the most severe form of employment adjustment (2 per cent) are on a par with or perhaps less than during the high yen recession (3 per cent) and clearly less than during the oil shock recession (5 per cent) (Source: 1994 *Labour White Paper* (*Heisei Rokunenban Rodo Hakusho*), p. 300, Table 11).

2. Level of employment adjustment

We are able to understand the scope of employment adjustment from the *Survey of Labour Economic Trends*, although these data do not give an adequate picture of its depth. The impact of employment adjustment on the workforce depends on the extent to which such reorganization is carried out in each business. More useful data are to be found in the *Survey of Employment Trends* (*Koyo Doko Chosa*), which samples Japanese businesses employing more than five non-temporary workers, distinguishing industry and size. In 1992 it surveyed 14,000 concerns.

Figure 8.2 shows the trend of the rate at which workers left their jobs through management decisions. It indicates the level of subtle (voluntary severance) and not-so-subtle (outright discharge) 'lay-offs' in total (i.e., inclusive of voluntary severance and lay-offs).

At the worst point of the recession that followed the first oil shock in 1975, the rate was 1.66 per cent, in the wake of the second oil shock in 1978 it was 1.25 per cent, and in the trough of the economic down-turn which followed the Plaza Accords in 1986 it peaked at 1.28 per cent. After that, an improvement in economic conditions saw the rate steadily decline. From 1992, however, the numbers started to rise again, in 1994 it reached 1.03 per cent and in 1995 1.25 per cent. Even so, it has not exceeded the peaks of the employment adjustment witnessed in the past.

Viewed from this perspective, the outstanding conclusion to be drawn about the current recession is that personnel adjustment does not appear to have been pursued through methods such as voluntary severance/retirement or dismissals. Instead, more moderate techniques have been relied on.

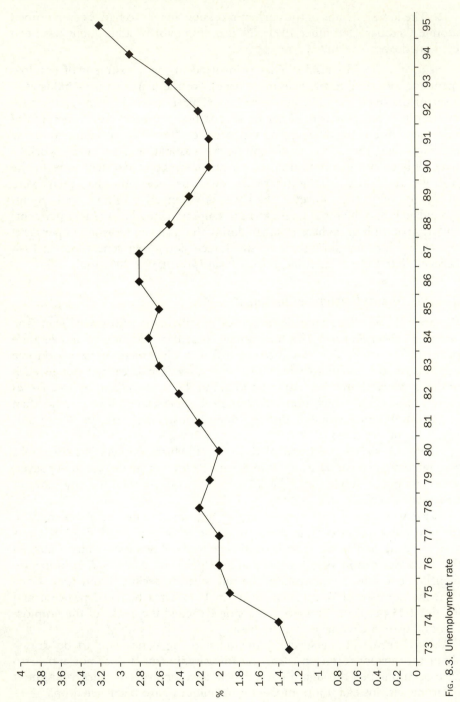

Fig. 8.3. Unemployment rate

It should be added that one of the weaknesses of an analysis like this, which uses the *Survey of Employment Trends*, is its unquestioning acceptance of the data given by the businesses surveyed. There is the possibility that businesses interpret and report numbers of workers who were dismissed for what are really managerial reasons as having quit or resigned. Even so, in analyses like this, where these same statistics are considered as time–series, this bias is not a great problem if it remains consistent.

Of course, it would be preferable to have the job-loss data of those workers who are actually on the receiving end of employment adjustment. What goes some of the way in filling this gap is the *Basic Survey of Work Structure (Shugyo Kozo Kihon Chosa)*. This is a survey of individuals that is thought not to suffer from the bias mentioned above. However, it is only conducted once every three years and it is not possible to use it in the analysis of recession periods. For reference, from the *Basic Survey of Work Structure* we can calculate that the percentage of the workforce who lost their jobs through personnel cutbacks and the dissolution or bankruptcy of companies was 0.6 per cent in 1992 (see the *Labour White Paper*, 1994, p. 84). This figure is not greatly different from the one arrived at in the *Survey of Employment Trends* for 1992, which put the proportion of workers who had lost employment through decisions of management, excluding those who had been sent on or returned from secondment, at 0.5 per cent.

3. The unemployment rate

As we have already seen from the data provided by the *Survey of Labour Economic Trends* and the *Survey of Employment Trends*, the employment adjustment taking place in the current recession is unusual both in its great scope and in the moderate nature of the methods being used. Also, it is noticeable that these responses have continued for a relatively long time. We can suppose that even quite moderate employment adjustment, if it continues over a long period, will increase the number of job losses and push up unemployment. This point is made clear by Figure 8.3, which shows the trends of the unemployed. The recent unemployment rate of 3.5 per cent (May 1996) is a record high, which indicates the seriousness of the current recession. Nevertheless, while rates of unemployment that exceed 3 per cent seem high, based on Japan's previous economic performance, these record-breaking figures do not, in themselves, point to structural change.[3]

4. The labour participation rate

Let us now turn our attention to the labour participation rate; that is, the ratio of the labour force to the population. In order to comprehend the shifts

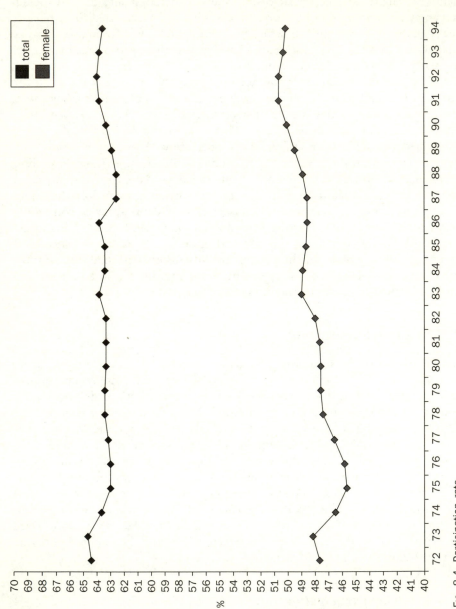

Fig. 8.4. Participation rate

in Japan's labour markets, it is necessary to look at the labour participation rate, especially as regards the proportion of females in the workforce. In previous recessions, the labour participation rate of females has been reduced with the result that increases in the overall unemployment rate have been kept in check. As far as the current recession is concerned, on the basis of the annual data for 1993 (Figure 8.4), there was no clear reduction in the participation rate of female workers. Looking at the monthly data for developments after 1993, we can see that the rate was 50.0 per cent in December 1993, it fell to 48.9 per cent in January 1994 and 48.6 per cent the following month, although it has recovered somewhat since. This corresponds to the movements in employment adjustment, and the role that reductions in female participation in the labour force play can be observed.[4] However, even this has been limited compared with the massive fluctuations in the ratio that followed the first oil crisis. It is also true that the fall in the participation rate of females has not had any pronounced effect in mitigating real rises in unemployment.

5. Working Hours

This being the case, how is it that enterprises have managed to survive this recession in which the production index in mining and manufacturing industries has registered minus values for two straight years (–6.1 per cent in 1992 and –4.5 per cent in 1993)? The control of working hours has played a very important role. As is shown in Figure 8.5, according to *Monthly Labour Statistics*, (*Maitsuki Kinro Tokei*), which surveys businesses of thirty workers and above, for the five years between 1989 and 1993, average hours worked per employee per month fell 16.5 hours. This figure breaks down as a reduction of 12 hours in regular working hours and a reduction of 4.6 hours in overtime. In the manufacturing industry, the role of overtime becomes much more significant. The reduction here translates as a fall of 10 fixed working hours versus 7.7 overtime hours.

If we see these as a direct response to economic fluctuations, the changes that took place in the years 1992 and 1993 are particularly important. During this period, the total average reduction in working hours per employee per month in all industries was 8.6 hours. This translates into a fall of 5.1 hours in regular hours and 3.5 hours in overtime. (Within the manufacturing industry the respective values were 9.8 hours, 3.4 hours, and 6.4 hours.) The relative importance of overtime within the changes in working hours during this period is clear.

In the longer term, the role of reductions in regular working hours becomes more important. Had regular working hours—which stagnated for a long period after the first oil crisis and then even increased—not been rapidly reduced after 1989, there is no doubt that the current moves to adjust

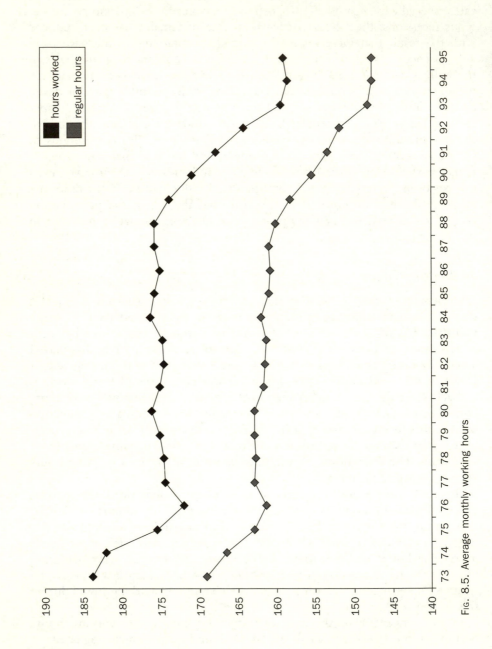

Fig. 8.5. Average monthly working hours

employment would have shown quite a different complexion. In this respect, we might also say that the effect of the movement to reduce working hours, which was begun in the second half of the 1980s and which the government and labour groups championed, brought about an unintended result: job sharing.

One may be critical of the *Monthly Labour Statistics* because the survey does not sufficiently get to grips with hidden hours that are worked, like those spent in entertaining clients, socializing with colleagues in the evenings, or in other forms of non-paid overtime. Once more, however, as far as this argument is concerned, so long as the distortion caused by such factors remains consistent, this is not an issue which need exercise our minds here.

Needless to say, it would certainly be preferable to have data that included statistics on working hours gathered on an individual basis. What can be used in this regard is the *Labour Force Survey (Rodoryoku Chosa)*. According to this survey, the rate of change for the average weekly working hours of males employed in industries other than agriculture and forestry can be calculated at 8.3 per cent (9.6 per cent in manufacturing).[5] This is little different from the 9.4 per cent rate of reduction (9.8 per cent in manufacturing) which is given in Figure 8.5. It shows the total hours worked by men and women in the industries surveyed over the same period. For the sake of comparison, also according to *Monthly Labour Statistics*, the rate of reduction in total hours worked monthly by male workers between September 1988 and September 1993 was 8.8 per cent in all industries, and 9.5 per cent in manufacturing. So, for the purposes of this argument, there is little qualitative difference in data from a survey that looks at the enterprise or at the individual.

For as long as these developments are not accompanied by cutbacks in pay, however, they involve an increase in hourly wage costs for the enterprise. If we consider the 'real pay per hour worked index' numbers which have been arrived at by dividing the Real Pay Index (calculated from the *Monthly Labour Statistics* and the Consumer Price Index, and which takes 1991 as the base year for earnings including bonuses and overtime pay) with the total hours worked taken from the same source, we see that it remained unchanged for a long period after the first oil shock. However, as Figure 8.6 reveals, following the improved economic conditions of 1987, there was a marked increase. This trend continued even into 1993 when at last there was a drop in the Real Pay Index. If it is remembered that the increases in general labour costs per hour carry with them also the consideration of benefit costs, then we should expect the impact of this rise to be all the greater. (During the period of the bubble economy, a wide-ranging improvement of benefits such as the introduction of new dormitories was planned to make it easier to employ younger workers.) This heightens the sense of burden that labour costs provoke in businesses and it may be one of the reasons why businesses regard their workforce as oversized.

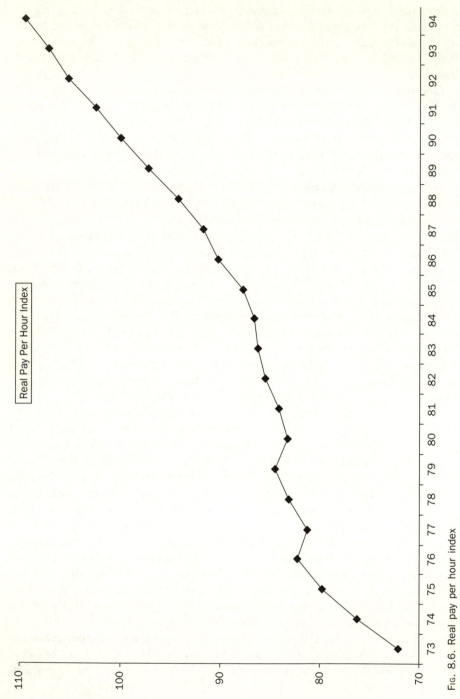

Real Pay Per Hour Index

FIG. 8.6. Real pay per hour index

6. White-collar over-employment

One outstanding feature of the recent changes in employment during the current recession has been the way employment adjustment has hit so-called white-collar workers, especially those in management positions. This has encouraged many to write the obituary of stable and cocooned white-collar employment in Japan. So that we can understand just what has been happening in the Japanese white-collar labour market, the changes in the occupation structure of the workforce have been mapped out in Figures 8.7 and 8.8 using data from the Labour Force Survey. Our findings may be summarized as follows:

(1) According to Figure 8.7, between 1986 and 1992 the number of those at work grew by 5.38 million (10 per cent). The three categories of white-collar workers (i.e., those in specialist/technical occupations, managerial occupations, and clerical occupations) increased by 4.48 million (28.2 per cent). Because of this expansion of white-collar workers, the share of these three types of workers in the total workforce rose from 30.6 per cent in 1986 to 34.8 per cent in 1992. The growth in white-collar workers was not unprecedented, however. For example, during the six years between 1977 and 1983, the number of the employed in total went up 3.91 million (7.3 per cent). At the same time, white-collar workers in the three categories increased by 2.59 million or 17.8 per cent. What was remarkable during the economic bubble, nevertheless, was the pace of the expansion of the white-collar stratum. In 1993, these three occupational categories registered zero growth, and their share among the total employed fell for the first time. The new graduates of Japan's universities felt the impact of these changes the most deeply.
(2) Figure 8.8 shows the trends displayed by those engaged in managerial occupations. Again, during the six years between 1977 and 1983, those in managerial occupations grew by only 30,000. In comparison, during the six years between 1986 and 1992, this group increased by some 460,000. Through 1993, this trend was reversed with a fall of 13,000, prompting doubts about the future of those in white-collar occupations. Many concerns were raised about the abolition of management status, job restructuring, the possibility of dismissal, and a clamp-down on promotions to management positions. Even in 1994, this is a trend that shows no signs of slowing. There are some indications that workers in white-collar occupations will increase in the future, but for the time being, the fall in the numbers of those employed as managers continues unabated.

While this has been the case, the post-bubble years have not been the first time that the numbers of managerial workers have decreased. Between 1977 and 1978, as well as 1982–5, large-scale reductions were recorded of 110,000 and 170,000 respectively. What we can say about the current situation is that reductions have been carried out on a large scale and with some urgency.

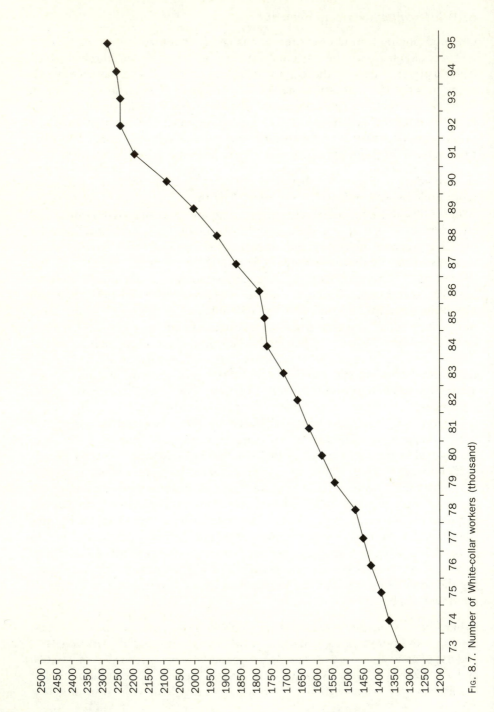

Fig. 8.7. Number of White-collar workers (thousand)

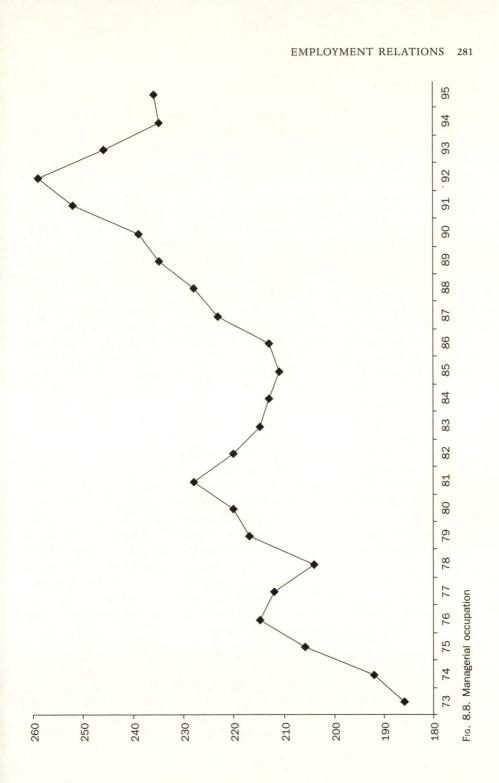

Fig. 8.8. Managerial occupation

III. Conclusions

The argument here has been that the adjustment of employment that accompanied the post-bubble recession in Japan has certainly been wide-ranging and has had an enormous influence on the livelihoods of workers. However, the measures taken have followed the typical Japanese employment adjustment formula by avoiding, where possible, dismissals, and by driving for voluntary severance/retirement. In the recent adjustments, reductions in working hours have provided management with their most important tool. Under these changes in employment and treatment, the most affected group has been employed in white-collar occupations. As such, concerns about the loss of management status or a slowdown in promotions have increased. These moves characterize the consolidation of the excessive white-collar employment and managerial appointments made during the bubble period. Many of those who argue that Japanese employment practices are disintegrating do so based on particular episodes where there has been friction in this adjustment process. What such characterizations fail to do is take in the whole picture of Japanese employment. That is not to understate the importance of the problems facing white-collar employment today, but it is clear that arguments of this type are limited in scope. Returning to the problem as set out at the beginning of this chapter, it has to be concluded that the evidence suggests that Japanese employment practices have undergone no fundamental change.

The question of whether this kind of employment adjustment is desirable or not is something that has to be debated as a matter of policy. It has been suggested that what adjustment there has been is moderate and takes time, making clear development and responses difficult for Japanese enterprises, and hindering the structural change of Japanese industry. This point is becoming a matter of increasing debate. Furthermore, when we consider the trends in Japanese employment and labour relations in the longer term, we should try to ascertain the impact of ongoing structural changes to the Japanese economy. It is still not clear how industrial adjustment, which accompanies deregulation and the high yen, will ultimately impact. When we embark on analyses in the future, the following points may be important references when we consider the prospects for Japanese employment:

1. It is important to differentiate between long-term structural change and the large-scale cyclical economic movements that are happening today. The former might occur through a large shift in the international economic structure and the realignment of international industrial sectors involving the Japanese economy, and would accompany, say, a rise of the Asian economies. The latter is comprised of factors that are peculiar to the collapse of the bubble.

It is essential to recognize this distinction as it is through the influence of the ill effects of the bubble that the debate concerning Japan's future has tended to become overly pessimistic.

2. Only with an accurate understanding of the structural characteristics of Japanese employment and labour relations is a meaningful debate concerning changes and shifts in these areas possible. Here, while we have restricted the discussion to the realities of employment adjustment, which are just one aspect of life-time employment, it has become evident that understandings of stereotypical Japanese employment practices greatly confuse the debate about change.

There is inertia in the system that will not change easily. Apart from predicting that change, it is important that we correctly understand what it is that underpins this inertia. By looking at the reality, we should also analyse how structural change is being realized, or whether it will indeed succeed in the future. For example, one important issue for today's Japanese economy is whether, in a situation of enormous upheaval in the stock and property markets, the current corporate governance structure, which is supported by the cross share-holding of enterprises, can effect rapid change. If we accept the fact that one important element that has structurally defined the pattern of Japanese labour relations is the special governance structure, then we can expect these kinds of changes to have a far-reaching influence on labour relations and employment practices (Aoki (1988), Nishiyama (1983), Nitta (1994)). So far, however, signs of a drastic change of this nature—not only in the structure of corporate governance, but also in the other organizations that support Japanese employment practices, such as in supplier networks—have been hard to detect.

References

Aoki, M. *Information, Incentives and Bargaining in the Japanese Economy*, (Cambridge, 1988).

Nakamura K. and Nitta M. 'Developments in Industrial Relations and Human Resource Practices in Japan', in Locke, R., Kochan, T., and Piore, M. (eds.), *Employment Relations in a Changing World Economy*, (Cambridge, Mass., 1995).

Nishiyama, C. *Datsu Shihonshugi Bunseki* (An Analysis of Post-Capitalism), (Tokyo, 1983).

Nitta, M. '*Koporeeto Gabanansu to Roshi Kankei*' (Corporate Governance and Labour Relations), *Jurisuto*, 1050 (1 August 1994).

Ono, A. *Nihonteki Koyo Kanko to Rodo Shijo* (Japanese Employment Practices and the Labour Market), (Tokyo, 1989).

Ujihara, S. 'Nenko Chingin Shogai Koyo Kigyo Betsu Kumiai wa Sanmi Ittai ka' (Seniority Pay, Career Employment and Enterprise Unions: A Trinity?) in *Nihon no Roshi Kankei to Rodo Seisaku* (Labour Relations and Labour Policy in Japan), (Tokyo, 1989).

Yoshikawa, Y. *Nihon Keizai to Makuro Keizaigaku* (The Japanese Economy and Macro Economics), (Tokyo, 1992).

9

Explaining the End of the Post-War Party System

HIWATARI NOBUHIRO

I. The Argument

The Murayama Socialist-led cabinet of 1994 marked the end of the post-war party system. Except for a brief interlude in 1947–8, this was only the second time, in nearly half a decade after the war, that the Socialist party[1] had been in power. Moreover, this time the Socialists were aligned in a three-party coalition with their rivals the Liberal Democratic party (LDP), who had been ousted only a year earlier after thirty-eight years of single-party rule. The post-war party system, in place since 1955, was characterized by one-party dominance by the LDP and enduring opposition by the Socialists. With the introduction of a new electoral system, legislated during the non-LDP government, an institutional break has occurred in the history of Japanese party politics.

Most conspicuous among the developments that led to these changes is the demise of the radical left-union opposition. After its almost accidental arrival in power, the Socialist party renounced what remained of its basic ideological tenets. The union arm of the party and the predominant national labour organization, Sohyo (the General Council of Japanese Trade Unions), had already ceased to exist in 1989. In contrast, the Liberal Democratic party still maintains most of its strength and has come to lead the government again in 1996. Ironically, what crippled one-party dominance and created a Socialist-led government was the demise, rather than the rise, of the Socialist–Sohyo bloc. In other words, the major political transformation in the last two decades was the demise of the radical left opposition, embodied by the Socialist–Sohyo bloc. This chapter explains what caused this demise, which enabled the Socialists to assume power, and examines the implications of this change for the comparative analysis of Japanese political economy.

I explain the demise of the radical left-union opposition as the result of adjustments made by market and political actors since the first oil crisis. At that time, facing a trade-off between either wage increases to compensate for inflation or else increased unemployment, the unions opted for co-ordinated wage restraint based on management-union collaboration. Because corporate-centred co-ordinated adjustment was no longer compatible with the strategies

of the predominant national union Sohyo, this decision led to the reorganization of the national labour movement under moderate auspices. In other
words, the golden years of high economic growth, in which national unions
could demand high wages and enjoy full employment, were over, and it was
the unions that had to make organizational adjustments. Unions of large corporations in the export sector provided leadership in this regard. However, since
only large corporations could guarantee employment security in exchange for
wage restraint, corporate-centred adjustment reinforced the cleavage between
large corporations, on the one hand, and smaller businesses and/or the self-
employed, on the other, instead of drawing a sharp line between business
and labour. Smaller businesses and the self-employed, most of which were
in domestic-oriented sectors, were dependent on government policies for
adjustment compensation.

This cleavage did not, however, deepen when the issue of scaling down
welfare commitments and strengthening the fiscal capacity of the state to
order to adapt to low economic growth reached the political agenda in the
1980s. Instead of exploiting this cleavage by taking sides, the government and
opposition parties competed to modify government reform proposals in
favour of small business and the self-employed. This was possible because the
state bureaucracy pre-co-ordinated the interests of large corporations with
those of small business and the self-employed in devising policy reforms.
This convergence of party positions across the government–opposition divide,
facilitated by the moderation of the labour unions, led to the demise of the
radical left-opposition and the realignment of the party system.

The two elements critical in explaining party system reorganization in
Japan—corporate-co-ordinated adjustment and bureaucratic pre-co-ordination
of policy reforms—and their impact on the trade union movement and the
opposition have not been fully accounted for in prevailing theories of comparative political economy. Corporate-co-ordinated adjustment and bureaucratic
pre-co-ordination explain why labour unification under moderate auspices and
labour inclusion in the policy process did not transform 'corporatism without
labour'[2] into either a neo-corporatist or a liberal market political economy.
Prevailing theories have difficulty in comprehending the characteristics of the
Japanese political economy because corporate-co-ordinated adjustment and
bureaucratic pre-co-ordination fall in the crack of the neo-corporatist vs.
pluralist dichotomy. Furthermore, focus on the unions and opposition parties
in explaining recent political change departs significantly from the dominant
perspective of Japanese political analysis, which has concentrated on the relations among the Liberal Democratic party, the bureaucracy, and business.
However, since major changes occurred in the union movement and the
opposition parties, while corporate-level industrial relations and government-
bureaucracy relations were stable, it is necessary to look into the former to
understand what caused a reorganization of the party system in Japan.

In what follows I examine, first, how adjustment by market actors in coping with the problems caused by the oil crisis led to the reorganization and
unification of the union movement. Stagflation, immediately after the first
oil crisis, made voluntary wage restraint an issue in most advanced industrial
democracies. In Japan management–union collaboration, based on the tacit
exchange of voluntary wage restraint for employment security and corporate welfare, was reinforced at oligopolistic firms in export-oriented industries.
Voluntary wage restraint at export-oriented industries had nationwide effects,
since the role of the oligopolistic firms in heavy metal industries as setters of
wage increases had been institutionalized in annual wage bargaining. Although
inter-industrial 'pegging' of wages had been in effect since the mid-1960s, it
was only when wage restraint and employment security became a trade-off that
management–union collaboration conflicted with the wage-maximizing strategy of Sohyo. Previously, during the high-growth years, large wage increases
and tight labour markets disguised the potential incompatibility between the
wage moderation strategy of export industries and the Sohyo strategy of wage
maximization.

Collaborative adjustment at oligopolistic firms in export-oriented industries
deepened the cleavage between such corporations and those firms that needed
assistance from the government to adjust. This cleavage was bridged by the
state bureaucracy, which negotiated plans to distribute the costs of employment and industrial policies for depressed firms. The bureaucracy played a
similar role in bridging the gap between large corporations and smaller
ones on policies demanded by the competitive sector, such as extending the
retirement age or introducing a five-day work week. In these cases, the
bureaucracy pursued a dual strategy of allowing large firms to implement such
measures while insisting that such policies should be put into law, despite
reservations from smaller firms. The export-sector unions lobbied the government to provide compensation for firms and workers in depressed sectors to
preserve the solidarity of the union movement.

Such lobbying only worsened the split between between export-sector
unions and Sohyo headquarters, a split that had become apparent since the
emergence of the wage-restraint issue. The 'anti-monopoly capitalism' line
of Sohyo, led by the public-sector unions, not only insisted on maximum
wage increases but also opposed bargaining with either business or government. Thus, to pursue wage restraint and lobby for compensation policies,
moderate union leaders had to contemplate the reorganization of the national
labour movement. The demands made by moderate union leaders, however,
could be assimilated by business and the state. Policy conflicts were settled
among market actors by corporate-co-ordinated adjustment, and between the
bureaucracy and market actors through bureaucratic co-ordination. In other
words, policy agreements detoured around the political parties and had a
distinctly non-partisan character.

Next, I explain how the de-radicalization of the union movement led to the moderation of the Socialist party. The decline of radical unionism led moderate opposition parties to collaborate with the ruling Liberal Democratic party instead of uniting to confront it. Such collaboration was facilitated by the near parity of government and opposition seats after the 1976 election, and was reinforced during the neo-liberal reforms, particularly social security and tax reforms. Furthermore, the large unions themselves, along with the moderate parties, pressed the Socialist leadership to jettison its Marxist ideology and de-radicalize. Such demands were intended partly to secure an alternative channel to government beside the LDP, and partly to secure the electoral success of union candidates.

The convergence among right and centre parties across the government–opposition line, facilitated by bureaucratic pre-co-ordination in carrying out neo-liberal reforms, compelled the Socialists to de-radicalize their policies to check right-centre collaboration while maintaining a populist stance to distinguish themselves from the moderate parties. In devising neo-liberal reforms, the bureaucracy co-ordinated the interests of large corporations with those of small businesses and the self-employed by redistributing the costs between the large corporations, who preferred less redistributive social security and direct taxes, due to supplementary corporate welfare, and smaller businesses and the self-employed, who were dependent on social security and government expenditures but wanted to transfer the costs to larger corporations. In devising a compromise between these two demands, bureaucratic co-ordination forestalled redistributive issues from becoming partisan ones. Moreover, neo-liberal reforms completed the unification of the union movement under moderate auspices because the privatization of public corporations and the social security reforms exacerbated conflicts within public-sector unions causing them to align with the private-sector unions.

As a result political parties across the government–opposition divide could compete to modify government proposals in favour of their core electoral constituents (mainly small businesses and the self-employed). This facilitated collaboration between the ruling party and moderate opposition parties. On the one hand, the ruling party could assimilate the demands of the moderate opposition parties and strengthen its 'catch-all' appeal. On the other hand, the moderate opposition parties could appeal to their constituents by extracting concessions from the government, while the Socialists could do the same by maintaining a populist stance of opposing any increases in social security burdens, cuts in benefits, or new taxes.

Despite its objection to government–moderate opposition compromises, the need to maintain ties with the moderate opposition in order to avoid isolation and marginalization compelled the Socialist party to abandon its ideological identity. Yet, the Socialists were unable to create a new identity and programme after abandoning the 'anti-monopoly capitalism' line. Thus, the differences among the parties from the LDP to the Socialists had become a matter of degree instead of a clear-cut contrast of policy or ideology. This made possible the realignment of coalitions across government–opposition lines and the reorganization of political parties. It also explains the paradox of the Socialists being ushered into power despite their decline in organizational and popular support.

II. Corporate-Co-ordinated Adjustment, Compensation Policies for Employees, and the Demise of Radical Left-Unionism

Two features stand out in Japan's response to the stagflation caused by the first oil crisis. First, management–union collaboration was reinforced at large corporations, where unions agreed to restrain wages in exchange for employment security for their members. Second, the government's employment policies became closely co-ordinated with its industrial policies and concentrated on 'structurally depressed' industries. Political parties competed to play a complementary role in expanding bureaucratically drafted policies for firms in structurally depressed industries/regions. In other words, the conflict among political parties in Japan was not over whether to impose austerity to cope with inflation, at the risk of high employment; or to guarantee employment, at the cost of rapid inflation and balance of payments problems, as seen typically in the UK and USA. Since the strategy of moderate unions—engaging in voluntary wage restraint and lobbying the government for adjustment compensation for the troubled industries—collided with Sohyo's 'anti-monopoly capitalism' strategy, which demanded high wage increases to compensate for high inflation and urged workers to confront the government and monopoly capital, the union leaders in the export industries started to reorganize the national union movement to suit their purposes.

Large corporations in competitive industries adjusted to the economic crisis by flexibly redeploying their workers and holding back wage increases. Corporate-centred employment adjustment was carried out by reducing overtime, cutting the number of new recruits, transferring or dispatching personnel to different positions or firms, and firing temporary workers. Corporate ties (*kigyo keiretsu*) were fully utilized in relocating workers.[3] For example, in the late 1970s the five major steel companies shed redundant workers by increasing temporary and permanent transfers. In the case of Nippon Steel, most of the temporary transfers went to nearby automobile and electric plants, including subsidiaries and subcontractors of oligopolistic parent companies. The parent auto or electric firms were consumers of steel products. Thus inter-corporate business ties were reinforced by personnel ties in the labour market.[4] As a result, Japan contained its unemployment rate after the oil crisis despite the lack of employment growth in either the public or private sector. This is in sharp contrast with both the Scandinavian neo-corporatist political economies, where full employment was achieved by expanding public-sector employment, and the pluralist political economies, where unemployment was high due to stagnation in the number of jobs in the private sector.[5]

Voluntary wage restraint, advocated by union leaders of oligopolistic firms in export industries, caused a major dispute within the national labour organization. Immediately after economic disruption hit the economy, during the annual spring wage offensive of 1975, the chairman of the steel industrial union strongly endorsed wage restraint. He was seconded by other export industry union leaders and the leaders of the moderate national organization, Domei, but harshly criticized by the leaders of Sohyo. Adhering to the 'anti-monopoly capitalism' line and under the strong influence of public-sector unions, leaders of Sohyo called for militant strikes to win wage increases comparable to the high inflation rates. However, the national wage-setting pattern prevailed whereby the major steel firms set the national wage increase standards, which were consolidated by oligopolistic firms in the auto, electronic, heavy machinery, and shipbuilding industries. The 1975 steel industry wage increase was 0.1 per cent below the 15 per cent guideline advocated by the employers' association, and the average wage increase was around 13 per cent. In stark contrast, unions had won an average 34 per cent wage increase in the 1974 spring offensive to compensate for price increases.[6]

Since the 1975 spring offensive, the moderate wage demands set forth by heavy and export-oriented industry unions have been the pattern. In 1976, the moderate unions set up their own wage committee (Chinto Kyoto Kaigi), independent of the usual committee sponsored by Sohyo (Shunto Kyoto Kaigi). The actual wage increase was set by the two leading companies of the four major heavy industries.[7] By 1977, the dominant role of the top unions in each of the four major metal-export industries in setting wages was consolidated. This was the result of the electronics union aligning itself with its counterparts in the metal industries. Annual wage demands thereafter, according to Tsujinaka, were in tandem with the rate of real productivity growth and the actual settlement was around 70 per cent of union demands. There is thus little doubt that wage increases were set so that they did not suppress investment in competitive industries. When deep and recurring hardships made it difficult for the steel industry to set the national wage standard after the mid-1980s, prosperous industries such as electronics and automobiles took over the role of national wage setting. However, moderate wage demands and uneventful wage bargaining, without strikes remained the basic pattern.[8]

In addition to the wage restraint issue, the demand for compensation policies to adjust to the post-oil crisis recession exacerbated the split within Sohyo between private- and public-sector unions. Parallel to the wage issue, the shift of leadership away from Sohyo to major private unions was seen in the policy activities of the unions. In 1977 a twin organization of the wage committee was launched to foster lobbying (Seisaku Suishin Roso Kaigi), especially for compensation policies. The members were almost identical in these two committees, and this structure became the nexus of a movement to create a new national labour organization, as the number of industrial unions joining the nascent group increased in the late 1970s at the expense of Sohyo.[9]

The basis of closer ties at the national level was the consolidation of industry–union collaboration. Just as company–union collaboration was based on the exchange of wage restraint for employment security, collaboration at the industry level was based on a trade-off between wage co-ordination and policy demands. Industrial union federations voiced demands in industrial policy, inflation control, income tax cuts, housing, education, and employment security. However, most exigent was the extension of the mandatory retirement age and the reduction of work hours, since both issues were related to employment security for union members. The retirement age for employees in large corporations had been 55 (older for employees in smaller firms), and criticism of long working hours was heard even from overseas. The issue of extending the retirement age and shortening work hours, as well as feasible ways to implement such policies, had been endorsed by a number of government advisory committees by the early 1970s. The role of competitive sector unions was mostly to press reluctant business leaders to accept such prescriptions. Shortly after the first oil crisis, the steel union federation revised its Second Term Wage Policy for 1975–80. Wage increase goals were gradually reduced from '6 per cent increase in real wages plus a 5 month bonus' (1975) to 'price increases as the minimum' (1977) and to levels 'economically compatible' with recovery, as the economic forecast for the industry worsened. In exchange for wage moderation, the union decided to pursue a 'comprehensive struggle for livelihood' and demanded corporate solutions to housing, education, medical care, and old age security problems, with the major focus on the retirement age. Furthermore, in 1979 the union announced its willingness to compromise on wage and personnel issues in exchange for increasing the retirement age from 55 to 60. The industrial union agreed to modify seniority wages so that wages would peak before retirement age, to increase the job-evaluation portion of wages, to lower the lump-sum retirement payment standards, and to accept more flexibility in manpower redeployment. As a result, in 1980 the top fifteen steel companies consented to change the retirement age from 55 to 60 under the following conditions. Employees were to retire from their supervisory positions at 55, the wage curve was to be flat after 50, lump-sum retirement payments were to be reduced, and the union was to accept further flexibility in manpower deployment. By 1989, this agreement was extended to thirty-three of the fifty members of the steel industry union as a result of the union's campaign to extend the benefits to smaller firms.[10]

Such efforts were not unique to the steel industry. Similar negotiations were carried out by the private railways and the textile industry. In 1979 the private railway federation demanded the extension of the retirement age from 57 to 60 without changes in labour conditions by the year 1985, and reached an agreement with major firms subject to the condition that modifications in wages and labour conditions would be hammered out. Similarly, in 1980 the textile union made age-60 retirement its top priority and decided to accept a freeze in seniority wages and lump-sum retirement payment increases. After negotiations, both sides agreed that the largest nine companies would extend retirement age to 57 by 1981 and to 60 by 1984. Furthermore, ninety-one smaller enterprise unions also won some kind of retirement age extension. Similar arrangements spread to the major firms in the electric power, chemicals, paper and pulp, foodstuff, department store, and life-insurance industries. Although the unions made concessions, it is undeniable that they played a positive role in forcing companies to accept policies widely regarded as necessary by the government and in business and academic circles. According to one survey, at 95.8 per cent of the firms surveyed, extension of the retirement age was proposed by the unions.[11]

At the level of national policy-making, corporate-co-ordinated adjustment prevented the trade-off between stable prices and full employment from becoming a contested partisan issue. As a result, the government was able to concentrate on industrial and employment policies for troubled industries. Demands for such adjustment compensation, moreover, were voiced not only by the unions but also by employers and the bureaucracy. The transformation of the unemployment compensation programme into active labour-market policy, for example, was triggered not by economic crisis but by the Ministry of Labour to rectify the insurance system, which disproportionately benefited seasonal labourers and unmarried women.[12] The 1974 Employment Insurance Act introduced a programme that subsidized employers' wage payments to temporarily laid-off employees. Naturally, private-sector unions welcomed such measures as a device to prevent dismissals. Sohyo, on the other hand, vehemently opposed the bill. Initially responding to the day-workers' and the construction workers' unions, whose interests would be harmed by the revision, Sohyo successfully defeated the bill with the help of the Socialists and Communists. It was intense lobbying by private-enterprise unions that led to the reintroduction and passage of the bill. Once major-sector unions became active, Sohyo changed its policy and endorsed the bill, which was passed by a government–opposition alliance (except for the Communists). The incident revealed conflicting interests among Sohyo members between the vocal day-workers and construction workers, on one hand, and the moderate enterprise unions on the other.[13]

With the 1974 Act as a watershed, programmes to encourage employers to retain, relocate, or retrain workers expanded rapidly in the late 1970s. The expansion of active labour-market policy, however, was based on bureaucratic co-ordination of business interests rather than through the adoption of union policies. Above all, the idea of creating a so-called Employment Stabilization Fund to assist employers in retraining and relocating employees in long-term structural, as opposed to cyclical, adjustments was proposed by the business community and echoed through government advisory committee reports.[14] Furthermore, the major issue in the expansion process was the funding mechanisms, particularly the proposed increase in unemployment insurance premiums. The business sector was split over successive increases in insurance premiums. Thus during the formulation of the 1977 revision of the Employment Insurance Act, the Ministry of Labour had to lower the proposed insurance rate hike (to 0.05 per cent) because of opposition from some business owners. Similarly, in a set of special measures to expand employment policies in 1977–8 to structurally depressed industries and regions, the government had to satisfy business by splitting another 0.1 per cent increase in unemployment insurance premiums between employers and employees and attaching a supplementary resolution stating that the employers' share of this increase would be abolished when the economy improved and the employment stabilization fund had become financially sound.

Finally, employment policy became linked to industrial policy. In the above-mentioned 1977–8 set of special measures to increase adjustment compensation to structurally depressed industries and regions, industrial policy provided government-guaranteed loans to industries engaged in cartels, along with price supports to assist the orderly disposition of abundant facilities.[15] The consent of unions to the firm's rationalization plan was necessary to enforce these cartels and for firms to receive additional subsidies in employment policy. To help firms shed redundant labour, the government relaxed the terms and extended the period of unemployment insurance, as well as providing extra subsidies to employers who reassigned, retrained, or hired redundant labour. Since structural adjustment by large corporations would affect the local economy, a second set of laws were put in place to assist employers and workers in depressed regions. Aid to local subsidiary firms and businesses dependent on a major corporation in structurally depressed industries were provided, as well as assistance in transferring or hiring redundant labour. These measures consolidated the basic structure of Japan's employment policies for adjustment. Though initially temporary, these measures remained in force in one form or another, throughout the 1980s.[16]

In the process of setting up policy frameworks for adjustment, there was little substantial disagreement among the unions or the political parties. Both of the two main rival national labour organizations, Sohyo and Domei, supported the reforms, which made possible a joint effort by all four national labour organizations on employment issues. Furthermore, both government and opposition parties were in accord in pressing the government for additional efforts on behalf of structurally depressed industries or regions. Thus the 1977–8 laws were proposed as Diet-member sponsored bills and were passed with the support of all major parties. These measures in effect merely eased eligibility requirements and increased benefits over existing levels. It was business that split over the expansion of employment programmes, since some firms opposed increased burdens. Against this backdrop, the Ministry of Labour pre-co-ordinated such differences prior to the involvement of political parties in order to forestall political intervention into policy matters. Although the policies proposed by the bureaucracy were in line with what was demanded by the parties, both MITI and the Ministry of Labour were reluctant to enact special laws for structurally depressed industries and regions, arguing that the necessary measures were available under existing laws. The bureaucracy preferred to pre-co-ordinate policies rather than let parties make policies that would undermine its autonomous control over such matters.[17]

The role played by the bureaucracy in co-ordinating conflicts within the business sector was seen in regulatory policies as well as state compensation, in such issues as retirement age and working hours. In both kinds of policy, bureaucratic intervention in effect prevented market differences from widening. Both the unions and the political parties were in favour of extending the retirement age and shortening working hours. It was business that was divided between the large and middle-sized firms.[18] Divisions within the business community did not become a partisan issue, however, since all parties favoured some form of regulation. By co-ordinating conflicts within business, the bureaucracy could assimilate the demands of the national union organizations and political parties.

Extending the retirement age and shortening work hours was initially endorsed in the early 1970s by a number of government advisory committees composed of government officials, business leaders, union leaders, and academics.[19] Although the measure was implemented at large corporations through management–union collaboration, it was not on the law books until the late 1980s. In the interim, the Ministry encouraged unions to negotiate retirement age extensions and provided incentives to employers to comply, while at the same time insisting on making the measure mandatory. As the number of firms extending the retirement age increased it became easier for the Ministry to argue for its legalization.

Subsidies to employers started with the announcement of this policy in 1972–3, resulting in the first wave of retirement age extensions, which were implemented at 38.1 per cent of firms with over 5,000 employees. The years 1977–8 witnessed another wave of reports by government-related research institutes and advisory committees urging for an agreement between management and labour to deflate the costs of retirement-age extension. Such measures included modification of the seniority wage system (so that wages would peak around 45 to 50), restraint in the increase of lump-sum retirement payments,

TABLE 9.1. Factors cited by management as obstacles to retirement age extension, 1974–80

	Reorganization of wage system		Revision of retirement payment		Job reorganization		Stagnation in promotion	
	1974	1980	1974	1980	1974	1980	1974	1980
All	16.8	14.2	11.7	9.7	32.0	14.5	17.4	7.0

Multiple answers

Source: Takehisa Hirao, '"Teinen Encho" to Jinji Kanri no Saihensei', in Shinichiro Kimoto (ed.), *Gendai Nihon Kigyo to Jinji Kanri* (Rodo Junpo-sha, 1981), 231.

improvements in early retirement and company pension schemes, and reorganization of promotion systems. Both unions and major business organizations expressed support in principle for government action to extend retirement age. Sohyo, which initially rejected the downgrading of lump-sum retirement payments as a condition of raising the retirement age and demanded some kind of restriction against early retirement schemes, began to accept some kind of compromise as retirement age extension spread to major companies. However, the union insisted that the extension should be realized by legislation. Similarly, employers' associations who had opposed a mandatory retirement age of 60, especially the Japan Employers' Group Association and the Tokyo Chamber of Commerce and Industry, joined the more 'enlightened' employers in favour of the measure.[20] The decline in perceived obstacles by managers to extend retirement is seen in Table 9.1. However, it was not until the third round of reports in 1984–5 that the path to legalizing age-60 retirement had opened. Moreover, this round of reports had another purpose: to link labour-market policy with pension reforms. Since the government was contemplating raising the pensionable age from 60 to 65, the reports recommended that firms, with assistance from the government, retain employees within the enterprise network (which included the *keiretsu* firms) until they reached their mid-60s. Thus, extending the retirement age was seen as a necessary step to raise the pensionable age.[21] The age-60 retirement was inserted in the 1986 Elderly Employment Stabilization Law. Even then, employers' associations opposed the bill and demanded that the government not apply the sanctions rigidly, citing the negative impact on the smaller firms.[22]

The issue of reducing working hours was basically a replay of the retirement age issue. The policy had been endorsed by several government advisory committees. Unions and political parties, as well as the Ministry of Labour, were in favour of reducing working hours by law, while the business sector was split. The Ministry of Labour allowed corporations to implement such practices while using the spread of reduced work hours as a justification for legalizing the practice and to overcome staunch opposition within business.

Finally, the measure was legalized but as a compromise that lacked strong enforcement provisions.[23]

Corporate-co-ordinated adjustment to stagflation and state intervention based on such corporate adjustment was, however, incompatible with the 'anti-monopoly capitalism' strategy of Sohyo. Sohyo opposed firm-level adjustment and demanded immediate legislative action to guarantee minimum wages, restrict dismissals, and limit redeployment of workers. But such slogans as 'safeguarding the vulnerable' and 'anti-monopoly struggle for livelihood,' which aimed to mobilize workers in smaller firms and the self-employed, conflicted with the propensity for market co-ordination among the major enterprise unions. As a result, private-sector unions started to exit Sohyo and joined the movement to reorganize labour.

Efforts by Sohyo to expand its support in the early 1970s exacerbated the divide within the organization. Having failed to mobilize opposition to the extension of the USA–Japan Security Treaty in 1970, Sohyo toned down political struggles focused on foreign policy and started to stress social and economic reforms. Proclaiming that 'the choice will be between guns and butter in the 70s', Sohyo started its 'livelihood struggles' to benefit 'unorganized workers, seasonal workers, day-workers, pensioners, the poor, and the handicapped'. Launched by its new leadership team in 1970, Sohyo's strategy focused on establishing nationwide minimum wages, reduction of working hours, opposition to rationalization of the workforce, improvement of social welfare benefits, and the recovery of the right to strike for public-sector workers. Such themes were officially incorporated in the 1973 spring wage offensive. However, the public-sector unions and the day-workers' and the construction workers' unions criticized this strategy, claiming that its fixation on wages still represented the 'egotism typical of big business unions'.[24] Thus attempts by Sohyo to mobilize support around socioeconomic policy themes actually exacerbated the divide within the union organization.

It was the union leaders of export-oriented industries rather than leaders of existing national unions who led the unification of organized labour. Ironically, it was the issue of employment policy that destroyed the chance of a unification based on the merger of existing organizations, such as Sohyo and Domei. The 1977 employment bill for workers in depressed industries had failed to pass the legislature because of Sohyo opposition. Although the bill had the approval of all major parties, Sohyo demanded that the Socialist party oppose the bill because it was packaged with two unpopular bills increasing fees for public railways and health care. The reason Sohyo pushed the Socialists to confront the government was to unite the party, ruptured by factional disputes over the replacement of its chairman and control of its left-wing group (see Section IV). The decision of Sohyo leaders to give priority on uniting the Socialists above co-operation with other labour organizations underestimated the importance of the employment issue for private-sector unions. As a result, Sohyo was not able to exert influence proportional to its size in the process of labour unification.

After this incident, it was the major industrial unions that led the reorganization process, with existing national unions checking each other to reduce their opponents' influence on the new organization. Leaders of private-industry unions, especially steel, automobiles, electronics, electric power, chemicals, and textiles, hammered out the details of the new group's organizational structure, principles, and policies. Steel and textile unions endorsed the unification of private-sector unions in 1978, despite their affiliation with Sohyo, and participated in the 'unification preparation group', which completed its work in late 1981 and released a statement to all private unions urging them to join the movement. Meanwhile, after the 1977 incident, the moderate Domei refused every request by Sohyo, to reconsider joint struggles. The efforts by a third and new national labour organization, Sorengo—created in 1979 when the remaining two minor labour confederations, Shin-sanbetsu and Chiritsu-roren, merged in order to 'became the catalyst of labour front unification'—to mediate between Sohyo and Domei were in vain. Instead, both Sohyo and Domei blocked each other's attempts to influence the new organization. Domei demanded that the new organization limit its membership to moderate private unions, exclude totalitarianism (read Marxism), join the International Confederation of Free Trade Unions, and debar the radical public-sector unions until they were 'democratic'. Sohyo, which was led by public-sector unions, rejected every one of these conditions and condemned 'discrimination' against any union that wished to join the new national centre.[25]

As a result, the new labour organization started as a liaison organization of private-sector unions in 1982 and eventually centralized its organization. By 1989, it was joined by most of the previously radical public-sector unions, completing the unification of the Japanese labour movement, with the exception of small minority groups. The demise of the radical, 'anti-monopoly capitalism' line can be seen from the fact that the new grouping of unions led to the departure of those claiming to preserve the essence of the Sohyo movement. As it became apparent that Sohyo-affiliated unions were determined to join the new organization, and that Sohyo leaders had decided to negotiate conditions to make the new organization open to Sohyo-affiliated unions, the radical factions within Sohyo decided to 'exit'. Although divided between the Communists and the left-Socialists, such groups vowed to re-establish a 'class-based' labour movement based on 'anti-monopoly capitalism' principles in the tradition of Sohyo. Thus, the left-Socialist group was created by three of the most prominent leaders in the history of Sohyo: Ota Kaoru, Iwai Akira, and Ichikawa Makoto. Particularly ironic is the fact that Ota was the inventor of the 'spring wage offensive' strategy, which turned into the basis of co-ordinated wage restraint. Ideologically, the left-Socialist groups were the true heirs of the mainstream Sohyo movement. However, they failed to reconstruct the labour movement based on the principles of militant economic struggles and close ties between the Socialists and the Communists. The left-socialist union leaders were unwilling to amalgamate forces with the Communists, so both turned into groupings of anti-mainstream minority factions in enterprise and industrial unions and remained a marginal force in the labour movement.[26]

Concomitant with this development, by the end of the 1970s Sohyo leaders themselves became politically committed to a centre-left coalition in national politics. During the 1979 election, major Sohyo-affiliated unions engaged in electoral co-operation with the centrist parties, despite the reservations of Sohyo and Socialist leaders. More than anything else, the ostracism of radical-left groups within the national labour movement and the change of Sohyo policies testifies to the dramatic demise of the radical-left unionism. Five years after the first oil crisis, what had been regarded as the mainstream of the post-war labour movement had become a marginalized and spent force.

III. Bureaucratic Co-ordination, Neo-Liberal Policy Reforms, and Political Parties

Following stagflation, Japan faced another set of problems common to most advanced industrial nations in the 1980s: the need to adjust welfare commit-ments to the reduced fiscal capacity of the state. This problem was intensified in Japan by large fiscal deficits, which accumulated in the late 1970s, and by a rapidly ageing population. Two features characterized the adjustment process during this period. First, efforts by the management and union of large corporations to secure employment for older employees and expand company welfare for retirees. These efforts were in line with the policies advocated by the government, whose goal was to keep the elderly in the labour market and shift part of the social security burden to the private sector. Thus the linkage between employment and social security policies was facilitated at both the corporate and governmental levels. Second, based on the response of the large corporations, the government, especially the Ministry of Health and Welfare, implemented social security—i.e., pension and health-care—reforms by engineering a compromise between large corporations, and other social groups who had to rely on state welfare. These reforms provided an opportunity for the government bureaucracy to address the cleavage between the large corporations, who preferred a smaller state, and small business and the self-employed, who preferred to redistribute the burden of social security to large corporations.

Bureaucratic co-ordination of this cleavage accelerated the de-radicalization of both the Socialist party and the public-sector unions. While the bureau-cracy designed the main outlines of social security reforms, political parties

concentrated on modifying the unpopular aspects of the government's proposals in favour of small businesses and the self-employed. Since the parties
all sought to modify government proposals in the same direction, the result
was increased collaboration between the government and moderate opposition parties. This collaboration served as a backdrop for the de-radicalization
of the public-sector unions, the unification of private- and public-sector unions,
and the moderation of the Socialist party.

By the end of the 1970s, discussion of employment security had started to
focus on older employees. As seen in the negotiation between the companies
and unions over the mandatory retirement age (Section II), securing employment for the elderly became intertwined with the broader issue of how to
support the income and health-care costs of the elderly. The government
reports of the mid-1980s emphasized the need for corporations to continue
employing workers over 60 and to supplement privately state pension and
health-care benefits. Furthermore, the unions themselves bargained for
employment security for elderly workers (including delaying retirement) and
readjustment of corporate welfare programmes (including lump-sum retirement payments) along the lines suggested by such reports. As a result, large
corporations extended the retirement age, became actively involved in finding
new jobs for retirees, and expanded employee health-care services to retirees.
Thus the linkage between employment and welfare policies was first seen in
the large-corporation sector, which made employees of such companies less
dependent on social security.

In addition to extending the retirement age, various measures were taken to
secure post-retirement employment for the employees of large corporations.[27]
The Labour Ministry exerted pressure on, and offered financial support to,
managers to retain or relocate employees after retirement age. Needless to
say, such labour relocation by major corporations is not possible without the
vast network of subsidiaries and *keiretsu* firms characteristic of the Japanese
economy. Furthermore, many major corporations went so far as to establish
new subsidiaries to provide employment for retired workers. Table 9.2*a* shows
that such firms started to increase rapidly after the late 1970s. These firms
performed activities closely related to the operation of the parent firm, or
provided service to the community where the parent firm was located, or

TABLE 9.2a. Dates of creation of subsidiary firms for re-employment of retired employees

	Prior to 1974	1974–1981/2	Unknown
A	19.8	79.6	3.9
B	26.4	65.3	8.3

Notes: A: Survey by Tokyo Municipal Government, Bureau of Labour Economy (1983).
    B: Survey by business magazine *Diamond* (18 Apr. 1981).

TABLE 9.2b. Number of companies established by major steel companies, 1983–91

	Nippon	NKK	Sumitomo	Kawasaki	Kobe	Subtotal
New Material, Electronics, and Information Technology						
1983	1	–	–	1	–	1
1984	–	2	–	1	1	4
1985	4	2	–	2	3	11
1986	5	4	4	2	5	20
1987	7	7	2	3	7	26
1988	7	1	4	6	1	19
1989	1	1	4	2	1	9
1990	–	–	1	2	1	4
1991	–	–	1	–	1	2
Subtotal	25	17	17	18	20	97
Chemicals, engineering, and metal related						
1983	1	–	–	–	1	2
1984	2	1	4	2	–	9
1985	2	–	2	1	–	5
1986	6	3	1	–	2	12
1987	6	4	4	5	2	21
1988	3	3	3	–	2	11
1989	2	–	4	5	–	10
1990	1	1	3	2	1	7
1991	–	–	–	–	1	2
Subtotal	23	12	21	14	9	79
Service						
1983	–	–	–	–	1	1
1984	–	–	–	–	1	1
1985	1	–	–	1	2	4
1986	2	1	4	–	4	11
1987	6	6	5	4	4	25
1988	4	1	4	–	–	9
1989	1	–	3	–	2	6
1990	1	2	1	–	1	5
1991	–	–	–	–	1	2
Subtotal	15	10	17	1	16	64
Leasing, finance, insurance						
1983	1	–	–	–	–	1
1984	–	–	–	–	1	1
1985	1	1	–	–	–	2
1986	1	–	–	1	–	2
1987	1	2	2	2	–	7
1988	–	–	–	–	–	0
1989	1	–	–	1	–	2
1990	–	–	–	–	–	0
1991	–	–	–	–	–	0
Subtotal	5	3	2	4	1	15

Source: Yoshiro Miwa (ed.), Gendai Nihon no Sangyo Kozo (Aoki Shoten, 1991), 193.

participated in totally new ventures. New subsidiaries for retired employees were created particularly when the parent firm had to undergo drastic rationalization. Table 9.2*b* shows that the major steel corporations created such subsidiaries when they had to rapidly reduce the number of their employees in order to adjust to the rapid appreciation of the yen after the 1985 Plaza Accord. However, such companies were not composed only of elderly employees; they usually hired younger employees from the labour market as well.[28] The unions usually welcomed the creation of such firms and bargained on the selection and labour conditions of the transferees, insisting that transferees not see drastic deterioration of their wages and working conditions and not have to go to subsidiaries against their will. The unions usually won a special allowance for accepting temporary transfers, compensation for wage differences between the new and the previous jobs, supplemental payments if workers had to work longer hours at their new assignment, and reimbursement of the overtime rate differences between the new and old assignments. According to one survey, 75.5 per cent of the transferees received wages according to the parent firms' standards. Similarly, 76.6 per cent of the transferees received bonus payments, 64.4 per cent received allowances, and 56.6 per cent received paid vacations according to the parent firm's standards. In short, the unions attempted to guarantee the same level of income and work conditions for their members who had to leave the company, either permanently or temporarily.[29]

New developments in company welfare were seen in tandem with those in employment. Under the banner of 'life-time planning' or 'comprehensive welfare', large corporations emphasized the need to put post-retirement considerations within company welfare and to achieve tighter co-ordination between private and public welfare. In corporate health care, the major development of the late 1970s was the extension of corporate benefits to retirees. This issue was negotiated at the firm level and the results differed significantly across industries. In contrast, the issue of post-retirement income security was debated at the industry level. Major industrial unions launched their pension reform plans between 1979 and 1980. In response to the then ongoing debate over public pension reform, the unions recognized company pensions (or lump-sum retirement payments) as an integral source of post-retirement income. Previously, the unions had insisted that lump-sum retirement allowances were deferred wages and refused to co-ordinate them with public pensions.[30] However, the growth of company pensions, especially among middle-sized firms (Table 9.3), made the unions more realistic in their demands.

Thus, as social security reform reached the political agenda, large corporations and enterprise unions were already making necessary adjustments. Thus, the government's plan linking employment and welfare policies by urging firms to retain elderly workers and internalize some of the social insurance burdens was realized at large firms. As a result, large corporations

TABLE 9.3. The increase in companies with company pensions (estimated percentages)

	1945	1954	1959	1963	1965	1966	1967	1968	1969	1971	1974	1975
A	1.0	2.4	8.0	19.9	29.5		44.6		55.2	61.0	66.8	
B												
Over 5,000						54.1		63.1				
										48.5		59.9
1,000–4,000						40.9		30.6				
All						13.5		29.4		28.7		32.9

Notes: A: Among large corporations.

B: Among all corporations with lump-sum retirement allowance classified according to number of employees.

Source: Kokumin Sekatsu Center (ed.), *Nenkin Seido to Korei Rodo Mondai* (Ochanomizu-shobo, 1977), 97.

and their employees preferred to cut back redistributive social insurance pro-grammes. Taking this into account, the Ministry of Health and Welfare was able to strike a compromise between large corporations and the small firms and/or the self-employed. Large corporations accepted cuts in social security benefits, since increased contributions were more likely to be redistributed to subsidize social insurance schemes for small firms and/or the self-employed. The employees of small firms and the self-employed, who did not have gen-erous corporate welfare and whose social insurance schemes were in financial trouble, preferred to protect social security benefits while transferring part of the costs to the large corporations through cross-subsidization. As a result, a combination of cuts in social security benefits, increases in burdens, and redistribution of costs between schemes became politically acceptable to both sides. As in the case of employment policy, we see the bureaucracy co-ordinating potential conflicts, though this time the policy covered not just employees but most of the population.

The government started preparing for social security reform immediately after the oil crisis. The problem was twofold. First, the cost of such pro-grammes was expected to become too high because of lower revenue growth, generous indexation of benefits, and upward revision of elderly population estimates. Second, under the divided post-war social insurance system,[31] the public pension and health-care schemes for small firms and/or the self-employed were in immediate trouble, despite being heavily subsidized by the state, because they enrolled a disproportionate number of the elderly. During the 1970s, the government tried to cope with the problem simply by propos-ing to increase contributions and cut benefits. In the face of strong opposi-tion and no support, the government had by the mid-1980s devised reforms that included redistribution of costs between schemes by cross-subsidization. More concretely, in health care the 1982 reform pooled and redistributed contributions from different schemes to pay for those over 70, while the 1984 reform proposed to keep retirees in their previous health-care scheme until they were 70. In public pension reform, the system was integrated into a two-tier universal system of basic pensions and superannuations (only for employees), in which government subsidies were to be consolidated with the basic pension.[32] Since the interests of the unions were in accord with those of their employers, the bureaucracy could focus on co-ordinating the interest of employers, without opposition from unions. Thus, although Sohyo maintained a populist position, opposing any cuts in social insurance benefits and any increases in its contributions, this position was in the interests of small business and the self-employed, and not necessarily in the interests of the core members of organized labour. Furthermore, after bureaucratic pre-co-ordination had done the spadework, political parties tried to modify unpopular portions of the reforms, namely increases in payments and cuts in benefits. In doing so, the parties were competing to cater to the interests of small business and the self-employed. All major social security reform bills of the 1980s were passed by an alliance of the government and the moderate opposition parties.

The 1982 Health Care Law combined benefit cuts (the most controversial being the ending of free health care for the elderly) and payment increases with the cross-subsidization of the costs for people over 70. The major objection came from employers' associations, unions, and health-insurance associations of large firms. Although they agreed to share the costs hitherto borne by National Health Insurance, they opposed the initial government plan to redistribute the health-care costs of the elderly (inversely proportional to the ratio of elderly in each scheme) on the grounds that it would be too much of a redistribution. On the other hand, employers and unions of large corporations (and the moderate Domei) agreed to abolish free health care for the elderly, agreeing to the government's reasoning that in order to reduce the growth of medical costs, self-reliance should be invoked, and the elderly should be discouraged from paying unnecessary visits and doctors from providing unwanted treatment. The compromise engineered by the Ministry of Health and Welfare prior to submitting the bill stipulated that only half of the health-care costs were to be redistributed among health-care schemes.[33]

The same combination of increased co-payments and cross-subsidization among insurance schemes characterized the health insurance reform of 1984. The government draft had three features. First, the reduction of compensation rate for the insured (from 100 to 80 per cent), a drastic reduction of government subsidies to National Health Insurance, and a series of increases on co-payment items as the increased payments/reduced benefits part of the reform. Second, the proposal to retain retirees in their previous health scheme ('Retiree Health Care') and reimburse 80 per cent of their health-care costs until they reached the age of 70. Finally, as a sweetener, the compensation rate for dependent family members was increased incrementally (up to 80 per cent). Again, it was the unions and the employee health insurance associations, both representing the interests of the large corporations, that initially opposed Retiree Health Care. However, they withdrew their opposition when the Ministry of Health and Education proposed a 20 per cent co-payment (to end the 100 per cent compensation for the insured) and revoking the ban on additional health care provided by insurance associations, since this meant that additional costs imposed by the Retiree Health Care scheme could be offset through money saved by the 20 per cent reduction in the compensation rate for the insured and that companies were to be free to set up individual health-care benefits. The fact that private retiree health-care schemes had already been installed by many companies and urged by labour confederations should have facilitated the acceptance of such plans by large corporations.

In public pensions, the key feature of the 1985 reform was the integration of the Employee and National pensions into a semi-universal two-tier system of basic and supplementary pensions (the latter provided only to employees). Furthermore, immediate contribution rates were raised, although future growth of pensions was stemmed, and government subsidies were to be concentrated in basic pensions at a reduced rate in order to ease the burden on the Treasury.[34] The integration of pension schemes in effect increased redistribution among occupation groups and increased government assistance to basic pensions, which catered to the self-employed. This compromise between large corporations, who opposed future increases in public pensions, and small firms and the self-employed, who had to face an alarming increase in contribution rates if they could not share the burden with others, was engineered by the Health and Welfare Ministry, which was worried that the National Pension scheme would become insolvent. Equally important is what was not included in this reform: raising the pensionable age to 65. This was because both large corporations and unions argued that the retirement age should be extended before raising the pensionable age. As with the health-care reform, it was the large corporations who opposed redistributive measures, while the idea of integrating pensions had wide support among unions and opposition parties. The unions had been proposing a two-tier universal pension scheme, comparable to the government's proposal, since the late 1970s. Thus the Ministry could broker a compromise by linking the redistribution issue with the scaling down of public pension expansion.[35]

Bureaucratic co-ordination was instrumental in forestalling the potential policy cleavage between the large corporations and smaller firms or the self-employed. It reinforced management–union collaboration, as employers and unions of large firms lobbied the government for their shared interests; and it facilitated the moderation and unification of organized labour by preventing the cleavage between large corporations and smaller firms, including their unions, from widening. Furthermore, since the bureaucracy had co-ordinated the interests of large corporations on the one hand, and small business and the self-employed on the other, political parties could focus on modifying government proposals to ease payment increases and benefit cuts, since small business and the self-employed were reliable sources of electoral support. As a result, the difference between the ruling and opposition policies became one of degree. However, while the ruling and moderate opposition parties wanted to ameliorate the unpopular aspects of government proposals without damaging the basic compromise co-ordinated by the bureaucracy, the Socialists took the populist position of opposing any increase in social insurance burdens and cuts in benefits. As a result, policy collaboration between the ruling party and the moderate opposition increased. All three of the above mentioned social insurance reforms—the 1982 and 1984 health-care reforms and the 1985 pension reform—were passed by this alliance.

During the legislative debates over the 1982 health-care reform, for example, the Liberal Democrats and the moderate opposition were eager to minimize co-payments by elderly patients, for fear of a possible voter backlash. Initially, all political parties were opposed to ending free medical care, which led to government concessions lowering the amount paid by elderly patients. Sohyo and the Socialists maintained their absolute opposition, while the ruling party negotiated several revisions with the Democratic Socialists and the Komeito (Clean Government party) to pass the bill. During this process, Domei and the Democratic Socialists accepted partial co-payments in exchange for redistribution of costs among health-care schemes. In the 1984 health-care reform, Domei consented to co-payments for the insured, which led to the final compromise. The Socialists maintained their opposition and demanded the expansion of full insurance coverage (100 per cent compensation) to dependent families. The final compromise between the three parties (the Liberal Democrats, the Democratic Socialists, and the Komeito) put the compensation rate at 90 (instead of 80) per cent for the time being, and discarded most of the proposed co-payment increases. Finally, the 1985 pension reform was also passed by a government–moderate opposition alliance with the support of the employers' associations and moderate unions. The demand by the Socialists and Sohyo to maintain previous benefit and government-subsidization levels was regarded as a manœuvre to check the moderate parties from allying with the ruling party. The pension reform, however, did not ignite such strong protests as health-care reform, probably because of the low maturity rate of public pensions, which meant that the number of retirees whose vested interests the political parties could cater to was relatively small.[36]

The social security reforms of 1984–5 marked the climax of government efforts to adjust to changed fiscal conditions and a rapidly ageing population.

Other efforts continued, however, along the lines debated during the late 1970s and early 1980s. The government revised the Elderly Health Care Law in 1986 to increase co-payments and to implement the original cross-subsidization proposal, which redistributed all of the medical costs for the elderly among each scheme. Opposition from the employers' association and the union confederations forced the government to delay its implementation. A further revision of the public pension system was carried out in 1989, which strengthened automatic cost-of-living indexation of pensions and made it mandatory for students to join the basic pension plan. However, the government was still prevented from achieving its main purpose by opposition from the unions and managers to raising the pensionable age to 65.[37]

The tax reform of 1986–9 was basically a replay of the social security reforms. After incrementally increasing corporate taxes and constraining expenditures during the 1980s, the Ministry of Finance regarded the introduction of a VAT tax and the shift from direct to indirect taxation as necessary in order to balance the budget and to stabilize revenue sources. When the Ministry failed to introduce a VAT in 1979 due to strong political opposition, it created a package that combined direct tax cuts with tax increases, especially the VAT, and distributed costs and benefits among relevant social interests. Large corporations were given tax cuts in exchange for supporting a VAT, so top business leaders rescinded their insistence on 'balanced budgets without tax increases' and accepted a VAT as a means of raising revenues. The demand for personal income tax cuts by unions and the opposition was also accommodated. Trade unions and opposition parties had been demanding tax cuts of 100 to 200 billion yen annually throughout the 1980s despite budget deficits. Finally, small businesses, the self-employed, and retailers were given generous loopholes because of their vocal opposition to the new tax.[38] Actually, being dependent on government expenditures and subsidies, they were likely to benefit from an expanded revenue base with the introduction of a VAT. Indeed, it was the demands made by such local constituents for increased expenditure that led LDP politicians to criticize the Finance Ministry for its cap on (or across-the-board reduction of) government expenditures, and to support the new sales tax. The original tax-reform package was enacted in two stages, and the government introduced further income-tax cuts and loopholes for small businesses when revising the bill, and also added several measures to ease the transition to the new system as a concession to the moderate opposition partes.[39] Thus, the tax bills were modified and enacted by agreement between the ruling and moderate parties, while the Socialists maintained their absolute opposition to the VAT. That the general public and small businesses were never placated by either bureaucratic pre-co-ordination of interests or additional concessions won by political parties was to cost the LDP and moderate opposition parties dearly in the 1989 upper house elections to the benefit of the Socialists.[40]

IV. The Demise of the Radical Left and the Transformation of the Opposition

The final stage in the demise of the radical-left opposition was characterized by two mutually reinforcing developments. One was the collapse of public-sector union unity—public-sector unions had been stronghold of radicalism in the unions throughout the post-war years. The other was the abandonment by the Socialists of their ideological tenets in response to strengthened collaboration between the ruling and moderate–opposition parties. As the policy differences between the ruling party and opposition became a matter of degree and with the Socialists abandoning their ideological tenets, the situation became conducive to party realignment across the government–opposition divide.

Within the union movement, the final stage in the demise of the radical left was seen in the public-sector unions, whose strongest members were two major public corporation unions—the unions of NTT (Nippon Telegraph and Telecommunications) and National Railways—and the government-employee unions. The relations among public corporation unions became strained by issues similar to those that enabled moderate leaders to consolidate their forces in the private sector. They were: whether to promote management–union collaboration and enhance efficiency when faced with threats of possible privatization; and how to fund pension schemes. As public-sector unions de-radicalized over these issues, government-employee unions, such as the local government workers' unions, teachers' unions, and postal workers' unions, also changed their basic policies. Fear of isolation and marginalization, as well as dependence on moderate parties in order to get their officials elected to the legislature, seem to have pushed government employee unions to de-radicalize. Thus, instead of changes in the market situation, it was changes in the political environment that led to the transformation of the public-sector unions.

The two major public-corporation unions had differed in the extent to which they were willing to collaborate with management. The historical origin of this difference was the 'productivity' movement of the late 1960s. The NTT union was co-operative, while the National Railways (JNR) unions fought tooth and nail, launching their 'anti-rationalization' movement, successfully stalling management plans to increase productivity. Thereafter, the telecommunications union became moderate and strengthened ties with other enterprise unions in favour of reorganizing the national labour movement, whereas the largest National Railway union (Kokuro) retained its radicalism and provided leadership and support for Sohyo. Under that leadership, Sohyo chose to concentrate on anti-government mobilization on political issues, such as struggles against the 1970 extension of the USA–Japan Security Treaty and to 'recover the right to strike' for public-sector unions, and showed disdain for bread-and-butter issues.[41] At the 1969 Sohyo convention, 'economic demands' were criticized as 'restricting union activities within the confines defined by monopoly capital and abandoning the duty [of the unions] to achieve class emancipation'. Such political struggles alienated major private-sector unions from Sohyo leadership. Such was especially the case during the protracted 'strike to "recover the right to strike"', which paralysed transportation for 10 days in 1975.

Differences between the two public corporations unions were exacerbated by two issues typical of the post-oil crisis era. One was public-sector pension reforms, and the other was the privatization of public corporations. Public-sector pension reform reached the political agenda because of two incidents.[42] The first, which isolated public-sector unions from their private counterparts, started in 1977 as a campaign ignited by a LDP Diet-member (Kato Koichi), who criticized public-sector employees for receiving extravagant retirement payments. Driven by media exposés of exorbitant retirement payments to top public officials, the criticism developed into a movement by business leaders, private-sector unions, and government and moderate opposition leaders that demanded elimination of 'inequality between the public and private sector'. Facing such criticism, the public-sector unions were unable to forge a united front because they were divided on the second issue: the imminent danger of bankruptcy of the National Railway pension fund caused by an exceptionally high maturity rate.[43] The government's plan was to integrate the independent insurance schemes of each public corporation and government agency into a single scheme in order to bail out the National Railway pension fund by cross-subsidization, and then to peg the benefits of the new private-sector pension scheme to their private-sector counterparts. Naturally, the cross-subsidization scheme caused resentment on the part of public corporations with low-maturity pension funds such as the NTT.

The issue of privatizing public corporations was the final straw that led to the demise of radicalism in its remaining stronghold. The management and union of NTT were not against privatization, since it meant new business opportunities for the high-tech giant with less regulations. In contrast, national railway unions were vehemently opposed. Failure to find allies led to factional disputes and thence to the de-radicalization and reorganization of the railway unions. To secure employment for their members after privatization the National Railway unions—including the most radical and militant new-left union, Doro—signed a 'joint proclamation' with management in 1986 pledging to co-operate with privatization. The exception was the predominant union Kokuro, which was dominated by die-hard radicals who had won an upset leadership election. As groups defected from Kokuro to join the pact with management, the union that had been a dominant force in the post-war Sohyo movement disintegrated.[44] Since Sohyo and Socialist leaders were deeply involved in negotiations over privatizing the National Railways in order to minimize the effects on workers and union organizations, they and other public-union leaders had little sympathy for the die-hard Kokuro leaders.

Furthermore, by this time, leaders of both Sohyo and the major public-sector unions were also preparing to join the unified private-sector union (Minkan Rengo). A voice in the new organization had been chosen over isolation. Public-sector union leaders were concerned with keeping their organizations intact in order to secure a large say after their merger with private-sector unions. However, acrimonious and protracted disputes erupted in all public unions between the leadership and minority radical factions, as in the teachers' union and the local government workers' union. The radicals defended the basic tenets of the postwar Sohyo movement and were eventually expelled, or else seceded to join either one of the marginal left-Socialist or Communist groups. The creation of Rengo (the Japan Trade Union Confederation) in 1989 concluded the demise of the radical-left line in the union movement and the unification of labour under moderate auspices.

The development in public-sector unions also enfeebled the radicals within the Socialist party. The abandonment by the Socialist party of its 'anti-monopoly capitalism' tenets in the latter half of the 1980s was the end product of a long and oscillating development which took off shortly after the first oil crisis and accelerated in the 1980s. The watershed was the 1976 general election. When the election reduced the LDP's majority to a thin margin, moderate opposition parties faced the choice of strengthening solidarity among the opposition, with the Socialists as the core, or co-operating with the ruling LDP to influence policy-making. Prior to 1976, the opposition parties shared radical rhetoric of pledging to create an 'anti-LDP' and 'anti-monopoly capitalism' government and to champion the interests of small businesses and the self-employed. Such was the case in party platforms during the 1974 upper house election. Even the moderate Democratic Socialists demanded the nationalization of the Bank of Japan and of major industries and the implementation of a land reform, tax reform, welfare expansion, agriculture and small business modernization, and administrative reform. Similarly, the Komeito demanded the democratization of banks, corporate tax hikes, and income-tax cuts. Naturally, the Socialists proposed economic planning, restrictions on monopoly capital, democratic control of banks and major industries, promotion of agriculture and small businesses, tax cuts for the masses, and welfare expansion. This emphasis on confrontation with the LDP and 'monopoly capital' was typical of the opposition during the high-growth period, in which the Socialists remained the dominant and pivotal party within the opposition camp. Thus, in the 1974 upper house elections, the Komeito joined electoral coalitions with the Socialists, and allowed the Socialists to do the same with the Communists, although the Komeito refused to align itself directly with the Communists.

In Parliament, 'bridge alliances' between the Socialists and Communists on the one hand, and the Socialists, Komeito, and the Democratic Socialists, on the other, were formed on major policy issues. One of the major themes of the so-called 'all-opposition alliance' was criticism of government economic policies for disregarding protection for small business and the expansion of social security. Efforts to maintain the alliance prevailed, despite signs of disruption. For example, a call by the chairman of the Socialist party to exclude the Democratic Socialists from the all-opposition alliance, a move to punish the latter for supporting the government's budget for fiscal year (FY) 1976 and to preserve the coalition's anti-LDP identity, was rejected by other opposition parties and unions alike. Similarly, a proposal by the Democratic Socialist leader to launch a right–centre coalition with the LDP was shot down by the moderate union Domei. However, prospects of a government defeat in a general election made unity among the opposition parties fragile. When the relationship between the Komeito and the Communists became acrimonious just before the 1976 general election, Sohyo issued a statement urging both parties to stop smearing each other with insults and co-operate for the sake of an 'all-opposition alliance' against the ruling party.[45]

The fact that the opposition was able to achieve a near-parity of seats in the 1976 general election led moderate parties to strengthen ties with the LDP in the legislature in order to extract concessions from the government, rather than to consolidate an anti-LDP and/or 'anti-monopoly capitalism' force. If we compare the politics of the unions in the 1976 and 1979 general elections, and examine the budgetary debates of the legislative sessions in between, it becomes clear that the moderation of the national union movement, along with competition among parties to cater to small business and the self-employed, had strengthened the right–centre *rapprochement* across government–opposition lines.

In the first place, by time of the 1979 and 1980 elections, even Sohyo leaders were pressing the Socialists to cut ties with the Communists in favour of electoral and parliamentary co-operation with the Komeito. Only three years earlier the moderate Domei had rejected the possibility of the Democratic Socialists establishing formal ties with the LDP and the radical Sohyo had endorsed the all-opposition alliance. The reason Sohyo pressed for strengthened centre–left ties, instead of a national front of Socialists and Communists, was to secure the election of union-endorsed candidates and to cripple the strength of 'anti-monopoly capitalism' minority groups in domestic disputes. Indeed, the 1979 general election was characterized by unofficial support of Sohyo-endorsed candidates by the Komeito, usually running on a Socialist ticket, and union support of Komeito candidates. Such co-operation spread, under the tacit approval of the Sohyo leadership, despite protests from the Socialist party. Typical cases of union–Komeito collaboration involved the NTT union, the postal workers' union, the private railways union, and the electronics union (although not a Sohyo member) in over ten electoral districts.

Electoral coalitions between the moderate parties increased considerably. Electoral coalitions between the Komeito and the Democratic Socialists were seen in 28 districts, and four-party coalitions (which included the New Liberal Club and Social Democratic League) were seen in more than ten districts. Furthermore, the defeat of the Socialists and the stagnation of the Liberal Democrats in the 1979 election elevated the position of the Komeito as the strategic centre of both opposition and government–opposition alliances. After the election, Sohyo leaders explicitly endorsed the fostering of Socialist–Komeito ties, even against the wishes of the Socialist party leader. Sohyo leaders made it clear that the Socialist–Sohyo bloc no longer had the power to elect union-endorsed candidates without the co-operation of the Komeito. Thus the policy of the Socialist party chairman—to keep the party's left open in order to remain a mediating force between the Communists and moderate parties—was overruled when the party convention in 1980 adopted a resolution calling for talks about a coalition with the Komeito. Such a move was justified on the grounds that it would check a right–centre coalition, and was strongly supported by Diet-members and Sohyo-affiliated union delegates, particularly those of the telecommunications and postal workers' union. Unable to defeat this motion, the left wing adopted a 'supplementary opinion', which stressed to preserve the party's commitment of abolishing the USA–Japan Security Treaty and working for the 'all opposition alliance' formula.[46]

In the second place, alliances between government and moderate opposition parties expanded during the 1976–9 legislative sessions, typically in budget negotiations. Although the opposition usually formed a united front demanding more income-tax cuts, expenditures for employment policies, and protective measures for small firms, and rejecting unpopular measures such as price increases, they competed among each other to reach agreements with the government. With the Communists choosing isolation and the Socialists remaining staunchly populist by criticizing government budgets for both too little social spending and too few tax cuts, moderate parties had a chance to extract budgetary concessions from the government for their constituencies. With the populist option taken by the Socialists, and budgetary agreements reached by the centre–right opposition and the government, the centre–left party became tempted to negotiate policy agreements directly with the government itself, so that it would get credit for concessions made by the government and thus undermine the position of the centre–right parties. During the FY 1977 budget deliberations, the New Liberal Club and the Democratic Socialists supported the budget and the government's policy of issuing deficit bonds, in exchange for additional tax cuts, which were demanded by all opposition parties. The FY 1978 budget was passed with the support of the New Liberal Club when the LDP made selective concessions to the opposition parties' demand for further tax cuts and increased social welfare expenditures. As a result, in the following year the Komeito attempted to out-manœuvre the Democratic Socialists and the New Liberal Club by entering budget negotiations with the Liberal Democrats. Although a formal LDP/Democratic Socialist/Komeito pact for the FY 1979 budget floundered at the last minute over formalities, the budget itself was a creature of the three-party agreement. With moderate opposition parties competing to enter policy alliances with the ruling party, the situation had come close to a formal coalition government.[47]

Right–centre *rapprochement* across government–opposition lines continued during the 1980s, despite an LDP landslide victory in the 1980 general election. All of the major neo-liberal reform bills (as explained in Section III) were passed with right–centre support. As a result, the Socialists were forced to abandon their radical tenets and narrow their differences with the moderate parties in order to keep moderate parties from competing to align with the LDP. This process was reinforced by the weakening of the public-sector unions of Sohyo and their decision to join their private counterparts, which decisively weakened the radical forces within the Socialist party. That the Socialists had to compromise on ideology and policy matters, however, caused intense inter-party struggles between their right and left wings. Externally, the basic issue was how to align with other opposition parties. The left wing called for resurrecting the 'all-opposition alliance' including the Communists, while the right wing criticized that as a spent alternative, since the moderate parties would not co-operate with the Communists. Internally, the issue was how to control the radical mass organization Shakaishugi Kyokai (Socialist League), and whether to revise the party's manifesto.

It took almost a decade for Socialist leaders to establish control over the *Shakaishugi Kyokai* and finish the re-examination of their party's manifesto. Since each issue was connected with the election of a new party chairman, compromises struck among competing factions contained the seeds for future disputes and power struggles. Moreover, the party had to depend on the intervention of Sohyo to settle its internal disputes. Despite such vacillation, however, by the mid-1980s the party had departed decisively from its Marxist past.

The influence of the Shakaishugi Kyokai as the backbone of left-wing power in the Socialist party reached its zenith in the mid-1970s. At that time, controlling the largest bloc of non-Diet-member delegate votes, the organization was able to influence party leadership elections and abort plans by right-wingers to strengthen ties with moderate parties. For example, when a moderate, Eda Saburo, co-sponsored a new political group with leaders of the Komeito and the Democratic Socialists in 1976, left-wing Diet-members successfully prevailed on the party to confirm its adherence to its revolutionary manifesto ('The Road to Socialism in Japan', or 'Road'), refuse any future ties with conservative forces or a right turn of the party, and uphold the anti-West foreign policy principles of proletarian internationalism, anti-hegemony, and the Five Peace Principles. It was only after a disillusioned Eda bolted from the party—when his report on the 1976 election defeat, in which he urged the party to present socio-economic policy alternatives instead of doctrinaire foreign policies, was rejected on the grounds that it lacked 'class perspectives'—and successive defections were seen among high-profile legislators disgusted with back-room deals over the election of a new party leader, that the Diet-member factions launched an assault on Kyokai and demanded a revision of the party's manifesto.

The issue of controlling the Kyokai by limiting its role as a research organ, abolishing its executive functions, and disclosing its publications, internal documents, and membership lists was closely connected with the confusing and protracted process of electing a new party chairman which dragged on for five months. Sohyo intervened in this process, signing an accord with Kyokai leaders in 1977. The leaders of the union were pressed to take this role in order to prevent this issue from splitting the party and the union itself. It should be recalled that this was a delicate period, when moderate union leaders had started to amalgamate their power. Consequently, those moderate union leaders denounced Kyokai activities within the party and criticized Sohyo leaders for striking a deal with Kyokai. Nevertheless, to aid the party leadership in its disarray, Sohyo went so far as to force the party to renege on its agreement with the government and the other opposition parties to pass bills increasing railway and health-insurance fees in exchange for a bill to help employment in structurally depressed industries. Sohyo carried out strikes and mass demonstrations, in alliance with the Communists, in opposition to the price hikes. Such manœuvres did successfully unite the party but at the cost of terminating joint struggles among national unions on employment issues, which caused Sohyo to lose its initiative in the reorganization of the national union. The influence of Kyokai, although weakened, continued until the death of its charismatic leader in 1985.

The revision of the 'Road' started after the election defeats of 1979 and 1980. Although the issue was straightforward, again the process became linked with factional intrigues aimed at bringing down the party leader, Asukata Ichio. As mentioned above, by 1979–80 Sohyo had realized that it had little alternative but to accommodate the shift of power toward unions of export industries and to support the strengthening of center–left ties in the political arena. Thus the union had upset Asukata's plans for keeping the party's left open. On the other hand, demands made by the Komeito—who leaned further toward the Liberal Democrats after disappointing returns in the 1980 general election—that the Socialists should approve Japan's role in the western bloc by recognizing the constitutionality of the Self-Defence Force and the USA–Japan Security Treaty backfired and strengthened the position of the left-leaning leadership. Thus, in 1981, Asukata was re-elected party chairman by pledging to 're-establish the party's identity of Non-armament Neutrality and Anti-Monopoly Democratic Reforms'. He also criticized segments of the opposition and unions for acquiescing in the government's plans to expand military forces, and reiterated his commitment to Anti-nuclear Peace Movements. However, his selection of a left-winger for the number-two position (secretary-general) of the party ignited strong protests from both the right wing and Sohyo. The situation became critical when a deputy leader resigned in late 1982, leading to demands for the resignation of both the chairman and the secretary-general. No longer was Sohyo merely an arbitrator of factional disputes, it was now a prime force in demanding the removal of party leaders and revision of the party's ideological commitments. As a concession, the left wing agreed to replace the secretary-general with a moderate. Six months later, however, the battered chairman himself resigned, taking responsibility for another election defeat. It was the election of a new chairman, committed to modernizing the party and strengthening right–centre ties, that cleared the final obstacles to the redefinition of the party's basic tenets.

The new manifesto of 1986 abandoned the role of the party as the vanguard of socialist revolution and denounced state socialism. Instead, it defined the party as a people's party, accepted the market economy (albeit without abandoning nationalization), and acknowledged the need to create a broad coalition, including conservatives, to gain power. Throughout the process, but especially at the final stages, the left wing resisted the changes and criticized the new manifesto for abandoning Marxist principles, lacking class analysis, accepting capitalism, and promoting an alliance with moderate parties. Nevertheless, although a drastic departure from the post-war character of the party, the revised manifesto reflected a compromise between the contesting wings. The 'Road' was not formally abolished but demoted to an 'historical document'. Furthermore, the party leader was not able to commit the party to recognizing the legality of the Self-Defence Force.[48]

Despite such problems, the abandonment by the Socialist party of most of its basic post-war tenets opened up a new era by changing the nature of party competition. Thereafter, the Socialists maintained their populist policy position of criticizing the government for neglecting the interests of small businesses and the self-employed. Since these groups were strongholds of LDP support, to which the government also wanted to cater, the policy differences between the ruling party and the opposition had become a matter of degree rather than of diametrically opposed ideologies. More than ever, the opposition now depended on the contingent dissatisfaction of the electorate toward the government rather than attracting supporters by its own policies or ideology. This is evidenced by the increased bipolarity in government–opposition competition during the 1980s. It was this bipolarity without fundamental policy differences that enabled the Socialist party to abandon, with relative ease, and without internal discussion, its final legacy of radicalism—denial of the

TABLE 9.4. Changes in electoral results

Lower House	LDP	Komeito	DSP	JSP	JCP
1958–60	−0.2		−1.4	−5.3	0.3
1960–3	−2.9		0.0	1.4	1.1
1963–7	−5.9		0.3	−1.1	0.8
1967–9	−1.2	5.5	−0.7	−6.4	2.0
1969–72	−0.7	−2.4	−0.7	0.4	4.3
1972–6	−5.1	2.4	−0.7	−1.2	0.2
1976–9	2.8	−1.1	−0.5	−1.0	0.1
1979–80	3.3	−0.8	−0.2	−0.4	−0.6
1980–3	−2.1	1.1	0.7	0.2	−0.5
1983–6	3.6	−0.7	−0.9	−2.3	−0.5
1986–90	−3.3	−1.4	−1.6	7.2	−0.8

constitutionality of the Self-Defence Force and desirability of the USA–Japan Security Treaty—once in government with the Liberal Democrats in 1994.

Increased bipolarity started to emerge in the 1980s after multipolarity stagnated in the mid-1970s. As can be seen in Table 9.4, until the 1976 elections the vote totals for both the Liberal Democrats and the Socialists declined to the benefit of the moderate parties and the Communists, thus strengthening multipolarity. After 1980, LDP and Socialist votes moved in the opposite direction, while the moderate parties stagnated, creating bipolarity. The nature of this bipolar system was seen clearly during the 1986 general and the 1989 upper house elections, which shared two characteristics. First, in both cases it was a landslide for one of the two poles. In the 1986 election, voters moved toward the ruling party; while in the 1989 election, LDP votes defected to the Socialists *en masse* in all demographic categories.[49] Second, the cleavage between the two poles was drawn between the LDP and moderates on the one side, and the Socialists on the other. Thus it was the Socialists who attracted discontented voters at the cost of both the ruling party and the moderate opposition parties. Ironically, the Socialists and their affiliates were able to score an unprecedented victory in the 1989 election because they had rid themselves of ideological differences to the extent that they could attract 'floating' protest votes against the newly introduced VAT. This can be seen from the fact that the Socialists could not retain their new support at either the 1990 general or the 1992 upper house elections, as most voters returned to the LDP fold. As political parties increasingly lacked distinct policy profiles, switch-voting between the two poles became easier, and it became more difficult for parties to maintain organizational coherence.

The de-radicalization of the Socialists and the diminishing of distinct party profiles exacerbated the dilemma of the moderate opposition parties. As voters switched between the ruling LDP and the populist Socialists, the strength of the moderate parties stagnated despite their success in winning concessions from the government. As a result, moderate parties sought to engage in power-sharing with the LDP. Several such attempts were made in the mid-1980s, when the moderate opposition negotiated possible government coalitions with LDP leaders. During these negotiations, it became clear that the ruling party would try to divide the opposition and co-opt the closest party (e.g., after the 1983 election defeat) unless the ruling party itself was split and its dissidents were pondering the possibility of joining hands with the opposition (as in the failed case of 1984). The latter occurred in 1993. However, since the leaders of the non-LDP coalition government kept demanding that the Socialists renounce their populist policy stance and control or expel their left wing, the Socialists, instead of endangering party unity, decided to undermine the leaders of the non-LDP coalition by aligning directly with the LDP in 1994.

Hence, it was changes in the nature of party competition after the Socialists buried their post-war manifesto and strengthened their populist profile that started a drive by moderate parties to seek a coalition government with the LDP, which triggered the reorganization of the party system itself. The fact that policy differences had become a matter of degree and that co-operation across government–opposition lines became the normal operation of the legislature in passing major reform bills in the 1980s made it easier for ambitious LDP groups to defect and join the opposition.

V. Conclusion: Implications of the Japanese Case

In explaining the transformation of the post-war party system, I have stressed the importance of two sets of actors who have not been fully accounted for in previous studies but have seen most drastic organizational changes in the last two decades. These are market actors, especially unions, and the political opposition. Furthermore, in connecting changes in the union movement with changes in the party system, I have provided a very different portrait of the state bureaucracy from the one found in prevailing theories. According to the analysis offered here, bureaucratic co-ordination in policy-making forestalled new policy cleavages from emerging once management–union collaboration was continued and de-radicalization took place in the union movement. The bureaucracy pre-co-ordinated potential conflicts between large corporations, on the one hand, and small businesses and/or the self-employed on the other. Apart from facilitating the unification of the labour movement under moderate auspices, this pre-co-ordination permitted political parties to focus on the assumed interests of small businesses and the self-employed and compete for their support. Both the decline of the radical left in the union movement and continued bureaucratic pre-co-ordination caused moderate opposition parties to collaborate with the government, which in turn pressed the Socialists to abandon their basic tenets. The abandonment of radical-left tenets by the Socialist party, on the one hand, exacerbated the dilemma of the moderate opposition parties, who were squeezed between the LDP government and populist Socialist opposition, and led them to aspire to coalition government with the LDP. On the other hand, it removed the obstacles for an LDP–Socialist alliance.

Prevailing theories of contemporary Japanese politics differ from the analysis presented here. Their focus has been on relations between the government party and the bureaucracy, and not unions or the opposition parties. Furthermore, the debate was over who governs: the parties or the bureaucracy.[50] Thus, the role of the bureaucracy as a co-ordinator of market or social interests, the notion of bureaucratic pre-co-ordination as the source of bureaucratic autonomy, and the compatibility of bureaucratic autonomy and party control have not been fully explored.

Dominant accounts of the Japanese political economy characterize it as 'corporatism without labour', emphasizing the exclusion of labour in a policy-making process dominated by the ruling party, the bureaucracy, and big business.[51] More recent accounts, however, characterize Japan as a 'co-ordinated market economy', similar to countries like Germany and Sweden, and different from 'liberal market economies' such as the UK and USA.[52] The difference between co-ordinated and liberal markets lies, first, in the fact of business-labour co-operation and, second, in its effect on public policy through wage restraint and flexible redeployment of labour. The argument presented in this chapter suggests that, in Japan, 'corporatism without labour' is compatible with being a 'co-ordinated market', and that one crucial factor that distinguishes types of co-ordinated market economies—e.g., between Japan, on the one hand, and Sweden and Germany on the other—is the role of the bureaucracy and of political parties.

In Japan, the exclusion of organized labour from policy-making is compatible with co-ordinated markets because the combination of bureaucratic pre-co-ordination and government–opposition collaboration were crucial in providing compensation policies. However, in frameworks derived from the German and/or Swedish cases, 'corporatism without labour' is an oxymoron. This is because political parties and trade unions were instrumental in providing compensation policies in neo-corporatist/co-ordinated market regimes. Hence, despite management–union collaboration in wage restraint, the unions and left parties had an independent role in installing active employment policies, shortening work hours, securing income for retirees, etc. In Japan, although the institutionalization of business–union co-operation at the firm level produced similarities with its neo-corporatist/co-ordinated market counterparts, labour was not able to carve out an independent role so that interests could not be represented or assimilated by business or the bureaucracy.

As a result, exclusive channels of interest representation were not established between unions and left-parties, notwithstanding the moderation of organized labour and its further participation in the policy process. Labour unification under moderate auspices and labour inclusion in the policy process did not transform 'corporatism without labour' into either a neo-corporatist/co-ordinated market economy of the European variety, or a liberal market economy; nor is it likely, contrary to mainstream interpretation of Japanese labour politics, to strengthen the role of organized labour in Japan.[53]

In Sweden and Germany, political parties provided state compensation in the form of employment and welfare programmes to employees. These programmes were sometimes extended to the self-employed through universal programmes. In Japan, compensation for adjustment was primarily provided through the market, and state compensation focused mostly on sheltered or declining sectors of the economy. Since collaborative unions did not have an exclusive political channel in Japan, the cleavage between large corporations who favoured a reduction in the role of the state, and small businesses and the self-employed, who depended on state redistribution and regulation, was co-ordinated by the bureaucracy. As a result, the role of political parties remained limited to representing the assumed interests of small businesses and the self-employed. By comparison, in Sweden and Germany, the above-mentioned cleavage was represented by different parties of the right and left and was solved through partisan competition, partisan compromise, and change of ruling coalitions.[54]

The above description of bureaucracy-party relations also challenges the traditional dichotomy of bureaucracy-dominance vs. party-dominance in Japanese studies. As is well known, the former has been represented by élitist theories and proponents of the developmental state, while the latter has been advocated by pluralist and rational choice theorists.[55] The arguments presented here show that the two views are not incompatible. Bureaucratic pre-co-ordination solves most of the critical problems that one would expect to be debated between the right and left parties in the UK or USA, especially regarding the issue of liberal markets/small state vs. interventionist state. In doing so, bureaucratic pre-co-ordination simultaneously preserves bureaucratic autonomy from political parties and prevents the bureaucracy from being captured by social interests. However, this does not support the bureaucratic-dominance view. Instead, it shows how bureaucratic co-ordination institutionalized skewed representation by political parties that competed to represent small businesses and the self-employed against 'monopoly capital'. A comparison of failed policy attempts of the late 1970s and the successful passage of reforms a decade later shows that the bureaucracy took into account the interests of both the ruling party and opposition parties. Furthermore, all major reform bills were revised again in the legislature by an alliance of government and opposition parties.

The symbiotic relations described in this chapter indicate why the expected drive toward bipolarity under the newly installed electoral reforms may not result in a party system based on the industrial cleavage between neo-liberalism and social democracy, as in the cases of the UK, Germany, or Sweden. Despite the seeming convergence in the left camp between Japan and the UK, as the result of the moderation of unions and the Socialist party in Japan, fundamental policy differences between the Tories and Labour remain in the UK, especially over the role of government in mitigating and correcting the problems of market competition. Such is the case even after Labour contained its left wing and took a centralist position after the 1983 election defeat, a centrism embodied in the Labour Policy Reviews and the party leadership of Neil Kinnock, John Smith, and Tony Blair. Labour in the UK reversed its electoral decline after 1983 by maintaining its commitment to employment, social welfare, and education. The transformation from class-based to regional-based voting, with Labour strongholds being the north and the inner cities, reproduced the policy cleavage between the Tories and Labour, whereby Labour has to maintain commitment to redistribution and planning by the state in order to cater to its core constituencies. In other words, political parties in the UK have the ability to mobilize voters and exploit social cleavages. This is the opposite of the Japanese case in the 1980s.[56]

The importance of societal and regional cleavages on party competition was also characteristic of Italy. On the surface, Italy resembles Japan in that the dominant party of the left abandoned Marxism. However, in the Italian case, it was the collapse of the ruling coalition rather than the transformation of the opposition that caused the reorganization of the party system. Moreover, there are indications that the north–south cleavage may be emerging as the basis of a new party cleavage.[57]

In Japan, the major left party still remains a major political force and the role of the bureaucracy has not gone through drastic changes. This is in contrast with cases where the reinforcement of old, or the emergence of new, policy cleavages, and the role of political parties in mobilizing social interests, have remained the basis of party competition. Examining the demise of the radical union-left in Japan not only explains the transformation of the post-war Japanese party system, but also provides a more nuanced view of political change in Japan, on which sets the basic institutional characteristics of the Japanese political economy within a common framework.

Notes

Unless otherwise indicated, place of publication of works cited in the Notes is Tokyo. Japanese names are ordered according to the convention of family name, followed by first name.

1. JAPAN AS A CREDITOR NATION: WHAT IS HAPPENING TO ITS NET EXTERNAL ASSETS?

1. The stock data published by the Ministry of Finance show that Japan's net external assets became positive in 1968 and have remained so ever since.
2. The big rise in the flow data in 1992–93 appears to be due to the rapid decline in the US Treasury bill interest rate from 5.41% in 1991 to 3.46–3.02% in the next two years.
3. The Ministry of Finance's publications state that major valuation adjustments include: (*a*) those due to exchange rate changes; (*b*) those of end-of-the-year outstanding positions where such data are available (particularly trade credits and securities investments); and (*c*) those of stocks held by non-residents due to stock price changes.
4. Since the rates of return on the government sector's net assets were likely lower than those on the private sector's net liabilities, this particular sectoral composition of net assets perhaps explains why Japan's overall rates of return on external assets were lower than those on external liabilities until the beginning of the 1980s.
5. Commercial banks were also engaged in cross-border securities investment by borrowing short abroad in the 1980s.
6. Each country's national statistics are supplemented by IMF statistics, which have recently been published in its *International Financial Statistics*. All statistics are end-of-the-year data, converted into US dollars at the end-of-the-year exchange rate. Since the US data are based on historical costs for 1970–75, current replacement cost for 1976–81, and market values for 1982–95, they are not strictly comparable over time.
7. Sinn (1990) estimates the stock of external assets and liabilities for 145 countries using flow transactions data. Although they differ from individual countries' national statistics, his estimates are useful for international comparisons of a larger number of countries until 1987.
8. The regression result is as follows:

$$X/Y = 14.12 - 3.44ln(E) - 6.40ln(D/D^*) - 0.73ln(P^{OIL}) + 0.036TIME$$
$$\quad (2.39) \quad (0.61) \qquad (2.00) \qquad\qquad (0.21) \qquad\qquad (0.009)$$
$$+ \; 0.71[X(-1)/Y(-1)],$$
$$\quad (0.04)$$

R-squared Adjusted = 0.95, Standard Error of Residuals = 0.274, DW = 2.25. Sample Period: 1975.I − 1996.IV.

Here X/Y is the nominal Japanese net export in the national income accounts as a percentage of GDP, E is a distributed lag of the IMF's relative normalized unit labour costs, D/D^* is a distributed lag of relative real domestic demand between Japan and six major industrialized countries, P^{OIL} is a distributed lag of real oil prices, and $TIME$ is a time trend. Numbers in parentheses are the estimated standard errors of coefficients. The variable D^* is constructed as the geometric weighted average of the real domestic demand indices for the United States (0.5251), Germany (0.1334), France (0.1061), Italy (0.0972), the United Kingdom (0.0873), and Canada (0.0509), where numbers indicate the nominal GDP shares of the respective countries in 1990. The variable P^{OIL} is defined by the US-dollar oil price divided by the US wholesale price index. The distributed lags chosen for E, P^{OIL}, and D/D^* are four.

9. It must be pointed out that beginning January 1996 the Bank of Japan started to publish new balance of payments statistics based on the fifth edition of the IMF's *Balance of Payments Manual* (1993), which is the corner stone of the established accounting principles. In the Bank of Japan's new balance of payments statistics, a distinction is no longer made between long-term and short-term capital flows and excludes capital transfers from the current account. In addition, the Bank of Japan publishes statistics only in terms of the yen. This makes it almost impossible for researchers to construct a long time series of balance of payments data based on the Bank of Japan's new statistics, since the latter are published only for the year 1991 and after. Appendix Table A2 and Appendix Table A3 are constructed by using old statistics whose information is partially available from the April 1996 issue of the Bank of Japan's *Balance of Payments Monthly*. Another way to construct a long-time data series would be to use IMF statistics published in *Balance of Payments Yearbook*.

10. A similar picture is depicted even if we use the statistics published by the IMF, particularly by using direct and portfolio net investment outflow (IMF statistics) instead of long-term net capital outflow (Bank of Japan statistics) and using other net investment outflow excluding errors and omissions and reserves and related items (IMF statistics) instead of private short-term net capital outflow (Bank of Japan statistics).

11. When the net outflow of long-term capital declined in 1990 and switched to a net inflow in 1991, all types of long-term capital, with the exception of direct investment, registered net inflows.

12. Detailed information about the composition of long-term capital transactions is given in Appendix Table A3. The rise and fall in net outflows of long-term capital in the 1980s and 1990s was principally the result of a big surge and decline in net outflows of securities investment. The rapid rise and the high level of securities investment abroad until end of the 1980s and again in 1994–5 was

through bonds; Japanese investment in stocks and shares abroad was relatively small throughout the 1980s and 1990s. One reason for this is that bonds are a more standardized and less information-specific financial asset and, hence, more easily managed than stocks and shares. Management of foreign stocks and shares, on the other hand, requires highly specialized knowledge, expertise, and information, which Japanese investors have yet to acquire to become global fund managers. The data on the geographical distribution of Japan's net capital out-flows (not reported) indicates that the net outflow of securities investments has largely been channelled toward the United States and the European Union (EU) countries. The preference for securities investment in the developed countries has clearly been due to the favourable investment environment—low country risk and a deep capital market in terms of size, instruments, maturity, and liquidity. Much of Japan's external assets held in the form of foreign securities has been placed in markets where expected yields were high and perceived risks low. The net outflow of direct investments has been directed to almost all regions, particularly the United States, EU countries, and East Asian economies.

13. See Kawai (1991) for more detailed discussion.

14. Japanese foreign direct investment in East Asia has contributed to the deepening of trade relationships within the region and thus has changed Japan's trade patterns significantly in recent years. Kawai (1997) and Kawai and Urata (1997) find that Japan's foreign direct investment and trade are reinforcing each other.

15. This is the well-known Feldstein–Horioka (1980) effect.

16. Among them are: (a) culture and tradition that encourage thrift and saving rather than spending (for example, the influence of Confucianism); (b) the young demographic structure of the population; (c) the high proportion of the self-employed; (d) the bonus system; (e) the unavailability of consumer credit; (f) the need to purchase land and housing; (g) the need to prepare the cost of education for children; (h) the intensity of competition among banks and other financial institutions for deposits; (i) the existence of the postal savings system; (j) the government's saving promotion policies such as tax breaks for savings as opposed to no tax breaks for borrowing; (k) the low level of social security benefits; (l) the rapid rate of economic growth; (m) the low level of initial assets as a result of wartime destruction and the post-war hyperinflation; and (n) the greater prevalence of earthquakes, volcanic eruptions, typhoons, and other natural disasters. See Horioka (1992).

2. THE INTERNATIONALIZATION OF THE JAPANESE FIRM: JAPANESE WORKING PRACTICES AND INDIGENOUS ASIAN WORKPLACES

1. Okamoto, Yasuo. '*Takokuseki Kigyo to Nihon Kigyo no Takokusekika*' (Multinational firms and the multinationalization of Japanese firms), *Keizai Gakuronshu*, Vol. 53, No. 1, 21.

2. Much research has had the objective of comparing Japanese firms located in other Asian countries. I would mention, as examples of studies based on large-scale questionnaire surveys, the work of the Ichimura Shinichi group and of Hiroshima University. The former produced two different Japanese texts and a report in English, which includes the results of the questionnaire survey. Ichimura Shinichi (ed.), *Nihon Kigyo in Ajia* (Japanese firms in Asia) (Toyo Keizai Shinposha, 1980). Ichimura Shinichi (ed.), *Ajia ni Nezuku Nihon-teki Keiei* (Japanese Management Rooted in Asia) (Toyo Keizai Shinposha, 1988). Ichimura Shinichi, and Yoshihara Kunio (eds.), 'Japanese Management Southeast Asia', *Southeast Asian Studies* (1985), 22–4, 23–1. The Hiroshima University surveys were also reported in an English book and a Japanese article, but in this case the Japanese report is more inclusive. Yamashita Shoichi (ed.), *Transfer of Japanese Management and Technology to the ASEAN Countries* (University of Tokyo Press, 1991). Yamashita Shoichi (ed.), 'ASEAN Shokoku ni okeru Nihongata-keiei to Gijutsu Iten ni Kansuru Keieisha no Iken Chosa' (Survey of Managers' Opinions on Technology Transfer and Japanese Management in the ASEAN Countries), Nenpo Keizaigaku, 10 (Hiroshima University, 1991). This is a lengthy text of 89 pages and reflects a laborious amount of work. However, there are serious problems, as mentioned above, in the essential survey structure. For example, the statement, 'Mark which of the following so-called Japanese-style management practices should be encouraged when engaging in commercial activities in Thailand: 1. Permanent employment. 2. Seniority promotion and wages. 3. Ringi (draft circulation) system. 4. Groupism. 5. Internal human resource training . . . 12. Job rotation.' was provided with the alternative responses: 'agree', and 'strongly agree' (p. 22). Is it acceptable for the survey to ignore how the respondents would interpret such ambiguous items? That problem, which is also a feature of the Ichimura survey, means that we cannot judge the real situation.

3. Koike Kazuo, *Shokuba no Rodo Kumiai to Sanka—Roshi Kankei no Nichibei Hikaku* (A Comparative Study of Industrial Relations on the Shop Floor in the United States and Japan) (Toyo Keizai Shinpo-sha, 1977), 103.

4. Koike Kazuo, and Inoki Takenori. *Jinzai Keisei no Kokusai Hikaku—Tonan Ajia to Nihon* (An International Comparison of Skill Formation: South-East Asia and Japan) (Toyo Keizai Shinpo-sha, 1987). Refer to Chapters 1 and 2.

5. Apart from the next section concerning Singapore, the main works, in addition to texts on Thailand and Malaysia, are: *ASEAN Kenkyu-kai, Indoneshia ni okeru Nikkei Kigyo no Romu Kanri to Roshi Kankei* (Personnel Management and Industrial Relations in Japanese-Indonesian Joint Ventures) (Kyoto: Kyoto Daigaku Keizai Kenkyujo, 1985). ASEAN Kenkyu-kai, *Indoneshia no Rodo Jijo* (Labour Conditions in Indonesia), (Nihon Rodo Kyokai, 1985).

6. Yahata Shigemi, and Mizuno Junko, *Nikkei Shinshutsu Kigyo to Genchi Kigyo to no Kigyo-kan Bungyo Kozo to Gijutsu Iten—Tai no Jidosha Sangyo o Jirei toshite* (Technology Transfer and Division of Labour between Japanese Joint Ventures and Indigenous Firms: Case Studies in the Thai Automobile Industry) (Ajia Keizai Kenkyujo, 1988) (Institute of Developing Economies).

7. Odaka Konosuke (ed.), *Ajia no Jukuren—Kaihatsu to Jinzai Ikusei* (Skills in Asia: development and human resources development), (1989). My commentary on this survey can be found in the August 1990 edition of *Ajia Keizai* (Asian Economies).

8. Shiba Shoji, *A Cross-National Comparison of Labour Management with Reference to Technology Transfer* (Institute of Developing Economies, 1973).

9. Koike Kazuo, and Inoki Takenori, *Skill formation in Japan and Southeast Asia and Japan* (University of Tokyo Press, 1990).

10. Ibid. Refer to Chapter 1.

11. Nihon Rodo Kyokai (Japan Institute of Labour) (ed.), *Kaigai Rodo Jijo—Shingaporu* (Labour Conditions Overseas: Singapore) (Nihon Rodo Kyokai, 1974).

12. Nihon Rodo Kyokai (Japan Institute of Labour) (ed.), *Shingaporu no Rodo Jijo* (Labour Conditions in Singapore) (Nihon Rodo Kyokai, 1983).

13. Imano Koichiro, and Yahata Shigemi, 'Shingaporu no Nikkei Shinshutsu Kigyo 1, 2, 3' (Japanese Joint Ventures in Singapore). *IE*, (February, March and April. Imano Koichiro, 'Shingaporu ni okeru Gijutsu Kyoiku to Nihon Takokuseki-Kigyo no Kyoiku Kunren' (Technical Training and Training by Japanese Multi-nationals in Singapore), *Tokyo Gakugei Daigaku Kiyo*, Dai 6, Bumon No. 32 (1979). Yahata Shigemi, and Imano Koichiro, 'Kaigai Shinshutsu Kigyo no Keiei Genchika to Genchijin Chukan Kanrisha. Kantokusha no Yakuwari—Shingaporu–Nikkei Shinshutsu no Baai 1, 2' (Singaporean–Japanese Joint Ventures as an Example of the Localization of Management by Multinational Companies). *IE*, (1980) November and December. Imano Koichiro, 'Zaigai Nihon Kigyo no Chingin Kanri—Shingaporu' (Wage administration in Japanese companies in Singapore), *Tokyo Gakugei Daigaku Kiyo*, Dai 6, Bumon No. 33 (1981). Imano Koichiro, 'Shingaporu ni okeru Nikkei Shinshutsu Kigyo no Romu Kanri' (Personnel Management in Japanese–Singaporean Joint Ventures), *Nihon Rodo Kyokai Zasshi*, No. 262 (Jan 1981). Imano Koichiro, 'Nikkei Shinshutsu Kigyo Keiei Genchika to sono Tokucho—Singaporu' (Some Characteristics of Appointment of Singa-poreans to Managerial Positions in Japanese–Singaporean Joint Ventures). *Rodo Mondai Kenkyo*, No. 59 (1983).

14. Nihon Boeki Shinkokai (Japan External Trade Organization), *Kaigai Rodo Jijo—Shingaporu no Rodo Jijo* (Labour Conditions Overseas: Singapore), (1974).
—— *Shingaporu ni okeru Rodo Funso* (Industrial Disputes in Singapore), (1976).
—— *Shingaporu ni okeru Gino Rodoryoku no Jukyu to Kongo no Mitoshi* (The Market and Prospects for Skilled Labour in Singapore), (1977).

15. Nihon Rodo Kyokai (Japan Institute of Labour) (1974), 150. See also Yahata and Imano (1980), 73.

16. Nihon Rodo Kyokai (Japan Institute of Labour) (1974), 12.

17. For example, ibid., 9.

18. For example, ibid., 12.

19. They have passed quite difficult national O-level examinations at the age of 16 years.

20. Koike and Inoki (1987). Refer to Chapter 1.

21. Koike and Inoki (1987).

22. The record of these interviews can be found in: Koike Kazuo (1982). *Skill Formation on the Shop Floor in Southeast Asian Countries—Foundations for Development* (Kyoto: Kyoto Institute of Economic Research, Kyoto University), Discussion Paper No. 169.

23. Koike and Inoki (1990).

24. Koike and Inoki (1990).

25. Koike Kazuo, *Chusho Kigyo no Jukuren* (Skill formation in small and medium-sized companies) (Dobunkan, 1981).

26. Koike and Inoki (1990).

27. One example is in: Koike Kazuo, 'Learning and incentive systems in contemporary Japanese industry', in Masahiko Aoki and Ronald P. Dore (eds.). *The Japanese Firm* (London: Oxford University Press, 1994).

28. Koike and Inoki (1990).

29. Inoki Takenori, 'Nihon no Tai–Bei Chokusetsu Toshi wa Kasoku suru ka— Chokusetsu Toshi to Koyo ni Kansuru Ichiko Satsu' (Will the Pace of Direct Investment in the USA Quicken? A Comment on Direct Investment and Employment), in *Kokusai Kankyoka ni okeru Koyo Mondai* (Kansai Keizai Kenkyu Senta, 1987). Also Inoki, 'Tai no Nikkei Kigyo no Pafomansu—1973–1988' (The Performance of Thai–Japanese Joint Ventures: 1973–1988), in *Kokusai Kankyoka ni okeru Koyo Mondai* (Kansai Keizai Kenkyu Senta, 1989). Finally, please see Kokusai Kangyo Rodo Kenkyu Senta, *Kaigai Nihon Kigyo no Koyo to Keiei ni Kansuru Chosa Kenkyu* (Survey Research on Employment and Management in Japanese Companies Overseas, 1989).

30. Shimada Haruo, Human Uea no Keizaigaku (The Economics of Human Resources) (Iwanami Shoten, 1988).

31. Wickens, Peter, *The Road to Nissan: Flexibility, Quality, Teamwork* (London: Macmillan, 1987), 123.

32. Ledford, Gerald C., Jr. 'Three case studies on skill-based pay', *Compensation and benefits review* (March–April, 1991).

3. FOREIGN WORKERS AND IMMIGRATION POLICY

1. Factual references in this chapter derived from the *Homu Nenkan* (Justice Annual) are limited to the Immigration Bureau entry each year, so the page quoted has been omitted except in particularly important cases. Also, see the statement by Kobayashi Shunji, Director of the Immigration Bureau, in 'Zadankai-Nyukokukanri no Genjo to Gaikokujin no Shuromondai' (Discussion on the Issue of Foreigners' Work and the Present State of Immigration Control), *Jurisuto* (Jurist), 7 (1 Feb. 1987).

2. The 1976 *Homu Nenkan* (Justice Annual) refers to the upward trend in activities outside residence status, commenting that 'the types of violations are becoming

worse and more devious', but in quantitative terms there were just 53 violators in 1973, 175 in 1974, 247 in 1975, and 241 in 1976, 186.

3. The 1986 edition of the Immigration Bureau's *Shutsunyukoku Kanri—Henbo suru kokusai kankyo no naka de* (Immigration Control in the Changing International Environment) had already attempted an analysis of the 'actual operation of illegal work', 107–10. See also Tanaka Shinya (of the Narita District Immigration Office of the Tokyo Regional Immigration Bureau), 'Zairyu Gaikokujin to Shutsunyukokukanri—Shutsunyukokukanri Genba kara no Hokoku' (Foreign Residents and Immigration Control: an on Site Report from Immigration Control), *Horitsu jiho* (Legal News) (July 1987), 28–32 and Machida Yukio, 'Fuhoshurogaikokujin no Jittai' (The Situation of Illegal Foreign Workers), *Jurisuto* (Jurist), (1 June 1988), 18–25.

4. *Kokusai Jinryu* (The Immigration Newsmagazine) (July 1994), 36–45.

5. Immigration Bureau, op. cit., 171.

6. See Sunobe Ryozo, Oonuma Yasuaki and Kim Kyong-Duk, 'Zadankai—Zainichi Kankoku/Chosenjin no Hoteki Chii "Kyotei Sansei" Mondai to Hirakareta Nihonshakai e no Tenbo' (Symposium on the legal status of Korean residents: 'the third generation of the agreement' and prospects for an open Japanese society), *Horitsu Jiho* (Legal News) (June 1990), 6–19.

7. See Yamazaki Tetsuo, 'Koshite Matomatta Zainichi Kankokujin Hoteki Chii Mondai—sono Keika to Naiyo' (How the Issue of the Legal Status of Korean Residents was Resolved: The Process and the Content) *Kokusai Jinryu* (The Immigration Newsmagazine) (Mar. 1991), 6–14. The memorandum confirmed the direction of the Japanese government's response in five areas: items related to the Immigration Law (permanent residence status, reasons for deportation, re-entry permits); items related to the alien registration law (fingerprinting, the obligation to carry alien registration certificate at all times); education issues (ethnic education); employment as teachers in government schools; and employment as civil servants in local governments. The memorandum also states that 'a request was made' by the South Korean government about 'local government voting rights'.

8. See *Kokusai Jinryu* (The Immigration Newsmagazine) (June 1991), 21–4 for the content of the special law. The special law also stipulates limits in the case of deportation of special permanent residents and exceptions to the period of validity of re-entry permits (paragraph 26, sections 3 and 4—one year becoming four and in the case of an extension two becoming five). On the situation regarding the legal status (i.e., residence status) of Koreans since they lost their citizenship, see the Immigration Bureau General Affairs Division, 'Zainichi Kankoku/Chosenjin no Hoteki Chii to Zairyu no Jokyo' (The Legal Status of Korean Residents and the Situation of Those Remaining), *Kokusai Jinryu* (The Immigration Newsmagazine) (Mar. 1991), 18–24.

9. On the factual history see the Immigration Bureau General Affairs Division's 'Zainichi Kankoku/Chosenjin no Hoteki Chii to Zairyu no Jokyo' (The Legal

Status of Korean Residents and the Situation of Those Remaining), *Kokusai Jinryu* (The Immigration Newsmagazine) (March 1991), 18–24.

10. Since the first lower house election after the war (in April 1946), the election law by-laws have included the regulation that 'the right of persons not subject to the Family Registration Law to participate in elections or to be elected is hereby suspended until further notice'. Koreans and Taiwanese, who did not belong to any family register of Japan proper, were not subject to the Family Registration Law. Despite still having citizenship, they were denied electoral rights. There have recently been increasing calls demanding that foreign long-term residents be permitted to participate in local council elections. In September 1990, second generation Korean residents of Osaka City launched an administrative suit on the grounds that 'not allowing foreign long-term residents the right to participate in local council elections is unconstitutional'. See the interview with So Yong-Dal on this in the morning edition of *Asahi Shimbun* (13 Jan. 1991). See also Hirowatari Seigo, 'Teijugaikokujin no Senkyoken' (Electoral Rights of Foreign Long-Term Residents), in *Horitsu Jiho* (Legal News) (Sept. 1986), 2–5, and *Futatsu no Sengoshakai to Ho no Aida—Nihon to Nishi Doitsu* (Between Two Post-War Societies and the Law—Japan and West Germany) (Ookurasho Insatsukyoku), 147–64, by the same author.

11. For a reference work which includes the claims one of the parties involved, see Choe Ch'ang-Hwa, *Kokuseki to Jinken* (Citizenship and Human Rights) (Sakaishoten, 1975).

12. *Horitsu Jiho* (Legal News) (June 1990), 20–4.

13. See, for example, Morita Kiriro (ed.), *Kokusai Rodoryoku Ido* (International Labour Movements) (University of Tokyo Press, 1987); Kuwahara Yasuo, 'Sekiyukikigo no Kokusai Rodoryoku Ido no Dotai—Gaikokujin Rodosha Mondai e no Shiza Settei no Tame ni' (Changes in International Labour Movements Following the Oil Crises—Establishing a Parallax for the Issue of Foreign Workers), *Nihon Rodokyokai Zasshi* (Journal of the Japan Labour Association) (Aug. 1988), 14–23; Higuchi Yoshio, 'Gaikokujin Rodosha Mondai no Keizaigakuteki Sokumen—Kokunai Koyo e no Eikyo' (Economic Aspects of the Foreign Worker Issue—the Impact on Domestic Employment), *Nihon Rodokyokai Zasshi* (Journal of the Japan Labour Association) (Aug. 1988), 34–47; Goto Jun'ichi, *Gaikokujin Rodo no Keizaigaku —Kokusai Boekiron Kara no Apurochi* (The Economics of Foreign Labour—an Approach from International Trade Theory) (Toyo Keizai Shinposha, 1990).

14. Ministry of Labour Employment Security Bureau, 'Gaikokujin Rodosha Mondai Kenkyukai Hokoku (Yoshi)' (Report of the Working Group on the Foreign Worker Problem) *Gekkan Nyu Porishii* (New Policy Monthly) (May 1988), 476–90.

15. There has been public debate recently about the admission of foreign workers that has centred on discussion of what are generally referred to as the 'open country' and the 'closed country'. Nishio Kanji, Tezuka Kazuaki, Oonuma Yasuaki, Miyajima Takashi, Koike Kazuo, Ishikawa Yoshimi, Komai Hiroshi, Shimada Haruo, Yano Toru, Hanami Tadashi, Ebashi Takashi, and Tanaka Hiroshi have

been the main participants. In this chapter, I will not attempt to follow that debate, but rather approach the issue of foreign workers from the perspective put forward here.

16. Miyazaki Shigeki, 'Gaikokujin' (Foreigners), in *Gendai no Kokka Kenryoku to Ho* (The Power of the Contemporary State and the Law) (Gendai Hogaku Zenshu (Contemporary Law Collection)) (Chikuma Shobo), 1978, 230, n. 1.

17. See Doi Takako (ed.), *Kokuseki o Kangaeru* (On Citizenship) (Jijitsushinsha, 1984).

18. On citizenship law, see Egawa Hidefumi, Yamada Ryoichi and Hayata Yoshio, *Kokusekiho* (Citizenship Law) (revised edition) (Yuhikaku, 1989).

19. See Hirowatari Seigo, 'Nishidoitsu no Gaikokujin to Gaikokujinseisaku' (Foreigner and Immigration Policy in West Germany), *Shakaikagaku Kenkyu* (The Journal of Social Science) 41/6, (1990).

20. Josef Isensee, 'Die staatsrechtliche Stellung der Ausländer in der BRD', *Veröffentlichungen der Vereinigung der Deutschen Staatsrechtslehrer*, No. 32 (1974), 64–5. Reference was also made to the translation by Saito Yasuo in *Jurisuto* (Jurist) (15 Oct. 1976), 137–8.

21. This issue was also raised at the deliberations over the revision of the Immigration Law. The government justification was that it was proceeding cautiously because ratification would require considerable correlation with domestic laws. See the record of the 116th House of Councillors Committee on Judicial Affairs No. 1 (30 Nov. 1989), 31–2, and No. 3 (7 Dec. 1989), 18.

22. Hosei University's Professor Ebashi Takashi, who appeared as a witness at the Immigration Law revision deliberations, has pursued the point that Japan's treatment of foreigners fails to address international human rights standards. See the record of the 116th House of Councillors Committee on Judicial Affairs No. 2 (5 Dec. 1989), 17–18.

23. Ikegami Tsutomu, Immigration Control Bureau Chief, *Hoteki Chii 200 no Shitsumon* (200 Questions on Legal Status) (Kyobunsha, 1965). Cited in Miyazaki op. cit., 244.

24. Isensee, op. cit., 68–71.

25. The idea for this theory of the typology of admission comes from Suwa Yasuo's chapter 2 of Hanami Tadashi, and Kuwahara Yasuo (eds.), *Asu no Rinjin— Gaikokujin Rodosha* (Foreign workers: the Neighbours of Tomorrow) (Toyo Keizai Shinposha, 1989).

26. Ulrich Wölker, 'Das Ausländerrecht in Frankreich', in J. A. Frowein/J. Wolf (eds.), *Ausländerrecht im internationalen Vergleich* (1985), 156 ff.

27. See Nyukankyokai (ed.), *Gokakoku Shutsunyukoku Kanri Saishin Jijo* (The Latest Situation in Immigration Control in Five Countries) (1990), 111 ff.

28. See Iyotani Toshio, 'Amerika Gasshukoku ni okeru Imin Rodo to Imin Seisaku' (Immigrant Labour and Immigration Policy in the United States of America), *Nihon Rodokyokai Zasshi* (Journal of the Japan Labour Association) (Aug. 1988), 49–50.

29. Rolf Grawert, *Staat und Staatsangehörigkeit. Verfassungsgeschichtliche Untersuchung zur Entstehung der Staatsangehörigkeit* (1973), 156 ff.

30. This point is cited in Ito Ruri, '"Dokanaki Togo" no Sodai na Jikken' (The Grand Experiment of 'Integration Without Assimilation') *Nihon ga Taminzoku Kokka ni Naru hi* (The Day Japan Becomes a Multi-ethnic State), Bessatsu Takarajima, No. 106 (1990), 227.

31. For full coverage of American immigration and citizenship law, see Nunoi Keijiro, *Beikoku ni okeru Shutsunyukoku Oyobi Kokusekiho* (Immigration and Citizenship Law in America) vols. 1–2 (Yuhikaku, 1985), and Kawahara Kenichi, *Amerika Iminho* (American Immigration Law) (Shinzansha, 1990). On the period since the 1986 revision to the Immigration Law, see Nyukankyokai (ed.), op. cit., 48–95.

32. On the background to establishment of the post-war Immigration Law, see Onuma Yasuaki, 'Shutsunyukoku Kanri Hosei no Seiritsu Katei' (The Process of Establishment of Immigration Control Legislation) in *Tan'itsu Minzoku no Shinwa o Koete* (Beyond the Myth of Mono-ethnicity) by the same author (Toshindo, 1986), 15–114.

33. Record of the 116th House of Councillors Committee on Judicial Affairs, No. 1 (30 Nov. 1989), 3.

34. On this see Dietrich Thränhardt, 'Die europäische Dimension der allgemeinen Ausländerpolitik in der Mitgliederstaaten der EG', in von M. Zuleeg (ed.), *Ausländerrecht und Ausländerpolitik in Europa* (1987), 17–22.

35. The statement of the lawyer Kim Kyong-Duk in 'Zadankai' (Symposium) (see note 5 above), 18.

36. On this issue, see Hirowatari Seigo, 'Doitsu ni okeru Gaikokujin Mondai to Kokuseki' (The Issue of Foreign Workers and Citizenship in Germany) in Momose Hiroshi and Ogura Michio (eds.), *Gendai Kokka to Imin Rodosha* (The Modern State and Immigrant Workers) (Yushindo, 1991) and Zainichi Chosenkankokujin Kyokai Kyoiku Kenkyujo (ed.), *Kika* (Naturalization) vols. 1–2 (Banseisha, 1989).

37. These 28 status of residence were Diplomat, Official, Professor, Artist, Religious Activities, Journalist, Investor/Business Manager, Legal/Accounting Services, Medical Services, Researcher, Instructor, Engineer, Specialist in Humanities/ International Services, Intracompany Transferee, Entertainer, Skilled Labour, Cultural Activities, Temporary Visitor, College Student, Pre-college Student, Trainee, Dependant, Designated Activities, Permanent Resident, Spouse or Child of Japanese National, Spouse or Child of Permanent Resident, Child of Resident under Law No. 126 of 1952, and Long-Term Resident. The Special Immigration Law of 1991 above mentioned brought this number of status to 27.

38. On the revised Immigration Law, see Sakanaka Hidenori, and Takaya Shigeru, *Kaisei Nyukanho no Kaisetsu—Atarashii Shutsunyukoku Kanri Seido* (The New Immigration Control System: A Commentary on the Revised Immigration Law) (Nihon kajo shuppan, 1991); Homusho Nyukankyoku—Gaikokujin Rodosha Mondai Kenkyukai (eds.), *Shinpan Gaikokujin no Shushoku/Koyo Q &A* (Q & A on

Work and Employment of Foreigners) (Nihon Kajo Shuppan, 1990). In parliamentary deliberations, the concern was raised that 'intra-company transferee' would be used as a loophole for allowing unskilled foreign workers into the country. The response was that eligibility was restricted to those engaged in work classified as 'Specialist in Humanities/International Services' or 'Engineer', thus excluding unskilled workers. The text of the legislation also reads that way. This was the response of Director of Immigration Bureau Matano to the question of Councillor Kidaira Noriko. See the record of the 116th House of Councillors Committee on Judicial Affairs, No. 1 (30 Nov. 1989), 30. Representative Ando Iwao also put the same question. See the record of the 116th House of Representatives Committee on Judicial Affairs, No. 3 (14 Dec. 1989), 18.

39. See Ministry of Justice Immigration Bureau, *Shutsunyukoku Kanri—Henbo suru Kokusai Kankyo no Naka de* (Immigration Control in the Changing International Environment) (1986 edn.), 157–61.

40. See Hanami and Kuwahara (eds.), *Asu no Rinjin—Gaikokujin Rodosha* (Foreign Workers: the Neighbours of Tomorrow), 58 ff. Permission was granted for the duties of buying foreign products (art buyers), and decorative design that assumed a foreign lifestyle (interior decorators). Employment began in 1982 and as at October 1988 the company had 69 foreign employees.

41. In the revised law, the new statuses of 'legal and accounting services' and 'Specialist in humanities and international services' were created, so almost all foreign students who were graduates of a university (or a graduate school) in the humanities now fall in these categories. Students in the physical sciences were able to be categorized as 'Engineer' (see *Kokusai Jinryu* (The Immigration Newsmagazine) (June 1991), 17–19).

42. Response of an officer of the Minister's secretariat of the Ministry of Labour. The record of the 116th House of Representatives Committee on Judicial Affairs, No. 2 (10 Nov. 1989), 19.

43. See Yamazaki Tetsuo (Ministerial Conductor, Immigration Bureau), 'Atarashii Shutsunyukoku Kanri—Kaisei "shutsunyukoku kanri oyobi nanmin ninteiho"' (The New Immigration Control: The Revised 'Immigration Control and Refugee Recognition Act') in Koido Yuji (ed.), *Gaikokujin Rodosha—Seisaku to Kadai* (Foreign Workers: Policies and Issues) (Zeimu Keiri Kyokai, 1990), 30–57.

44. The statement of Professor Tanaka Hiroshi, who appeared at the deliberations of the House of Councillors as a witness, is a good example. See the record of the House of Councillors Committee on Judicial Affairs, No. 2 (5 Dec. 1989), 13–15. The House of Councillors Committee on Judicial Affairs adopted the following appended resolution, which was the joint proposal of all parties and non-aligned members with the exception of the Democratic Socialists and the Communists: 'that, in view of the fact that labour-related laws and ordinances should be observed even in the case of foreign workers, efforts be made to expand the legal support system and the system of consultation regarding issues such as that of the human rights of foreign workers, in addition to humane consideration being

given to issues relating to the working conditions of foreigners during their employment, such as outstanding wages'. The record of the House of Councillors Committee on Judicial Affairs, No. 3 (7 Dec. 1989), 27.

45. The record of the 116th House of Councillors Committee on Judicial Affairs, No. 3 (7 Dec. 1989), 3–5. Kurata's essay (*Hanrei Taimusu* (The Judicial Case Times) No. 694) expresses the aim of the creation of punitive regulations as 'the destruction of the forces pulling illegal foreign workers to Japan and the destruction of elements constituting the driving force in that pull', stating that 'admitting unskilled foreign workers means admitting immigrants. To do so would induce change in Japan's unique culture and national character. To be swayed by cheap humanism or incomprehensible terms like "human internationalization" and rush to ease regulations without any policy which takes the future into consideration would be a gross transgression against our descendants.' The perception that foreign unskilled workers are detrimental is blatant, but this does put the finger on the essence of the problem. It is fundamentally in accord with the assertion of Nishio Kanji. Whether it is to become a 'gross transgression against our descendants' or a 'gift to our descendants' will depend on the creation of a 'policy which takes the future into consideration'.

46. The record of the 116th House of Representatives Committee on Judicial Affairs, No. 4 (17 Nov. 1989), 13–14.

47. This point, unfortunately, did not appear in the parliamentary deliberations.

48. See, for example, Hinago Akira's report, 'Kaette Kita Nanbei Imin' (South American emigrants who came back), in *Nihon ga Taminzoku Kokka ni Naru Hi* (The Day Japan Becomes a Multi-ethnic State) (see n. 29 above), 173–82.

49. 'Sasho—Ima Gaikokujin Rodosha wa' (What Foreign Workers are Doing about Visas), *Asahi Shimbun* (1 Aug. 1990).

50. Akagi Kazushige, 'Naze Karera wa Nihon o Mezasu no ka—Burajiru Nikkeijin no Dekasegi to Nikkei Shakai no Genjo' (Why do They Come?—Brazilian Workers of Japanese Descent and the Situation in the Japanese Community), *Kokusai Jinryu* (The Immigration Newsmagazine) (July 1990), 9. The official statistics of the Ministry of Foreign Affairs report that at the end of 1989 in Brazil there were 108,518 permanent residents who hold Japanese citizenship, and 529,310 people of Japanese descent. On the historical changes in emigration to Brazil from Japan, see 'Tokei ni Yoru Nihonjin no Kaigai Iju' (Japanese emigration through statistics) *Kokusai Jinryu* (The Immigration Newsmagazine) (July 1990), 20–8.

51. 'Zairyu Nikkei Burajirujin nado no Kadojokyo ni Kansuru Jittai Chosa no Jisshi ni Tsuite' (On the Administration of a Survey of the Situation Regarding Utilization of Japanese Brazilians and Others in Japan) (13 Apr. 1990), *Nyu Porishii Detabesu* (New Policy Database), 900423006.

52. With situations like the charging of the Kanagawa prefecture personnel agency Sankyokogyo in July 1989 with violation of worker secondment legislation in regard to the employment and secondment of Brazilians, it appears that employers have become somewhat cautious.

53. The comment of Toda Katsunori, Planning Officer of the Ministry of Foreign Affairs. See *Kokusai Jinryu* (The Immigration Newsmagazine) (July 1990), 11–12.

54. See Akagi's essay referred to in n. 50 above.

55. *Gekkan Nyu Porishii* (New Policy Monthly) (Feb. 1991), 469–74.

56. *Gekkan Nyu Porishii* (New Policy Monthly) (June 1991), 445–64, particularly 456.

57. See Maeyama Takashi, 'Nikkei Gaikokujin Rodosha no sono go?—"Nihonkokumin" to wa dare ka' (What of the Foreign Workers of Japanese Descent Afterwards?: Who *are* Japanese Nationals?), *Kokusai Jinryu* (The Immigration Newsmagazine) (July 1990), 2–6.

58. *Kaisei Nyukanho no Kaisetsu* (A Commentary on the Revised Immigration Law) (see n. 62 above), 105–6. See Tanaka Kiyoshi, 'Gaikokujin Kenshusei no Genjo to Mondaiten' (The Situation of and Problems with Foreign Trainees), in Ebashi Takashi (ed.), *Gaikokujin Rodosha to Jinken—Nihon/Tai Kankei Kenkyu no Genba kara* (Foreign Workers and Human Rights: an On-Site Report on Research in Japan–Thai Relations) (Hosei Daigaku Shuppankyoku, 1990), 95–119.

59. 'Gaikokujin Kenshusei ni Kakawaru Kenshu Jisshi Kigyo ni Kansuru Jittai Chosa Kekka ni Tsuite' (Results of a survey on the actual conditions of corporations involved in training foreign trainees), *Gekkan Nyu Porishii* (New Policy Monthly) (Sept. 1989), 158–61.

60. See Keizaikikakucho sogokeikakukyoku (ed.), *Gaikokujin Rodosha to Keizaishakai no Shinro* (Foreign Workers and Directions for the Economy and Society) (1989), 30–1.

61. This established standards for among other things requirements for trainees, requirements for institutions providing training, requirements for institutions sending trainees, requirements for institutions mediating for trainees, requirements for training content, items to be stipulated in training contracts, and the requirements for training allowances, as well as specifying that spouses would not be granted entry and that the number of trainees should be in about the ratio of one to every twenty employees.

62. For example, Immigration Bureau Director Matano's answers to Councillor Shirahama Kazuyoshi in the record of the 116th House of Councillors Committee on Judicial Affairs, No. 1 (30 Nov. 1989), 15–16, and answers of an officer of the Minister's Secretariat of the Ministry of Justice, Yonezawa, to questions from Representative Ando Iwao in the record of the 116th House of Representatives Committee on Judicial Affairs, No. 2 (10 Nov. 1989), 30–1.

63. The record of the 116th House of Councillors Committee on Judicial Affairs, No. 3 (7 Dec. 1989), 25.

64. The record of the 116th House of Representatives Committee on Judicial Affairs, No. 3 (14 Nov. 1989), 12. In his statement (pp. 5–7), Kato also proposed the following three conditions for intake of foreign workers: harmony with domestic employment and labour; preparation of Japanese society and its various systems for reception of foreigners; and the agreement of the people. He also sought the prior agreement of labour unions in the case of the intake of trainees. On the whole, his ideas are worthy of attention.

65. The record of the 116th House of Representatives Committee on Judicial Affairs, No. 3 (14 Nov. 1989), 4–5.

66. 'China' here includes Chinese from both Hong Kong and Taiwan.

67. See *Kokusai Jinryu* (The Immigration Newsmagazine) (Dec. 1990), 36–9.

68. See the comment of the Immigration Bureau on the announcement: '"Kenshu" ni Kansuru Homu Daijin Kokuji ni Tsuite' (On the Minister of Justice's Notification Regarding 'Training'), *Gekkan Nyu Porishii* (New Policy Monthly) (Sept. 1990), 200 and *Kaiseinyukanho no Kaisetsu* (see n. 62 above), 114–32.

69. (Zai) Chusho Kigyo Keieisha Saigai Hosho Jigyodan, 'Gaikokujin Kenshusei Ukeire Kikan Setsuritsu Koso ni Tsuite' (On the Concept of Establishing an Institution for the Intake of Foreign Trainees) (3 July 1990), in *Nyu Porishii Detabesu* (New Policy Database), 900705051.

70. *Asahi Shimbun* (27 June 1991), morning edition.

71. 'If we accept the idea that we ought to contribute to the economic and social development of other countries through, *inter alia*, technology transfer, then as well as increasing the intake of students and technical trainees we must consider allowing foreigners to work for the purpose of practical training for a specified period where required, in order to put into practice the knowledge and skills they have acquired as the outcome of their schooling or training.' Ministry of Labour Employment Security Bureauu, 'Gaikokujin Rodosha Mondai Kenkyukai Hokoku(Yoshi)' (Report by the Working Group on the Foreign Worker Problem (summary)) (26 March 1988), *Gekkan Nyu Porishii* (New Policy Monthly) (May 1988), 476–90, particularly 482. Also Chairman Koike Kazuo's 'Koyo Kyokasei no Teisho' (A Call for an Employment Permit System), *Jurisuto* (Jurist) (1 June 1989), 9.

72. *Kokusai jinryu* (The Immigration Newsmagazine) (May 1993), 32–8.

73. See Hachiya Takashi, 'Ajia Rodosha no Ukeire to Seifu, Sangyokai no Tachiba' (Admitting Foreign Workers and the Positions of Government and Industry), in *Gaikokujin Rodosha to Jinken—Nihon/Tai Kankei Kenkyu no Genba kara* (Foreign Workers and Human Rights: an On-Site Report on Research in Japan–Thai Relations) (see n. 83 above), 16–50, and Go Munechika's chapter 6 'Keizaikai no Taio' (The Response of the Business World), *Gaikokujin Rodosha—Seisaku to Kadai* (Foreign Workers: Policies and Issues) (see n. 43 above).

74. This is from Kansai Keizai Rengokai Gaikokujin Rodosha Mondai Tokubetsu Iinkai, 'Gaikokujin Rodosha Ukeire Mondai ni Tsuite' (On the Issue of Admission of Foreign Workers) (Apr. 1990), in *Nyu porishii detabesu* (New Policy Database), 900420046, 24, 25.

75. Ibid.

76. See Tokyo Shoko Kaigisho '"Gaikokujin Rodosha Jukuren Keisei Seido" no Sosetsu nado ni Kansuru Teigen' (Statement on the Establishment of a 'Foreign Workers Skill Formation System' (Dec. 1989), *Gekkan Nyu Porishii* (New Policy Monthly) (Jan. 1990), 579–80.

77. Kansai Keizai Rengokai Gaikokujin Rodosha Mondai Tokubetsu Iinkai, 'Gaikokujin Rodosha Ukeire Mondai ni Tsuite' (see nn. 74 and 75). The conditions for the

permit were to include a shortage of labour in the type of work; suitability of the worker (Japanese language, desire to work); no deterioration in domestic working conditions; that the employer had endeavoured to find workers; and that responsibility would be taken for observance of labour laws and standards and guaranteeing a place of residence for the worker. Furthermore, the state, self-governing bodies, industry groups, and corporations were to set up a system of accountability for the return of workers to their own countries.

78. For example, Kansai Keieisha Kyokai Kokusaika Taio Kenkyu Iinkai, '"Koyo Kyoka Seido" ni Tai suru Iken' (A Response to the 'Employment Permit System') Gekkan Nyu Porishii (New Policy Monthly) (Aug. 1988), 637.

79. See Gaikokujin Rodosha to Keizaishakai no Shinro (see n. 85), 81–95.

80. A comparison of the results of the Opinion Poll Regarding the Issue of Foreign Workers conducted by the Public Relations Room of the Cabinet Secretariat in November 1990 with those of similar surveys conducted in July 1980 and February 1988 shows (1) increased interest in the issue of foreign workers; (2) more tolerance of illegal work; and (3) a greater tendency for the public to support the admission of foreign workers. On (1), for example, the percentage of people aware of the limits on residence status of foreigners was 46 per cent in 1980, 63.6 per cent in 1988, and 72.8 per cent in 1990; on (2), the percentage of people who thought illegal work bad was 39.4 per cent in 1988 and 32.1 per cent in 1990, while that of those who thought it bad but inevitable was 45.4 per cent in 1988 and 55.0 per cent in 1990; on (3), the percentage supporting a continuation of the policy of not permitting unskilled workers to enter Japan was 24.2 per cent in 1988 and 14.1 per cent in 1990, those who would permit conditional entry were 51.9 per cent in 1988 and 56.5 per cent in 1990, while those who would permit unconditional entry in the same way as for Japanese was 14.9 per cent in 1990 (the same question was not asked in 1988). Kokusai Jinryu (The Immigration Newsmagazine) (May 1991), 21–8.

81. This does not mean simply a transfer from a type B state to a type A state, nor from a non-immigrant country to an immigrant one. In both types of state we see the friction between individual state sovereignty and universal human rights, and it is the reconstruction of the relational structure between these two that is the issue of today. The scene and phase of the problem will, of course, possibly vary from type to type.

4. ECONOMIC CO-OPERATION IN PLACE OF HISTORICAL REMORSE: JAPANESE POST-WAR SETTLEMENTS WITH CHINA, RUSSIA, AND KOREA IN THE CONTEXT OF THE COLD WAR

1. Asahi Shimbun (12 Sept. 1948).

2. Takeuchi Yoshimi, Gendai Chugokuron (On Contemporary China) (Kawade Shobo Shimin Bunko, 1951), 8.

3. Ibid., 10–11.

4. The San Francisco Treaty is referred to in Mainichi Shimbun (ed.), *Tainichi Heiwa Joyaku* (The Peace Treaty with Japan) (1952), 3–22.

5. Hosoya Chihiro, *San Francisco Kowa e no Michi* (The Road to the San Francisco Treaty) (Chuo Koronsha, 1984), 279–301.

6. These facts are documented in the excellent research covering both Taiwanese and Japanese texts by Ishii Akira. Kawada is mentioned by Ishii Akira, 'Nikka Heiwa Joyaku Teiketsu Kosho wo Meguru Jakkan no Mondai' (Several Problems Concerning the Negotiation of the Sino-Japanese Peace Treaty), *Tokyo Daigaku Kyoyogakubu Kyoyogakka Kiyo*, Issue 21 (1988) (further to be cited as Ishii I), 78–9. Kawada Isao wrote an autobiography, *Kawada Isao Jijoden* (Kawada Isao Jijoden-hakkokai, 1965), but its narrative stops at the end of the war.

7. Ishii I, 79–80.

8. Japanese Ministry of Foreign Affairs, *Nikka Heiwa Joyaku Kankei Ikken* (Files Concerning the Sino-Japanese Peace Treaty), i. 412. All citations are taken from the English texts which have been made public by the foreign ministries of both countries. Slight corrections have been made by the author.

9. Ibid., 417.

10. Ibid., iii. 28–9.

11. Ibid., i. 449.

12. Ibid., 450.

13. Ibid., 451.

14. Ibid., 451.

15. Japan's preliminary draft has been published in its entirety by Ishii (1988) 'Nikka Heiwa Joyaku no Kosho Katei—Nihongawa Dai-ichiji Soan wo Megutte' (The Process of Negotiation of the Sino-Japanese Peace Treaty), in *Chugoku—Shakai to Bunka*, iii. 207–9.

16. *Nikka Heiwa Joyaku Kankei Ikken*, iii. 15–18.

17. Ishii I, 86.

18. *Nikka Heiwa Joyaku Kankei Ikken*, i. 460.

19. Ishii I, 86–7.

20. *Nikka Heiwa Joyaku Kankei Ikken*, iii. 21–2.

21. Ishii I, 88.

22. Ibid., 88.

23. *Nikka Heiwa Joyaku Kankei Ikken*, i. 497–8.

24. Ishii I, 88–9.

25. Ibid., 89.

26. *Nikka Heiwa Joyaku Kankei Ikken*, i. 571–2.

27. Ibid., 575–6.

28. Ibid., 611–12.

29. Ibid. iii. 36.

30. Ibid., ii. 7–8.

31. Ibid., iii. 194.

32. Ibid., 305.

33. Ibid., 228.

34. Ibid., ii. 294.

35. Ibid., 298.

36. Kashima Heiwa Kenkyujo (ed.), *Nihon Gaikoshi* (The Diplomatic History of Japan) vol. 28 (1973), 238–9.

37. *Asahi Shimbun* (8 June 1952; 5 Sept. 1952, evening edition).

38. Ibid. (26 Jan. 1952).

39. Ibid. (1 Aug. 1952).

40. It is well known that Dulles used Article 26 to threaten Shigemitsu, but the fact that three years later, that is after 28 April 1955, Japan would no longer have to offer the Soviets the same treaty conditions as the San Francisco treaty was first mentioned on 16 February 1955 in a memo from McLurkin, head of the Northeast Asian Affairs Dept., the US Department of State, to Snow, the legal adviser to the Far Eastern Issues Section. Snow agreed with this interpretation. *Foreign Relations of the United States (FRUS), 1955–1957*, vol. 23, part 1, pp. 19–21.

41. The Hokkkaido Shimbun obtained and published this document from the Hatoyama Ichiro Papers. The entire text is reproduced in Wada Haruki, 'Hopporyodo Mondai wo Saiko suru' (The Northern Territory Problem Revisited), *Sekai* (Feb. 1992), 223–4.

42. *Department of State Bulletin* (18 Oct. 1954), 579–86.

43. Ibid. (29 Nov. 1954), 811.

44. *FRUS, 1952–1954*, xiv. 1793.

45. Telex dated 10 Jan. 1955 from Dulles to US Ambassador Allison in Tokyo, *FRUS, 1955–57*, vol. 23, part 1, pp. 5–6.

46. Ibid., 59.

47. Ibid., 65–8.

48. US National Archive, 661.94/10–2055. First discovered by Kajiura Atsushi, 'Hopporyodo, Ryukyu no Kizokumondai wo Meguru Beikoku no Senryaku' (The US Strategy Concerning the Problem of Belongings of the Northern Territory and the Ryukyu), Ph.D. Dissertation (University of Tokyo, 1993), 318.

49. Ambassador Allison's report dated 1 June 1955, US National Archive, 661.94/6–255. Because the original was a telegram, gramatical corrections have been inserted by the author.

50. For further consideration of reference materials and evidence see Wada Haruki, *Hopporyodo Mondai wo Kangaeru* (The Northern Territory Problem) (Iwanami Shoten, 1990), 145–8.

51. For further detail of this process see ibid., 156–71.

52. Matsumoto Shunichi, *Mosukuwa ni Kakeru Niji* (Rainbow Reaching to Moscow) (Asahi Shimbunsha, 1966), 51.

53. *FRUS, 1955–57*, vol. 23, part 1, pp. 122–3.

54. Imamura Takeo, *Koizumi Shinzo-den* (The Biography of Koizumi Shinzo) (Bungei Shunju, 1973), 371–3.

55. *Asahi Shimbun* (9 Oct. 1955).

56. Ibid. (22 Oct. 1955, evening edition).

57. Ibid. (13 Nov. 1955).

58. Kubota Masaaki *Kremlin e no Shisetsu: Hopporyodo Kosho 1955–1983* (Mission to Kremlin) (Bungei Shunju, 1983), 157.

59. *FRUS, 1955–57*, vol. 23, part 1, p. 203.

60. Kubota Masaaki, '"Okinawa Fuhenkan" no Dulles Keikoku' (Dulles's Warning of No Return of Okinawa), *Kankai* (Sept. 1981), 180–1.

61. Memo from the US Department of State to the US Embassy in Japan, believed to have been dated 27 Aug. 1956, *FRUS, 1955–57*, vol. 23, part 1, pp. 210–11.

62. Ambassador Allison's report dated 30 Aug. 1956, ibid., 212–13.

63. From a report submitted by Spielman on 1 Sept. 1956, ibid., 217.

64. Report given by Radford to Robertson, Assistant Secretary of State, on 29 Aug. 1956, ibid., 221–2.

65. Ibid., 216–20.

66. Ibid., 226.

67. Tanaka Takahiko, *Nisso Kokko Kaifuku no Shiteki Kenkyu* (Historical Research on the Recovery of Soviet-Japanese Diplomatic Relations) (Yuhikaku, 1993), 275–7.

68. Matsumoto, op. cit., 143–7.

69. *Zoku Shigemitsu Mamoru Shuki* (Shigemitsu Mamoru Papers, Part II) (Chuo Koronsha, 1983), 800.

70. *Asahi Shimbun* (28 Nov. 1956).

71. Hara Yoshihisa, *Nichibei Kankei no Kozu* (The Framework of US–Japanese Relations) (Nihon Hoso Shuppan Kyokai, 1991), 66–70.

72. *Department of State Bulletin* (8 July 1957), 72.

73. Refer to Hara Yoshihisa, op. cit., pp. 138–87.

74. *Daisanjuku Kokkai Shugiin Yosan Iinkai Kaigiroku* (Records of the 39th Diet House of Representatives Budgetary Committee), part 2, pp. 15, 22, 24, 25. At the time of discussion for ratification of the Peace Treaty in the Diet on 19 October 1951 Nishimura Kumao, in response to the question of a Diet member, stated that the government thought the reference to the Kurils Islands in the text of the Treaty was inclusive of both the Northern and the Southern Kurils. *Daijunikai Kokkai Shugiin Heiwajoyaku oyobi Nichibei Anzenhosho Joyaku Tokubetsu Iinkai Kaigiroku* (Records of the 12th Diet House of Representatives Special Committee on the Peace Treaty and the US–Japanese Security Pact), part 4, p. 18.

75. *Daisanjuku Kokkai Shugiin Yosan Iinkai Kaigiroku*, iii. 1.

76. *Zoho Kaitei Hopporyodo Mondai Shiryoshu* (The Enlarged Collection of Materials Concerning the Northern Territory Problem) (Hopporyodo Mondai Taisaku Kyokai, 1972), 234.

77. Ibid., 232.

78. One of the best works on this problem is Yi Won-tok, 'Nihon no Sengo Shori Gaiko no Ichikenkyu Nikkan Seijoka Kosho (1951–1965) wo Chushin ni'

(The Negotiations for the Normalization of Japanese–Korean Relations: A Study of the Japanese Post-war Settling), Ph.D. dissertation (University of Tokyo, 1993).

79. *Nihon Gaiko-shi*, 28, 33–34.

80. Yu Chin-ho, '*Hanil hoetam*' (Japanese–Korean Negotiation), *Chungang ilbo* (26 Sept. 1983).

81. Ibid.

82. *Nihon Gaiko-shi*, 28, 39–40.

83. *Yu Chin-ho, Chungang ilbo* (23 Sept. 1983).

84. *Nihon Gaiko-shi*, 28. *Hanir kwankye saryochip* (Collection of Documents of the Japanese–Korean Relations), vol. 1 (Institute of Asian Affairs, Korea University, 1976), 92–4. At the first conference, basic issues concerning the treaty were discussed, as mentioned by Takasaki Soji, 'Nikkan Kaidan no Keika to Shokuminchika Sekinin—August 1945–April 1952' (the Process of Korean–Japanese Negotiations and the Responsibility of Colonization), in *Rekishigaku Kenkyu* (Sept. 1985), 10–11.

85. *Hanil Kwankye saryochip*, 1, 108–9. The debate over Kubota's statement is reconstructed from various sources by Takasaki Soji, '*Mogen*' *no Genkei: Nihonjin no Chosenkan* (Prototypes of Shameless Utterings) (Kisosha, 1990), chapter 2.

86. *Asahi Shimbun* (22 Oct. 1953).

87. Wada Haruki, *Kankoku Minshu wo Mitsumerukoto* (Looking at the Korean People) (Sojusha, 1981), 157–8.

88. On 21 October 1957 Dulles informed Kono Ichiro that he had been unable to persuade Syngman Rhee. *FRUS, 1955–1957*, vol. 23, part 1, p. 526.

89. *Hanir kwankye saryochip*, 1, 136–7.

90. Yamamoto Takeshi, 'Nikkan Kokko Seijoka' (The Normalization of Japanese–Korean Diplomatic Relations), in *Sengo Nihon Gaikoshi* (The Postwar Diplomatic History of Japan), vol. 2 (Sanseido, 1983), 325–6. The report is somewhat confused.

91. *Hanil kwankye saryochip*, 1, 142–6.

92. *Nihon Gaiko-shi*, vol. 29 (1973), 327–8.

93. Ibid., 282–7.

94. Ibid., 301–5.

95. Kim Tong-jo, 'Hanil hoetam', *Chungang ilbo* (2 Sept. 1984).

96. Ibid. (3 Sept. 1984).

97. Ibid. (3 Sept. 1984).

98. *Asahi Shimbun* (21 Feb. 1965).

99. *Sangiin Kaigiroku* (Minutes from the House of Councilors Meeting), vol. 8 (19 Nov. 1965), 82.

100. Nicchu Kokko Kaihuku Sokushin Giinrenmei (ed.), *Nicchu Kokko Kaifuku Kankeishiryoshu* (Collection of Documents Concerning the Recovery of Sino-Japanese Diplomatic Relations) (1972), 141–2.

101. *Asahi Shimbun* (28 Aug. 1972, evening edition).

102. Matsumoto Hirokazu, 'Nicchu Kokko Seijoka' (The Normalization of Sino-Japanese Diplomatic Relations), *Sengo Nihon Gaiko-shi*, 2, 230–1. Tanaka Akihiko, *Nicchu Kankei 1945–1990* (Sino-Japanese Relations 1945–1990) (University of Tokyo Press, 1991), 80.

103. *Nicchu Kokko Kaifuku Kankei Shiryoshu*.

104. Ibid.

105. Comparative studies of Chou and Tanaka's speeches are made by Takeuchi Yoshimi, 'Zenji Fubo, Koji no Shi' (Do not Forget the Mistakes of the Past, Learn for the Future), in *Takeuchi Yoshimi Zenshu* (Works of Takeuchi Yoshimi), vol. 11 (Chikuma Shubo, 1981).

106. *Nicchu Kokko Kaifuku Kankei Shiryoshu*.

107. Matsumoto Hirokazu, op. cit., 233, 234. Tanaka, op. cit., 80–1.

108. *Yomiuri Shimbun* (27 Aug. 1982).

5. THE FEMINIZATION OF THE LABOUR MARKET

1. Claudia von Werlhof, 'Women's Work: The Blind Spot in the Critique of Political Economy,' in Maria Mies, Veronica Bennholdt–Thomsen, and Claudia von Werlhof, *Women, The Last Colony* (London: Zed Books Ltd., 1988).

2. Un'ei-iinkai (Steering Committee), 'Joron—Gendai Nihon Shakai no Kozo to Tokushusei' (The Structure and Characteristics of Contemporary Japanese Society: Introduction), Tokyo Daigaku Shakaikagaku Kenkyusho (The Institute of Social Science (ISS), University of Tokyo) (ed.), *Gendai Nihon Shakai: 1 Kadai to Shikaku* (Contemporary Japanese Society, 1: Problems and Perspectives) (University of Tokyo Press, 1991), 3–5, 13, 15–16.

3. Baba Hiroji, 'Gendai Sekai to Nihon Kaisha Shugi' (Japanese Companyism and the Contemporary World), in ISS (ed.), op. cit.; Watanabe Osamu *'Yutakana Shakai' Nihon no Kozo* (The Structure of Japan, an 'Affluent Society') (Rodo Jumposha, 1990).

4. Baba, op. cit., 62, 71–2.

5. Watanabe, op. cit., 53, 56, 68.

6. Baba, op. cit., 74.

7. Watanabe, op. cit., 95.

8. Baba, op. cit., 78–80.

9. Ibid., 63.

10. Sumiya Mikio, 'Nihonteki Roshikankei ron no Saikosei—sono Zentaizo no Kochiku no Tame ni' (Reconstruction of Japanese Industrial Relations Theory), *Nihon rodo Kyokai Zasshi* (The Japan Institute of Labour Journal), vol. 26, No. 4/5 (1984).

11. Ibid., particularly p. 6.

12. Takenaka Emiko, Sengo Joshi Rodo Shiron (A History of Women's Work since the War) (Yuhikaku, 1989).

13. Nakanishi Yo, 'Keizaigaku to "Kazoku"' (Economics and the 'Family'), *Kazokushi Kenkyu* (History of Family), No. 6 (1982), 75.

14. Werlhof, op. cit.

15. The Ministry of Labour Women's Bureau's Annual, *The Labour Conditions of Women*, offers relatively easy access to these numbers, to which I will not make detailed references.

16. Somucho (Management and Co-ordination Agency), *Kokumin no Seikatsu Kodo: Showa 61 nen Shakai-Seikatsu Kihon Chosa no Kaisetsu* (Survey on Time Use and Leisure Activities) (1988).

17. Nakamura Masanori (ed.), *Gijutsu Kakushin to Josei Rodo* (Technological Innovation and Women's Labour) (United Nations University and University of Tokyo Press, 1985), particularly table 2 of the introductory chapter and table 2 of chapter 5.

18. The 1991 *Labour White Paper* focused on women and youth in its Part 2, *Josei Rodosha, Jakunen Rodosha no Genjo to Kadai* (Women and Young Workers' Current Situation and Policy Objectives), but in analysing wage differences between women and men it relies solely on the *Basic Survey on Wage Structure*. This is in order to observe differences among full-time workers, excluding part-timers. Rodosho (Ministry of Labour), *Rodo Hakusho* (Labour White Paper), (Japan Institute of Labour, 1991), 132. In order to know the causes of these differences, however, it would seem necessary to analyse the various factors that compose them, so to the extent that a process of first analysing and then viewing comprehensively data for part-time workers is lacking in the *White Paper*, it is difficult to say that there is any real grasp of the nature of these gender-based wage differences.

19. Among the countries that report separate male/female wage statistics to the ILO, the USA and European countries report either hourly wage proportions or earned income per hour worked, but Japan reports on a monthly basis the total actual wage derived from *The Monthly Labour Survey*. Cf. ILO, Yearbook of Labour Statistics.

20. Koyo Shokugyo Sogo Kenkyusho (National Institute of Employment and vocational Research) (ed.), *Joshi Rodo no Shin Jidai* (The New Era of Women's Labour) (University of Tokyo Press, 1987), 149 f.; Walby, Sylvia (ed.), *Gender Segregation at Work* (Philadelphia: Open University Press, 1988), 1.

21. Ishikawa Tsuneo, 'Chingin Niju-kozo no rironteki kento' (A theoretical examination of the dualism in wage structure), in Tsuchiya Moriaki, and Miwa Yoshoro (eds.), *Nihon no Chusho Kigyo* (Middle and Small-sized Companies in Japan) (University of Tokyo Press, 1989), 47.

21a. Ibid.

22. Koike Kazuo, *Shigoto no Keizaigaku* (Economics of Occupation) (Toyo Keizai Shinposha, 1991), 48, 142–3.

23. OECD (Organization for Economic Co-operation and Development), *The Integration of Women into the Economy* (Paris: OECD, 1985), 68.

24. Koike, op. cit., chapter 8.

25. Kumazawa Makoto, *Portraits of the Japanese Workplace, Labor Movements, Workers, and Managers*, ed. Andrew Gordon, trans. Andrew Gordon and Mikiso Hana (Boulder, Colo.: Westview Press, 1996), 170–2; Takenaka, op. cit., 276–7.

26. Kumazawa, op. cit., 151–2.

27. Osawa Mari, 'Nihon no "Paatotaimu Rodo" towa Nanika' (What is So-called Part-Time Work in Japan?), *Kikan Rodoho* (Quarterly Journal on Labour Law), No. 170 (1994).

28. Rodosho (Ministry of Labour), Rodo-daijin kambo seisakuchosabu (ed.), *Heisei 2-nen Paatotaimu no Jittai: Paatotaimu Rodosha Sogo Jittai Chosa Hokoku* (The Actual Situation of Part-Time Workers in 1990: a Report of a Comprehensive Survey on Part-Time Workers) (Ministry of Finance Printing Bureau, 1992).

29. Nagase Nobuko, 'Kikon Joshi no Koyo-Shugyo Keitai no Sentaku ni Kansuru Jissho-Bunseki' (Part-Time and Full-Time Work in Japan: Work Selection and Wages), *Nihon Rodo Kenkyu Zasshi* (The Monthly Journal of the Japan Institute of Labour), No. 418 (1994).

30. Nagase Nobuko, ' "Paato" Sentaku no Jihatsusei to Chingin Kansu' (An Analysis of Involuntary 'Part-Time' Workers and their Wages), *Nihon Keizai Kenkyu* (JCER Economic Journal), No. 28 (1995).

31. Hanami Tadashi, 'Nihonteki Sabetsu no Kozo: 5-nen de Towareru Fujin Gyosei' (The Structure of Japanese-style Discrimination: Public Administration for Women Fraught with Problems Five Years after the Implementation of the Eqaul Employment Opportunity Law), *Juristo*, No. 988 (1991).

32. Wanda Anasz, Ueda Hirofumi, and Yamamoto Kiyoshi, 'Industrial Structures in Japan: Pyramidal Organization in the Automobile and the Electrical/Electronics Industries', *Annals of the Institute of Social Science*, No. 28 (1987).

33. Chuo Daigaku Keizai Kenkyusho (Institute of Economics of Chuo University), *ME Gijutsu Kakushinka no Shitauke Kogyo to Noson Henbo* (Subcontracting Industries and Social Change of Rural Districts as a Result of ME Innovation) (Chuo daigaku shuppankai, 1985), 221–2.

34. Ibid., 30–3.

35. Ibid., chapter 2.

36. Tokunaga Shigeyoshi, and Sugimoto Noriyuki (eds.), *FA kara CIM e: Hitachi no Jirei Kenkyu* (From FA to CIM: A Case Study of Hitachi) (Dobunkan, 1990), 351–2.

37. Ibid., 232–4, 237–40.

38. Ibid., 240, 239.

39. Ibid., 302.

40. Josei Shokugyo Zaidan (Japan Institute of Women's Employment), *Joshi Kanrishoku Chosa Kekka Hokokusho* (Report of a Survey on Female Managers in Large Companies) (1990).

41. Somucho, op. cit.

42. Asahikasei Tomobataraki Kazoku Kenkyujo (Asahikasei Institute for Study of Dual-Income Families), *Tomobataraki Kazoku/Sengyo Shufu Kazoku Hikaku Chosa*

Hokokusho (Report of a Comparative Survey of Dual-Income Families and Single-Income Families) (1989), 22–3.

43. Keizai Kikakucho (Economic Planning Agency) (ed.), *Seikatsu Jikan no Kozo Bunseki: Jikan no Tsukawarekata to Seikatsu no Shitsu* (A Study of Time Budget Structure: Time Use and Quality of Life) (1975), 31.

44. Ito Setsu and Amano Hiroko, *Seikatsu Jikan to Seikatsu Yoshiki* (Time Use and Mode of Life) (Koseikan, 1989), 174.

45. Sorifu (Prime Minister's Office), *Fujin no Seikatsu to Ishiki, Kokusai Hikaku Chosa Kekka Hokokusho* (International Comparative Survey on Life and Attitudes of Women in Six countries) (1984), 174–209.

46. Asahikasei Tomobataraki Kazoku Kenkyujo (Asahikasei Institute for Study of Dual-Income Families), *Tokyo, Nyu Yoku, Rondon, Tomobataraki Kazoku no Seikatsu Hikaku Chosa* (Report of a Comparative survey on Life and Work of Dual-Income Families in Tokyo, New York, and London) (1990), 8, 12, 14–16.

47. Sorifu, op. cit.; cf. Gisela Erler, 'The German Paradox, Non-feminization of the Labor Force and Post-industrial Social Policies', in Jane Jensen, Elisabeth Hagen, and Ceallaigh Reddy (eds.), *Feminization of the Labour Force, Paradoxes and Promises* (Cambridge: Polity Press, 1988).

48. Cf. Fujisaki Hiroko, 'Katei wa Kosoku ka Supringubodo ka: Katei no Jokyo ni Sayu Sareru Josei' (Is Family Restraint or a Springboard for Women), in Sodei Takako and Yano Masakazu (eds.), *Gendai Josei no Chii* (The Status of Women Today) (Keiso shobo, 1987), 142.

49. Koyo Shokugyo Sogo Kenkyusho (National Institute of Employment and vocational Research), *Josei no Shokuba Shinshutsu to Kazokukono no Henka ni Kansuru Chosakekka Hokokusho (Zoku): 4, 5-Saiji wo Motsu Fubo wo Taisho to Shita Chosa Kara* (An Investigation of Changes in the Function of the Family Unit in Relation to Women's Participation in the Workforce: Continued) (1986), 21.

50. Sylvia Walby, *Theorizing Patriarchy* (Oxford: Basil Blackwell, 1990), 83.

51. Sechiyama Kaku, 'Kafuchosei o Megutte' (On Patriarchy), in Ehara Yumiko (ed.), *Feminizumu Ronso: 70 Nendai kara 90 Nendai e* (Debates in Feminism, from 1970s to 90s) (Keiso shobo, 1990).

52. Ueno Chizuko, *Kafuchosei to Shihonsei—Marukusu-Shugi Feminizumu no Chihei* (Patriarchy and Capitalism: the Horizon of Marxist Feminism) (Iwanami shoten, 1990), 25, 51, 66, 181–182.

53. Ibid., 58, 126.

54. Walby, op. cit., 24.

55. Mori Tateshi, *Koyo kankei no seisei* (The Formation of the Employment Relationship) (Bokutakusha, 1988), 5–7, 41–3.

56. Christine Delphy, *Close to Home: A Materialist Analysis of Women's Oppression* (London: Hutchinson, 1984), 20, also cf. Walby (ed.), *Gender Segregation at Work*, 22.

57. Hayashi Chiyo, 'Showa 63-Nendo Zenkoku Boshi Setai to Jittai Chosa Kekka no Gaiyo (Koseisho Jido Katei Kyoku) o yonde' (On Reading the Summary Report

of 1988 National Survey on Female-Headed Households), *Fujin Tsushin* (Women's Newsletter) (October 1990).

58. Koseisho (Ministry of Health and Welfare), *Kosei Hakusho: Showa 61-Nen Ban* (Health and Welfare White Paper for 1986) (Kosei Tokei Kyokai, 1987), 165.

59. Apart from the Sapporo Television documentary entitled *Kaasan ga Shinda* (Mum has Died), books and articles as follow have been published in relation to this incident. Terakubo Mitsuyoshi, *Fukushi ga Hito o Korosu Toki* (When Welfare Administration Kills People) (Akebi Shobo, 1988); Mizushima Hiroaki, *Kaasan ga Shinda* (Mum has Died) (Hitonaru shobo, 1990); Hisada Megumi and Nakagawa Kazunori, '"Kaasan ga Shinda" no Uso' (Lies in 'Mum has Died'), *Bungei Shunjyu* (Aug. 1992); Osawa Mari, 'Bye-bye Corporate Warriors: The Formation of a Corporate-Centred Society and Gender-Biased Social Policies in Japan', *Annals of the Institute of Social Science*, No. 35 (1993).

60. Cf. Osawa Mari, *Igirisu Shakai Seisaku Shi—Kyuhinho to Fukushi Kokka* (A History of Social Policy in Modern Britain: From Poor Law to the Welfare State) (University of Tokyo Press, 1986).

6. THE AGEING SOCIETY, THE FAMILY, AND SOCIAL POLICY

1. The Ministry of Health and Welfare, too, devoted the 1986 edition of its annual report, *Kosei Hakusho* (White Paper on Welfare) (January 1987), to the discussion of the same theme. It should also be pointed out that matters pertaining to social security have traditionally been regarded as basically falling under the jurisdiction of the national government.

2. According to statistics compiled in 1993 by the French INSEE, the percentage share of family allowances in social security benefits as recently as in 1991 was a minuscule 0.9% in Japan, compared with 10.3% for Denmark, 9.6% for Britain, 8.2% for France, and 6.0% for Germany.

3. According to the 1995 edition of the *White Paper on Welfare* (a table on p. 327), social security benefits as percentage of National Income in different countries compared as follows as of 1989: Sweden 44.2%, France 33.6%, former West Germany 28.4%, Britain 22.1%, the United States 15.7%, and Japan 13.9%.

4. For instance, the 1993 edition of the *White Paper on Welfare* adopted the subtitle 'For Children Who are to Open up a New Future: A Search for Ways of Providing Social Support to Child-Raising'.

5. Harada Sumitaka, '"Nihongata Fukushi Shakai" Ron no Kazokuzo' (The Image of the Family Assumed by the Thesis on 'Japanese-style Welfare Society'), the Institute of Social Science, University of Tokyo (ed.), *Tenkanki no Fukushi Kokka* (Welfare States at the Turning Point), Vol. 2 (University of Tokyo Press, 1988).

6. For a more detailed exposition and notes of the author's main contentions in this paper, see Harada Sumitaka, 'Koreika Shakai to Kazoku' (Ageing Society and the Family), in the Institute of Social Science, University of Tokyo (ed.), *Gendai Nihon*

Shakai, 6 (Contemporary Japanese Society, 6) (University of Tokyo Press, 1992); Harada Sumitaka, 'The Aging Society, the Family, and Social Policy', *Occasional Papers Series in Law and Society*, No. 8, Institute of Social Science (University of Tokyo, 1996).

7. To put it briefly, the 'principle of neutrality' principle asserts that the state should not be concerned—through its implementation not simply of the social security laws, but also of the Civil Code's Family Law—with trying to influence the choices which direct private behaviour affecting the family but with a closer examination of the social situations that result from these choices.

8. The 'household' system was a family system founded upon a family registration system which required a family consisting of three generations of relatives of a direct lineage, or a family group of a more extensive coverage, to register on a 'house-by-house' basis. Members of each house were subject to rule by its 'house head' by virtue of his holding the 'headship of the house', with the property of the house being in its entirety from one generation of house head to the next (usually the eldest son), along with the headship of the house. The right to be supported by, and the duty to support, members of the house were meticulously defined, centred around the duty of relatives of a lineal relationship to live together, in the following order: (1) lineal ascendants; (2) lineal descendants; (3) spouse; (4) relatives by affinity belonging to the same 'house'; (5) brothers and sisters; and (6) other members.

9. Prior to the mid-1960s, when the traditional practices associated with three-generation families composed of lineal relatives were still influential, divorce cases where the husband took charge of the children within the framework of the 'house' with the wife leaving the 'house' alone outnumbered those where the wife took charge of the children. In contrast, it is practically impossible for the husband in the nuclear family to take the children under his custody upon divorce, even if he wanted to do so. The establishment in 1962 of a scheme for paying child-rearing allowance for the guardian contributed significantly to the increased economic independence of the wife after a divorce.

10. The recommendation entitled 'Asu no Kateiseikatsu no Tameni' (For a Family Life Tomorrow). The Council was a consultative body to the Minister of Welfare.

11. Especially important among these are (*a*), (*b*), and (*c*), but (*g*), too, is noteworthy in the sense that the policy documents announced during this period identified social welfare services as constituting an important policy area of its own, distinct from that of public assistance to be provided to people in distress. Consequently, government outlays for social welfare services began to increase by leaps and bounds with the years 1971–2 as the turning point, and outpaced public assistance outlays in 1974. However, see also n. 14.

12. It should be kept in mind, none the less, that this decision was meant to pay off the long overdue 'bills' that had accumulated over years, and as such was in accord with the intent of employers' associations which were eager to restrain increases in burdens of retirement allowances.

13. The National Census of 1970 found that 53.3% of the families with people aged 65 or older were three-generation families, while approximately three-quarters of all the aged people were living with their children.

14. Social welfare benefits increased at much lower rates than pension and medical care benefits. Consequently, the share of social welfare benefits, including those paid as public assistance, in the total social security outlays showed a gradual decrease from 17–18% in the mid-1970s to approximately 10% in 1990.

15. Throughout the remaining years of the 1980s, a ceiling remained to be imposed strictly on annual increments in social security outlays.

16. A spouse's legally guaranteed portion in the inheritance used to be set at one-third in case the child[ren] and the spouse were the successors, and one-half in case a lineal ascendant or ascendants and the spouse were the successors; the ratios were respectively raised to one-half and two-thirds. The same revision of the Civil Code put into effect a new arrangement whereby the inheritor who has done much to care for and nurse the inheritee should be entitled to receive a portion of the inheritance as a special 'compensation' for his/her caretaking contribution.

17. Fukutake Tadashi, 'Katsuryokuaru Fukushi Shakai to Shakai Hosho' (A Vigorous Welfare Society and Social Security), in Shakai Hosho Kenkyusho (ed.), Shakai Hosho no Kihon Mondai (Fundamental Problems of Social Security) (University of Tokyo Press, 1983), 210, 215.

18. Koseisho Daijin Kambo Seisakuka (Policy Division, Minister's Secretariat, Ministry of Health and Welfare) (ed.), 21-Seiki Fukushi Bijon (Vision of Welfare in the Twenty-first Century) (Daiichi Hoki, 1994), 86.

19. The figure is the estimate presented in a December 1994 report of the Study Group on the Support System for the Nursing and Self-Reliance of the Elderly, to be referred to in IV-1 (3)-iv. The remaining 40% of the costs is taken up by the costs for institutional services (35%) and the costs for services provided to aged persons being taken care of at home (5%).

20. Mainichi Shimbun's nationwide polls on family planning reveal that, on the question of 'children taking care of their aged parents', 26% of the respondents in 1975 thought this to be a 'good custom', and 49% thought it to be a 'natural duty', but that the percentages precipitated during the 1980s, declining to 17% and 32%, respectively, by 1992.

21. Prime Minister's Office, 'Koreiki no Seikatsu Imeji ni taisuru Yoron Chosa' (An Opinion Poll on the Image of One's Life in Old Age) (1993).

22. This does not mean to deny the important role the family can perform in the care of the aged by its very existence and by showing concern for the aged. The author's intent is to question the idea of linking this important role directly with the traditional principle of the family's self-help, because the family's show of concern for its aged members can be meaningful by itself, even when this is not linked up with traditional values.

23. Between 1965 and 1993, the average age of the first marriage for women rose from 24.5 to 26.1 years, and the percentage of unmarried women of between 25 and 29 years increased from 19.0% to 44.6%.

24. See, for instance, the 1993 edition of the *White Paper on Welfare*, 58, and the 1994 edition, 207.

25. For instance, the recent recommendation compiled by the Advisory Council on the Social Security System (July 1955) defines the basic task of policy measures in support of childrearing to be 'the creation of an environment in which working women can reconcile their domestic tasks and occupational duties with ease, and the creation of an environment in which women can give birth to children with pleasure and hope, and in which the children can grow healthily' (pp. 22–3).

26. Among various policy documents, the 1991 edition of the *White Paper on Welfare* explicitly upheld this view by stressing the need for establishing 'a comprehensive family policy' for the first time (p. 100), but subsequent policy documents have, for some unknown reason, obscured this view and failed to develop it any further.

27. This is corroborated, for instance, by the fact that various phenomena characteristic of the changes taking place in the family in western Europe—such as a significant increase in the divorce rate, a decrease in the rate of marriage coupled with an increase in *de facto* marriages, and an increase in the number of illegitimate children—have not yet manifested themselves very clearly in Japan; in other words, even though the first marriage age is getting higher, the 'disinstitutionalization' of the marriage system and the family system themselves has not yet progressed too far, nor has the practice of viewing the family relationship as one of 'contract' taken root in Japan. Another piece of corroborating evidence is that the percentage of aged parents living with their children, though on the decline, still remains much higher than in western Europe, as demonstrated in Table 6.7.

7. THE PROBLEM OF LAND USE AND LAND PRICES

1. This particularly affected commercial properties in the wake of the 'Iwato keiki'.

2. Koyama, 'Daitan na shiken seigen o' (Toward a bold restriction of private rights), *Chuo koron* (Aug. 1972), 205.

3. During this period, the National Land Use Planning Law was enacted. The introduction of filing and permit requirements for land transactions was aimed at controlling land prices through restrictions imposed on trade, and as such reflected a partial adoption of the former approach referred to in the main text. As indicated in the Report of the National Land Agency Round Table referred to in the next footnote, 'The reason for introducing a policy of strict control is that, the land problem having worsened, there are limits to the policy of promoting supply that have been pursued to this point. Our attention fell to the demand side, and in order to restrict demand, it was necessary to introduce

restrictions at the point where land transactions take place.' In fact, the 'land price stability' from 1982 to 1986 is difficult to ascribe to the system of advisory notification, limited as it is to large-scale transactions. As will be discussed in greater detail later, the impact of the advisory notification system of that time was extremely mild in practice.

4. Kokudocho Tochikyoku (National Land Agency, Land Bureau), 'Asu no Tochi o Kangaeru—Tochi Mondai Kondankai no Teigen' (Thinking of Tomorrow's Land: Report of the Land Problem Roundtable) (June 1983), 23–5.

5. However, there was a clear difference in the timing in Tokyo and Osaka, the former experiencing the worst of the rise in 1987–8, the latter in 1988–90.

6. Concerning this, see Kaneko, 'Kigyo Shakai no Keisei: "Shisan Shoyu Minshu Shugi" no Kiketsu' (The Structure of Industrial Societies and the Society of Japan: The End of the 'Property Owning' Democracy) Gendai Nihon Shakai (Contemporary Japanese Society), vol. 5 (1992). This work dedicates considerable space to the appraisal of Japanese housing policy in the post-war period, and is rich in insights; it is highly recommended as a reference.

7. Hashimoto, 'Dai Kigyo Taisei no Keizai Kozo' (The Economic Structure of Large Corporate Organizations), Gendai Nihon Shakai (Contemporary Japanese Societly), vol. 5 (1992), 117.

8. From a Tokyo branch office of a certain urban bank it has been heard that it was common for the banks themselves to search out properties to sell, and put a deal together explaining to a client with a capital base that a future sale would be sure to turn a profit; lend that client a sum nearly equal to the purchase price; wait and watch as the price of the land rose, while searching for a further piece of land for the client to buy in part exchange for the original property; and line up a separate client to purchase the original property. In these circumstances, it is thought that internal audit procedures broke down, the separation of managers became impossible to maintain, and various inappropriate loans came to be made as a result.

9. For example, the Interim Report on Tax Reform published 28 April 1988 stresses, concerning the 'basic way of thinking' on this issue, that 'in principle, the tax system influences economic activity through the market; it cannot have the direct influence enjoyed, for instance, by rules concerning land use. Therefore, if the tax system is to be used to direct the behaviour of individuals and enterprises in accordance with particular policy aims, it is essential that detailed provisions be prepared in advance in the areas of city planning etc. In this sense, this Committee has emphasized the supplementary and directive role of tax measures.'

10. The entire amount is taxable if the land had been held for less than three years prior to the sale. For land held more than three years, one half of the amount is taxed. This measure was introduced in the tax reform of 1964.

11. Effective 1 January 1974. However, properties acquired after 21 April 1973 are subject to this provision from the date of acquisition. In this case, income on short-term transfers is considered by have been earned after 1 January 1969.

12. Zeisei Chosakai (Investigatory Committee on the Tax System), 'Tochi Zeisei no Arikata ni Tsuiteno Kihon Hoshin' (Basic Report on the State of the Land Tax System), 33.

13. This was compiled from a simple five-year average of figures contained in '1989: Yearly Report on Land Price Trends', 61, 72 ff.

14. Nihon Fudosan Kenkyujo (Japan Real Estate Institute), *Shigaichi Kakaku Shisu* (Urban land price index) (Dec. 1991).

15. Apart from this, Nihon Fudosan Kanteishi-kai (Japan Association of Real Estate Appraisal), *Tokyo-to Chika Doko Chosa* (Survey of land price trends in Tokyo) (Dec. 1991), prepared for the City of Tokyo, price movements in Tokyo from 1 October 1989 to 1 October 1990 showed a drop of 3.6% among commercial properties in the 23 wards, and 6.0% among residential properties. This differs sharply from the figures used in preparing this article. This is presumably due to a difference in the properties and districts used in sampling. This figures do match, however, with respect to residential properties.

16. Afterward, three types of districts were added, to make seven in all. The added district types were: Prospective Urban Renewal Project Districts (1974); Promotion Areas (1975); District Plans (1980).

17. Inamoto, 'Toshi to nochi 1968–88 (Cities and Agricultural Land, 1968–88)', Nosei chosa iinkai [Research Committee on Agricultural Policy] (ed.), *Kihon Ho Nosei ka ni Okeru Nogyo/Nosei to Kongo no Kadai* (Agriculture under current policy, and emerging agricultural issues) (Mar. 1988). For recent work on the establishment and operation of the line-drawing system, see Ishida Y., *Toshi Nogyo to Tochi Riyo Keikaku* (Urban agriculture and city planning) (1990), Tashiro Y., *Keikaku-teki Toshi Nogyo e no Chosen* (Toward a systemmatic approach to urban agriculture) (1991).

18. When district boundaries are drawn under the City Planning Act, the aims for 'preparation, development, and preservation' are spelled out in the Act. Toshi Keikaku Ho (City Planning Law) § 7(4) (Law no. 100 of 1968). Given the uncertainty over the legally binding nature of this language, and the ways in which it is applied in practice, it is not appropriate to view these provisions as constituting a 'master plan'. There is also a need to specify exactly what subordinate plans are to be governed by such a master plan. In the current re-examination of the City Planning Act, consideration is being given to strengthening the provisions on 'preparation, development, and preservation', making these matters the subject of a master plan by governors. As a complementary measure, local councils would establish local 'master plans'. Under this structure, a detailed plan would consist of 'land-use zones' specified by the former, and 'district plans' (*chiku keikaku*) set down by the latter authorities. In this way, it would be possible to set up a multi-layered system of planning control.

19. The 'limitation of private rights' referred to here is a corollary to liberalization. For instance, working on the assumption that some loss of solar access on account of a loosening of height restrictions and floor space area limitations ought to be tolerated, low-rise residential zoning is criticized, and conversion to

    mid-rise residential and commercial use is encouraged. It should be marked carefully that this does not entail a restriction of rights of private ownership, but on rights of use.

20. Another important event in the liberalization that took place during this period may be found in the easing of restrictions in the guidance issued by local authorities on residential development projects (reducing the burden to be born by developers). This issue is not treated in this article. For a criticism of liberalization in this area, and a consideration of the diverse models that might be applied to this problem, see Igarashi, *Toshi Saisei no Senryaku—Kisei Ho kara Sozo Ho e* (Strategies for regenerating the city—from restrictive laws to creative laws) (1986). This piece should be read together with other works by the same author.

21. 'District planning based upon separate floor space restrictions for each use-district' was settled upon as a variation upon the general scheme of 'district planning'.

22. The master plan referred to here might be either a plan developed by local authorities under the aegis of superior wide-area planning regulations, or a plan introduced for regulatory purposes by a superior adminstrative body.

23. Concerning use of the district planning system, at the time of writing (March 1990), 225 local authorities have introduced district plans. The total number of districts is 698, with a total area of 21,953 hectares. By prefectural unit, the distribution of districts is comparatively large in Tokyo (119 districts); Saitama (81 districts); and Chiba (69 districts). There are 21 redevelopment districts (including 6 in Tokyo and 5 in Osaka), amounting to 572 hectares. These figures show that the system is stalled at the experimental stage at present. All proposals put forward to date have been approved unanimously by those with an interest in land in the affected districts; because of the large number of persons with an interest in land, in many cases 'district planning' is extremely time-consuming. On the other hand, it is said that in the case of redevelopment district planning, because such projects often involve vacant industrial land, and because the number of parties with an interest in land is smaller in such areas, often consisting primarily of companies, setting up the agreement is easier.

24. The term 'land myth' is not a recent coinage. The person who first used this phrase to refer to the social conditions underlying the current land problem was Hanayama Ken, in 'Tochi shinwa no jidai' (The Age of the Land Myth), published in three parts is *Ekonomisuto* (28 August, 4 September, and 11 September 1979). Since the publication of *Chika to Tochi Seisaku (Land Prices and Land Policy)* with Shinzawa, the students of the land problem have been greatly in his debt.

25. Zeisei Chosakai (Investigatory Committee on the Tax System), Tochi Zeisei no Arikata ni Tsuite no Kihon Hoshin (Basic Report on the State of the Tax System), 11.

26. According to the report cited in the previous footnote, the fact that 'on account of the various special exclusions applicable to land, and the special regulation on serial purchase, there is great potential for lightening the tax burden on land, and this makes it more attractive than other types of assets', the fact that 'the risk of

a drop in property values is small, the timing of sale can be chosen with a view to postponing income from the transfer', and the fact that 'valuation for inheritance tax purposes is below the actual value, and because of the exclusion of a portion of the assessed valuation in the case of small commercial and residential properties, it has special attractions.' The report further stated, 'in a time of spiralling land price inflation, land has come to be worth more than it will produce in income, with the result that the cost of holding the land compares quite favourably to the cost of acquiring it.' Investigatory Committee on the Tax System, Basic Report on the State of the Tax System, 11–12.

27. There is a partial misunderstanding on this point. See, e.g., the various articles that appear in *Tochi Kihon Ho o Yomu* (Reading the Basic Law on Land) (Homma et al., eds.). These sources assert that it was pressure from financial circles that caused the fourth point (restoring the profit from capital gain to society) to be quashed, and the fifth alone (burdens to be borne by the recipient of benefit) was adopted; but the facts differ. In an announcement, members of Keidanren (Federation of Economic Organizations) opposed the Special Enterprise Tax (or Large City Office Tax) that was the subject of discussion in the preparation of the Interim Report. But they did not particularly object to the inclusion of the capital gain and burden-and-benefit language that was the topic of so much discussion in the Basic Land Law. The National Land Agency, having put so much effort into refining the drafting of point five, might have assumed that it would be clearly understood; but there seem still perhaps to be some problems following its meaning. Kokudocho, Tochi Kyoku [National Land Agency, Land Bureau], *Chikujo Kaisetsu Tochi Kihon Ho* (The Basic Law on Land, Line by Line).

28. Translator's note: throughout this article, 'capital gain' is a translation of *kaihatsu rieki*. While this term translates literally as 'development benefit', it is clear from the context that capital gain—increase in the value of an asset that is not offset by an endogenous development cost—conveys what is intended.

29. Interim Report, 31.

30. The French Declaration of the Rights of Man, Article 2. For the theoretical premises of the Declaration, see Sieyès, *Reconnaissance et exposition raisonnée des droits de l'homme et du citoyen, Archives parlementaires*, t. VIII, pp. 256 et seq.; Inamoto, '1789 nen no/Hito oyobi shimin no kenri no sengen' (The 1789 Declaration of the Rights of Man), *Kihon-teki Jinken no Kenkyu* (Studies in Basic Human Rights), 109 (ed.) (Shakai Kagaku Kenkyujo (Institute of Social Science).

31. Ishii, 'Tochi no "Shiyu" to wa Nani ka' (On the Private Ownership of Land), *Chuo koron* (June 1979). See also the debate with Ryotaro Shiba at Ishii and Shiba, 'Nihon ni okeru "ko" to "shi"—tochi mondai o megutte' (Public versus Private in Japan—the land problem), *Chuo Koron* (Jul. 1976). In Professor Ishii's view, the duties associated with control exerted over land by the aristocratic order (*noblesse oblige*) lie at the foundation of the western sense of land ownership, and hence the early modern concept of absolute ownership, when introduced, did not deny the imposition of restrictions in the interest of the wider society. In Japan, on the

other hand, there was no sense of duty to counterbalance control over 'one's own thing', and so, backed up by a legal concept of absolute ownership, a popular conception of 'absolute ownership' spread through society at large.

32. Translator's note: In the original text, pre-Civil Code terms are used for 'land-lord' and 'tenant'; use of these particular terms in this translation does not imply anything about the proper classification of such relationships under *modern* law.

33. Concerning conditions at the time, and subsequent changes to the system of land leases, see the outline given in Inamoto, 'Shakuchi hosei temmatsu gaiyo' (A Comprehensive Overview of the Land Lease System), *Tochi Jutaku Mondai*, 163, 32 ff.

34. Apart from additional remarks concerning fixed-term leases, I will not elaborate on the revised Land and Building Lease Act here. On my views on this new legislation, see the following: *Horitsu Jiho Tokushu: Shakuchi, Shakuya Ho Kaisei no Mondai ten* (Special issue: Issues in the Revision of the Land Lease and Building Lease Laws) (1986); *Horitsu jiho Tokushu: Shakuchi, shakuya ho kaisei mondai no ronten* (Special issue: Points of Debate in the Revision of the Land Lease and Building Lease Acts) (1989); *Ho to minshu shugi Tokushu: Shakuchi, Shakuya Ho Kaisei Mondai o Kangaeru* (Special issue: Considering the Revision of the Land Lease and Building Lease Laws) (1987); Inamoto, 'Kenkyu Noto: Shakuchi Ho, Shakuya Ho to Shoji Chintaishaku' (Research note: The Land Lease Act, the Building Lease Act, and commercial leases), *Shakai Kagaku Kenkyu*, 42; Inamoto, 'Kenkyu noto: Teiki Shakuchi ken seido no kento (1–4) [Research notes: Examination of a Fixed-term Land Lease Right]', *Shakai Kagaku Kenkyu*, 42.

35. Watanabe Y., *Tochi to Zaisan Ken* (Land and Rights over Property), (1977) 106.

36. Inamoto, 'Tochi no Shiken Seigen o Megutte' (On the Limitation of Private Rights to Land), *Chiho Zaimu*, 29 (1987).

37. This provision reads as follows:

The right to own or to hold property is inviolable.
Property rights shall be defined by law, in conformity with the public welfare.
Private property may be taken for public use upon just compensation therefore.

38. This is essentially the position taken in the statement cited above concerning 'carefully respecting rights of land ownership while limiting rights of land use'.

39. This latter basically follows the wording proposed by the Report of the Ad Hoc Investigatory Committee, with the exception that the term 'land use' in the Report was replaced by simply 'land'.

40. Kokudocho, Tochi Kyoku (National Land Agency, Land Bureau), *supra* note 27.

41. Among these points, thanks to an opposition amendment, the law does at least reflect a desire for citizen participation in a reference, in section 11 (3), to solicitation of citizen opinion and feedback.

42. See Inamoto, 'Shakuchi Ho Kaisei to Tochi Shoyu Kan' nen' (Revision of the Land Lease Law and the Concept of Land Ownership), *Shakai kagaku kenkyu*, 42, 225.

43. The response to the draft revision of the land and building lease laws done by the non-profit organ Nihon Jutaku Sogo Centre (to be found in Homu Sho Minji Kyoku Sanjikan shitsu, *Shakuchi ho, shakuya ho kaisei yoko shian nitaisuru iken-shu*, 911 (1988)) summarizes the position from this perspective.

44. Translator's note: This is a contrived word in English, but accurately convey's Professor Inamoto's meaning.

8. EMPLOYMENT RELATIONS AFTER THE COLLAPSE OF THE BUBBLE ECONOMY

1. If we accept the argument of macroeconomists that, ultimately, the exchange rate is determined by differentials in productivity, and also that the future equilibrium for the exchange rate can be predicted from the macroeconomic factors, and if we agree with the judgement that the yen is currently (1995) over-valued against the dollar, then we would have to conclude that the yen will not continue to trade at such high levels in the future. On the determination of the exchange rate see Yoshikawa (1992).

2. In his discussion of Japanese employment practices, Ujihara (1989) has introduced the idea that Japanese employment and labour relations are organized and governed by the four dimensions which he distinguishes as 'normative assumptions', 'the objective system (rules)', 'ideology' and 'the economic basis/effects'. For a discussion of the 'Japanese model' within this framework see Nakamura and Nitta (1995).

3. Concerning the upwards tendency of the unemployment rate since the 1970s, there is considerable research which suggests that a large proportion of the rise is made up of increases in frictional unemployment. If these conclusions are accurate, it would not be appropriate to argue in terms of increases or decreases through a comparison of the unemployment rate of the 1960s, which was at about the 1% level, with that of recent years that has ranged between 2 and 3%. If it is remembered that even at the height of the economic bubble in 1990 and 1991, the unemployment rate was around 2.1%, it is obvious that such an argument has merit. On this point see Ono (1989), especially ch. 11.

4. See the *Labour White Paper* for 1994, 22–8, which reached conclusions similar to the ones outlined in this chapter. I analysed the monthly changes in the workforce as seen in the relationship between shifts in economic conditions and the gender and age of the labour force.

5. Among the employees covered by the Labour Force Survey are included 'temporary (in the original sense) employees' and family workers, who are taken on for an undetermined period. The movements of this type of employee, in terms of their numbers, has an influence on the average number of hours worked and it makes it harder to understand the real changes in hours worked. When looking at male workers among whom such 'temporary workers' are only a small proportion, it is appropriate to adopt a comparison of time–series data.

9. EXPLAINING THE END OF THE POST-WAR PARTY SYSTEM

1. In Japanese, the Socialists were Nippon Shakai-to (Japanese Socialist party) until 1996 when they changed the name to Shakai Minshu-to (Social Democratic party), although the English title of the party had earlier been changed to the Social Democratic Party of Japan.

2. 'Corporatism without labour' has been the standard characterization of labour exclusion in Japanese political economy. See T. J. Pempel and Tsunekawa Keiichi 'Corporatism without Labour: The Japanese Anomaly?', in Phillipe C. Schmitter and Gerhard Lehmbruch (eds.), *Trends toward Corporatist Intermediation* (London: Sage, 1979).

3. Akita Nariaki, 'Koyo Kanko to Haichi Tenkan, Shukko' (Employment Practices and Redeployment, Transfers), in Nariaki Akita (ed.), *Nihon no Koyo Kanko no Henka to Ho* (Changes in Japanese Employment Practices and the Law) (Hosei Daigaku Shuppan-bu, 1993), 87–91; Ogata Taka'aki, 'Koyo Seisaku no Genjitsu' (The Reality of Employment Policy), in Ando Kikuo et al. (eds.), *Nihon-teki Keiei no Tenki* (The Development of Japanese Management) (Yuhikaku, 1980), 227–39.

4. Ishida Mitsuo, 'Nihon Tekko-gyo no Roshi Kankei—B Seitetsu-jo no Jirei Chosa (Industrial Relations in the Japanese Steel Industry: Field Research of B-Steel Mill), *Shakai Kagaku Kenkyu* (Social Science Research), Vol. 38, No. 2 (1986), 145–50.

5. See Manfred Schmidt, 'The Politics of Labor Market Policy', in F. Castles et al. (eds.), *Managing Mixed Economies* (Berlin: Walter de Gryunter, 1984).

6. On the 1975 Spring Offensive, see Shinkawa Toshimitsu, '1975-nen Shunto to Keizai Kiki Kanri' (Economic Crisis Management during the 1975 Spring Offensive), in Hideo Otake (ed.), *Nihon Seiji no Soten: Jirei Kenkyu ni yoru Seiji Taisei no Bunseki* (Issues in Japanese Politics: Case Study Analysis of the Regime) (Tokyo: Sanichi Shobo: 1984), 191–232; Shinkawa Toshimitu, *Nihon-gata-Fukushi no Seiji Keizaigaku* (The Political Economy of Japanese Welfare) (Sanichi Shobo, 1993), 199–216, Tsujinaka Yutaka, 'Kyuchi ni tatsu "Rodo" Seisaku Katei' (Labour Policy Making Trouble), in Nakano Minoru (ed.), *Nihon-gata Seisaku Kettei no Henyo* (Changes in Japanese Policy Making) (Toyo Keizai Shinposha, 1986), 285–8; Murakami Hiroharu et al. *Sohyo Rodo Undo 30-nen no Kiseki* (The Trajectory of 30 Years of Sohyo Labour Movement) (Rodo Kyoiku Senta, 1980), 383–416; Kozuma Yoshiaki, *Shunto* (The Spring Offensive) (Rodo Kyoiku Senta, 1976), 235–8, 281–8.

7. Discussion Group of Eight Companies was composed of representatives of the steel industry (Nippon Steel and NKK), automobiles (Toyota and Nissan), electronics (Hitachi and Toshiba), and heavy machinery-shipbuilding (Mitsubishi Heavy Machinery and IHI).

8. Tsujinaka, op. cit., 278–80, Undoshi Henshu Iinkai (ed.), *Yutakana Asu o Hiraku: Denki Roren Undoshi*, Vol. 4 (1982–1991) (Opening a New Future: The History of the Electronics Industry Union Vol. 4) (Zen-Nihon Denki-kiki Rodo-kumiai Rengokai,

1992), 77–9, Nihon Tekko Rodo-kumiai Rengo-kai, *Tekko Roren-shi* Vol. 3 (The History of the Steel Union Federation) (Nihon Tekko Rodo-kumiai Rengo-kai, 1991), 146–75, 222–30.

9. Hosei Daigaku O'hara Shakai Mondai Kenkyujyo (ed.), *Nihon Rodo Nenkan 1982* (Annals of Japanese Labour 1982) (Rodo Junposha, 1983), 59–60. Hereafter referred to as *NRN*. *NRN* appears the following year as stated in the title (eq: *NRN 1982*, is published in 1983).

10. Nihon Tekko Rodo-kumiai Rengo-kai, op. cit., 92–102, 149–50, 186–209, 216–20.

11. *NRN 1981*, 54–7; *NRN 1982*, 490–2.

12. Seasonal workers, usually farmers employed during the winter as construction workers, made up 40% of insurance recipients, despite being 3% of the insured, and received one-third of all unemployment insurance payments. Similarly, young unmarried women were the second largest group of insurance recipients, despite the fact that most of them had left the labour force to get married with no intention of returning in the near future. Ujihara Shojiro, *Nihon Keizai to Koyo Seisaku*, (Japanese Employment Policy and the Economy) (University of Tokyo Press, 1989), 101–12; Kume Ikuo, 'Rodo no Sanka naki Shori?' (Victory without Participation for Labour?), *Leviathan*, Vol. 11 (1992), 180–1; *NRN, 1975*, 529–32; Takanashi Masaru, *Aratana Koyo Seisaku no Tenkai* (The Development of Employment Policy) (Romu Gyosei Kenkyu-jyo, 1989), 41–90.

13. Ujihara, op. cit., 116–20, Kamayama Naoyuki, 'Rodo Kumiai no Koyo Hosho Seisaku (Employment Security Policy of Labour Unions),' in *'Kozo Kiki' ka no Shakai Seisaku* (Social Policy under Structural Crisis) (Ochanomizu Shobo, 1979), 55–6, 169–82; *NRN, 1976*, 500–2; Shakai Hosho Undo-shi Henshu Iinkai, *Shakai Hosho Undo-shi* (The History of Movements for Social Welfare) (Rodo Junposha, 1982), 557–8; Sohyo 40-nen-shi Henshu Iinkai (ed.), *Sohyo 40-nen-shi* (The 40 Year History of Sohyo), Vol. 2 (Sohyo 40-nen-shi Henshu Iinkai, 1993), 711–12; Takanashi, op. cit, 120–34.

14. Such as the Ministry of Labour's Employment Policy Research Group (Koyo Seisaku Chosa Kenkyukai) and the Employment Study Group (Koyo Shingikai).

15. They were the Special Measures Law for Workers Leaving Designated Depressed Industries of 1977 and the Special Measures Law to Stabilize Designated Depressed Industries of 1978 for depressed industries, and the Special Measures Law for Workers Leaving Designated Depressed Areas and the Special Counter-Measures Law for Small Businesses in Designated Depressed Areas both of 1978 for depressed regions.

16. For details see Mark Tilton, *Restrained Trade: Cartels in Japan's Basic Materials Industries* (Ithaca, NY: Cornell University Press, 1996); Robert M. Uriu, *Troubled Industries: Confronting Economic Change in Japan* (Ithaca, NY: Cornell University Press, 1996); and Hong W. Tan and Haruo Shimada, *Troubled Industries in the United States and Japan* (London: The Macmillan Press, 1994).

17. Ujihara, op. cit., 121–7; Kamayama, op. cit., 56–9; Shinozuka Hideko, *Nihon no Koyo Chosei* (Employment Adjustment in Japan) (Toyo Keizai Shinposha, 1989),

110–14; Takanashi, op. cit., 91–119, 135–65; *NRN, 1978,* 537–9; *NRN, 1979,* 543–5; *NRN, 1980,* 483–7; *NRN, 1980,* 483–7.

18. For employees of large corporations the retirement age was 55, although most continued to work by transferring to other smaller firms or by re-negotiating their terms of employment. As a result, small firms employed a comparatively large number of elderly workers. Thus extending the retirement age was an issue mostly for large and medium-sized firms.

19. In 1972, the Research Group for Employment Policy (*Koyo Seisaku Chosa Kenkyu-kai*), an informal advisory committee of the Minister of Labour, reported that retirement age should eventually be set at 65, but proposed an interim goal of 60. Other private advisory committees of the Labour Minister, such as the Wage Study Group (Chingin Kenkyu kai), and the Discussion Group for Livelihood Plans of Workers (Rodosha Seikatsu Vision Kondankai), made similar proposals. On the policy coalition of employers and employees, see also Ito Mitsutoshi, 'Daikigyo Roshi Rengo no Keisei' (The Formation of Management–Labour Alliances in Large Corporations), *Leviathan,* Vol. 2 (Spring 1988).

20. In 1977, the Labour Ministry-affiliated Wage System Research Group released its report, which was followed by the Interim Labour Policy Discussion Group in 1978 and was incorporated in the Fourth Basic Employment Plan of the government in 1979. *NRN, 1981,* 42–5, 48–9, 72–3; Hirao Takehisa, '"Teinen Encho" to Jinji Kanri no Saihensei' ('Retirement Extension' and Personnel Management), in Kimoto Shinichiro (ed.), *Gendai Nihon Kigyo to Jinji Kanri* (Personnel Management at Contemporary Japanese Corporations) (Rodo Junposha, 1981), 222–40.

21. In 1982 a government advisory committee (the Research Group on the Problems of Aging Society) report focused on employment between the retirement age of 60 and the pension age of 65. The reports of the 'Research Group for the Employment of those in their Mid-sixties', issued in 1984 and 1985, also encouraged the use of corporate ties, retraining within the firm, and government assistance to secure continued employment for those in their mid-60s. Similar arguments were made at the Employment Research Committee, in 1985. *NRN, 1984,* 467–8; *NRN, 1986,* 436–40.

22. *NRN, 1983,* 279; *NRN, 1987,* 134–5.

23. See Kume Ikuo, 'Shin Hoshushugi no Jidai ni okeru Nihon no Rodo Seiji; Daraku ka, Atarashi Kanoseika' (Japanese Labour Politics in the Neo-Conservative Era—Decline or New Possibilities?), *Leviathan,* Vol. 17 (1995).

24. Kozuma, op. cit., pp. 281–8; Murakami et al., op. cit., 383–5, 395–416. Mori Kenji, 'Rodo Kumiai to Kokumin Seikatsu' (National Livelihood and the Unions), in Kurita Ken (ed.), *Gendai Nihon no Roshi Kankei* (Contemporary Japanese Industrial Relations) (Rodo Kagaku Kenkyu-jo Shuppan-kyoku, 1992), 40–7.

25. *NRN, 1979,* 186–9; *NRN, 1982,* 60–3, 67–73; *NRN, 1983,* 200–7; *NRN, 1984,* 197–9; *NRN, 1988,* 34–9.

26. Asami Kazuhiko, 'Toitsu Rosokon no 15-nen' (15 Years of the Unified Labour Congress), in Hosei Daigaku O'hara Shakai Mondai Kenkyu-jo (ed.), *'Rengo Jidai' no Rodo Undo* (Labour Movement of the 'Rengo' era) (Sogo Rodo Kenkyu-jo, 1992), 83–7; Kinoshita Takeo, 'Sangyo-betsu Zenkoku Soshiki no Bunretsu, Saihen to "Rengo" e no Michinori' (Splits and Reorganization of Nationwide Industrial Unions and the Road to Rengo), in Hosei Daigaku O'hara Shakai Mondai Kenkyujo (ed.), ibid., 177–9; *NRN, 1979*, 189; *NRN, 1982*, 65–7, 72–3; *NRN, 1983*, 200–7; *NRN, 1984*, 199–200; *NRN, 1986*, 172–3; *NRN, 1988*, 34.

27. Post-retirement included redeployment, retraining, re-employment, and employment extension. When re-employed, the worker would be given lower pay and benefits; whereas in the case of extension, the person received basic pay and benefits but for a fixed period.

28. Subsidiaries were created not only in technologically advanced areas (such as new materials, electronics, and information technology) or areas related to steel production (such as chemicals, engineering, or metals), but also in areas unrelated to steel, such as service or finance, building maintenance, car dealing, catalogue retail, strawberry cultivation, mushroom cultivation, fish breeding, sleeping mat cleaning, gardening, printing, electric wiring, restaurants, and funeral parlours.

29. John Creighton Campbell, *How Policies Change: The Japanese Government and the Aging Society*, (Princeton: Princeton University Press, 1992), 254–8, 260–7; Koyo Shokugyo Kenkyu-jyo, *Shukko, Tenseki no Genjo to Kadai* (The Reality and Problems of Transfers and Re-employment) (Koyo Shokugyo Kenkyu-jo, 1989), 7–10, 44–5; Ujihara Shujiro, 'Koreika Shakai ni okeru Kigyo no Taio' (Corporate Responses to Ageing Society), in Tokyo Daigaku Shakai Kagaku Kenkyu-jo (ed.), *Fukushi Kokka*, Vol. 5—*Nihon no Keizai to Fukushi* (Welfare State, Vol. 5: Welfare and the Japanese Economy) (University of Tokyo Press, 1985), 373–85, 406–17, 421; Kanbayashi Chieko, 'Dai-kigyo to Chusho-kigyo no Koreisha Taisaku' (Policies for the Elderly in Large and Small-Medium Sized Corporations), in Hosei Daigaku O'hara Shakai Mondai Kenkyu-jo (ed.), *Gendai no Koreika Taisaku* (Contemporary Policy for the Elderly) (Sogo Rodo Kenkyu-jo, 1985), 48–9; *NRN, 1982*, 277–80; *NRN, 1983*, 27–9; *NRN, 1984*, 467–8; *NRN, 1987*, 154; *NRN, 1988*, 137–8, 180–2.

30. Otani Tsuyoshi, 'Sogo Fukushi no Kigyo-nai Tenkai' (The Development of 'Comprehensive Welfare' within Firms), *Shakai Mondai Kenkyu*, (Research on Social Issues), Vol. 31–1 (1981), 151; Otani Tsuyoshi, 'Taishokusha Iryo-seido no Gutai-ka' (Implementing Retiree Heath-Care Schemes), *Shakai Mondai Kenkyu*, (Research on Social Issues), Vol. 32–2 (1983), 135–45; Iwao Namie, 'Sogo Shakai Seisaku no naka no Kigyo Fukushi to Roshi Karkei' (Industrial Relations and Corporate Welfare in the Context of Comprehensive Social Policy), in Nishimura Hiromichi (ed.), *Gendai no Fukushi Seisaku to Rodo Mondai* (Contemporary Welfare Policies and Labour Issues) (Keibunsha, 1983), 141–2; Kiriki Itsuo, '"Fukushi Seisaku" to "Rodo Fukushi"' ('Welfare Policy' and 'Labour Welfare'), in Nishimura Hiromichi

(ed.), op. cit., 100–2; Romu Kenkyujo (ed.), *Roshi ni okeru Koreisha Fukushi Taisaku no Jittai* (Cases of Elderly Welfare Policies by Management and Labour) (Romu Kenkyujo, 1981), 153–95, 205–16, 239–66.

31. Prior to the reform of the 1980s, Japan's welfare regime can be characterized as a divided system that generated four clusters of interests as summarized in the table below. One problem was that most retirees joined National Health Insurance, which drastically increased the number of the elderly in this scheme. The other problem was that the members of the schemes for the small firms and the self-employed were older and needed more benefits but could no longer contribute.

Employees	Pensions	Health Care
Large Corporation	Employee Pensions	Associational Employee Health Insurance + Company Pensions + Corporate Benefits
Small Firm	Employee Pensions	National Health Insurance
Self-Employed	Mutual Assistance Associations	National Health Insurance
Public Sector	National Pensions	Government Employee Health Insurance

32. Kato Junko, 'Seisaku Katei Kenkyu no Riron to Jissho' (Theory and Evidence of Policymaking Research), *Leviathan*, Vol. 8 (1991), 171; Kato Junko, 'Nihon no Seisaku Kettei Katei—Rieki Sakugengata Shisaku no Seiko' (Policymaking in Japan: Success in Interest Reduction Policies) (Unpublished manuscript, 1986), 65; Yamazaki Hiroaki, 'Kosei Nenkin Seido no "Bappon Kaisei" Katei' (The 'Fundamental Reform' of the Employee Pension System), in Tokyo Daigaku Shakai Kagaku Kenkyu-jo (ed.), *Tenkan-ki no Fukushi Kokka*, Vol. 2 (The Welfare State at Crossroads, Vol. 2) (University of Tokyo Press, 1988), 92–104; Shakaihosho-undo-shi Henshu-iinkai (ed.), op. cit., 452–67; *NRN, 1976*, 314–18, 528–30; *NRN, 1977*, 570–4; *NRN, 1981*, 66–8, 74–5.

33. Yokoyama Kazuhiko and Tada Hidenori (eds.), *Nihon Shakai Hosho no Rekishi* (The History of Japanese Social Security) (Gakubun-sha, 1991), 280–4, Shinkawa, op. cit., (1993), 163–74; *NRN, 1982*, 328–9; Campbell, op. cit., 290–7, 302–4.

34. Another major feature of this reform was to establish pension rights for women (especially housewives). On the other hand, mutual assistance associations, which provided health care and pensions for public-sector workers, were not included in this unification.

35. The unions favoured a fixed amount basic pension with an incomes-proportional superannuation, both of which were to be paid from the age of 60 and indexed to wage increases (instead of cost-of-living). Murakami Kiyoshi, and Yamazaki Yasuhiko, *Koreika Shakai to Nenkin* (The Ageing Society and Pensions) (Chuo Hoki Shuppan, 1981), 121–8; Soneda Ikuo, *Nihon no Kigyo Nenkin, Showa 60 nendo-ban*

(Japanese Corporate Pensions: FY 1985 Edition) (Toyo Keizai Shinposha, 1985), 114–32; Kato, op. cit. (1986), 66–7; Shakaihosho-undo-shi Henshu-iinkai (ed.), op. cit., 467–71; *NRN, 1977*, 361–5; *NRN, 1978*, 581–3; *NRN, 1979*, 357–8; *NRN, 1981*, 74–8.

36. Kato, op. cit. (1986), 86–9, 161–7; Kato, op. cit. (1991), 172–9; Takahashi Hideyuki, 'Nihon Ishikai no Seijikodo to Ishikettei' (Decision Making and Lobbying of the Japan Medical Association), in Nakano Minoru (ed.), op. cit., 250–5; Hayakawa Sumitaka, 'Fukushi Kokka o Meguru Seijikatei' (Political Process of the Welfare State), *Komazawa Daigaku Hogaku Ronshu* (Komazawa University, Papers in Law), Vol. 43 (1991), 37–50; Hayakawa Sumitaka et al., 21-seiki no Iryo Hoken wa Tenbo Dekitaka' (Is the Health-Care for the 21st Century in Sight?), *Handai Hogaku* (Osaka University, Law and Politics) (1986), 195–211; Shakaihosho-undo-shi Henshu-iinkai (ed.), op. cit., 307–9, 362–3; Shinkawa, op. cit. (1993), 163–8, 174–7; Yamazaki, op. cit., 108–47; Yokoyama and Tada, op. cit., 280–90; *NRN, 1980*, 316–18, 512–18; *NRN, 1982*, 326–9; *NRN, 1984*, 328–9, 497–501, 512–13; *NRN, 1985*, 310–13, 535–7; *NRN, 1986*, 286–91.

37. Yamazaki, op. cit. (1988), 79; Yokoyama and Tada (eds.), op. cit., 294–6, 317–21; *NRN, 1987*, 140–2, 365–70, 500–2; *NRN, 1988*, 469–70.

38. Smaller firms were allowed to report a certain portion of their sales as their tax base (instead of the actual amount sold), and some were allowed to retain the tax they collected.

39. Concessions hammered out between the ruling party and the bureaucracy between the first and second stages of the tax reform included additional income tax cuts, reduction of the sales tax rate (from 5 to 3%), and generous loopholes for small businesses. As a result, the tax reforms became a genuine tax cut instead of being revenue-neutral. Further concessions to opposition parties included a half-year delay in the implementation of the new tax, an income tax exemption of up to 100,000 yen in this period, an increase in tax exemptions for retirement funds, implementation of special cost-of-living adjustments for pensions, and a special stipend for welfare recipients. The government also promised to increase expenditures on social services for the elderly, tax exemptions for families with bed-ridden elderly, and the amount of non-contributory pensions.

40. Sato Susumu, and Miyajima Horoshi, *Sengo Zeisei-shi (Dai-ni Zoho-ban)* (Post-war History of the Tax System (Second Enlarged Edition)) (Zaimu Keiri Kyokai, 1990), 414–20; Mizuno Masaru, *Shuzei Kyokucho no Sen-Sanbyaku Nichi* (1300 Days as the Tax Bureau Director) (Okura Zaimu Kyokai, 1993), 101–51, 153–75, 275–367; Takahashi Toshio, *Nihon no Zesisei Kaikaku to Sozei-ron no Tenkai* (Tax Reform and the Development of the Tax System in Japan) (Keiso Shobo, 1994), 78–85; Takeshita Noboru, *Shogen Hoshu Seiken* (Testimony: Conservative Government) (Yomiuri Shinbun-sha, 1991), 186–206; Tanaka Zen'ichiro, 'Nakasone Seiken to Tenkanki no Kokkai' (The Nakasone Government and the Legislature at Cross-roads), in Uchida, Kinbara, Furuya (eds.), *Nihon Gikai Shiroku*, Vol. 6 (History of the Japanese Legislature, Vol. 6) (Dai'ichi Hoki, 1990), 218–20.

41. The public-sector unions were deprived of their right to strike by the Occupation Authorities in 1948.

42. Public-sector employees, along with private-school employees, had independent pension and health-care schemes. See n. 25.

43. This was because the National Railways had a large number of retirees who had worked in the pre-war public railways of former colonies.

44. Hideo Otake, 'Jiyu-shugi Kaikaku no naka no Corporatism' (Corporatism within the Context of Liberal Reforms), *Leviathan* (Special Edition, 1992), 123–7, 130–6; Kinoshita, op. cit., 32–40; Kato, op. cit. (1986), 67–8, 100–1; Shakaihosho-undo-shi Henshu-iinkai (ed.), op. cit., 471–3; Takagi Tadao, and Hayakawa Sei'ichiro (eds.), *Kokutetsu Rodo Kumiai* (National Railways Union) (Nihon Hyoron-sha, 1993), 4–5, 16–32; *NRN, 1980*, 319–20, 512–14; *NRN, 1981*, 330; *NRN, 1983*, 506–7; *NRN, 1984*, 326–7, 506–7; *NRN, 1985*, 192–3; *NRN, 1986*, 172–5; *NRN, 1987*, 234–8, 244–5; *NRN, 1988*, 56–8.

45. Masumi Jun'nosuke, *Gendai Seiji*, Vol. 2 (Contemporary Politics, Vol. 2) (University of Tokyo Press, 1985), 540–1, 650–3; *NRN, 1975*, 446–51, 455–9, 487–9; *NRN, 1976*, 470; *NRN, 1977*, 473–4; *NRN, 1978*, 464–9.

46. Soma Masao (ed.), *Nihon no Sosenkyo 1979–1980* (Japanese Elections 1979–80) (Seiji Koho Senta 1982), 182–90; *NRN, 1981*, 421, 430–8, 450–5.

47. *NRN, 1977*, 475–6; *NRN, 1978*, 508, *NRN, 1979*, 452–62; *NRN, 1980*, 414–15.

48. Masumi, op. cit., 546–55; *NRN, 1975*, 467–68; *NRN, 1976*, 442–3; *NRN, 1977*, 475–6, 488–9; *NRN, 1978*, 477–97; *NRN, 1989*, 468–80.

49. See Kabashima Ikuo, '89-nen Saninsen' (The 89 Upper House Election), *Leviathan*, (Special Issue, 1992).

50. See, for example, Chalmers A. Johnson, *Japan: Who Governs?: The Rise of the Developmental State* (New York: Norton, 1995).

51. See n. 2.

52. See David Soskice, 'The Institutional Infrastructure for International Competitiveness: A Comparative Analysis of the UK and Germany', in A. B. Atkinson and R. Brunetta (eds.), *The Economics of New Europe* (London: Macmillan, forthcoming); David Soskice, 'Finer Varieties in Advanced Capitalism: Industry versus Group-Based Co-ordination in Germany and Japan', (Mimeo, 1995).

53. For the dominant view which stresses the increased strength of labour in policy-making, see Shinoda Toru, ' "Rengo" Jidai ni okeru Seisaku Sanka' (Policy Participation in the 'Rengo' era,) in Hosei Daigaku O'hara Shakai Mondai Kenkyujo (ed.), op. cit., (1992); Shinoda Toru, 'Yuigi na Tasha—Gendai Nihon no Rodo Seiji' (The Significant Other: Contemporary Japanese Labour Politics), *Leviathan*, Vol. 14 (1994); Tsujinaka Yutaka, 'Rodokai no Saihen to 86-nen Taisei no Igi' (Reorganization of Labour and the Implications of the 1986 System), *Leviathan*, Vol. 1 (1987).

54. For the Swedish and German cases, see Leif Lewin, *Ideology and Strategy: A Century of Swedish Politics* (Cambridge: Cambridge University Press, 1988), 204–25, 274–304; Andrew Martin, 'Trade Unions in Sweden: Strategic Responses to

Change and Crisis', in P. Gourevitch et al., *Unions and Economic Crisis: Britain, West Germany, and Sweden* (London: George Allen & Unwin, 1984), 192–202, 213–16, 225–30; Peter J. Katzenstein, *Small States in World Markets* (Ithaca, NY: Cornell University Press, 1985); Fritz W. Sharpf, *Crisis and Choice in European Social Democracy* (Ithaca, NY: Cornell University Press, 1987); Peter Swenson, *Fair Shares: Unions, Pay, and Politics in Sweden and West Germany* (Ithaca, NY: Cornell University Press, 1989), 111–76.

55. On the pluralist school and its critique of the bureaucracy–dominance theme, see Muramatsu Michio, *Sengo Nihon no Kanryosei* (Post-war Japanese Bureaucracy) (Toyo Keizai Shinposha, 1984); Sato Seizaburo and Matsuzaki Tetsuhisa, *Jiminto Seiken* (The LDP Government) (Chuo Koronsha, 1986) and Inoguchi Takashi, and Iwai Tomoaki, *Zoku-Giin no Kenkyu* (A Study of 'Zoku' Members) (Tokyo: Nihon Keizai Shinbun-sha, 1987). On the rational choice critique of the bureaucracy–dominance theme, see Mathew D. McCubbins and Gregory W. Noble, 'The Appearance of Power', in Peter F. Cowhey and Mathew D. McCubbins (eds.), *Structure and Policy in Japan and the United States* (Cambridge: Cambridge University Press, 1995), and J. Mark Ramseyer and Frances McCall Rosenbluth, *Japan's Political Marketplace* (Cambridge, Mass.: Harvard University Press, 1993), chs. 6–7.

56. Content analysis of party platforms shows policy convergence among parties in Japan, especially since the mid-1970s, which is the opposite of the UK and USA where parties maintained their policy distances. See Ian Budge et al., *Ideology, Strategy, and Party Change: Spatial Analysis of Post-war Election Programmes in 19 Democracies* (Cambridge: Cambridge University Press, 1989). On the British electoral behaviour and party system, see Ivor Crewe, 'The Electorate: Partisan Dealignment Ten Years on', *West European Politics*, Vol. 6, No. 3 (1983), 188–92, 206–13; David T. Denver, *Elections and Voting Behaviour in Britain* (London: Philip Allen, 1989), 57–8; Anthony Heath et al., *Understanding Political Change: The British Voter 1964–87* (Oxford: Pergamon Press, 1991), 23, 79–81, 95, 102–17, 122–30, 168. On the British Labour Party see Patrick Seyd, *The Rise and Fall of the Labour Left* (London: Macmillan, 1987); Eric Shaw, *The Labour Party since 1979: Crisis and Transformation* (London: Routledge, 1994); Martin J. Smith and Joanna Spear (eds.), *The Changing Labour Party* (London: Routledge, 1992).

57. Although the direction of political change in Italy is yet to be determined and accounts remain sketchy, see Gianfranco Pasquino and Patrick McCarthy (eds.), *The End of Post-War Politics in Italy* (Boulder, Colo.: Westview Press, 1993); Carol Mershon and Gianfranco Pasquino (eds.), *Italian Politics: Ending the First Republic* (Boulder, Colo.: Westview Press, 1995); and Mark Gilbert, *The Italian Revolution: The End of Politics Italian Style?* (Boulder, Colo.: Westview Press, 1995).

Index